PAY LESS TAX LEGALLY

If you have any questions concerning any changes in form numbers or line numbers, call your local Internal Revenue Service office or your professional accountant. Some of the examples in this book have been computed on the basis of preliminary information. Consequently, there may be some minor discrepancies in the final figures.

PAY LESS TAX LEGALLY

BY

BARRY R. STEINER
Certified Public Accountant

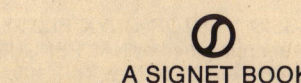

A SIGNET BOOK
NEW AMERICAN LIBRARY

ACKNOWLEDGMENTS

Many thanks to those who made
Pay Less Tax Legally a reality:

Dominick Abel for his talents as a literary agent; Arnold Dolin for his wisdom and guidance as an editor; Eric S. Kaplan, CPA, for his tax expertise in review; Jeanne King for a great job in research and typing; Kathleen Moloney for her patience and gift as an editor; and my wife, Faye, for being a friend when I needed one.

Publisher's Note

This publication is designed to provide accurate and authoritative information in regard to the subject matter covered. It is published and put on sale with the understanding that the publisher is not engaged in rendering legal, accounting, financial, or other professional service. If expert assistance is required, the services of a competent professional person should be sought.

NAL BOOKS ARE AVAILABLE AT QUANTITY DISCOUNTS
WHEN USED TO PROMOTE PRODUCTS OR SERVICES. FOR
INFORMATION PLEASE WRITE TO PREMIUM MARKETING
DIVISION, THE NEW AMERICAN LIBRARY,
1633 BROADWAY, NEW YORK, NEW YORK 10019

Copyright © 1975, 1976, 1977, 1978, 1979, 1980, 1981, 1982, 1983, 1984, 1985, 1986, 1987
by Second Tax Co., Inc.
All rights reserved.

SIGNET TRADEMARK REG. U.S. PAT. OFF. AND FOREIGN COUNTRIES
REGISTERED TRADEMARK—MARCA REGISTRADA
HECHO EN CANTON, OHIO, U.S.A.

SIGNET, SIGNET CLASSIC, MENTOR, ONYX, PLUME, MERIDIAN
and NAL BOOKS are published by NAL PENGUIN INC.,
1633 Broadway, New York, New York 10019

First Printing, December, 1987

1 2 3 4 5 6 7 8 9

PRINTED IN THE UNITED STATES OF AMERICA

Contents

Introduction 5
How to Use This Book 5
The 1987 Tax Law in a Nutshell 6
Summary of New Tax Laws Affecting Individuals 11
The New Tax Reform Law, A to Z 12
An Overview of Tax Reform 13
Financial and Estate Planning 14
Investments—Changes under Tax Reform 15
The New Tax Law A–Z 16
Compute Your Own Taxes—Worksheet 30
Tax Rate Tables 31

Commonly Asked Income Tax Questions and Where to Find the Answers in *Pay Less Tax Legally* 32

PART I
SAVE MONEY NOW
A Complete Guide to the Deductions, Credits, and Tax-Saving Opportunities You Can Make Use of on This Year's Taxes 39

Important Tax Dates for 1988 40

1 Your Income Tax Return: Basic Guidelines 41
Who Must File? 41
Children's Tax Forms 42
What You Need in Order to File 44
Where to File and Pay 45
When to File 45
Form W-4EZ 45
When Penalties for Underwithholding Are Waived 45

v

Form W-2   46
The "Short Forms": Form 1040A and Form 1040EZ   50

2   Form 1040: Basic Information   51

Changes in Form 1040   51

Choosing Your Filing Status   54
Single   54
Advantages of Married Filing Separately   55
Head of Household   55
Qualifying Widow(er) with Dependent Child   56

Exemptions   57
Personal Exemptions   57
Elderly and/or Blind Taxpayers   57
Exemptions for Dependents   57
Income Shifting   61

3   Reporting Your Income   62

Schedule B—Interest and Dividend Income   62
Determining Your Gross Income   64

The One-Minute Taxman: Nontaxable Income   64

The One-Minute Taxman: Taxable Income   65

The Income Section   66
Wages, Salaries, and Tips   66
Interest Income   66
Tax-Exempt Interest Income   67
Dividends   67
Taxable Refunds of State and Local Income Taxes   67
Alimony Received   67
Business Income or Loss   67
Capital Gain or Loss   67
Other Gains or Losses   68
Pensions, IRA Distributions, and Annuities   68
Rents, Royalties, Partnerships, Estates, Trusts, etc.   68
Farm Income or Loss   68
Unemployment Compensation Benefits   68
Social Security Benefits   69

Income Other Than Wages, Dividends, and Interest   71
Prizes, Awards, and Premiums   71
Gambling Winnings   71
Exclusions from Income   71
Foreign Income   72

Contents **vii**

 Reporting Business Income or Loss: Schedule C   73

Actors and Actresses 73
Schedule C 73

The One-Minute Taxman: Business Expenses   75

Net Operating Losses 76
Method of Accounting—Cash or Accrual Basis 76
Income 76
Gross Receipts 76
Cost of Goods Sold and/or Operations 77
Deductions 77
Car and Travel Expenses 77
Depreciation and Section 179 Deduction 77
Mortgage Interest Paid to Financial Institution 78
Rent on Business Property 78
Repairs 80
Entertainment Expenses 80
Travel Expenses 82
Targeted-Jobs Credit 83
Other Business Expenses 84
Net Profit or Loss 86
Cost of Goods Sold and/or Operations 86
Inventories 86
Purchases Less Cost of Items Withdrawn for Personal Use 87
Depreciation 87
Business Autos 87
New Depreciation Rules 88

5 Capital Gains and Losses and Reconciliation of Form 1099-B: Schedule D   90

Tax Planning Checklist: Assets and Investments 91
Securities, Stocks, and Bonds 91
Capital Assets 91
Long-Term vs. Short-Term Gains and Losses 94
Short-Term Gains and Losses 94
Non-Business Bad Debt 94
Business Bad Debt 95
How to Handle Dividend Reinvestment Stock 96
Long-Term Capital Gains and Losses 96
Sale of Inherited Property 96
Sale of a Patent 97

viii   Contents

    Part III: Summary of Parts I and II 97
        Alternative Tax Computation (Part IV) 97
        Avoiding Gain on Condemnation 98
    Capital Losses (Part V) 98
    Sale on the Installment Method 98
        Nontaxable Exchanges 99
    Recapture Rules 100
    Sale or Exchange of Principal Residence 100

> **The One-Minute Taxman: Buying or Selling Homes** 102

        Conversion to Rental Property 104
        55-or-Older Exclusion 105
        Lump-Sum Distributions 105

Supplemental Income: Schedule E   106

    Passive Losses and Credits 106
        Passive Income/Losses 107
        Real Estate Investments 110
        Passive Loss Rules 110
    Form 8582 (Passive Activity Loss Limitations) 111
    Rent and Royalty Income or Loss 114
        Mortgage Interest Paid to Financial Institution 114
        Rental Expenses 115
    Depreciation 116

> **The One-Minute Taxman: Rental Income and Expenses** 117

    Depletion 118

Adjustments to Income   122

    Form 2106 122
        Changes on Form 2106 122
    Employee Business Expenses 123
        Temporary Away-from-Home Deductions 126
        Automobile Deductions 127
        Charitable and Educational Travel Costs, Cruises 129
        Employee Travel Expenses 129
        Meals and Entertainment Expenses 130
        Business Meals While Traveling 132
    Individual Retirement Accounts 132

Contents ix

The One-Minute Taxman: Employee Business Travel Expenses 133

  IRAs Under Tax Reform 135
  Deductible and Nondeductible IRAs 135
  Form 8606 135
  Inherited IRAs 140
  Where to Invest Funds 140
  Tax-Free Rollovers 141
  IRA Early Withdrawals 142
  IRA Rollovers 142

Self-Employed Health Insurance Deductions 143

Self-Employed Retirement Plans 144
  Keogh Retirement Plan and Self-Employed (SEP) Deductions 144
  Simplified Employee Pension (SEP) Plans 145

Tax-Planning Checklist: Retirement 145

Penalty on Early Withdrawal of Savings 146

Alimony Paid 146
  Legal Fees 147
  Alimony and Tax Reform 148

8 Itemizing Your Deductions 149

Itemize or Claim the New Standard Deduction? 149

Changes in Schedule A—Itemized Deductions 150

Medical and Dental Expenses 150

The One-Minute Taxman: Medical Expenses 152

Taxes as Deductions 154
  State and Local Income Taxes 154
  Real Estate Taxes 155
  Other Taxes, Including Personal Property Tax 155

Interest Expense 155
  Interest: Is It Deductible? 155
  Home Mortgage Interest 156
  Qualified Residence Interest 161
  Mortgage Interest as a Deduction 162
  Contingent Interest 163
  Points Charged by Banks 164
  Consumer Interest 164
  Other Deductible Forms of Interest 165
  Limitation on Interest Deduction 166
  Investment Interest 166
  Margin Interest Limited 169

Contributions 169
    Cash Contributions 169
    Noncash Contributions 170
    Charitable Contributions 171
    Deducting the Cost of Private School 171

Casualty and Theft Gains and Losses 171

The One-Minute Taxman: Contributions 174

The One-Minute Taxman: Casualty Losses 178

Moving Expenses 180
    Foreign Country 181
    Form 3903—Moving Expenses 181
    Moving Expenses Limited 183
    Self-Employed Persons 184

Miscellaneous Deductions 184
    Employee Business Expenses 184
    Union and Professional Dues 186
    Tax Return Preparation Fee 186
    Other Miscellaneous Deductions 186

The One-Minute Taxman: Miscellaneous Business and Professional Expenses 187

The One-Minute Taxman: Educational Expenses 190

The One-Minute Taxman: Other Miscellaneous Deductions 190

The One-Minute Taxman: Investment Expenses 191

⑨ Putting It All Together 192

Computing Your Tax 192

Itemize or Claim the New Standard Deduction? 192
    Married Persons Filing Separately 193
    Filing Returns for Dependent Children 193

Tax Tables 193
    Computing Your Tax with the Tables 194

Tax Rate Schedules 194

Lump-Sum Distributions 194
    Ten-Year Averaging 196

Forward Averaging 196
Capital Gain Option 197

Summary of Federal Tax Rules on Lump-Sum Distributions and Qualifying Partial Distributions 198
Rollovers—60 Day Limit 198
Special Tax Treatment for Lump-Sum Distributions 199
Other Taxes 200

Tax Credits 201
Refundable Credits 201
Nonrefundable Credits 201

Child and Dependent Care Credit (Form 2441) 202
Employment-Related Expenses 202
Computing the Credit 202
Limitation on the Credit 202

Credit for the Elderly and the Permanently and Totally Disabled (Schedule R) 204
Determining the Initial Amount 204
Reductions to the Initial Amount 204

General Business Credit 208
Determining the Maximum Tax Liability 208
Carry-Backs and Carry-Forwards of Unused Credits 208

Rehabilitation Tax Credits 208

Investment Tax Credit 209

Windfall Profits Tax Credits (Oil Royalties) 209

Self-Employment Tax (Schedule SE) 209

Alternative Minimum Tax (Form 6251) 211
Incentive Stock Options 213

Earned Income Credit 213
Claiming the Credit 213

10 Last-Minute Filing Tips and Special Filing Situations 215

Last-Minute Filing Tips 215
Last-Minute Tax Forms 216
Checking on Your Refund 216
If You Don't Have the Money to Pay Your Taxes 216
Interest Rates 216
Proper Postage 216

Special Filing Situations 216
Filing a Late Return 216
Filing Very Late 218
Filing an Amended Return 218
IRS Interest Charges 219

xii   Contents

      Problems Resolution Office 219
          Back Taxes: Negotiating Installment Agreements 222
          Paying Off the IRS 222

11 IRS Audits (And How to Avoid Them) 223

      Audits Under Tax Reform 223

      Types of Audit 228
          Correspondence Audits 228
          Office Audits 228
          Field Audits 228
          TCMP Audits 228

      What Triggers an Audit 228
          Chances of Being Audited 230

      Audit Tolerances 231

      IRS Examinations Guidelines 231

      Where Will the IRS Be Concentrating This Year? 232

      Dealing with an Audit 232

      Criminal Tax Cases 238

PART II

SAVE MONEY LATER

An In-Depth Analysis, Arranged Alphabetically by Subject,
of Tax-Planning Opportunities That Will
Save You Hard-Earned Dollars Both Now and Later On 239

      Introduction 240

      Four Tax-Planning Strategies 240
          Strategy 1: Generating Tax-Free Income 240
          Strategy 2: Claiming Everything to Which You Are Entitled 240
          Strategy 3: Lowering Your Tax Bracket 241
          Strategy 4: Deferring the Tax 241

      Combining Various Tax Strategies 241

      Avoiding Tax Penalties 242

      How Much Does Tax Saving Cost? 242

      Accountants 242
          Choosing an Accountant 242

      Advertising People, Deductions for 244

      Audit Lottery 245
          Understanding the Rules 245
          How to Play 245

Audit-Proofing Your Return 246
Auto Expense 246
Business vs. Hobby 247
Casualty Losses 247
Charitable Donations 247
    More Deductible Contributions 248
    Charitable Deductions for Future Payments 249
College Expenses 249
Computers 251
Conventions 251
Divorce 251
Educational Expenses 252
Estate Planning 253
    Estate Tax: Unified Credit 253
    Estate Tax: Marital Deduction 253
    Gift Tax: Annual Exclusion 254
Estimated Tax (Form 1040-ES) 255
Executives—Financial Planning 256
    401(K) Plan 258
    Split-Dollar Life Insurance 259
    An Executive Checklist 259
    Retirement Planning 259
    IRAs 260
Family Members on the Payroll 261
Filing Status Tax Tips 261
Fringe Benefits 262
Gift Leasebacks 262
Gifts of Appreciated Property 263
    Alternative Minimum Tax 263
Home Office 264
    Home Office "Focal Point" Test 264
    Benefitting from a Home Office 264
Home Ownership 265
    Supporting Parents 265
    College Child 266
    Sale Under Age 55 266
    Home Office 266
    Vacation Property Traps 266
Home Rental 267
Income Shifting 267
    Zero Coupon Tax Exempts 267
    The High/Low Spread 268
    The Under-Age-14 Rules 268

Incorporation 269
Individual Retirement Accounts 270
Interest Income 270
Intra-Family Loans 271
Investment Loss 271
Investments 271
Job Hunting 274
Loan Service Charges 274
Loss Carryovers/Carrybacks 274
Marriage vs. Living Together 274
Medical Expenses 275
  Some Unusual Medical Tax Tips 275
Medical Reimbursement Plan 278
Miscellaneous Deductions 278
Passive Income 279
Passive Losses 279
Record-Keeping 279
Refund Claims 280
Retirement Planning 280
Salary Reduction Plans 283
Sale of Residence 283
Savings Bonds 284
Single-Premium Life Insurance as a Tax Shelter 284
Tax Planning under Tax Reform 285
Tax-Sheltered Investments 287
  Your Home As a Tax Shelter Under Tax Reform 288
Ten Tax Loopholes That Work 291
Travel Deductions 291
Trusts 292
Union Membership 293
Vacation Homes 294
Index 296

From the desk of
BARRY R. STEINER, C.P.A.

Dear Taxpayer,

Tax Reform was <u>supposed</u> to make life simpler—streamlining tax computations by eliminating deductions, reducing rates, and taxing more of our income at a lower rate—but, of course, Tax Reform is proving to be anything but simple. In fact, it has made many people's financial decisions significantly more complicated. With or without Tax Reform, however, everyone's goal remains the same: <u>to pay less tax legally.</u>

The book you have in your hand is a step-by-step guide to doing just that, but before you take that first step, take a moment to look at the ''big picture'' under Tax Reform. The following pieces of advice are ones I give to all my clients, and they are explored in depth in PAY LESS TAX LEGALLY. Keep them in mind as you make your way through the book and discover that there <u>is</u> life after Tax Reform.

INVEST IN REAL ESTATE. Even with the new restrictions under Tax Reform—an increase in the number of years over which you may depreciate real estate and a stricter limit on the deductions to which you are entitled (to the amount for which you are ''at risk'')—real estate is still considered by many to be a sound investment. The two types of real estate investments that make the most sense under Tax Reform are:

- Buying a house in a stable neighborhood and renting it out. Under the new law this is considered a ''passive activity,'' but if you earn less than $100,000 and actively participate in managing the property (approving repairs, checking out tenants, etc.), you may deduct up to $25,000 of any net loss against your other income. The deduction is phased out between $100,000 and $150,000 of adjusted gross income. If you owned the property before the passage of the Tax Reform Act, you may deduct a decreasing share of any loss through 1990, no matter what your income bracket is.
- Converting a rental property into a second residence (even if you rent it out part of the year). You will be allowed full mortgage interest deductions on the property.

—over—

DEFER YOUR TAXES. One of the best ways to end up with more money is to defer taxes—earning something on the money the IRS would have had and paying later with ''cheaper'' dollars. (Income deferral is not always advisable—if you are subject to the alternative minimum tax or if you have an expiring net operating loss in 1987, for instance.) Under Tax Reform there are still many recommended ways to defer taxes:

- Enroll in a retirement plan at work. The best kind allows you to deduct the money you pay into the fund.
- Shift income to family members in lower tax brackets. This is harder to do under Tax Reform than it was in the past, but a few things you can still do are: choose investments for your children that don't produce income but do increase in value (sell after the child turns 14); make tax-exempt investments, such as zero-coupon tax exempts, until your child turns 14; employ your children in the family business; buy tax-deferred investments, such as U.S. Series EE Savings Bonds, timing the purchase so that the maturity date occurs after the child's fourteenth birthday; and buy tax-free municipal bonds, the interest income of which is tax-free.
- Ask your employer to defer salary or bonuses to 1988 or even later.
- Invest in six-month Treasury bills purchased after June 30 (the interest is not taxable until maturity, in 1988).
- If you are self-employed, time the invoices you send out so that you'll receive payment in 1988 instead of 1987.
- If you are the owner of a closely held corporation, delay the payment of dividends until next year.

ACCELERATE YOUR DEDUCTIONS. Because tax rates are dropping and because deductions are worth less when rates are low, accelerating your deductions produces the same effect as deferring your income. It makes sense to accelerate all deductible expenses into 1987. For example, if you are planning to make a contribution to a charity for the next five years, think about donating all five years' worth this year. Or consider refinancing your home in order to get a fully deductible mortgage interest.

BUY LIFE INSURANCE. Life insurance is still a viable tax shelter. There is no tax on the investment buildup in the policy unless you cash it in during your lifetime, and when your beneficiaries cash it in after your death, there will be no income tax to pay.

KEEP USING YOUR IRA. Under Tax Reform it still makes sense to use your IRA to the maximum. Save as much as you can for

—over—

retirement and forget about taxes. Taxpayers covered by a company retirement plan who earn more than $35,000 ($50,000 if married) may not deduct IRA contributions, but they may invest in a nondeductible IRA, the earnings of which will be tax-deferred. An IRA funded entirely with nondeductible contributions will be virtually tax-free upon its withdrawal at retirement, because the tax will already have been paid.

PAY OFF YOUR DEBTS. In 1987 you were entitled to deduct 65 percent of the interest you pay on personal loans, credit cards, etc. In 1988 the percentage will go down to 40, in 1989 it will be 20, and in 1990 it will be reduced to 10 percent. After that, none of your personal interest expense will be deductible. You can get around this phase-out by paying your debts in advance whenever possible. Some of the advantageous ways to do this are:

- Use your savings to pay off debts. You'll lose the interest you would have earned from a savings account, but remember, you would have had to pay tax on that interest.
- Borrow against the equity in your home. This interest will be fully deductible, because Tax Reform allows the deduction of interest on mortgages on your principal or second residence (up to the cost plus improvements).
- Borrow against the margin account you have with your stockbroker. The charges you incur may be as many as 10 points lower than those you would pay with a credit card.

REVIEW YOUR INVESTMENT STRATEGIES. There is no question that Tax Reform has forced many taxpayers to re-evaluate their financial plans. Some of the facts to keep in mind as you devise (and revise) your strategy are:

- As of 1988 preferential treatment of capital gains is eliminated; capital gains will be taxed as ordinary income. Because of the loss of the capital gains advantage, some people are getting out of the stock market and buying fixed-income securities and letting them grow, while others are turning to quality common stocks.
- In 1987 short-term gains are taxed at your top rate (up to 38.5 percent), and long-term gains are taxed at only 28 percent. In 1988 short- and long-term gains will be taxed at the same rate. Consider taking long-term gains this year and postponing short-term gains until next year (but only if you do not expect a change in the market to offset the tax advantage).
- Yields on tax-exempt municipal bonds are expected to range between 85 percent and 100 percent of the yields on long-term treasury bonds. Naturally, as these bonds become more popular, the price will go up, and the return will go down.

-over-

- If you plan to buy municipal bonds for a child who is not subject to the alternative minimum tax, look at private-purpose municipals issued to finance multi-family housing and airports. These bonds currently yield about a point more than ordinary public-purpose municipals, because interest on them is not subject to the alternative minimum tax.
- If you have passive losses, charitable donations of appreciated property, certain types of depreciation, and other items singled out by the tax law, you may be subject to the alternative minimum tax.
- If you are self-employed, you may contribute a significant part of your income to a Keogh plan. Under Tax Reform, this is still an excellent idea.

Now, with these facts in mind, it's time to learn _more_ about how to pay less tax legally.

Barry R. Steiner, C.P.A.

INTRODUCTION

How to Use This Book

Pay Less Tax Legally contains not only the tax law necessary to file an accurate income-tax return but also timely tax advice on how to get around the tax law—legally.

The book follows Form 1040 itself, in most instances line for line, so that even if you are a novice at preparing your tax return you should have no difficulty following along *and* saving taxes. Sample forms and schedules are filled out and included after their first mention in the text. (Some forms were not available when this book went to press. However, since no major changes are expected on these forms, last year's forms have been used for the purpose of illustration.) The book is basically organized in two columns—tax law and tax loopholes; an additional mini-column at the left-hand margin identifies the line number of the form being discussed. As you read *Pay Less Tax Legally,* you will find examples of actual court cases that were "against the grain"; they can be followed if the facts appear to be sufficiently close to your own.

Pay Less Tax Legally consists of two main sections:

I. Save Money Now

A complete, easy-to-follow instructional guide to deductions, credits, and tax-saving opportunities to use on this year's taxes.

II. Save Money Later

An in-depth analysis, arranged alphabetically by subject, of tax-planning opportunities to save next year's hard-earned dollars.

In addition, throughout the book you will find many tax-planning checklists called "The One-Minute Taxman." By filling out these checklists and using the data to prepare your tax return, you will find that you have gone a long way toward completing the forms you will need.

"Save Money Now" discusses who must file a return, how to claim an exemption, and which filing status to select. It then covers the reporting of income, supplemental income, business income, and capital gains and losses. Once you have arrived at your *total income,* you are permitted to deduct certain expenses regardless of whether you itemize or claim the standard deduction. These deductions are referred to as *adjustments to income* and include reimbursed employee business expenses, Individual Retirement Accounts, self-employed retirement plan deductions, forfeited interest, and alimony payments. These items are subtracted from total income to arrive at a figure known as *adjusted gross income.* At this juncture you have to decide whether to itemize or claim the standard deduction (and the only way to make that decision is to determine your deductions and see how much they total).

Now comes the moment of truth—the actual tax computation. Using the tax tables or the tax-rate schedules, compute your total tax on the basis of income minus the amount paid in during the year, either through quarterly estimated tax payments or amounts that have been withheld from your salary. That's when you learn whether you have either broken even with Uncle Sam, owe him money, or, with any luck and the information this book provides, have a refund coming.

The 1987 Tax Law in a Nutshell

As you have no doubt heard, 1986 was the last year with the old tax rates, and 1988 is the first year under the new tax rates. That makes 1987 the year in between.

New Tax Rates

Here are the 1987 rates. To compute your tax, find your status and income, multiply the excess over the lower end of your bracket by the rate for that bracket, and add the amount next to the rate to find your tax.

Joint Returns	Tax	Single Returns	Tax
0 to $3,000	0 + 11%	0 to $1,800	0 + 11%
$3,000 to 28,000	$330 + 15%	$1,800 to 16,800	$198 + 15%
$28,000 to 45,000	$4,080 + 28%	$16,800 to 27,000	$2,448 + 28%
$45,000 to 90,000	$8,840 + 35%	$27,000 to 54,000	$5,304 + 35%
over $90,000	$24,590 + 38½%	over 54,000	$14,754 + 38½%

● For heads of households, the brackets are about 85 percent of the joint rate. See Tax Rate Schedule Z on page 321 for specifics.

● Net long-term capital gain has a special top rate of 28 percent with the alternate tax.

● Marrieds under $28,000 income (AGI) and singles under $16,800 taxable AGI are fully taxed at 11 percent and 15 percent.

● For 1987, the 60 percent capital gains exclusion is repealed.

● Short-term gains are taxed as ordinary income at rates up to 38½ percent.

Standard Deductions for 1987

Beginning in 1987, you can claim the new standard deduction or total itemized deductions, whichever is greater. The standard deduction amounts are:

$3,760—married filing jointly or surviving spouse
$2,540—single or head of household
$1,880—married filing separately

For taxpayers who are blind or elderly, the standard deduction amounts are:

$5,000—married filing jointly or surviving spouse
$3,000—single
$4,400—head of household
$2,500—married filing separately

A married taxpayer filing jointly who is both elderly and blind may claim an additional $600; if both spouses are elderly and blind, they may claim a total of $1200 in addition to the $5,000 standard deduction.

A taxpayer who files as single or head of household and is either blind or elderly may claim an additional $750; if he or she is elderly *and* blind, he or she may deduct an additional $1,500 in addition to the $3,000 or $4,400 standard deduction.

Personal Exemptions

Personal exemptions for 1987 increased to $1,900, with no extra exemption at age 65; nonitemizers who are 65 and over get a larger standard deduction instead. Beginning in 1988, exemptions will phase out at higher brackets.

Earnings of Children

Dependents claimed on another person's return don't get a personal exemption, but they do get a standard deduction (same as singles). For children, the amount of income earned free of tax is limited to $500, and the full standard deduction can only be claimed against earned income.

Items No Longer Included

These items have been eliminated for 1987 by the Tax Reform Act:

1. Income averaging
2. Two-earner deduction
3. Charitable deduction for nonitemizers
4. Installment sales (now generally treated as ordinary income)
5. Casualty losses (not deductible if an insurance claim could be filed)
6. Moving expenses (unless itemized)
7. Unemployment compensation exclusion (unemployment compensation is now fully taxable)
8. Political contributions credit
9. Ten-year averaging for lump-sum distributions (exception: taxpayers born before 1936 may use it once); replaced with 5-year averaging.
10. $100/$200 dividend exclusion
11. State and local sales taxes
12. Adoption expenses (no more deduction for hard-to-place children)

Medical Expenses

The 5 percent floor has been increased to 7½ percent.

Interest Expense

Interest expenses on mortgages obtained before August 16, 1986, are fully deductible. Only 65 percent of the interest on most types of consumer loans can be deducted in 1987, even if the money was borrowed in 1987. This does not apply to plan loans made (or modified) after 1986 to key employees or an employee secured by a voluntary 401(k) plan.

Miscellaneous Deductions

Miscellaneous Deductions fall into 2 categories: those that are fully deductible and those that are partially deductible—to the extent that the total exceeds 2 percent of the AGI—adjusted gross income.

Fully Deductible

1. Estate taxes on income (taxed to estate)
2. Excess gambling losses (over winnings)
3. Some short sales costs
4. Impairment-related work expenses of the handicapped
5. Amortizable bond premiums
6. Some costs paid by a cooperative housing corporation

Partially Deductible

1. Job-hunting costs
2. Home office expenses
3. Safe deposit box fees
4. IRA custodial fees
5. Professional and investment journals
6. Union dues
7. Professional dues
8. Tax advice costs
9. Job-related education
10. Investment advice fees
11. Unreimbursed business meals and entertainment

Hobby Losses

If a hobby shows a profit in 3 out of 5 years, it is presumed to be for profit. Any loss incurred is deductible.

Foreign Income

The exclusion for income earned abroad dropped from $80,000 to $70,000.

Scholarships as Income

Scholarships not used for tuition or books (e.g., a grant for room and board) are taxed.

Individual Retirement Accounts

Taxpayers in the following income groups can make deductible pay-ins to an IRA of up to $2,000 (but not in excess of income). This may increase to $2,250 if the spouse does not work.

1. Couples with an adjusted gross income under $40,000. Deduction is phased out $1 for every $5 from $40,000 to $50,000, with a minimum deduction of $200 per person.
2. Singles with an adjusted gross income below $25,000. The phase-out is $1 for every $5 from $25,000 to $35,000, with the $200 minimum.
3. Employees not currently in a retirement plan (regardless of income).

If one spouse is in a qualified plan, IRA rules consider both to be in a plan, and combined income must be below $50,000 in order to qualify for an IRA deduction.

In 1987, employees whose income prohibits IRA deductions may claim a nondeductible IRA pay-in (marrieds, $50,000; singles, $35,000).

IRAs may be used to purchase new U.S. gold and silver bullion coins; the coins must be held by a trustee.

Contributions to Pension Plans—401(k) and 403(b) Annuities

Pay-ins decreased for 1987. The maximum is now $7,000 for 401(k)s, with tight new nondiscrimination rules. On 403(b)s, the maximum is $9,500, with nondiscrimination rules delayed until 1989.

Passive Losses

Any taxpayer who partly or completely owns an interest in a passive activity in which he or she does not regularly participate may be affected by the new passive-loss rule.

Passive losses cannot offset salary, interest, or other income.

The law says *all* income and loss of limited partners is passive, regardless of the size or operation of the business.

Most rental real estate (office buildings, apartments, homes) is affected.

When fewer than 6 individuals own more than half a company, the passive-loss ban will hurt. Owners of S corporations who are not active in the business will feel the pinch.

Unused passive losses can be used to offset the gain when the property is sold.

The passive-loss rule overrides interest deduction rules, so interest paid with regard to passive activities is netted with income and other expenses, and the interest expense is not deducted separately.

Deductible passive losses are subtracted from investment income (thereby reducing how much investment interest may be deducted).

Exceptions

There is an overall exception: a phase-out. In 1987 65 percent of passive losses are deductible; in 1988, it goes to 40 percent and stays there until phased out in 1990 (*after* using the $25,000 exception on real estate—see below). Investments made after October 22, 1986, do not qualify for this exception.

A more specific exception is the real estate exception. An owner can deduct combined rental losses up to $25,000 against other income, phasing out when the adjusted gross income exceeds $100,000; to zero loss when AGI reaches $150,000. To qualify for this $25,000 maximum loss, the individual must be active in operating the real estate (even through owner-directed agents). If the property is considered low-income or a rehab, the phase-out range is higher, and there does not have to be any personal involvement.

Finally, there is the oil and gas exception. Working interests in these ventures are not affected.

Estimated Taxes

You must prepay either 90 percent of actual 1987 tax or an amount equal to your 1986 tax (whichever is less) if you don't want to face an underpayment penalty. If the tax is under $500, a prepayment is not required.

Use of Calendar Year

S corporations, partnerships, personal service corporations, and most trusts will have to shift to a calendar tax year in 1987 because using a fiscal year will take away their ability to defer income and tax.

A special rule spreads the income from the short 1987 tax year over the next 4 years so that owners and trust beneficiaries do not have to report 2 years' income on the 1987 returns (income from the current tax year ending in 1987 plus income from the short year that ends December 31, 1987).

Standard Mileage Rate

The standard mileage rate for cars used for business purposes has been increased to 22.5 cents per mile, up from 21 cents per mile for the first 15,000 miles of business usage. The rate for business usage over 15,000 miles stays at 11 cents per mile.

Summary of New Tax Law Affecting Individuals

Law Affected	Old Tax Law	Tax Reform	Effective Date of Change
Charitable Deductions	Fully deductible for itemizers and non-itemizers	Deductible only for itemizers	1-1-87
Deferred Savings Plans (401(k))	Allows up to $30,000 a year	Limited to $7,000 a year	1-1-87
Income Averaging	Allowed	Not allowed	1-1-87
Individual Retirement Account Contributions	$2,000; $250 for non-working spouse. These amounts can be split in any proportion as long as no more than $2,000 is credited to one individual's account.	$2,000 deductible for low- and middle-income workers; phased out for upper-middle- and high-income workers with pension plans	1-1-87
Interest Deductions	$10,000 plus amount equal to investment income	Consumer interest not deductible; investment interest deductible up to amount of investment income	5-year phase-in
Long-term capital gains	20% top rate	28% top rate	1-1-87
Medical deductions	Deductible in excess of 5% of adjusted gross income	Deductible in excess of 7.5% of adjusted gross income	1-1-87
Miscellaneous deductions	Fully deductible	Deductible in excess of 2% of AGI	1-1-87
Mortgage Interest	All mortgages, including home equity loans, fully deductible	Principal and second residence interest fully deductible; interest on home equity loans deductible if used for home purchase, home improvement, medical, or educational expenses	8-16-86
Pension benefits	Up to 3 years to recover contributions	New retirees who contributed to their own pension plan start paying tax immediately on their benefits	1-1-87

Law Affected	Old Tax Law	Tax Reform	Effective Date of Change
Personal exemption	$1,080	$2,000 ($1,900 in 1987, $1,950 in 1988); phased out for incomes above $149,250.	3-year phase-in
Tax rates	14 rates from 11% to 50%	2 rates in 1988: 15% up to $29,750 (marrieds); $17,850 (singles); generally 28% tax over these amounts. There are "blended" tax rates for 1987.	3-15-87
Short-term capital gains	50% top rate	28% top rate	1-1-88
Standard deduction	Joint filers, $3,670; head of household, $2,480; singles, $2,480.	Joint filers, $5,000; head of household, $4,400; singles, $3,000	1-1-88
State and local taxes	Fully deductible	Deductible except for sales taxes	1-1-87
Tax shelters	No limits on using losses from "passive" investments to offset other income	Prohibits use of losses from "passive" investments to offset other income	5-year phase-in for existing investments
Two-earner deduction	Yes	No	1-1-87

The New Tax Reform Law, A to Z

About 4 out of 5 taxpayers should benefit from the Tax Reform Act by receiving a tax cut. Generally speaking, the tax cut will result from significant cuts in personal income tax rates. In addition, personal exemptions and the standard deduction amounts have been significantly increased.

When President Reagan assumed office, in 1981, the highest marginal individual tax rate was 70 percent. This rate was reduced to 50 percent in 1981. The current legislation goes considerably further by cutting it back to 28 percent, the lowest tax marginal tax rate since the development of the modern tax code, in 1916.

These changes in tax rates in the personal exemption and standard deduction amounts will not be fully implemented until 1988. Therefore, although individuals can, on average, expect a slightly lower tax bill in 1987, their 1988 tax bill should be lowered even more.

For this year, there are 5 marginal tax rates ranging from 11–38½ percent. When the new individual income tax rates are fully implemented in 1988, there will be only 2 tax rates, 15 percent and 28 percent, based upon taxable income as follows:

	15 PERCENT	28 PERCENT
Single Taxpayers	$0–17,850	$17,850–over
Married Taxpayers	$0–29,750	$29,750–over
Head of Household	$0–25,288	$25,288–over

Although at first blush the new maximum rate of 28 percent appears very attractive, it is somewhat misleading. In their quest for revenue, Congress added to the new tax code provisions that raise the marginal tax rate in many cases to 33 percent, and in some cases to as high as 49.5 percent. Basically, these provisions raise the rate for high-income taxpayers by phasing out the benefit of the lower 15 percent bracket (for 1988), thereby taxing all income at the 28 percent rate for such taxpayers (and killing once and for all the notion of a graduated-rate approach to taxation), and also by phasing out the ability of high-income taxpayers to claim personal exemptions for themselves, their spouses, their children, and other family members. The phase-out of these benefits (for 1988) is accomplished by placing a surcharge of 5 percent on income between $43,150 and $89,650 for singles, or between $71,900 and $149,250 for married couples, which effectively raises the tax on the first bracket of income from 15 percent to 28 percent, and by thereafter placing a further 5 percent surcharge on income beyond $89,650 for singles and $149,250 for marrieds until all personal exemptions are eliminated. Again, this is for 1988.

The deep cuts in individual tax rates do not, unfortunately, come without a price. Basic mathematics tells us that when we reduce the rate at which income is to be taxed, we must increase the amount of income subject to tax if the bill is to remain revenue-neutral. Thus, although the latest version of tax reform will produce a net reduction in individual income tax collections (to be matched by a corresponding increase in business tax collections), the legislation has made dramatic revisions to the definition of what income is taxable at the newly reduced rates. For example, the new tax bill strictly limits writeoffs for tax shelters, reduces other tax breaks, and does away with the time-honored reduced tax rate for long-term capital gains. Therefore, depending upon your financial circumstances, you may make out better or worse than under the current tax code.

An Overview of Tax Reform

The increased personal exemptions will look good to many taxpayers ($1,900 in 1987 will increase to $2,000 in 1989). Nonitemizers will benefit a little from the increased standard deduction ($5,000 in 1988 for couples; $3,000 for singles).

For all intents and purposes, deductible IRA contributions are eliminated ($50,000 AGI for a married couple covered under a company qualified pension or profit-sharing plan), and contributions to pensions have dropped from a ceiling of $30,000 to $7,000. Sales taxes, consumer interest, the married worker deduction, political contributions credit, income averaging, and the dividends exclusion will no longer be around. Medical expenses now have a 7½ percent floor instead of 5 percent. Most miscellaneous itemized deductions and some reimbursed employee business expenses now must exceed 2 percent of AGI to be deductible.

Interest on home mortgages can be deducted on only 2 residences and only to the extent of loans up to the original purchase price of the residence plus cost of improvements (except for borrowing for education or medical expenses). Investment interest is deductible only to the extent of investment income (no longer $10,000 maximum).

Once the new tax rate reductions are fully phased in (in 1988), ordinary income will be subject to a top tax rate of 28 percent, including long-term capital gains. As of 1987, individual taxpayers are subject to a new 21 percent alternative minimum tax, which now includes as a tax preference certain tax-exempt interest and appreciation on charitable gifts. Tax shelters will be hard to come by and perhaps not even necessary.

Because of tough new rules, small businesses may have to close out their pension plans. There are several cutbacks in family income-splitting and the use of spousal remainder trusts; the end of the use of Clifford trusts is in sight.

Accountants will be busy keeping up with phase-outs (the 15 percent bracket, personal exemptions, the $25,000 rental real estate maximum, passive losses connected with pre-1986 investments, consumer interest deductions) and with phase-ins for the new standard deductions and personal exemptions.

In addition to routine year-to-year tax planning, there are 5 tax brackets in 1987 and the 28 percent top rate for capital gains to deal with.

Some expenses that have been considered fully deductible are being limited for the first time: for example, the 2 percent floor on expenses for production of income and the 80 percent maximum deduction for business meals and entertainment.

On the plus side, there will no longer be the 14 tax brackets to contend with; however, upper income earners will have their problems. As the 15 percent bracket is phased out, there will be a 33 percent marginal rate. As personal exemptions are phased out, there will be another series of brackets, depending on the number of exemptions claimed. The phase-out of IRA deductions, passive losses, and the $25,000 rental real estate maximum will cause still more tax brackets to appear.

Financial and Estate Planning

Here is a checklist of provisions of the 1986 Tax Reform Act that affect financial and estate planning.

1. *Standard deduction.* For 1988, the standard deduction is $5,000 joint, surviving spouses; $4,400 head of household; $3,000 singles; and $2,500 on separate returns. The standard deduction is increased for the elderly and for the blind.
2. *Itemized deductions for state and local sales taxes.* These have been eliminated.
3. *Personal exemptions.* Increased to $1,900 for 1987; $1,950 for 1988; $2,000 for 1989. If a child is eligible as a dependent on another's return, there is no exemption, but the dependent is allowed a standard deduction of $500 (or earned income, whichever is greater). There is no additional exemption for the elderly or blind.
4. *Tax rates.* For 1988, there are basically 2 brackets: 15 percent and 28 percent. The 28 percent bracket applies to income over $29,750 on a joint return. The 15 percent bracket is phased out by applying a 5 percent rate adjustment (on joint returns, for income between $71,900 and $149,250). For 1987, a 5-rate

structure exists with a top of 38.5 percent on income over $90,000 for marrieds filing jointly.

5. *Unearned income of child under 14.* All unearned income over $500 is taxed to a child at the parents' top marginal rate. This income can be reduced by the $500 standard deduction so that only unearned income over $1,000 will be taxed at the parents' rates.
6. *Personal interest.* Repealed but phased in over 5 years, with 65 percent allowed in 1987, reduced to zero in 1991. Qualified first- and second-home interest and interest on loans secured by residence are deductible, but not in excess of the original cost (plus improvements) or for medical and educational expenses.
7. *Miscellaneous deductions.* Items such as investment expenses, certain employee business expenses, and the cost of tax advice are deductible only to the extent that they exceed 2 percent of the adjusted gross income. Some expenses, such as administration expenses of estates and trusts and gambling losses, are not subject to this 2 percent floor.
8. *Income averaging.* Gone.
9. *Charitable deduction for nonitemizers.* Gone.
10. *Married worker deduction.* Gone.
11. *Employee awards.* Limited exclusion for employee awards for length of service or safety achievement.
12. *Hobby losses.* If the activity is profitable in 3 out of 5 years, it is considered a for-profit enterprise.
13. *Moving expenses.* Changed to an itemized deduction instead of allowed before adjusted gross income. Not affected by new 2 percent floor.
14. *Itemized medical deductions.* Floor increased from 5 percent to 7.5 percent of AGI.
15. *Travel expenses for attending conventions.* Not deductible when attending a convention or seminar for investment purposes.
16. *Nonbusiness casualty losses.* Allowed *only* if insurance claim is filed.
17. *Estimated tax.* Changed from 80 percent to 90 percent which must be paid in order to avoid penalty.
18. *Charitable travel deductions.* Not allowed unless you can prove *no* element of personal pleasure, vacation, or recreation when away from home.
19. *Home office deductions.* Deductions are limited to net income from the business. (Disallowed deductions may be carried forward to later years.) Limits on employee leasing portion of home to employer.
20. *Charitable contributions.* As result of elimination of capital gains preference, any tax deduction is limited to the donor's cost basis in the property.
21. *Interest on installment payments of life insurance.* The $1,000 annual exclusion for interest received by a surviving spouse is gone.
22. *Unemployment compensation.* Fully taxable.
23. *Investment tax credit.* Scale-down of carryover.

Investments—Changes under Tax Reform

1. *Dividend exclusion.* $100/$200 dividend exclusion is repealed.
2. *Investment interest.* Generally limited to amount of net investment income.

16 Introduction

When you compute net investment income, passive losses allowed under the 5-year phase-in of losses are deducted from investment income. Deductions for investment income are no longer limited to investment income plus $10,000.

3. *Capital gains.* Taxed at same rate as ordinary income but no higher than 28 percent during 1987.
4. *Passive losses.* Net losses from passive activities may not be deducted against ordinary income (except investment income) to the extent that they exceed income from all such activities.

One exception involves rental real estate activities in which an individual actively participates. In that case, up to $25,000 of losses may be applied against nonpassive income; however, the $25,000 of losses is phased out between $100,000 and $150,000 of adjusted gross income.

5. *Rehab credits.* Rehabilitation credits and low-income housing credits may be used to offset tax on up to $25,000 of nonpassive income regardless of whether the taxpayer actively participates. These rehab credits are subject to a phaseout between $200,000 and $250,000 AGI.

Tax Reform replaces the previous three-tier credit with a two-tier credit. Buildings built before 1936 (except certified historic structures) qualify for 10 percent, and certified historic structures are eligible for 20 percent. Their tax basis is reduced by the full amount of any credit. These new rules are effective for property placed in service after 1986.

6. *Penalties on withdrawal of deferred annuity contracts.* Beginning in 1987, the early withdrawal penalty is increased from 5 percent to 10 percent.
7. *At risk rules.* New rules are extended to real estate activities and apply to property acquired in 1987 and after. The at-risk rules are subject to an exception for qualified nonrecourse financing secured by real property used in the activity. Qualified nonrecourse financing comes from traditional lenders as opposed to seller financing.
8. *Credit for low-income housing.* Owners of residential rental property that provides low-income housing get a new tax credit, which replaces existing incentives (5-year amortization of rehabilitation expenses, special treatment of construction period interest and taxes, and preferential depreciation). There are separate credits for new construction and rehabilitation of low-income housing and for certain costs to purchase existing housing for low-income individuals.

Credits allowed must be reduced by the amount of any rehabilitation credit for which the property is eligible. The basis for depreciation is not reduced by the amount of low-income housing tax credits claimed.

Credits are claimed each year for 10 years. For property placed in service in 1987, the annual credit is 9 percent for new construction (and rehabilitation) and a maximum of 4 percent for acquiring existing housing.

The low-income housing credit is effective for property placed in service after 1986 and before 1990, with an exception for certain property placed in service after 1989.

The New Tax Law A–Z

On the following pages, in alphabetical order, are some of the many areas in which tax law changes may affect your return. After you've had a chance to go through them, try your hand at computing your taxes under the current and future tax codes on the worksheet appearing on page 30. Good luck!

Adoption

Expenses in connection with adoption of a child with special needs are no longer deductible.

Alternative Minimum Tax

Anyone whose tax liability is more under the new minimum tax (than under the regular tax) must pay the minimum tax. After adding back certain tax preferences to taxable income, $40,000 is then exempted for marrieds; $30,000 for singles. The tax on the remainder is 21 percent.

For high-income taxpayers, the exemptions will be phased out. For each dollar of income over $150,000 for marrieds ($112,500 for singles), the exempted amounts will be reduced by 25 cents, which will result in roughly a 26 percent alternative minimum tax to those in the phase-out range.

Awards

All employee awards and bonuses are included in income except those of tangible personal property up to $400 given for longevity or safety achievement.

Barriers to the Handicapped

Provisions for deducting the costs of removing barriers to the handicapped (as well as to spouses of Vietnam MIAs) have been extended.

Business Meals/T & E

Only 80 percent of business meals and entertainment is allowed, and deductions are limited for luxury water transportation—e.g., cruises. Deductions will be phased out for luxury skyboxes at stadiums and are eliminated completely for educational travel as well as travel costs to attend investment conventions or seminars.

Capital Gains and Losses

The net capital gains exclusion is repealed, so capital gains are taxed the same as ordinary income. Losses can offset other income by no more than $3,000 a year. For 1987, the tax on capital gains is no more than the top individual tax rate (which became effective on July 1). The top capital gains rate is limited to 28 percent, even though the initial mixed top individual rate could be as high as 49.5 percent.

Certified Historic Structures

Certified historic structures qualify for a 20 percent rehabilitation investment tax credit. Other buildings placed in service before 1936 get a 10 percent investment tax credit for qualified rehabilitation expenses.

Charitable Deductions

The charitable deduction for nonitemizers is eliminated.

Children's Earnings

Clifford trusts are eliminated. Generally, a minor's unearned income over $1,000 is taxed to the child at the parent's top tax rate. In addition, children claimed as dependents by their parents cannot claim a personal exemption a second time on their own returns.

The new tax bill requires taxpayers to show the Social Security number of every person claimed as a dependent who is over age 5, which should discourage divorced parents from both claiming the same child.

Credits

Business credits: These can be used only to offset tax liability up to $25,000, plus 75 percent of tax liability in excess of $25,000.

Jobs credit: This credit is extended three more years; however, second-year wages are not eligible for the credit.

Incremental research tax credit: This credit is extended four more years. The general business credit limitation applies, and research for credit purposes will be defined.

Depreciation

Autos and light trucks are written off over 5 years (instead of 3). Most manufacturing *equipment* is written off over 7 years (instead of 5); long-life equipment, 10 years. There are 7 new categories of assets, and investments in some short-lived assets can be written off over 3 years.

Depreciation on luxury autos is limited to $2,560 in the first year, $4,100 for the second, $2,450 for the third, and $1,475 for each succeeding year.

Most equipment writeoffs are calculated using the 200 percent declining balance method (instead of 150 percent), permitting faster writeoffs in the initial years.

Residential rental property is written off with the straight-line method over 27.5 years. Nonresidential real estate is written off over 31.5 years.

Small businesses can write off up to $10,000 cost of equipment per year. This fast writeoff will be phased out for businesses investing more than $200,000 annually.

Dividend Exclusion

The $100/$200 dividend exclusion is eliminated.

Earned Income Credit

The earned income credit is increased to help low-income families with children. The new credit is limited to $800 and is phased out for workers earning between $9,000 and $17,000.

Educational Travel

No deduction will be allowed for the cost of educational travel; however, the cost of traveling to and from school to take classes is fully deductible.

Elderly or Blind

The elderly and blind get an additional standard deduction of $600 if married; if single, it's $750. This is in addition to the credit for the elderly and the permanently and totally disabled.

Employee Business Expenses

Unreimbursed employee business expenses will be deductible only by those who itemize and only to the extent that total expenses exceed 2 percent of adjusted gross income. Handicapped employees get a special tax break for certain business expenses.

Energy Tax Credits

The solar energy credit is extended at 20 percent for 1987 and 20 percent for 1988.

Estimated Tax Payments

The amount of estimated tax payments increases from 80 percent to 90 percent of the current year tax liability.

Exclusions of Awards and Prizes

The exclusion for certain awards and prizes is allowed only when the recipient assigns payment of the award or prize to a tax-exempt charity.

Exemptions

The personal exemption increases from $1,080 to $1,900 in 1987; to $1,950 in 1988; and to $2,000 in 1989. These amounts will be phased out in 1988, however, for taxpayers with higher income. The phase-outs are: for marrieds, between $145,320 and $185,320; for heads of household, between $111,400 and $151,400; and for singles, between $87,240 and $127,240.

The extra exemption for the blind and elderly is eliminated and replaced by a $600 additional standard deduction for marrieds; if single, $750.

Children eligible to be claimed as dependents on their parents' return will not be allowed to claim a second personal exemption on their own returns.

Expensing Business Assets in One Year

A maximum $10,000 cost of tangible personal business property can be written off in one year; however, when the taxpayer's total investment in such property exceeds $200,000 (for the year), the $10,000 maximum will be phased out.

Farm Financing

Financing on depreciable farm property is allowed up to a maximum of $250,000 cost of property for any principal user.

Foreign Income

The foreign earned income exclusion is reduced to $70,000 and is no longer available to citizens of the U.S. who live and work in a foreign country. It may be wise for someone working abroad to take a credit directly against U.S. tax for foreign tax paid (on the income) instead of using the optional foreign earned income exclusion. Americans living in a foreign country who have not fully used the housing cost exclusion may be able to offset that exclusion against their income.

General Business Credit

Limits on the amount of income tax liability over $25,000 that can be reduced by business tax credits are reduced from 85 percent to 75 percent.

Green Card

Permanent U.S. resident aliens applying for renewal of a green card will have to show that they filed income tax returns during the years since the last renewal application, or that they were exempt from filing.

Health Insurance

Self-employeds can deduct one-half the cost of health insurance premiums under a nondiscriminatory plan.

Hobby Losses

The new law places limits on claiming recurring business losses referred to as hobby losses. An activity (other than horseracing or breeding) will be assumed not to be a hobby if it is profitable in 3 out of 5 consecutive years.

Home Office Deductions

Under the new law, home office expenses, all other unreimbursed employee business expenses, and miscellaneous itemized deductions must be lumped together and are deductible only to the extent that the total exceeds 2 percent of adjusted gross income.

Leasing of Home Offices: Under the new law, when a portion of the taxpayer's home is leased to an employer, a home office deduction cannot be claimed. An independent contractor is considered an employee, and the person(s) he worked for is/are considered employer(s).

Income Averaging

Generally, income averaging is eliminated. However, 5-year averaging is available for some recipients of lump-sum distributions.

Income Shifting

The unearned income over $1,000 of a child under age 14 is taxed to the child at the parents' tax rate.

Indexing

Indexing of exemptions and deductions is suspended.

Information Reporting

On real estate sales, royalty payments, and federal contracts, more detailed information reporting will be required.

Interest Expense

Beginning in 1987 (and phased in over 4 years), no deduction is allowed for interest paid on any consumer purchases except home mortgages. For consumer interest writeoffs, 35 percent is disallowed in 1987, 60 percent in 1988, 80 percent in 1989, 90 percent in 1990, and 100 percent in 1991 and thereafter.

Except for interest paid on deferred estate tax, interest on income tax underpayments will become nondeductible.

Interest—Home Mortgage

The new tax law eliminates interest deductions on consumer loans but still allows an interest deduction on mortgage interest. In an effort to close the potential loophole of taxpayers "abusing" homeowner loans, the new law limits the deductibility of mortgage interest. It permits an interest writeoff only on principal and second homes, with the loan amount limited to the original purchase price plus improvements. The only exceptions are for the inclusion of educational and medical costs in the loan amount. However, there is no deduction for interest on loans secured by appreciated value of the property.

The interest on a mortgage (or home equity loan) incurred before August 16, 1986, remains deductible in full. Interest on mortgages taken out after this date are subject to the new limitations.

It may become a way of life for homeowners to use home-equity loans for consumer purchases, vacations, or a new car purchase, even though consumer interest is not deductible under the new law. There are usually no prepayment restrictions or penalties on home-equity loans, and, once a credit line is established with a bank, money can be borrowed any time. Some banks are already informing their mortgage customers about the new tax bill and suggesting ways to utilize a credit line through the bank.

Interest Rates

There is a one percent differential between interest rates paid on refunds and collected on deficiencies by the IRS, naturally in favor of the IRS.

Investment Interest

There are greater limitations on deducting investment interest not in connection with a taxpayer's business, limited to net investment income only.

Net Lease Provisions: If certain rental deductions are less than 15 percent of rental income, the property will be treated as investment property. Under the new law, the 15 percent test will include the value of the taxpayer's personal management and repair services as well as actual out-of-pocket expenses.

Phase-In: Due to the 5-year phase-in, taxpayers have some time to decide what to do with their investment property. The phase-in percentages are: 35 percent of investment interest disallowed in 1987, 60 percent in 1988, 80 percent in 1989, 90 percent in 1990, and 100 percent in 1991 and thereafter.

Carry-overs: Any disallowed investment interest may still be carried over and treated as investment interest in the following tax year. In this way excess investment interest will not be lost, only deferred.

Investment Seminars

No deduction will be allowed for the cost of investment seminars or conventions.

IRA Contributions

All taxpayers may continue contributing to an Individual Retirement Account. However, effective January 1, 1987, the contributions to the IRA may no longer be deductible. Regardless of whether the IRA contribution is deductible, earnings from IRA contributions will still be tax-free until withdrawn. The penalty for early withdrawal increases from 10 percent to 15 percent (except for distributions in the form of a single life or joint and survivor annuity).

For those employees covered by qualified employer pension plans, deductions for IRA contributions will begin phasing out at $25,000 income for singles and $40,000 for married couples. No IRA deductions are allowed after $35,000 income for singles and $50,000 income for married couples.

Taxpayers who are denied IRA deductions can still make nondeductible IRA contributions up to $2,000 and defer taxes on earnings from the IRAs.

IRA contributors may acquire certain gold and silver coins issued by the United States.

Low-Income Housing Credit

There is a new tax credit for low-income housing, depending on the median income of the tenants.

Lump-Sum Distributions

A one-time election of 5-year forward averaging after age 59½ replaces 10-year averaging for lump-sum distributions. Capital gains treatment of the pre-1974 portion will be phased out over 6 years. For those age 50 by January 1, 1986, a special transition rule applies allowing election of either the 5-year or the 10-year averaging, regardless of the age 59½ requirement.

Married Worker Deduction

The married worker deduction is eliminated.

Medical Expenses

The medical expense floor increased from 5 percent to 7½ percent of adjusted gross income, and self-employed taxpayers can deduct 25 percent of the health insurance premiums paid for themselves and their dependents under a nondiscriminatory employer-provided health plan.

Miscellaneous Itemized Deductions

Deductions for safe deposit boxes, income tax preparation fees, union dues, etc., are deductible to the extent that they exceed 2 percent of adjusted gross income. Exceptions to this 2 percent floor are employment-related expenses for disabled employees, certain expenses for adopting children with special needs, and moving expenses.

The new tax law exempts actors from the 2 percent floor, since they rely heavily on being able to deduct employee business expenses. Actors with an adjusted gross income of less than $16,000 will be treated as independent contractors.

Moving Expenses

Only taxpayers who itemize may claim moving expenses, without the 2 percent floor.

Penalties

The negligence penalty is increased from 5 percent to 10 percent, and the fraud penalty increased from 50 percent to 75 percent; however, only the underpayment attributable to the taxpayer's negligence (or fraud) will be subject to the increased penalty.

Penalty for failure to pay tax on time doubled to 1 percent per month.

Pensions and Annuities

Plans involving nondeductible employee contributions have new basis recovery rules on money distributions. For pension distributions received after the annuity starting date, the 3-year basis recovery rule is eliminated, which means that part of each payment would be considered income; the remainder, a recovery of employee contributions.

For pension distributions before the annuity starting date, employee contributions would be recovered pro rata. For instance, if an employee has contributed $12,000 to his pension and the total benefits are valued at $60,000, one-fifth of the withdrawal would be treated as a recovery of employee contributions. The balance would be fully taxable as income.

Pensions—Premature Distributions

In the case of pension distributions before age 59½, disability, or separation from service, there is a 15 percent premature withdrawal penalty, except for (1) distributions in the form of single life (or joint and survivor annuity), (2) distributions following early retirement after age 55, and (3) distributions in the case of unforeseen hardship.

Retirement Pay-Out Options: Taxpayers who reached age 50 before January 1, 1986, may choose between 10-year or the new 5-year averaging on lump-sum distributions. Government and private sector workers who retired after June 30, 1986, and contributed to their pension start paying tax immediately on their benefits.

Political Contributions Credit

The political contributions tax credit is repealed.

Rates of Tax

Tax Rates for 1987

Singles:

INCOME	RATE
$0–1,800	11%
$1,800–16,800	15%
$16,800–27,000	28%
$27,000–54,000	35%
over $54,000	38½%

Marrieds Filing Jointly:

INCOME	RATE
$0–3,000	11%
$3,000–28,000	15%
$28,000–45,000	28%
$45,000–90,000	35%
over $90,000	38½%

Tax Rates for 1988: The tax rates for 1988 will be 15 percent and 28 percent, with a 5 percent rate adjustment for phasing out the lower rate. (The 5 percent adjustment would start at taxable income of $43,150 for singles and $71,900 for marrieds filing jointly.)

Rehabilitation Tax Credit

Under the new law, nonhistoric structures placed in service before 1936 get a 10 percent credit; certified historic structures, a 20 percent credit. The new credit applies to property on which rehabilitation was completed after January 1, 1987.

Research and Development

The credit for increases in research and development spending is reduced from 25 to 20 percent.

Return-Preparer Fees

Return-preparer fees, cost of tax publications, and investment fees are not deductible in 1987 unless they are business expenses and they exceed 2 percent of AGI.

Salary Reduction Plans (401(k))

The maximum elective deferral is lowered from $30,000 to $7,000. Salary reductions above $7,000 are included in gross income.

An employer making excess contributions is subject to a 10 percent excise tax unless the excess (plus earnings on that excess) was distributed within 2½ months after the close of the company's tax year.

Hardship withdrawals from a salary reduction plan will be permitted without penalty only on elective deferrals, not on income earned on the deferrals. If the 401(k) plan was terminated, distributions would be allowed without penalty, but only if there was no successor plan and the distribution consisted of the total balance in the employee's account.

Sales Tax

State and local sales taxes are no longer deductible. However, businesses may include sales tax in the depreciable basis of purchased property, and may continue to deduct sales tax as a business expense. Sales tax paid by a business when acquiring depreciable property is not deductible; it is treated as part of the cost of the property to be depreciated.

Scholarships

Special awards and prizes granted for achievement in fields such as charity, arts, or science no longer have a special exclusion. Even Nobel prizes are now subject to tax.

Scholarships and fellowships are taxable except for amounts spent on tuition, course-required equipment (for degree candidates), or incidental travel, research, clerical, and equipment expenses (for non-degree candidates).

Standard Deduction

Under the new law, the standard deduction is not built into the rate tables; it is subtracted from income before taxes are computed. The standard deduction will be adjusted each year after 1988 to reflect inflation.

The elderly or blind get an additional $600 deduction if married ($750 if single) in addition to the standard deduction.

The standard deduction for 1987 is $3,760 for marrieds filing jointly, and $2,540 for singles and heads of households. The standard deduction for 1988 will be $3,000 for singles; $5,000 for marrieds filing jointly; and $4,400 for heads of households.

Standard Mileage Rate

Increased to 22.5 cents per mile for the first 15,000 miles of business usage, 11 cents thereafter.

Straddles

Under new loss deferral rules, a qualified covered call option is denied a taxpayer who fails to hold an option for 30 days after the related stock is sold at a loss. This only affects straddles wherein a gain on the sale is included as income the following year.

Targeted Jobs Credit

The targeted jobs credit (for employers who hire economically disadvantaged employees) is extended for 3 years.

Tax Shelters

A loss from a non-participatory business activity cannot be used against other income (i.e., salary or investment income), but can only offset a gain from another passive activity.

Unused tax writeoffs can be carried forward and used against a gain at the time of sale of the entire investment.

This limitation of losses is to be phased in over 5 years for existing investments, with 35 percent of the loss disallowed in 1987, 60 percent in 1988, 80 percent in 1989, 90 percent in 1990, and 100 percent starting in 1991. New investments will be subject to the disallowance rule immediately.

A taxpayer who is actively participating in rental activities (e.g., collecting rents, repairing, and decorating) will be allowed to use losses (and credits) from the rentals to offset up to $25,000 of nonpassive income, e.g., salary. Taxpayers with adjusted gross income from $100,000 to $150,000 must phase out even this $25,000 loss.

Investment Interest: Investment interest is deductible only to the extent of investment income. Excess investment interest disallowed could be carried indefinitely. This rule will be phased in over a 5-year period.

At-Risk Rules: This has been extended to include real estate investments, but it does not include new recourse debt extended by qualified third parties.

Recovery Period: Increased to 27½ years for depreciating residential realty and 31½ years for commercial property. Additional depreciation would be straight-line.

Rehabilitation Credits: Buildings over 50 years old are eligible for a 10 percent rehabilitation credit, and certified historic structures are eligible for a 20 percent credit.

Low-Income Housing: The new law creates a special credit for projects using federal, state, or local housing funds.

Tax-Exempt Bonds: Interest on bonds issued by government for building schools or highways continues to be tax-free.

Travel Expenses

Deductions in connection with luxury water travel—cruises, for instance—are limited to twice the highest federal per diem rate for travel in the United States.

Unemployment Compensation

The partial exclusion for unemployment compensation benefits has been eliminated. All unemployment benefits are taxable.

Widow's Exclusion

The $1,000 annual exclusion ends for interest and installment insurance payouts.

How Will You Come Out Under the New Tax Law?

Take out a copy of your 1986 tax return and use this guide to estimate how the new tax changes will affect you. Complete the worksheet on page 30 to see how you come out on 1987 and 1988 taxes.

Income

1. *Wages, salaries, tips:* No real changes from old law.
2. *Interest income:* No changes except that certain private-purpose, tax-free bonds issued after 8/7/86 may affect the minimum tax.
3. *Dividends:* The $100/$200 dividend exclusion is out. Report all dividends.
4. *Capital gains:* In 1987 and 1988 columns, no capital gain exclusion is allowed, which means that all long-term gains are taxable. Capital losses are still limited to $3,000 a year.

5. *Rents, royalties, partnerships:* Tax shelter and rental losses will no longer be allowed, with a 4-year phase-out (in 1987, you can claim 65 percent of losses; in 1988, 40 percent; after 1989, zero). However, there is an exception for oil and gas drilling partnerships in which investors have a "working interest."

    A taxpayer who owns (and manages) rental property with an adjusted gross income of less than $100,000 can claim only up to $25,000 in rental losses. With an adjusted gross income of $100,000 to $150,000, the loss limit is phased out, and no deduction will be allowed for taxpayers reporting an adjusted gross income of over $150,000.

    If an investor has tax credits from low-income housing (or historic rehabilitation projects) the $150,000 maximum is increased to an adjusted gross income of $200,000 and phases out with an adjusted gross income of $200,000 to $250,000.
6. *Unemployment compensation:* There is no partial exclusion of benefits; in 1987 and 1988 the entire amount will be taxable.
7. *Excess 401(k) contributions (Salary Reduction Plan):* Only the first $7,000 contributed can be excluded from income; amounts over $7,000 should be entered in 1987 and 1988.
8. *Social Security Benefits:* The same calculations will be used as in 1986. The number in 1987 and 1988 will be unchanged.
9. *Other income:* The exclusion of certain awards and prizes is repealed. Business income is subject to changes in depreciation and limitation of other business writeoffs. Lump-sum pension distributions will no longer qualify for 10-year averaging. (See page 194 for exceptions.)
10. *Total income:* Add items 1 through 9 to arrive at total income.

Adjustments to Income

11. *Moving expenses:* Moving expenses can be claimed only as an itemized deduction, but not subject to the 2 percent floor.
12. *Employee business expenses:* Only itemizers can claim most types of employee business expenses. Only amounts reimbursed by an employer will be deductible as adjustments. Enter these figures in 1987 and 1988. Enter all other employee business expenses as itemized deductions.
13. *Keogh plan deduction:* No change.
14. *Two-earner deduction:* The married worker deduction is repealed.
15. *Other adjustments:* No major changes.

Adjusted Gross Income Before IRA Deduction

Subtract all adjustments (lines 11 through 15) from total income (line 10) and enter amount on line 16.

IRA Deduction

Taxpayers not covered by a company pension plan continue to deduct up to $2,000 a year and an extra $250 for a nonworking spouse.

Single employees covered by a company pension plan earning between $25,000 and $35,000 (couples between $40,000 and $50,000) only get a partial IRA deduction; for each $1,000 of income over those limits, they lose $200 of the maximum IRA writeoff.

Employees covered by a company plan who earn more than $35,000 ($50,000 for

28 *Introduction*

couples) can set aside $2,000 annually for an IRA but may not claim it on their taxes. However, the interest will accumulate tax-free until the funds are taken out.

Adjusted Gross Income

Subtract any IRA deduction (line 17) from the figure for "Adjusted gross income before IRA deduction" (line 16) and enter the total on line 18.

Itemized Deductions

19. *Medical expenses:* The floor is 7.5 percent of adjusted gross income.
20. *State and local income, real estate, and personal property taxes:* No change from the old law.
21. *State and local sales taxes:* No more deductions are permitted under the new tax law.
22. *Mortgage interest:* Interest paid on first and second homes is still deductible, limited to original purchase price plus cost of home improvements. The only exceptions are for amounts borrowed against the equity for educational or medical expenses.
23. *Other interest:* No deductions are allowed for interest on charge cards, car loans, or other consumer purchases. On loans used to finance investments, the interest deduction is limited to investment income. This disallowance of consumer interest will be phased in over 5 years (in 1987, claim 65 percent of consumer interest; in 1988, claim 40 percent).
24. *Charitable contributions:* No changes for itemizers.
25. *Casualty and theft losses:* No changes except that an insurance claim must be filed.
26. *Moving expenses:* Can be claimed only as an itemized deduction but not subject to a 2 percent floor.
27. *Miscellaneous deductions and employee business expenses:* Your deduction must exceed 2 percent of adjusted gross income, except for gambling losses, certain expenses incurred by handicapped employees, and moving expenses.

Total Itemized Deductions

Add lines 19 through 27 and enter total on line 28.

Minus Standard Deduction

29. Under the new tax law, the standard deduction is not built into the tax tables, so for 1987 and 1988 enter your total projected itemized deductions (from line 28).

Deductions for Nonitemizers (Before Standard Deduction)

30. *Charitable contributions:* No deduction is allowed for nonitemizers in 1987 or 1988. (Place zero on line 30.)
31. *Standard deduction:* For 1987, enter $3,760 for joint filers or $2,540 for both singles and heads of households. For 1988, enter $5,000 for joint filers, $4,400 for heads of households, or $3,000 for singles.
    Taxpayers who are either blind or over age 65 may claim an extra $600 (if married) or $750 (if single) in addition to the standard deduction.

Total Deductions for Nonitemizers

Add lines 30 and 31 and enter total on line 32.

Personal Exemptions

In 1987 the personal exemption is $1,900, and in 1988, $1,950. The blind and elderly will not get to claim an extra personal exemption (it has been replaced by an extra standard deduction).

Taxable Income Before Capital Gains Adjustment

Subtract the greater of line 29 or 32 and personal exemptions from adjusted gross income on line 18, and enter result on line 34.

1987 capital gains adjustments: Taxpayers falling into the 35 percent or 38.5 percent bracket (for 1987) will have some adjustment to make sure that no more than 28 percent tax is paid on capital gains. Enter amount on line 35.

Taxable Income After 1987 Capital Gains Adjustment

Subtract capital gains adjustment (line 35) from taxable income (line 34) to arrive at total to enter on line 36.

Tax Computation

37. Enter tax from tables.
38. *Upper-Income Surcharge for Phase-Out of 15 Percent Bracket:* Add a surcharge for 1988 of 5 percent of taxable income from $71,900 to $149,250 (jointly), $43,140 to $89,560 (singles), or $61,115 to $126,867 (unmarried heads of households).
39. *Upper-Income Surcharge for Phase-Out of Personal Exemptions:* Upper-income taxpayers are subject to a 5 percent surcharge (maximum $546 per exemption) on taxable income over $149,250 (joint), $89,560 (singles), and $126,867 (unmarried heads of households).

Tax Before Credits

For 1988, add any surcharges (lines 38 and 39) to total tax computed from tables (line 37), and enter amount on line 40.

41. *Child and dependent care expenses:* No change.
42. *Elderly and disabled credit:* Same.
43. *Political contributions credit:* Repealed.

Total Credits

Add lines 41 through 43, and enter total on line 44.

Total Taxes Owed

Subtract total credits on line 44 from "Tax Before Credits" (line 40) and enter result on line 45.

Compute Your Own Taxes—Worksheet

	1986	New Tax Law 1987	1988
1. Wages, salaries, tips, etc.			
2. Interest income			
3. Dividends			
4. Capital gains			
5. Rents, royalties, partnerships			
6. Unemployment compensation			
7. Excess 401(k) contributions			
8. Taxable Soc. Security income			
9. Other income			
10. TOTAL INCOME			

ADJUSTMENTS TO INCOME

	1986	1987	1988
11. Moving expenses		out	out
12. Employee business expenses			
13. Keogh plan deduction			
14. Two-earner deduction		out	out
15. Other adjustments			
16. ADJUSTED GROSS INCOME (pre-IRA)			
17. IRA deduction			
18. ADJUSTED GROSS INCOME			

ITEMIZED DEDUCTIONS

	1986	1987	1988
19. Medical expenses			
20. State and local income, real estate, personal prop. taxes			
21. State/local sales taxes		out	out
22. Mortgage interest			
23. Other interest			
24. Charitable contributions			
25. Casualty & theft losses			
26. Moving expenses	out		
27. Miscellaneous deductions & employee business expenses			
28. TOTAL ITEMIZED DEDUCTIONS			
29. MINUS STANDARD DEDUCTION			

DEDUCTIONS FOR NONITEMIZERS

	1986	1987	1988
30. Charitable contributions		out	out
31. Standard deduction			
32. TOTAL NONITEMIZER DEDUCTIONS			
33. PERSONAL EXEMPTION			
34. TAXABLE INCOME—Precapital Gains			
35. 1987 Capital Gains Adjustment			
36. 1987 TAXABLE INCOME			

COMPUTING YOUR TAXES

37. Tax from tables (see below) _____ _____ _____
38. Upper-income surcharge for phase-out of 15% bracket   _out_ _out_ _____
39. Upper-income surcharge for phase-out of personal exemptions   _out_ _out_ _____
40. TAX BEFORE CREDITS   _____ _____ _____

CREDITS

41. Child & dependent care expenses credit   _____ _____ _____
42. Elderly & disabled credit   _____ _____ _____
43. Political contributions credit   _____ _out_ _out_
44. TOTAL CREDITS   _____ _____ _____

45. TOTAL TAXES DUE   _____ _____ _____

Tax Rate Tables

	Single filers			Joint filers			Head of household	
If your taxable income is above:	You will pay a base of:	Plus this % of taxable income:	If your taxable income is above:	You will pay a base of:	Plus this % of taxable income:	If your taxable income is above:	You will pay a base of:	Plus this % of taxable income:

Tax Law, 1987

$0	$0	11%	$0	$0	11%	$0	$0	11%
$1,800	$198	15%	$3,000	$330	15%	$2,500	$275	15%
$16,800	$2,448	28%	$28,000	$4,080	28%	$23,000	$3,350	28%
$27,000	$5,304	35%	$45,000	$8,840	35%	$38,000	$7,550	35%
$54,000	$14,754	38.5%	$90,000	$24,590	38.5%	$80,000	$22,250	38.5%

Tax Law, 1988

$0	$0	15%	$0	$0	15%	$0	$0	15%
$17,850	$2,678	28%	$29,750	$4,463	28%	$23,900	$3,585	28%
$43,150	$9,762	33%	$71,900	$16,265	33%	$61,650	$14,155	33%
$89,560	$25,077	28%	$149,250	$41,790	28%	$123,790	$34,661	28%

100 Commonly Asked Income Tax Questions and Where to Find The Answers in *Pay Less Tax Legally*

Topic	Question	Answer (Page)
Advertising People	I work for a large advertising agency and have been told that there are special tax tips for admen. What are they?	244
Allergy	My son suffers from various allergies. The doctor suggested installing central air conditioning. Is there any way we can write off the cost on our taxes?	275
Alternative Minimum Tax	We sold a block of stock at a $50,000 profit last year. We understand we may overlook the alternative minimum tax due to Tax Reform. Is this true?	211
Audit Lottery	My accountant mentioned something about the audit lottery. Do we want to take part in it, and where do we buy tickets?	245
Auto Expense	Someone told us we could write off the first $2,560 cost of a new car if we used it for business. How does that work?	87
	I purchased a new car last year for business. Can I still claim the sales tax as a deduction?	154
	We use our car for business purposes. From the tax point of view, would we be better off claiming actual expenses or mileage?	77
Baby-sitter	I pay my mother $50 every week to baby-sit our 2 kids while we work. Can we get child care credit for this even though it is paid to a relative?	202
Bad Debt	Last year I lent $500 to my wife's brother, and I can't collect. Can I get a tax writeoff?	95
Bond Premiums	Is there a special way of reporting bond premium income? Where do I do it?	66
Business	We started a small business last year and will be filing our first return. Do we have a choice of filing on either the cash or the accrual basis?	76
	We give our 9-year-old son a $10 per week allowance. He occasionally helps out in the business. How do we deduct his allowance against the business?	261
	We have a small family business and seem to be paying quite a bit of tax. Can we split up the business among our 4 children and have them report the income on their returns?	261

Casualty Loss	While we were on vacation, our house was burglarized. Insurance covered everything except my wife's jewelry, which she had inherited from her mother. If we claim a loss on our taxes, what records will we need?	171
Child Care	Can I deduct the cost of summer camp for my child if I work?	202
Children	Will my kids have to pay tax on their investment income this year?	42
Closing Costs	We bought a new home last year. The realtor told us that loan service charges are deductible. Is she right?	164
College Costs	Our daughter will graduate from high school next year and go on to a church-affiliated college. Can we write off any part of her tuition as a charitable contribution?	171
Computers	We are thinking of buying a personal computer, which we may eventually be able to tie into the business. Any way of writing it off now?	251
Contributions, Charitable	How much in the way of charitable contributions can we claim on our taxes without getting called in?	229
	Our son attends private school. The administrator sent out a memo saying that under some circumstances tuition might be deductible as a charitable contribution. Under what circumstances?	171
	We don't have enough deductions to warrant itemizing. What percentage of our contributions are deductible?	247
	We are senior citizens and are thinking about donating our home to our church. What tax benefits can we expect, if any?	248
	I own some land that has gone up in value over the last several years. Instead of paying capital-gain tax, may I donate the land and get a tax writeoff for the fair market value?	247
	My wife is active in many charitable organizations. She incurs quite a few out-of-pocket expenses, which we'd like to write off. Which expenses are deductible?	248
	How do we value the old clothes we gave to the Salvation Army last year?	169
Conventions	I am going to be attending a business convention in the spring, and would like to take my wife along. May I write off her expenses?	128
Custodian Accounts	How do we make gifts to minors using custodian accounts? Do the children need their own Social Security numbers?	249
Deferring Income	How can I go about deferring investment income from this year into next year?	267
Delayed Refund	Last year we filed our tax return in February but did not receive a refund check until July. If we have that problem again, whom can we contact?	216

34 Introduction

Dependents	My wife and sister-in-law support their father, who is in a nursing home. Each provides about the same amount of money. Who gets to claim him at the end of the year?	58
	My son attends a local college during the day and works evenings and weekends. Last year he earned $3,000. Should he file his own return? Does that mean we can no longer claim him as a dependent?	58
Depreciation	We just bought a 3-flat apartment building. We hope to improve it and put it back on the market within the next few years. How do we go about claiming depreciation?	116
Disaster	Our home was damaged by floods last January. Can we write off the loss on last year's taxes?	171
Divorce	I am in the process of getting divorced. Are there any special tax breaks for singles?	54
	My wife and I are separated. I earn about $50,000 per year and pay $10,000 in unallocated support. May I deduct the entire amount as alimony?	146
Educational Travel	I am a history teacher and traveled to Europe last summer. Can I write off the trip if I simply visited a few museums?	126
Estimated Tax	I am retired and live off investments. Each year I seem to be penalized for not sending in enough estimated tax. Any suggestions?	255
Exchanging Property	I recently read that I could exchange some vacant land I own for some other property without paying any tax. How does that work?	99
Exemptions	I am recently divorced. The divorce decree does not specify who gets to claim our daughter on the tax returns. What are the rules?	251
Extensions	If I can't file my tax return by April 15, is there any problem in getting an extension?	216
Family Trusts	Is it still wise to set up a trust for our minor children? If so, how do we go about it?	254
Filing Status	I recently got married. Is it better to file a joint return or married filing separately?	54
Freelance Income	I work for a company that takes no deductions and am considered self-employed. How should I report my income?	73
Fringe Benefits	I am single and looking for a new sales position. Should I be looking for a substantial salary increase, or would I be better off with a comparable salary and better fringe benefits?	256
Gambling	We won a tidy sum of money in our state lottery. I know this has to be reported, but can I write off gambling losses, or the trip to Las Vegas?	71

Gifts	What is the maximum value of deductible gifts we can give to our grandchildren?	254
Gifts— Property	I own some land that has gone down in value and want to give it to my daughter. Would I be better off making the gift or selling outright and giving her the proceeds?	104
Ground Rent	We pay redeemable ground rent on our home. Is this tax-deductible?	162
Hobby	I collect, buy, and sell stamps. At what point can I transform my hobby into a business in order to get some tax benefits?	86
Home	We are currently renting a home but are considering buying. What are the tax breaks for homeowners?	265
Home Improvements	We recently invested a considerable amount of money in home improvements and are now thinking of selling. What records do we need?	102
Home Loss	We are thinking of selling our condominium but would incur a loss if we did. How can we write off the loss?	104
Home Office	I set up an extra bedroom in my home as an office. What are the necessary guidelines for being able to write off the office?	264
Home Sale	We had trouble selling our home and had to rent it out, although we bought another home in the interim. What effect will a sale of the first home have on our taxes?	104
	I am 54, my wife is 49, and we live in a home worth approximately $250,000. We built it in 1960 for a little over $100,000. We are thinking about selling in order to move into something smaller. Do we have to wait until we are both over age 55 to avoid paying tax on the gain?	105
Incorporation	We have a small business and are thinking of incorporating. What are the advantages to being incorporated?	269
	I am an artist and have generated quite a lot of freelance income this year. Should I be incorporating?	269
Interest Income	Should I report money-market earnings as dividends or interest?	62
Investment Club	My wife belongs to an investment club. She attends seminars and lectures. Are her membership dues deductible?	186
IRA	We have several thousand dollars tied up in our IRA accounts. How can we borrow the money without being penalized?	142
IRA Custodial Fees	The bank charged us a $25 custodial fee for managing our IRA. Is this deductible, as well as the $2,000 contribution?	134
Job-Hunting	If I go out of town looking for a new job, which expenses are deductible, and what records should I keep?	186
Job Insurance	My insurance agent told me there's a new form of job insur-	

36 Introduction

	ance which will pay my salary if I am fired. Are the premiums tax-deductible?	188
Job Skills	I take marketing courses at a local university. If the courses are job-related, may I write off the cost of tuition?	188
Legal Fees	I had to take my ex-husband to court to collect overdue child support. Are my attorney's fees deductible?	147
Loans	Are there any tax benefits if I lend money to friends or relatives and can't collect?	95
Lump-Sum Distributions	I am planning on retiring next year. I will be getting a sum of money from my pension plan. How should I handle its distribution?	194
Medical Expenses	Our son is retarded and in an institution. Can we deduct airfare and hotel charges when we visit him?	276
	Our son has dyslexia, which causes a reading problem, and he attends a special school. Is the tuition deductible?	275
Moving Expenses	My husband was transferred, and we moved to a new location. The job did not work out, and we ended up moving a second time in the same year. Can we deduct the cost of both moves?	180
Office Expenses	I am a project engineer for a large computer company and am expected to prepare projects at home. Can I write off my incidental office expenses?	264
Partnership	My wife and I operate a small business. Is there any tax advantage to our forming a legal partnership?	73
Patent	I developed a good idea, patented it, and sold it to a large company. Can I claim long-term capital gains on the profit?	97
Points	We refinanced our home last year. Are the points still deductible?	164
Prepayment Penalty	We sold our home last year, and the bank charged us 2 months' interest as a loan prepayment penalty. Is that amount deductible?	164
Recreational Vehicle	We have a 30-foot motor home sitting in our driveway which we occasionally rent out. Can we get some tax benefits?	81
Rental Property	We own a 2-flat apartment building, live on the first floor, and rent out the second floor to my niece. Do we have to charge her the same rent as an outsider?	116
Salary Reduction Plans	My company is offering a new pension plan that involves salary reduction. If I join, am I still eligible for my own IRA?	135
Sales Tax	We refurnished our home last year and spent quite a bit on items that had sales tax added. May we still write off sales tax?	154
Securities	Is it better to sell stock at a profit this year or wait until next year when tax rates may be lower?	271

Self-Employment Tax	My wife earned $350 selling cosmetics part-time. Does she have to pay Social Security tax on that amount?	209
Shifting Income	Can we still shift income to our children in order to save on taxes?	267
Single Parents	I am divorced and have custody of 2 boys. What special tax breaks are there, if any, for single parents?	56
Singles	I am single and own my own home. I usually receive a large tax refund. Can I claim more than one exemption on my W-4 form?	48
Social Security	I understand that Social Security benefits may be partially taxable, depending on my income. How much can I earn before having to pay tax on my Social Security benefits?	69
Stock	I bought stock when the market was high. Now the stocks have decreased in value. When is the best time to sell?	271
	Are there any rules keeping me from selling stock at a loss and buying it right back?	271
	Can I still get long-term capital gain on my investments without holding onto them for more than 6 months?	94
Support	Can I claim my married daughter on my return if I am still supporting her?	57
Tax-Free Bonds	Both my wife and I work and have substantial income. At what point does it make sense to consider tax-free bonds?	287
Tax Reform	Is there a quick way I can tell how Tax Reform is going to affect me?	30
Travel for Business	I spend about 2 weeks per month on the road as a commissioned salesman and always seem to be dipping into my own pocket for expenses. How do I write them off on my taxes?	130
	I'm an engineer and work in different locations for extended time periods. Are my living expenses deductible?	128
Trusts	How can I make use of trusts in order to save the most tax dollars?	254
Unemployment Compensation	I collected unemployment compensation and had a few temporary jobs. Do I have to declare the money from unemployment benefits as income?	68
Vacation	Is there any way I can write off the cost of a vacation by calling it job-hunting?	186
Vacation Home	We own a vacation condo, which we rent for part of the year to help defray expenses. Can we write our expenses off on our taxes?	294
Worthless Stock	My wife has some worthless bonds she purchased many years ago. How and where do we write them off on our taxes?	98
Year-End Tax Planning	Are there any year-end tax tips that can save me money?	291

PART I

Save Money Now

A Complete Guide to
the Deductions, Credits,
and Tax-Saving Opportunities
You Can Make Use of on
This Year's Taxes

Important Tax Dates for 1988

January 15 — Due date for your final payment of 1987 estimated tax unless you file your return by January 31.

February 1 — If you file your 1987 income tax return by this date, the deadline for final payment of your 1987 estimated tax is extended to this date. W-2 and 1099 information statements due by today from employer, bank, broker; and if you hire and pay unincorporated workers, you must send out these forms by this date.

April 15 — Form 1040 for 1987 income tax and self-employment tax due with payment of tax. Extension requests must be filed today if you need extra time.
IRA and SEP contributions can be made through today for 1987. The first installment on your 1988 estimated tax is due.

June 15 — Second installment of 1988 estimated tax is due.

August 15 — If you received an extension of the April 15 deadline, your tax return is due today; or you can file for an additional extension.

September 15 — Time to pay the third installment on your 1988 estimated tax.

October 15 — If you were granted a second extension, your income tax return is due today—final deadline.
Start your year-end tax planning.

December 15 — Attend to year-end transactions so they will be finished in time to report as 1988 transactions.

December 31 — Your filing status for 1988 is determined by whatever your marital status is on this date.
Keogh and SEP plans must be established by today for 1988.

YOUR INCOME TAX RETURN: BASIC GUIDELINES

Too many taxpayers make the mistake of waiting until the last minute to assemble their records and prepare their tax returns. This procrastination often leads to a great deal of frustration, not to mention the loss of valuable tax deductions. While you are preparing to fill out this year's tax return, begin to plan for next year as well. Collect all your records in a handy place all year round.

Who Must File?

You must file a tax return if you are:

Single and have a gross income of (1) $4,440 or more if you are under 65; (2) $5,650 if you are 65 or older; (3) $5,660 if you are a surviving spouse under 65; or (4) $7,650 if you are a surviving spouse 65 or older. Children under age 14 with income should see page 42.

Married and (1) both spouses are under 65 with a combined income of $7,560 or more; (2) one is 65 or older with a combined gross income of $9,400; (3) both are 65 or older with a combined gross income of $10,000; or (4) the spouses are not living together at the end of the tax year and the filer has a gross income of $1,900 or more. The first 3 requirements apply only if the couple lives together at the end of the taxable year and files jointly, and if neither is the dependent of another person (see page 251 for a discussion of the status of divorced or separated couples).

If your income is more than $1,900, you must file a return if:

1. You are a nonresident alien
2. You are married filing separately
3. You are a U.S. citizen entitled to the exclusion of income from a U.S. possession
4. You file a return for less than 12 months or change your accounting period
5. You are either a student or dependent child with unearned income of $1,900 or more
6. You claim advance payments of the earned income credit from your employer
7. You are self-employed and your net income is $400 or more. (Although you may not owe income tax, you may be liable for self-employment tax.)

Single persons who could be claimed as dependents on a parent's return (for example, students) must file a return if they have a gross income of $1,900 or more, including interest, dividends, and other unearned income. A return is required even if tax is not due (see page 192 for limitation on standard deductions). Single taxpayers whose total income is less than $4,440 (including passive income under $1,900) and who do not expect to owe any tax for 1988 should write "exempt" on line 6b of Form W-4, filed with the employer, to prevent withholding tax from being deducted from their paycheck. They still must pay Social Security tax.

If earned income is less than the average amounts as stated above, you should file to take advantage of the earned income credit (see Chapter 9).

Children's Tax Forms

The amount and source of your child's income will determine which 1987 tax forms you need to use.
1. *1040-A.* This is the one most often used, but not in the case of trust income.
2. *1040-EZ.* This is suitable if interest income is $400 or less.
3. *8615.* If the child is under age 14 and has investment income over $1,000, you should file this form; however, you must figure *your* taxes first because they will determine how much your child pays.
4. *1040.* This is the form for children with complicated returns.

Form 8615—The "Kiddie Tax" Form

Children under age 14 who had investment income of more than $1,000 and whose parents' marginal tax rate is greater than the child's must use Form 8615.

IRS has found a way to eliminate income shifting (from the parents' higher tax bracket to the child's lower tax bracket) by taxing the child's unearned income over $1,000 at the parents' higher rate.

Unearned income includes interest, rents, dividends, royalties, capital gains, annuity or pension income, and income received as a beneficiary of a trust. It is also referred to as investment income.

The child is allowed a standard $500 deduction against the first $500 of unearned income, and the second $500 is taxed at the child's rate. Everything over that is taxed at the parents' rate.

If you have a child for whom you need to complete a Form 8615, you must first complete your own tax return because your taxable income must be determined and placed on line 6 of Form 8615 before it can be completed. In addition, you must show on line 7 the investment income of all other children in the family.

Form 8615—Line-by-Line Instructions

On line 1, place the total investment income for the child. If the total is $1,000 or less, do not complete the form.

On line 2, enter $1,000 if the child does not itemize.

Subtract line 2 from line 1. If the result is zero, *Stop* and attach this form to the child's return. If the result is other than zero, enter the result on line 3 and continue.

On line 4 enter the child's taxable income from Form 1040 or other return form.

On line 5 enter the amount on line 3 or line 4, whichever is smaller.

On line 6 enter the parents' taxable income from his or her return.

On line 7 show the total of all net investment income from line 5 of other Forms 8615 of any other children in the family (same parents).

Add lines 5, 6, and 7, and enter the total on Line 8.

On line 9 show the tax applicable to the amount on line 8, based on the child's tax

Form 8615
Computation of Tax for Children Under Age 14 Who Have Investment Income of More Than $1,000

Department of the Treasury
Internal Revenue Service

▶ See Instructions below.
▶ Attach to the Child's Form 1040, Form 1040A, or Form 1040NR.

OMB No. 1545-xxxx
1987
Attachment Sequence No. 33

General Instructions

Purpose of Form.—Before 1987, the tax law allowed income-producing property to be given to children so that the investment income from the property could be taxed at the children's lower tax rate. The law was changed for 1987 and later years so that, for children under age 14, investment income (such as interest and dividends) over $1,000 will be taxed at the parent's rate if higher than the child's rate.

Do not use this form if the child's investment income is $1,000 or less. Instead, figure the tax in the normal manner on the child's income tax return. For example, if the child had $900 of interest income and $200 of income from wages, Form 8615 is not required to be completed and the child's tax should be figured on Form 1040A using the Tax Table.

If the child's investment income is more than $1,000, use this form to see if any of the child's net investment income is taxed at the parent's rate and, if so, to figure the child's tax. For example, if the child had $1,100 of interest income and $200 of income from wages, Form 8615 should be completed and attached to the child's Form 1040A.

Investment income.— As referred to in this form, the term investment income includes all taxable income other than earned income as defined on page 2. It includes income such as interest, dividends, capital gains, rents, royalties, etc. It also includes pension and annuity income and income received as the beneficiary of a trust.

Who Must File.—Generally, **Form 8615** must be filed for any child who was under age 14 on December 31, 1987, and who had more than $1,000 of investment income. However, if neither parent was alive on December 31, do not use Form 8615. Instead, figure the child's tax based on his or her own rate.

Additional Information.—For more information about the tax on investment income of children, please get **Publication 922**, Tax Rules for Children and Dependents (Rev. Nov. 1987).

Child's name as shown on return: **MARCIE JOY DOUGH**
Child's social security number: **004 19 6420**

Parent's name (first, initial, and last) (**Caution:** See Instructions before completing.): **Barry DOUGH**
Parent's filing status:
Parent's social security number: **329 04 1040**

Step 1 — Figure child's net investment income

1	Enter the child's investment income, such as interest and dividend income (see Instructions). (If this amount is $1,000 or less, stop here; do not file this form.)	**1275**
2	If the child DID NOT itemize deductions on Schedule A (Form 1040 or Form 1040NR), enter $1,000. If the child ITEMIZED deductions, see the Instructions.	**1000**
3	Subtract the amount on line 2 from the amount on line 1. Enter the result. (If zero or less, stop here; do not complete the rest of this form but ATTACH it to the child's return.)	**275**
4	Enter the child's taxable income (from Form 1040, line 36; Form 1040A, line 17; or Form 1040NR, line 35)	**1250**
5	Compare the amounts on lines 3 and 4 and enter the **smaller** of the two amounts ▶	**275**

Step 2 — Figure tentative tax based on the parent's tax rate

6	Enter the parent's taxable income (from Form 1040, line 36; Form 1040A, line 17; Form 1040EZ, line 7; or Form 1040NR, line 35)	**36004**
7	Enter the total, if any, of the net investment income from Forms 8615, line 5, of ALL OTHER children of the parent listed above	**0**
8	Add the amounts on lines 5, 6, and 7. Enter the total	**36279**
9	Tax on the amount on line 8 based on the parent's filing status (see Instructions). Check if from ☒ Tax Table, ☐ Tax Rate Schedule X, Y, or Z, or ☐ Schedule D	**6397**
10	Enter the parent's tax (from Form 1040, line 37; Form 1040A, line 18; Form 1040EZ, line 9; or Form 1040NR, line 36)	**6327**
11	Subtract the amount on line 10 from the amount on line 9. Enter the result. (If no amount is entered on line 7, enter the amount from line 11 on line 13.)	**70**
12a	Add the amounts on lines 5 and 7. Enter the total 12a **275**	
b	Divide the amount on line 5 by the amount on line 12a. Enter the percentage	12b **1 x 00**
13	Multiply the amount on line 11 by the percentage on line 12b. Enter the result ▶	**70**

Step 3 — Figure child's tax

14	Subtract the amount on line 5 from the amount on line 4. Enter the result . 14 **975**	
15	Tax on the amount on line 14 based on the **child's** filing status (see Instructions). Check if from ☒ Tax Table, ☐ Tax Rate Schedule X, or ☐ Schedule D	**109**
16	Add the amounts on lines 13 and 15. Enter the total	**179**
17	Tax on the amount on line 4 based on the **child's** filing status. Check if from ☒ Tax Table, ☐ Tax Rate Schedule X, or ☐ Schedule D	**139**
18	Compare the amounts on lines 16 and 17. Enter the **larger** of the two amounts here and on Form 1040, line 37; Form 1040A, line 18; or Form 1040NR, line 36. Be sure to check the box for "Form 8615" ▶	**179**

rate. (Indicate whether you used tax table, tax rate schedule X, Y, Z, or Schedule D, as requested.)

On line 10 enter the parents' tax from your return.

Subtract line 10 from line 9 and enter the result on line 11.

Line 12a is the total of lines 5 and 7.

Line 12b: Divide line 5 by line 12a and show the percentage on line 12b.

Multiply line 11 by the percentage on 12b and enter the result on line 13.

Subtract line 5 from line 4 and enter the result on line 14.

On line 15 enter the amount of tax for line 14, based on the child's tax rate. Indicate whether you use tax table, Schedule D, or Tax Rate Schedule X, as requested.

Add line 13 to line 15 and enter the total on line 16.

On line 17 show the amount of tax on line 4 amount (taxable income), and indicate what table or schedule used.

On line 18 enter either the amount on line16 or the amount on line 17, whichever is larger. Also show this amount on Form 1040 or other return being used for the child. Check the box "Form 8615" on the return.

Here are some additional tips in completing Form 8615:

● Re "parents' tax rate" on the child's return: When the parents are married and filing jointly, there is no problem determining the parents' tax rate; however, when the parents are treated as unmarried (live apart for the last half of the year), divorced, or legally separated, use the tax rate of the parent who has custody of the child for the greater part of the year.

● When married parents file separate returns, use the tax rate of the parent with the larger taxable income.

● If both parents have deceased prior to the end of the year, the "kiddie tax" does not apply to the child.

● The Social Security number of the parent whose tax rate is used must be included in the space provided on the form. If the parents' taxable income changes after Form 8615 has been filed, the child must file an amended tax return (Form 1040X). The parent should sign the return in the child's name, then sign his or her own name and the word "parent." Failure to do this may result in penalties.

What You Need in Order to File

Basically, here's what you will need in order to file your return:

1. *Tax returns from the past few years.* These may bring to mind deductions that could otherwise be overlooked.
2. *W-2 forms.* No later than January 31, you should receive 3 copies of this form from each employer you worked for during the year. The W-2 form details salary/wages and federal and Social Security taxes paid during the year. (Be sure to attach all Copy A W-2s to your federal return when you file.) If you have not received your W-2 forms by February 1, contact your employer. If you are still having a problem, call your local IRS office and they will see that your W-2 forms are mailed. If you receive an incorrect W-2 from your employer, contact them immediately to issue a corrected one.
3. *1099 forms* (for dividends, interest, and certain other kinds of income).

4. *Checkbook registers, paid bills, canceled checks, end-of-year charge account statements and other financial records.*

Reporting Whole Dollars

You need not report pennies on your tax return. Eliminate the cents by rounding off ($1.01 to $1.49 becomes $1; $1.50 to $1.99 becomes $2) and reporting only whole dollars.

Where to File and Pay

Use the addressed envelope that came with your return. If you do not have one, or if you moved during the year, mail your return to the **Internal Revenue Service Center** for the place where you live. No street address is needed.

If you are located in:	Use this address:
Alabama, Florida, Georgia, Mississippi, South Carolina	Atlanta, GA 31101
New Jersey, New York City, and counties of Nassau, Rockland, Suffolk, and Westchester	Holtsville, NY 00501
Illinois, Iowa, Missouri, Wisconsin	Kansas City, MO 64999
Delware, District of Columbia, Maryland, Pennsylvania	Philadelphia, PA 19255
Connecticut, Maine, Massachusetts, Minnesota, New Hampshire, New York (all other counties), Rhode Island, Vermont	Andover, MA 05501
Kentucky, Michigan, Ohio West Virginia	Cincinnati, OH 45999
Kansas, Louisiana, New Mexico, Oklahoma, Texas	Austin, TX 73301
Alaska, Arizona, California, (counties of Alpme, Amador, Butte, Calaveras, Colusa, Contra Costa, Del Norte, El Dorado, Glenn, Humboldt, Lake, Lassen, Marin, Mendocino, Modoc, Napa, Nevada, Placer, Plumas, Sacramento, San Joaquin, Shasta, Sierra, Siskiyou, Solano, Sonoma, Sutter, Tehama, Trinity, Yolo, and Yuba), Colorado, Idaho, Montana, Nebraska, Nevada, North Dakota, Oregon, South Dakota, Utah, Washington, Wyoming	Ogden, UT 84201
California (all other counties), Hawaii	Fresno, CA 93888
Arkansas, Indiana, North Carolina, Tennessee, Virginia	Memphis, TN 37501
American Samoa	Philadelphia, PA 19255
Guam	Commissioner of Revenue and Taxation Agana, GU 96910
Puerto Rico (or if excluding income under section 933) Virgin Islands: Nonpermanent residents	Philadelphia, PA 19255
Virgin Islands: Permanent residents	V.I. Bureau of Internal Revenue P.O. Box 3185 St. Thomas, VI 00801
Foreign country: U.S. citizens and those filing Form 2555 or Form 4563, even if you have an A.P.O. or F.P.O. address	Philadelphia, PA 19255
A.P.O. or F.P.O. addresses of:	Miami—Atlanta, GA 31101 New York—Holtsville, NY 00501 San Francisco—Fresno, CA 93888 Seattle—Ogden, UT 84201
Foreign country U.S. citizen and those excluding income under section 911 or 931	Philadelphia, PA 19255

Tax payers who owe should write their daytime telephone number on any checks in case the check gets separated from the tax return.

When to File

Individual returns must be filed on or before April 15 for calendar-year taxpayers. Your tax return will be considered on time if postmarked on the due date. Registered- and certified-mail receipts will constitute proof of delivery. However, if you mail your return on the last day, don't use a postage meter—you may have problems with the IRS if delivery is delayed. If you file at the last minute, have the post office hand-cancel your return, and ask for a proof-of-mailing certificate.

Be sure to put proper postage on your tax return; if you owe tax and your return is sent back for postage, you will be charged penalties for late filing.

There is a new address check box in case you moved during the year.

There may be an advantage to waiting until the last minute to file your return (see page 216).

Form W-4A

When Penalties for Underwithholding Are Waived

Individuals who did not have enough federal income tax withheld from their wages and filed Form W-4 (or W-4A) with their employers by June 1, 1987, will have their underpayment penalties waived.

46 SAVE MONEY NOW

    This waiver does not apply to nonwage income (self-employment or investment). You must prove that you didn't meet the estimated tax requirements because you relied on a timely filed 1987 Form W-2 or W-2A.

    For 1987 you must pay at least 90 percent of the current year's tax (or 100 percent of the tax liability for the preceding year) or be subject to penalty for underpayment. Wages withholdings are considered a payment of estimated taxes, so if your withholding in 1987 at least equals the total tax as shown on the 1986 return, there will be no underpayment penalty.

Form W-2

Form W-2, Wage and Tax Statement, is an Internal Revenue Service form prepared by your employer. If you worked until the end of the year, your employer must provide Form W-2 to you by January 31 of the following year. If you worked for only part of the year, you may have received this statement from your employer soon after you left your job, but you must receive it no later than January 31 of the following year. However, if you ask to have the form earlier than January 31, your employer must give it to you within 30 days of your request or within 30 days after your last wage payment, whichever is later. Every employer you work for during the year is required to have information on your W-2 on file at his place of business. Most employers mail out the W-2s to their employees; request it from your employer if you have not received it by February 1.

    The W-2 form is important because it provides a record of the wages you received. If you are required to file an income tax return, you must attach Copy A of Form W-2 to your return. If you had more than one employer, attach Copy A of all your W-2s to your return. Keep Copy C of your W-2s for your records. In most states, you will get additional copies (Copy B) to attach to your state and local income tax returns.

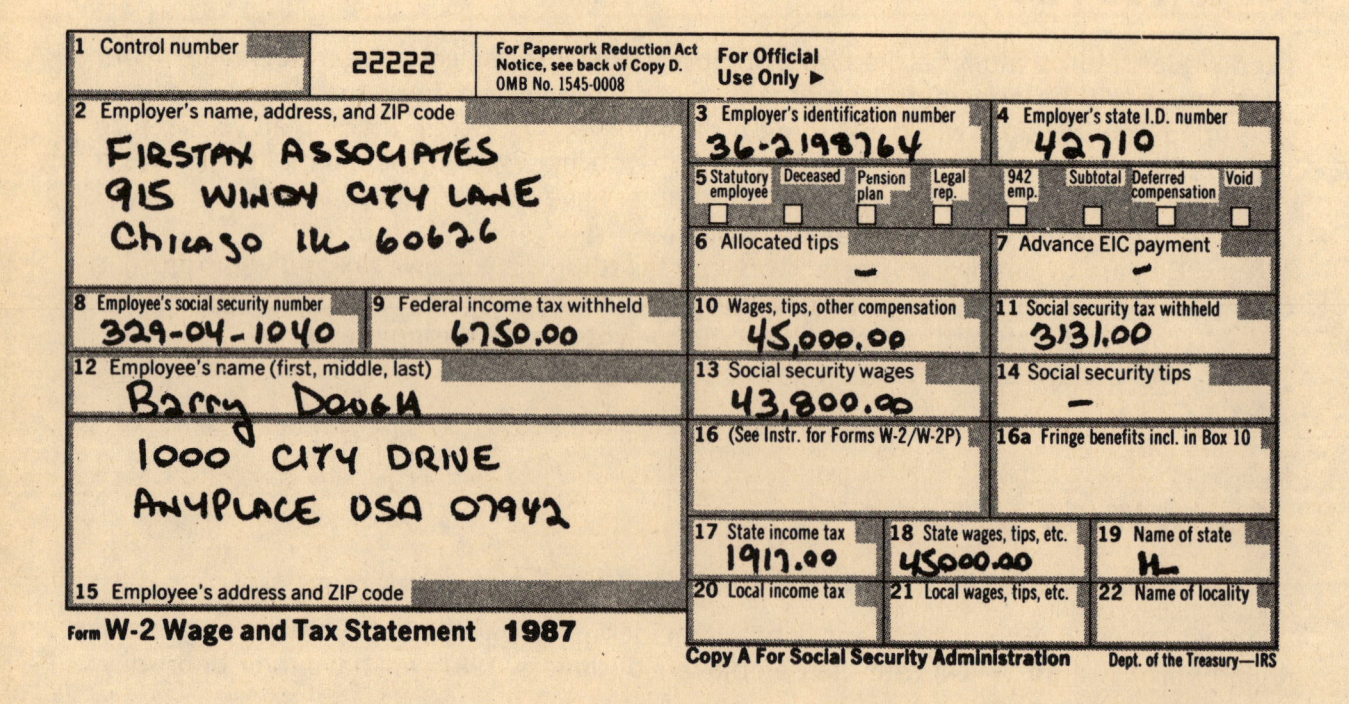

1 Control number	22222	For Paperwork Reduction Act Notice, see back of Copy D. OMB No. 1545-0008	For Official Use Only ▶	
2 Employer's name, address, and ZIP code FIRSTAX ASSOCIATES 915 WINDY CITY LANE CHICAGO IL 60626		3 Employer's identification number 36-2198764	4 Employer's state I.D. number 42710	
		5 Statutory employee / Deceased / Pension plan / Legal rep. / 942 emp. / Subtotal / Deferred compensation / Void		
		6 Allocated tips —	7 Advance EIC payment	
8 Employee's social security number 329-04-1040	9 Federal income tax withheld 6750.00	10 Wages, tips, other compensation 45,000.00	11 Social security tax withheld 3131.00	
12 Employee's name (first, middle, last) Barry Dough 1000 CITY DRIVE ANYPLACE USA 07942		13 Social security wages 43,800.00	14 Social security tips —	
		16 (See Instr. for Forms W-2/W-2P)	16a Fringe benefits incl. in Box 10	
		17 State income tax 1917.00	18 State wages, tips, etc. 45000.00	19 Name of state IL
15 Employee's address and ZIP code		20 Local income tax	21 Local wages, tips, etc.	22 Name of locality

Form **W-2 Wage and Tax Statement**   **1987**   **Copy A For Social Security Administration**   Dept. of the Treasury—IRS

Form 4852 (Revised October 1984)
Dept. of the Treasury
Internal Revenue Service

SUBSTITUTE FOR FORM W-2, WAGE AND TAX STATEMENT OR FORM W-2P, STATEMENT FOR RECIPIENTS OF ANNUITIES, PENSIONS, RETIRED PAY OR, IRA PAYMENTS
◀ Attach to Form 1040, 1040A, 1040EZ or 1040X

OMB No. 1545-0458
Expires 10-31-87

1. NAME (First, middle, last): FAYE DOUGH

2. SOCIAL SECURITY NUMBER: 004-19-7912

3. ADDRESS (Number, street, city, State, ZIP code): 1000 CITY DRIVE ANYPLACE USA 07942

4. PLEASE FILL IN THE YEAR AT THE END OF THIS STATEMENT:
I have been unable to obtain or have received an incorrect Form W-2, Wage and Tax Statement, or Form W-2P, Statement for Recipients of Annuities, Pensions, Retired Pay, or IRA Payments, from my employer or payer named below, and have so notified the Internal Revenue Service. The amounts shown below are my best estimates of all wages or payments paid to me and the Federal taxes withheld by this employer or payer during 19____.

5. EMPLOYER'S OR PAYER'S NAME, ADDRESS, AND ZIP CODE:
FIRSTRAVEL
1960 1ST AVENUE
ANYWHERE USA 07942

6. EMPLOYER'S OR PAYER'S IDENTIFICATION NUMBER (If known): 59-6179204

7. ADVANCE EIC (Earned Income Credit) PAYMENTS RECEIVED	8. FEDERAL INCOME TAX WITHHELD	9. WAGES, TIPS, OTHER COMPENSATION OR PAYMENTS (See note below)	10. SOCIAL SECURITY TAX WITHHELD	11. SOCIAL SECURITY WAGES	12. SOCIAL SECURITY TIPS
	1619.00	12,000.00	858.00	12,000	0

NOTE: Include the total of (1) wages paid, (2) noncash payments, (3) tips/reported, and (4) all other compensation before deductions for taxes, insurance, etc.

13. How did you determine the amounts in items 7 through 12 above?
PER PAY STUBS

14. Give reason Form W-2, W-2P (or W-2C, Statement of Corrected Income and Tax Amounts) was not furnished by employer, or payer, if known, and explain your efforts to get it.
EMPLOYER OUT OF BUSINESS - NO FORWARDING ADDRESS

Paperwork Reduction Notice
We ask for this information to carry out the Internal Revenue laws of the United States. We need it to ensure that taxpayers are complying with these laws and to allow us to figure and collect the right amount of tax. You are required to give us this information.

Under penalties of perjury, I declare that I have examined this statement and, to the best of my knowledge and belief, it is true, correct, and complete.

15. Your signature: Faye Dough

16. Date: 1/19/88

1987 Form W-4A

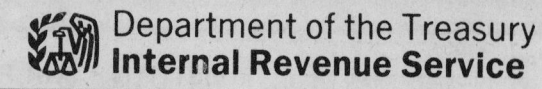

Department of the Treasury — Internal Revenue Service

What is Form W-4A? This form is an easier way to figure your withholding than the 4-page 1987 Form W-4. If you have already given your employer a Form W-4 this year, **do not** file a new Form W-4A unless you wish to change your withholding.

Caution: Form W-4A may cause more or less tax to be withheld from your wages than you wish because it adjusts your withholding only for pay you receive after it takes effect. If not enough tax was withheld earlier in the year, you can increase your withholding by reducing the allowances claimed on line 4 of the form or by requesting that more money be withheld on line 5 of the form.

Exemption From Withholding— Important Change in Law. If you are a dependent of another person (for example, a student who can still be claimed on your parents' return), you are not exempt if you have any nonwage income (such as interest on savings) **and** expect your total income to be more than $500.

What Do I Need To Do? Exempt employees can skip the Worksheet and go directly to line 6 of Form W-4A. All others must complete lines A through G. Many employees can stop at line G of the Worksheet.

Nonwage Income? If you have a large amount of income from other sources (such as interest or dividends), you should consider either using the 1987 Form W-4 or making estimated tax payments using Form 1040-ES. Call 1-800-424-3676 (in Hawaii and Alaska, check your local telephone directory) for copies of the 1987 Form W-4 and **Publication 919**, "Is My Withholding Correct?"

When Should I File? File as soon as possible to avoid underwithholding problems. If you do not file by October 1, 1987, your allowances may be adjusted to "1" if single or "2" if married and your take home pay may be reduced.

Two-Earner Couples? More Than One Job? To figure the number of allowances you may claim, combine allowances and wages from all jobs on one worksheet. File a Form W-4A with each employer, but do not claim the same allowances more than once. Your withholding will usually be more accurate if you claim all allowances on the highest paying job.

W-4A Worksheet To Figure Your Withholding Allowances

A	Enter "1" for **yourself** if no one else can claim you as a dependent	A 1
B	Enter "1" if: { 1. You are single and have only one job; or 2. You are married, have only one job, and your spouse does not work; or 3. Your wages from a second job or your spouse's wages (or the total of both) are $2,500 or less. }	B 1
C	Enter "1" for your **spouse** if no one else claims your spouse as a dependent	C ___
D	Enter number of **dependents** other than your spouse that you will claim on your return	D ___
E	Enter "1" if you want to reduce your withholding because you or your spouse is at least **age 65 or blind** and you do not plan to itemize deductions	E ___
F	Enter "1" if you want to reduce your withholding because you have at least $1,500 of **child or dependent care expenses** for which you plan to claim a credit	F ___
G	Add lines A through F and enter total here	G 2

- If you plan to **itemize or claim other deductions** and wish to reduce your withholding, turn to the Deductions Worksheet on the back.
- If you have **more than one job or a working spouse** AND your combined earnings from all jobs exceed $25,000, or $15,000 if you are married filing a joint return, turn to the Two-Earner/Two-Job Worksheet on the back if you want to avoid having too little tax withheld.
- If **neither** of the above situations applies to you, **stop here** and enter the number from line G on line 4 of Form W-4A below.

------- Cut here and give the certificate to your employer. Keep the top portion for your records. -------

Form W-4A — Employee's Withholding Allowance Certificate

Department of the Treasury — Internal Revenue Service
► For Privacy Act and Paperwork Reduction Act Notice, see reverse.

OMB No. 1545-0010
1987

1 Type or print your full name: FAYE DOUGH
2 Your social security number: 000-19-7912

Home address (number and street or rural route): 1000 CITY DRIVE
City or town, state, and ZIP code: ANYPLACE USA 07912

3 Marital Status: ☐ Single ☒ Married ☐ Married, but withhold at higher Single rate
Note: If married, but legally separated, or spouse is a nonresident alien, check the Single box.

4 Total number of allowances you are claiming (from line G above, or from the Worksheets on back if they apply): **2**
5 Additional amount, if any, you want deducted from each pay: $ ___

6 I claim exemption from withholding because (check boxes below that apply):
a ☐ Last year I did not owe any Federal income tax and had a right to a full refund of **ALL** income tax withheld, **AND**
b ☐ This year I do not expect to owe any Federal income tax and expect to have a right to a full refund of **ALL** income tax withheld. If both a and b apply, enter the year effective and "EXEMPT" here ► Year 19___
c Are you a full-time student? ☐ Yes ☐ No

Under penalties of perjury, I certify that I am entitled to the number of withholding allowances claimed on this certificate or, if claiming exemption from withholding, that I am entitled to claim the exempt status.

Employee's signature ► _Faye Dough_   Date ► 7/__, 1987

7 Employer's name and address (Employer: Complete 7, 8, and 9 only if sending to IRS):
FIRSTRAVEL
1960 1ST AVE ANYWHERE USA 07912

8 Office code: ___
9 Employer identification number: 59-6179204

Form W-4A (1987) Page 2

Deductions Worksheet

NOTE: Use this Worksheet only if you plan to itemize or claim other deductions.

1. Enter an estimate of your 1987 itemized deductions. These include: home mortgage interest, 65% of personal interest, charitable contributions, state and local taxes (but not sales taxes), medical expenses in excess of 7.5% of your income, and miscellaneous deductions (most miscellaneous deductions are now deductible only in excess of 2% of your income) .... 1 $ _____

2. Enter: { $3,760 if married filing jointly or qualifying widow(er) / $2,540 if single or head of household / $1,880 if married filing separately } .... 2 $ _____

3. **Subtract** line 2 from line 1. Enter the result, but not less than zero .... 3 $ _____

4. Enter an estimate of your 1987 adjustments to income. These include alimony paid and deductible IRA contributions .... 4 $ _____

5. **Add** lines 3 and 4 and enter the total .... 5 $ _____

6. Enter an estimate of your 1987 nonwage income (such as dividends or interest income) .... 6 $ _____

7. **Subtract** line 6 from line 5. Enter the result, but not less than zero .... 7 $ _____

8. **Divide** the amount on line 7 by $2,000 and enter the result here. Drop any fraction .... 8 _____

9. Enter the number from Form W-4A Worksheet, line G, on page 1 .... 9 _____

10. **Add** lines 8 and 9 and enter the total here. If you plan to use the Two-Earner/Two-Job Worksheet, also enter the total on line 1, below. Otherwise **stop here** and enter this total on Form W-4A, line 4 on page 1 .... 10 _____

Two-Earner/Two-Job Worksheet

NOTE: Use this Worksheet only if the instructions at line G on page 1 direct you here.

1. Enter the number from line G on page 1 (or from line 10 above if you used the Deductions Worksheet) ... 1 _____

2. Enter "1" if you are married filing a joint return and earnings from the lower paying jobs held by you or your spouse exceed $3,000. Otherwise enter "0" .... 2 _____

3. **Subtract** line 2 from line 1 and enter the result here. If you entered "1" on line 2 and combined earnings from all jobs are less than $40,000, enter the result on Form W-4A, line 4, page 1, and **do not** use the rest of this worksheet. Otherwise, continue .... 3 _____

4. Find the number in **Table 1** below that applies to the **LOWEST** paying job and enter it here .... 4 _____

5. If line 3 is **GREATER THAN OR EQUAL TO** line 4, **subtract** line 4 from line 3. Enter the result here (if zero, enter "0") and on Form W-4A, line 4, page 1. **Do not** use the rest of this worksheet .... 5 _____

6. If line 3 is **LESS THAN** line 4, enter "0" on Form W-4A, line 4, page 1, and enter the number from line 4 of this worksheet .... 6 _____

7. Enter the number from line 3 of this worksheet .... 7 _____

8. **Subtract** line 7 from line 6 .... 8 _____

9. Find the amount in **Table 2** below that applies to the **HIGHEST** paying job and enter it here .... 9 $ _____

10. **Multiply** line 9 by line 8 and enter the result here .... 10 $ _____

11. **Divide** line 10 by the number of pay periods each year. (For example, divide by 26 if you are paid every other week.) Enter the result here and on Form W-4A, line 5, page 1 .... 11 $ _____

Table 1: Two-Earner/Two-Job Worksheet

Married Filing Jointly		All Others	
If wages from **LOWEST** paying job are—	Enter on line 4, above	If wages from **LOWEST** paying job are—	Enter on line 4, above
0 - $6,000	0	0 - $4,000	0
6,001 - 10,000	1	4,001 - 7,000	1
10,001 - 13,000	2	7,001 - 11,000	2
13,001 - 16,000	3	11,001 - 14,000	3
16,001 - 20,000	4	14,001 - 17,000	4
20,001 - 23,000	5	17,001 - 23,000	5
23,001 - 26,000	6	23,001 - 30,000	6
26,001 - 29,000	7	30,001 and over	7
29,001 - 35,000	8		
35,001 - 50,000	9		
50,001 and over	10		

Table 2: Two-Earner/Two-Job Worksheet

Married Filing Jointly		All Others	
If wages from **HIGHEST** paying job are—	Enter on line 9, above	If wages from **HIGHEST** paying job are—	Enter on line 9, above
0 - $30,000	$300	0 - $17,000	$300
30,001 - 47,000	500	17,001 - 28,000	500
47,001 and over	700	28,001 and over	700

Privacy Act and Paperwork Reduction Act Notice.—We ask for this information to carry out the Internal Revenue laws of the United States. We may give the information to the Department of Justice for civil or criminal litigation and to cities, states, and the District of Columbia for use in administering their tax laws. You are required to give this information to your employer.

The "Short Forms": Form 1040A and Form 1040EZ

Form 1040A may be used by anyone regardless of income or filing status if his or her total income is derived solely from wages, salary, bonuses, and tips.

However, Form 1040A is not for everyone. It contains no provisions for claiming itemized deductions. If you elect to use Form 1040A, you must use the standard deductions. You will not be able to claim certain credits and adjustments to income—for example, credit for the elderly, interest expenses, moving expenses, employee business expenses, or alimony payments. If you are entitled to any of these, it may be to your advantage to file Form 1040. You are, of course, permitted to use whichever method will result in the greatest deduction and the corresponding lowest tax.

FORM 1040: BASIC INFORMATION

Changes in Form 1040

Naturally, the changes in the tax law have been reflected in the forms that must be filled out. Here is a breakdown of the significant changes that have been made in Form 1040.

Exemptions

- If you are age 65 or over (or blind) you are no longer entitled to claim an additional personal exemption for age or blindness but are entitled to an additional standard deduction on line 33.
- Dependent children over the age of 5 must have their own Social Security numbers.
- This year there are no dependency exemptions allowed to individuals who can be claimed as an exemption on someone else's tax return.

Income

- Be sure to indicate any tax-exempt interest on line 9. Although this tax-exempt interest is not taxable, reporting the amount will help compute taxable Social Security and alternative minimum tax.
- The full amount of dividends is to be reported on line 10.
- There is no more preferential treatment of long-term capital gains, so there is no longer a need to enter 40 percent for capital gain distributions.
- If you received capital gain distributions but do not need Schedule D to report any other gains (or losses) or to figure your tax, enter your capital gain distributions on Form 1040, Line 14. Write "CGD" on the dotted line to the left of line 14.

Adjustments to Income

- *IRAs.* To make things easier in keeping track of nondeductible IRA contributions, IRA deductions are now claimed on 2 lines—24a and 24b—one for the taxpayer and one for the spouse.
- The married worker deduction has been eliminated.
- Moving expenses are no longer reflected on page 1 of the 1040 Form; now they are to be treated as an itemized deduction (but not subject to the 2 percent floor).

Reimbursed Business Expenses—Line 23

- Only reimbursed employee business expenses from Form 2106 are to be deducted on page 1 to the extent of any reimbursement. *Un*reimbursed business expenses (from Form 2106) are to be claimed as miscellaneous deductions on Schedule A, Itemized Deductions, and are subject to the 2 percent floor.

Form 1040 — U.S. Individual Income Tax Return 1987

Department of the Treasury—Internal Revenue Service

For the year Jan.–Dec. 31, 1987, or other tax year beginning , 1987, ending , 19

OMB No. 1545-0074

Label (Use IRS label. Otherwise, please print or type.)

- Your first name and initial (if joint return, also give spouse's name and initial): **Barry R & Faye**
- Last name: **Dough**
- Present home address: **1000 City Place**
- City, town or post office, state, and ZIP code: **Anyplace USA 07942**
- Your social security number: **329 04 1040**
- Spouse's social security number: **004 19 79Q**

Presidential Election Campaign
- Do you want $1 to go to this fund? Yes ☐ No ☑
- If joint return, does your spouse want $1 to go to this fund? Yes ☐ No ☑

Filing Status (Check only one box.)

1. ☐ Single
2. ☑ Married filing joint return (even if only one had income)
3. ☐ Married filing separate return. Enter spouse's social security no. above and full name here.
4. ☐ Head of household (with qualifying person). (See page 6 of Instructions.) If the qualifying person is your child but not your dependent, enter child's name here.
5. ☐ Qualifying widow(er) with dependent child (year spouse died ▶ 19). (See page 7 of Instructions.)

Exemptions

- 6a ☑ Yourself
- 6b ☑ Spouse

Caution: If you can be claimed as a dependent on another person's tax return (such as your parents' return), do not check box 6a. But be sure to check the box on line 32b.

No. of boxes checked on 6a and 6b ▶ **2**

c Dependents:

(1) Name (first, initial, and last name)	(2) Check if under age 5	(3) If age 5 or over, dependent's social security number	(4) Relationship	(5) No. of months lived in your home
Miriam Dough		059 40 6217	Daughter	12
Marcie Dough		325 70 0007	Daughter	12

No. of children on 6c who lived with you ▶ **2**

No. of children on 6c who didn't live with you due to divorce or separation ▶

No. of parents listed on 6c ▶

No. of other dependents listed on 6c ▶

d If your child didn't live with you but is claimed as your dependent under a pre-1985 agreement, check here ▶ ☐

e Total number of exemptions claimed (also complete line 35)

Add numbers entered in boxes above ▶ **4**

Income

Line	Description	Amount
7	Wages, salaries, tips, etc. (attach Form(s) W-2)	57000
8	Taxable interest income (also attach Schedule B if over $400)	1912
9	Tax-exempt interest income (see page 9). DO NOT include on line 8	0
10	Dividend income (also attach Schedule B if over $400)	675
11	Taxable refunds of state and local income taxes, if any, from worksheet on page 10 of Instructions	
12	Alimony received	
13	Business income or (loss) (attach Schedule C)	1205
14	Capital gain or (loss) (attach Schedule D)	3000
15	Other gains or (losses) (attach Form 4797)	
16a	Pensions, IRA distributions, annuities, and rollovers. Total received	
16b	Taxable amount, if any (see page 10)	
17	Rents, royalties, partnerships, estates, trusts, etc. (attach Schedule E)	<1849>
18	Farm income or (loss) (attach Schedule F)	
19	Unemployment compensation (insurance) (see page 11)	
20a	Social security benefits (see page 11)	
20b	Taxable amount, if any, from the worksheet on page 12	
21	Other income (list type and amount—see page 11)	
22	Add the amounts shown in the far right column for lines 7, 8, and 10–21. This is your **total income** ▶	61943

Adjustments to Income

Line	Description	Amount	
23	Reimbursed employee business expenses from Form 2106		
24a	Your IRA deduction, from applicable worksheet on page 13	2000	
24b	Spouse's IRA deduction, from applicable worksheet on page 13	2000	
25	Self-employed health insurance deduction, from worksheet on page 14	350	
26	Keogh retirement plan and self-employed SEP deduction		
27	Penalty on early withdrawal of savings	90	
28	Alimony paid (recipient's last name and social security no.)		
29	Add lines 23 through 28. These are your **total adjustments** ▶		4440

Adjusted Gross Income

30. Subtract line 29 from line 22. This is your **adjusted gross income**. If this line is less than $15,432 and a child lived with you, see "Earned Income Credit" (line 56) on page 18 of Instructions. If you want IRS to figure your tax, see page 14 of Instructions ▶ **57503**

Page 2

	31	Amount from line 30 (adjusted gross income)		31	57503

Tax Computation

32a Check if: ☐ You were 65 or over ☐ Blind; ☐ Spouse was 65 or over ☐ Blind.
Add the number of boxes checked and enter the total here ▶ | 32a |

b If you can be claimed as a dependent on another person's return, check here ▶ 32b ☐

c If you are married filing a separate return and your spouse itemizes deductions, or you are a dual-status alien, see page 15 and check here ▶ 32c ☐

33a **Itemized deductions.** See page 15 to see if you should itemize. If you itemize, attach Schedule A, enter the amount from Schedule A, line 26, and skip line 33b. | 33a | 23156

b **Standard deduction.** Enter amount shown below for your filing status, unless Caution to left applies.
Filing status from page 1 { Single or Head of household, enter $2,540 / Married filing jointly or Qualifying widow(er), enter $3,760 / Married filing separately, enter $1,880 } | 33b |

Caution: If you completed line 32a, b, or c and you don't itemize, see page 15 for the amount to enter on line 33b.

34	Subtract line 33a or 33b, whichever applies, from line 31. Enter the result here	34	34347
35	Multiply $1,900 by the total number of exemptions claimed on line 6e or see chart on page 16	35	7600
36	**Taxable income.** Subtract line 35 from line 34. Enter the result (but not less than zero)	36	26747

Caution: If under age 14 and you have more than $1,000 of investment income, check here ▶ ☐ and see page 16 to see if you have to use Form 8615 to figure your tax.

37	Enter tax. Check if from ☒ Tax Table, ☐ Tax Rate Schedules, ☐ Schedule D, or ☐ Form 8615	37	3889
38	Additional taxes (see page 16). Check if from ☐ Form 4970 or ☐ Form 4972	38	
39	Add lines 37 and 38. Enter the total ▶	39	3889

Credits (See Instructions on page 16.)

40	Credit for child and dependent care expenses (attach Form 2441)	40	960		
41	Credit for the elderly or for the permanently and totally disabled (attach Schedule R)	41			
42	Add lines 40 and 41. Enter the total			42	960
43	Subtract line 42 from line 39. Enter the result (but not less than zero)			43	2929
44	Foreign tax credit (attach Form 1116)	44			
45	General business credit. Check if from ☐ Form 3800, ☐ Form 3468, ☐ Form 5884, ☐ Form 6478, ☐ Form 6765, or ☐ Form 8586	45			
46	Add lines 44 and 45. Enter the total			46	
47	Subtract line 46 from line 43. Enter the result (but not less than zero) ▶			47	2929

Other Taxes (Including Advance EIC Payments)

48	Self-employment tax (attach Schedule SE)	48	148
49	Alternative minimum tax (attach Form 6251)	49	
50	Tax from recapture of investment credit (attach Form 4255)	50	
51	Social security tax on tip income not reported to employer (attach Form 4137)	51	
52	Tax on an IRA or a qualified retirement plan (attach Form 5329)	52	
53	Add lines 47 through 52. This is your **total tax** ▶	53	3077

Payments
Attach Forms W-2, W-2G, and W-2P to front.

54	Federal income tax withheld	54	8369		
55	1987 estimated tax payments and amount applied from 1986 return	55	3000		
56	Earned income credit (see page 18)	56			
57	Amount paid with Form 4868 (extension request)	57			
58	Excess social security tax and RRTA tax withheld (see page 18)	58			
59	Credit for Federal tax on gasoline and special fuels (attach Form 4136)	59			
60	Regulated investment company credit (attach Form 2439)	60			
61	Add lines 54 through 60. These are your **total payments** ▶			61	11369

Refund or Amount You Owe

62	If line 61 is larger than line 53, enter amount **OVERPAID** ▶	62	8292
63	Amount of line 62 to be **REFUNDED TO YOU** ▶	63	8292
64	Amount of line 62 to be applied to your 1988 estimated tax ▶	64	
65	If line 53 is larger than line 61, enter **AMOUNT YOU OWE.** Attach check or money order for full amount payable to "Internal Revenue Service." Write your social security number, daytime phone number, and "1987 Form 1040" on it	65	

Check ▶ ☐ if Form 2210 (2210F) is attached. See page 19. Penalty: $

Please Sign Here

Under penalties of perjury, I declare that I have examined this return and accompanying schedules and statements, and to the best of my knowledge and belief, they are true, correct, and complete. Declaration of preparer (other than taxpayer) is based on all information of which preparer has any knowledge.

Your signature ▶ *B. Dough* | Date 4/1/88 | Your occupation EXECUTIVE

Spouse's signature (if joint return, BOTH must sign) *Faye Dough* | Date 4/1/88 | Spouse's occupation TRAVEL AGENT

Paid Preparer's Use Only

Preparer's signature ▶ | Date | Check if self-employed ☐ | Preparer's social security no.

Firm's name (or yours if self-employed) and address ▶ | E.I. No. | ZIP code

Tax Computation

- Nonitemizers can no longer deduct charitable contributions.
- The standard deduction (line 33b) replaces the zero bracket amount and is no longer reflected in the tax tables or tax rate schedules.
- Personal exemptions have been increased and reflected on line 35.
- Children under age 14 receiving more than $1,000 of unearned income (e.g., interest or dividends) will be taxed at the parents' rate and must check off a box on line 36.

Choosing Your Filing Status

There are different tax-rate schedules, each depending on marital status. For tax purposes, you are either: (1) single; (2) married filing jointly; (3) married filing separately; (4) unmarried head of household; or (5) widow(er) with dependent child.

Single (Line 1)

You are considered single for tax purposes if you are:

1. Unmarried at the end of the year
2. Married to a nonresident alien (a U.S. citizen married to a nonresident alien can file a joint return, but only if all income both here and abroad is taken into account)
3. Separated from your spouse under a final decree of divorce (or under a decree of separate maintenance).

Tax Planning for Singles (and for Those Who Think They Have No Writeoffs)

Single individuals often overlook tax breaks that can affect their taxes. When their income isn't as high as that of a family unit or they do not have the interest and real-estate tax writeoffs that accompany home ownership, they tend to assume that there is no need for tax planning. While singles may find it difficult to itemize their deductions, with proper planning they may be able to exceed the standard deduction at least every other tax year. How? By planning ahead.

All taxpayers should anticipate expenditures a year in advance whenever possible. Toward the end of the year, consider whether certain deductible items should be paid before December 31 for that year's taxes or after January 1 in order to double up on deductions and be able to itemize the following year.

There are always a number of tax deductions available to singles (and those who think they have no writeoffs), many of which you may not have considered. For instance, the interest paid on credit cards and school loans is partially deductible. If you are looking for another job (not your first), your job-hunting expenses, including travel, hotel, motel, laundry, dry cleaning, and meals (while out of town only) are deductible. So are telephone calls, newspapers, and the cost of producing and sending out résumés (typing, printing, and postage). The costs of continuing education and travel between your job and school (or to a second job) are tax-deductible as miscellaneous itemized deductions subject to a 2 percent floor.

Advantages of Married Filing Separately

Even if you have filed jointly in the past, because of the Tax Reform Act, you may want to reconsider. The two-wage-earner deduction is gone, there are adjustments to the standard deduction, and the tax rate schedules have been changed.

Medical expenses must exceed 7½ percent of AGI; on a joint return, they might not exceed 7½, but by filing separately, the spouse with large medical expenses may save the deduction. In addition, since miscellaneous deductions now have a 2 percent floor, a spouse with large unreimbursed miscellaneous business expenses may be better off filing separately.

Compute your tax both ways and file whichever way is the most beneficial.

Example

Faye has an adjusted gross income of $30,000 and itemized deductions of $8,000 ($5,000 for medical and $3,000 for unreimbursed miscellaneous expenses). Barry has $60,000 AGI with $9,000 itemized deductions (of which $4,000 are unreimbursed miscellaneous expenses). If they file jointly, their tax will total $19,690, as follows:

Adjusted gross income	$90,000
Less exemptions	(3,800)
Itemized deductions	(10,200)
Taxable income	$76,000
Tax	$19,690

If Faye files separately, her tax will be $4,577, as follows:

Adjusted gross income	$30,000
Less exemptions	(1,900)
Itemized deductions	(5,150)
Taxable income	$22,950
Tax	$ 4,577)

If Barry files separately, his tax will be $14,566 as follows:

Adjusted gross income	$60,000
Less exemptions	(1,900)
Itemized deductions	(7,200)
Taxable income	$50,900
Tax	$14,566

The net tax saving by filing separately is $547.

Head of Household (Line 4)

Head-of-household rates fall almost directly between those of single and joint returns. In order to qualify as a head of household you must:

1. Be single as of the end of the tax year and have living with you a child, stepchild, or other relative (whether you claim them as exemptions or not)

2. Pay more than half the living cost of running that household. The child living with you must have lived in the household throughout the year, with the exception of temporary absences (e.g., summer camp).

If the relative is someone other than a child or stepchild, you must be able to claim him or her as an exemption in order to get the benefit of head-of-household rates. The relative must have total gross income of less than $1,900, and you must have provided more than 50 percent of the support.

Special Rules for Taxpayers Supporting Parents

If you support one or both of your parents and wish to qualify for head-of-household rates, you must be able to claim them as exemptions. Your parents need not live with you, provided that they each have less than $1,900 in gross income and you provide more than 50 percent of their support and household costs—mortgage payments, utilities, taxes, repairs, and so forth.

Special Rules for an Abandoned Spouse

An abandoned spouse is treated as a single person for purposes of the zero-bracket amount and may be eligible to use head-of-household tax rates and claim the child-care credit without regard to deductions claimed by the other spouse. To qualify:

1. The taxpayer must file a separate return.
2. The taxpayer must furnish over one-half the cost of maintaining a household that was used for more than 6 months of the year as the principal residence of a dependent child or stepchild.
3. The dependent child must have lived in the taxpayer's household for the entire year.
4. The taxpayer's spouse cannot have been a member of the household during the last 6 months of the year. In a recent case, however, a taxpayer was permitted to file as a single person even though the couple was separated for only 6 months during the year.

There is no longer a requirement that the custodial parent be entitled to claim the child's exemption if:

1. There is a waiver of the exemption; or
2. There is a pre-1985 separation or divorce agreement awarding the exemption to the noncustodial parent.

Qualifying Widow(er) With Dependent Child (Line 5)

When a spouse dies during the tax year, the surviving spouse can file a joint return for the year of death and is entitled to use joint return rates for the next 2 years, provided:

1. The surviving spouse supports at least one dependent child or stepchild—that is, a child or stepchild for whom the parent provides more than 50 percent of his or her support.
2. The surviving spouse provides more than 50 percent of the costs of operating the household during each of the 2 years following the spouse's death.

Exemptions (Line 6)

You are entitled to a deduction of $1,900 for each exemption claimed on your return. There are 2 distinct types of exemptions: those for you and your spouse (personal exemptions) and those for children and relatives (exemptions for dependents).

Personal Exemptions (Lines 6a and 6b)

No matter what your filing status is, you can always claim at least one exemption for yourself. Personal exemptions are now $1,900 for yourself, your spouse, or dependents. The extra exemption for the blind and elderly is eliminated and replaced with a $600 additional standard deduction for marrieds and a $750 deduction for singles.

If your spouse died during the year and you did not remarry by December 31, you are entitled to claim his or her exemptions on a joint return—including the additional standard deduction for old age and blindness—the same as if your spouse had lived the entire year. If you were due a refund, you must file Form 1310 and attach a copy of the death certificate to your form when you file.

If at the end of the year you were divorced or separated under a final decree, you lose your spouse's exemption. If, however, you were separated under an interlocutory decree, you still may claim your spouse's exemption, but only if both signatures appear on the return. If you are married but file separately, you cannot claim your spouse's exemptions on your return.

Elderly and/or Blind Taxpayers

Taxpayers who are age 65 or over or blind will no longer be able to claim an additional personal exemption for age or blindness. Instead, only those who *do not itemize* will be entitled to an additional standard deduction in 1987, as follows:

	Basic Standard Deduction	One 65 or over	Both 65 or over
Married filing jointly and surviving spouses	$5,000	$5,600	$6,200
Married filing separately	2,500	3,100	—
Singles	3,000	3,750	—
Head of household	4,400	5,150	—

A married taxpayer filing jointly who is both elderly and blind may claim an additional $600; if both spouses are elderly and blind, they may claim a total of $1,200 in addition to the $5,000 standard deduction.

A taxpayer who files as single or head of household and is either blind or elderly may claim an additional $750; if he or she is elderly *and* blind, he or she may deduct an additional $1,500 in addition to the $3,000 or $4,400 standard deduction.

Exemptions for Dependents (Line 6c)

You can claim a $1,900 exemption for anyone who qualifies as a dependent during the year.

Who Is a Dependent?

1. A relative or member of your household who is either a citizen or resident of the United States, Mexico, or Canada. Citizens of other countries do not qualify unless they are residents of the United States. A relative other than a parent, grandparent, child, or grandchild must have lived in your home for the full year.
2. A person for whom you contributed more than 50 percent of his or her support. Support is the amount of money actually spent on behalf of the individual—not necessarily the same amount as he or she earns. Support includes any funds spent for necessities (food, shelter, clothing) but does not include money spent for incidentals (toys, recreation, automobiles). Amounts spent by an individual in making long trips to care for an invalid parent have been considered in determining support. Medicare and Medicaid benefits are no longer calculated in determining support. If you claim a dependent who has outside income (taxable or otherwise), you must have proof of the expenditures of both the money you gave the dependent and the dependent's own money.
3. A person who has earned less than $1,900 during the year, or a child or stepchild under 19 years of age or a full-time (day) student for any 5 months of the year regardless of the amount of money earned. School attendance limited exclusively to night classes when the child works full-time during the day *does not* qualify him or her as a full-time student. However, the taking of night classes as part of a full-time day course does not disqualify him or her as a full-time student. You must still prove that you contributed more than half of the child's support. A solution to this problem may be to have the child start a savings account and to deposit in that account as much in earnings as possible. Money saved is not considered as having been spent by a child toward his own support.

In order for you to claim a dependent, all three requirements must be met.

Filing for Dependents

Anyone claimed as a dependent on someone else's return is not allowed a personal exemption on his or her own return. A child claimed on his parents' return (as a dependent) may not claim a second personal exemption on his or her own return.

A dependent may use the standard deduction to offset (1) $500 or (2) the amount of unearned income, whichever is greater.

This limit on the standard deduction does not apply to the additional deduction for the elderly or blind. Individuals who are age 65 or older (or blind) may take an extra $750 deduction ($600 each in the case of married couples), which may be used to offset unearned income over $500.

Example: If you claim your elderly parent as a dependent on your return, he or she still may use the $2,540 standard deduction to offset income (earned or unearned) up to $500. In addition, your parent may use the additional standard deduction of $750 (over age 65) to offset remaining income, earned or unearned. You claim your elderly parent as a dependent, and your parent is still allowed $3,290 standard deduction against income.

A tax return must be filed if there is gross income over the standard deduction (including the additional standard deduction) or if there is unearned income over $500 (plus the additional standard deduction).

If your parent is over age 65, if his or her gross income is over $3,290 (the $2,540 standard deduction plus the $750 additional standard deduction) or if his or her unearned income is over $1,250 ($500 unearned income plus $750 additional standard deduction), he or she must file a tax return.

Exemptions for the Disabled

Income received by a permanently and totally disabled individual in a sheltered workshop can be ignored in determining the dependency exemption, if: (1) the income earned arose solely from activities at the sheltered workshop, and (2) the principal purpose of the individual's presence at the workshop is for medical care. A sheltered workshop is defined as a tax-exempt school, operated by either a charity or state or local government, which provides special training to alleviate disability.

Death of a Dependent

If a child was born alive at any time during the year (and all the dependency tests are met), the full $1,900 exemption may be claimed. This holds true if the child lives for only a few moments but not if the baby is stillborn. If a dependent dies during the year (and all the dependency tests are met for the part of the year he or she lived), the full $1,900 exemption may be claimed. See Form 1310 on next page. If the deceased was a spouse over 65 years old or blind, you may claim the appropriate additional exemptions.

Multiple Support Agreements

If 2 or more persons furnish more than 50 percent of the support of a dependent (on a combined basis) and either of those persons provides more than 10 percent of that support, either may claim that person as an exemption on his return provided that the person not claiming the exemption submits Form 2120 (Multiple Support Declaration) indicating that he or she will not claim the person in question. The signed form must then be filed with the return of the person claiming the exemption.

In the case of parents supported by children, the children have the right to switch the parental exemptions among themselves from year to year in order to give each child some tax benefits.

Only one exemption may be claimed for each person when an exemption is claimed under a multiple support agreement. A child cannot claim an extra standard deduction for old age or blindness on the part of his or her parents. The old-age and blindness standard deductions are personal exemptions and may only be claimed by the taxpayer on his or her own return.

Divorced parents often have problems connected with claiming the children as exemptions; in many cases, both parents try to claim the same exemptions. If the parents or the court specify in the divorce decree or separation agreement which party can claim the children as exemptions, the specified parent can claim them on his or her return. Unless stated otherwise in the agreement, exemptions are claimed by the parent with custody.

A dependent's medical bills paid by a parent may be included in that parent's deductible medical expenses regardless of whether that child is the parent's dependent for tax purposes.

Form 1310 (Rev. September 1985)
Department of the Treasury
Internal Revenue Service

Statement of Person Claiming Refund Due a Deceased Taxpayer

OMB No. 1545-0073

Tax year decedent was due a refund:
Calendar year **1987**, or other tax year beginning _____, 19___, and ending _____, 19___

Name of decedent: **ERMA DOUGH**	Date of death: **1-17-87** — Social security number of decedent: **322 07 1492**
Name of person claiming refund: **MAURICE DOUGH**	
Address (number and street): **800 ANYPLACE LANE**	
City or town, state, and ZIP code: **NOWHERE USA 00794**	

I am filing this statement as (check only one box):

- **A** ☐ Surviving spouse, claiming a refund based on a joint return. (See **Death of Taxpayer** in instructions for Form 1040 or Form 1040A.)
- **B** ☐ Decedent's court appointed personal representative. Attach a court certificate showing your appointment. (See instructions on back of form.)
- **C** ☐ Person, other than **A** or **B**, claiming refund for the decedent's estate. Complete Schedule A and attach a copy of the death certificate or proof of death. (See instructions on back of form.)

Please attach requested information and sign below. If you checked Box C, also complete Schedule A.

Schedule A (To be completed only if you checked Box C above.)

	Yes	No
1 Did the decedent leave a will?		X
2a Has a personal representative been appointed by a court for the estate of the decedent?		X
b If "No," will one be appointed?		X
If 2a or 2b is answered "Yes," do not file this form. The personal representative should file for the refund.		
3 As the person claiming the refund for the decedent's estate, will you pay out the refund according to the laws of the State where the decedent was a legal resident?	X	

If "No," a refund cannot be made until you submit a court certificate showing your appointment as personal representative or other evidence that you are entitled, under State law, to receive the refund.

Signature and Verification

I request a refund of taxes overpaid by or on behalf of the decedent. Under penalties of perjury, I declare that I have examined this claim and to the best of my knowledge and belief, it is true, correct, and complete.

Signature of person claiming refund ▶ *Maurice Dough*   Date ▶ **4/1/88**

Form 2120 (Rev. April 1986)

Department of the Treasury—Internal Revenue Service

Multiple Support Declaration

OMB No. 1545-0071
Expires 1-31-89

During the calendar year 19**87**, I paid more than 10% of the support of

JACKIE DOUGH
(Name of person)

I could have claimed this person as a dependent except that I did not pay more than 50% of his or her support. I understand that this person is being claimed as a dependent on the income tax return of **JOHN DOUGH**
(Name)

1850 ANYPLACE LANE
(Address)

I agree not to claim an exemption for this person on my Federal income tax return for any tax year that began in this calendar year.

Brian Dough   **504 12 2007**
(Your signature)   (Your social security number)

4/3/88   **1933 ANYPLACE LANE   ANYWHERE USA 00793**
(Date)   (Address)

Income Shifting

For many years, income shifting to children under the age of 14 has been a popular strategy for placing income in a lower tax bracket. Now, thanks to Tax Reform, it is generally no longer available to avoid paying taxes. As a matter of fact, Tax Reform penalizes prior transfers since there is no distinction as to the taxability of income based on when the assets were transferred.

Now only the first $1,000 of a child's net unearned income is taxed at the child's marginal tax rate. The first $500 is offset by the standard deduction, and the second $500 is taxed at the child's rate. Any amount in excess of $1,000 is taxed at the parents' marginal tax rate.

Computation of tax

The child's tax is the greater of (1) the tax on his total income or (2) the sum of the tax on his total income (reduced by net unearned income) plus his share of the parents' tax.

Net unearned income

The child's net unearned income is his unearned income less $500 plus either (1) $500, or, if the child itemizes, (2) amount of allowable deductions directly connected with production of unearned income. Of course, the difference cannot exceed his taxable income for the year.

This tax applies to a child who is not age 14 by the last day of the tax year and who has at least one parent alive at the end of the same tax year. If the child's parents are unmarried, the tax rate of the custodial parent applies. If the married parents file separately, the rate of the one with the greater taxable income is used.

Some are calling this the "kiddie tax." Although this tax puts income shifting in a different light, there are still some planning strategies that may be effective:
1. Invest in securities for children that are tax-exempt until the child is age 14 (because it helps in estate planning).
2. Invest in Series EE bonds that will mature after the child is age 14. The tax is payable only when the bond is redeemed.
3. Take advantage of the annual gift-tax exclusion. You can invest in income-producing property. Even though you will not realize current tax savings, you can transfer a substantial sum without having the gift tax imposed on the funds.
4. Purchase an annuity that will be payable after the child reaches age 14.
5. Invest in growth stocks that will pay little or no dividends. (When the stock is sold—when the child is 14—the gain will be taxed at the child's rate.)
6. Employ the child in the family business. The child's standard deduction will be $500 or his earned income, whichever is greater. The employer-parent could also deduct the salary as a business expense. (Salary paid must be reasonable for services performed.)

The parent's return should be completed simultaneously with the child's return, and the parent must provide his child with the parent's taxpayer identification number, which is included on the child's return.

3

REPORTING YOUR INCOME
WAGES, SALARIES, AND TIPS • DIVIDEND INCOME • INTEREST INCOME

You must report all income earned during the year. The column headed "Gross Wages" on Form W-2 notes the total amount of income to be reported on Form 1040, line 7. The amount under "Federal Income Tax Withheld" represents the federal tax withheld from your pay. Enter this amount on line 54. If you live in a state that has a state income tax, this too may have been taken out of your pay and will appear on your W-2 form. Any state tax can be taken as an itemized deduction on your federal return and as a direct credit against your tax on the state return. If you received a state income tax refund, you must report it as income on line 11, provided you claimed the state tax paid as an itemized deduction in the prior year and actually realized a tax benefit from the deduction.

If you worked for more than one employer during the year, or if your spouse worked, you must include that additional income as well. However, if either of you worked for more than one employer during the year and your total individual income was more than $43,800, you may have had too much Social Security taken from your pay. To determine if that occurred, add the Social Security withheld from all W-2s, subtract $3,131 (the maximum), and enter this amount on line 58.

If you received dividend income during the year, Form 1099 from the payor will tell you the amount to report. Even if you fail to receive Form 1099, you are still obligated to report the income on line 10. If your gross dividends exceed $400, report them on Schedule B.

If you received interest income during the year, you must report it on line 8. If your interest income exceeds $400, report it on Schedule B. Interest income would include money received on bonds, savings accounts, and personal loans whether or not you received Form 1099. You must enter tax-exempt interest on line 4.

If you have income from a business, refer to Chapter 4; you will be required to file Schedule C.

If you sold stock, a home, or other investments during the year, consult Chapter 5; you will have to file Schedule D.

If you had income from pensions, annuities, or rents and royalties, you will need to fill in Form 1040, lines 16a and b, regarding pensions, or Schedule E to report rents, royalties, and income gain or loss from partnerships, estates, trusts, and small business corporations, or windfall profits tax credits.

If you received Social Security benefits and have substantial other income, part of your Social Security benefits may be taxable (see page 69).

Schedule B—Interest and Dividend Income

The form is substantially the same. If you received a Form 1099-IND (or 1099-OID) from a broker, list the firm's name and the total of either interest or dividends received, in Part I.

Name(s) as shown on Form 1040. DOUGH

Your social security number: 329:04:1040

Schedule B—Interest and Dividend Income

Attachment Sequence No. 08

Part I Interest Income

(See Instructions on pages 9 and 24.)

Also complete Part III.

Note: If you received a Form 1099–INT or Form 1099–OID from a brokerage firm, enter the firm's name and the total interest shown on that form.

If you received more than $400 in taxable interest income, you must complete Part I and list ALL interest received. If you received, as a nominee, interest that actually belongs to another person, or you received or paid accrued interest on securities transferred between interest payment dates, see page 24.

Interest Income		Amount
1 Interest income from seller-financed mortgages. (See Instructions and list name of payer.) ▶	1	
2 Other interest income (list name of payer) ▶ 1ST BANKERS	2	1912
3 Add the amounts on lines 1 and 2. Enter the total here and on Form 1040, line 8. ▶	3	1912

Part II Dividend Income

(See Instructions on pages 9 and 24.)

Also complete Part III.

Note: If you received a Form 1099-DIV from a brokerage firm, enter the firm's name and the total dividends shown on that form.

If you received more than $400 in gross dividends and/or other distributions on stock, complete Part II. If you received, as a nominee, dividends that actually belong to another person, see page 24.

Dividend Income		Amount
4 Dividend income (list name of payer—include on this line capital gain distributions, nontaxable distributions, etc.) ▶ FIRSTAX	4	675
5 Add the amounts on line 4. Enter the total here	5	675
6 Capital gain distributions. Enter here and on line 13, Schedule D.*	6	
7 Nontaxable distributions. (See Schedule D Instructions for adjustment to basis.)	7	
8 Add the amounts on lines 6 and 7. Enter the total here	8	
9 Subtract line 8 from line 5. Enter the result here and on Form 1040, line 10 ▶	9	675

*If you received capital gain distributions but do not need Schedule D to report any other gains or losses or to figure your tax (see the Tax Tip under Capital gain distributions on page 10), enter your capital gain distributions on Form 1040, line 14. Write "CGD" on the dotted line to the left of line 14.

Part III Foreign Accounts and Foreign Trusts

(See Instructions on page 24.)

If you received more than $400 of interest or dividends, OR if you had a foreign account or were a grantor of, or a transferor to, a foreign trust, you must answer both questions in Part III.

	Yes	No
10 At any time during the tax year, did you have an interest in or a signature or other authority over a financial account in a foreign country (such as a bank account, securities account, or other financial account)? (See page 24 of the Instructions for exceptions and filing requirements for Form TD F 90-22.1.)		X
If "Yes," enter the name of the foreign country ▶		
11 Were you the grantor of, or transferor to, a foreign trust which existed during the current tax year, whether or not you have any beneficial interest in it? If "Yes," you may have to file Forms 3520, 3520-A, or 926.		X

Proof of August 13, 1987

If your securities were held by a big firm, be sure to include the firm's name and total dividends from Form 1099-DIV in Part II.

Determining Your Gross Income

To compute your tax properly you must know your total income. The starting point is Form W-2. If you worked for more than one employer, you will need a separate W-2 Form from each. Now answer the following questions:

1. Are you filing a joint return? Did your spouse work during the year? If so, you must include his or her income on your return.
2. Did you have other items of income? Interest on savings or stock dividends? Did you cash any bonds or sell any stock? Did you receive any Form 1099s?

The One-Minute Taxman: Nontaxable Income

Accident insurance proceeds
Advances by employer to be repaid
Allotment paid by government to families of servicemen
Allowance for moving expenses
Bad-debt recovery that did not reduce tax in a prior year
Bequests
Board and lodging if on the employer's premises and as a condition of the job (e.g., clergyman, hotel manager)
Car pool receipts
Damages: for injuries, alienation of affection, breach of promise, slander, or libel
Death benefits received by an employee's beneficiary (maximum $5,000)
Disability pay
Dividends on life-insurance policy
Dividends paid in stock
Gains from sale of residence (if replaced)
Gifts
Group life insurance premiums paid by employer (maximum $50,000 coverage)
Health insurance proceeds where the expense was not deducted
Insurance proceeds (casualty and loss)
Interest on state and municipal bonds
Legacies
Life insurance proceeds
Meals furnished by employer on the premises if not for the employee's convenience
Old Age survivors' insurance benefits
Railroad Retirement benefits
Rebates on auto purchased
Scholarships, unless in the form of compensation
Social Security benefits (but see page 69)
Supper monies
Tax rebates
Transportation furnished by employer
Workmen's Compensation benefits

The One-Minute Taxman: Taxable Income

Look over the following checklist of taxable income. If you spot a particular income item you received last year, place a check in the box to the left of the entry. Enter the amount when you know what it is or when you receive your 1099 forms. Total all taxable income. This worksheet will simplify the job of reporting your income on your return.

Amount   *Amount*

- ☐ Alimony and separate maintenance payments received periodically _____
- ☐ Annuities (taxable portion) _____
- ☐ Awards _____
- ☐ Back pay _____
- ☐ Bad debt recovery (deducted in a prior year) _____
- ☐ Bequests, income from, but not the bequest itself _____
- ☐ Board and lodging (in certain cases) _____
- ☐ Capital gains _____
- ☐ Christmas bonus _____
- ☐ Commissions _____
- ☐ Compensation for services _____
- ☐ Dividends paid in cash or property (other than stock in the same company) _____
- ☐ Gain from sale or exchange of property _____
- ☐ Gambling gains _____
- ☐ Income from a gift (but not the gift itself) _____
- ☐ Insurance premiums paid by employer, where the employee and family are beneficiaries (not group term life insurance) _____
- ☐ Interest received, excluding municipal bond interest _____
- ☐ Jury fees _____
- ☐ Overtime pay _____
- ☐ Partnership income _____
- ☐ Pension income _____
- ☐ Prizes in contests _____
- ☐ Profits from business or profession _____
- ☐ Rental income _____
- ☐ Retirement pay _____
- ☐ Rewards _____
- ☐ Royalties _____
- ☐ Salaries and wages _____
- ☐ Severance pay _____
- ☐ Social Security benefits (see page 69) _____
- ☐ Tuition paid by employer _____
- ☐ Unemployment compensation _____

Total _____

Line	Tax Law	Pay Less Tax Legally

The Income Section

Line 7 — *Wages, Salaries, and Tips*

You must report wages, salaries, tips, and commissions received during the year. State income tax refunds are only taxable for years that you itemize.

If an income payment was mailed to you in late December 1987 but received in January, you can report it as income for 1988 and not pay taxes on it until next year. *Tip:* Keep the envelope the payment came in. The payer will report the payment in 1987 by issuing a 1099 Form, and you can explain why you didn't report the income on your tax return.

- If a large employer can demonstrate that the actual tip rate of his restaurant is less than 8 percent, the IRS may lower the percentage allocated to tips to as low as 5 percent. Also, employers (or a majority of the employees) can petition the IRS for permission to allocate tips based on a rate as low as 2 percent.

- Waiters and waitresses should record tips, or the IRS may reconstruct income to show earnings greater than actually received. The IRS will frown on anything short of a daily written log as record-keeping for waiters or waitresses—no matter the size of the restaurant, bar, or hotel.

Line 8 — *Interest Income*

Savings Bond Interest

You may elect to report interest on savings bonds in either of 2 ways: (1) you may wait until cashing in the bond to report the interest, or (2) you may report the earned portion of the interest each year until maturity. Waiting until maturity to declare income from savings bonds is usually best, unless bunching the income will put you in a much higher tax bracket.

Certificates of Deposit, Treasury Bills, and Notes

If you purchase a bank certificate of deposit, you must report interest earned each year—even if none of the money was received. The bank will send you a Form 1099 showing the interest earned.

In the case of Treasury bills and notes, interest income is taxable whether you receive a Form 1099 or not.

- Treasury bill interest is earned "up front"—i.e., you receive the "discount" at the beginning of the term and hence are actually receiving more interest money than rates would indicate.

Deep Discount Bonds

Deep discount bonds are bonds purchased on the open market, usually at a large discount.

Tax-Exempt Interest Income (Line 9)

List any tax-exempt interest income, but do not add it to line 8. This is for determining taxable Social Security benefits and alternative minimum tax.

Imputed Interest—Loans from Your Parents

If your parents lend you money interest-free—say, for a down payment on a new house—it is considered imputed interest income to your parents. Under the old law, you could deduct interest expense. Under Tax Reform, you get no interest writeoff, and your parents have interest income to report.

Dividends (Line 10)

Itemize all dividend income. If the total is above $400, attach Schedule B; if it is less than $400, you need only enter the total on Form 1040, line 10. Even if you fail to receive Form 1099 from the dividend payor, you are still responsible for reporting the income.

The IRS has a 1099 computer matching program which sends automatic notices proposing adjustments. More often than not, these notices are incorrect inasmuch as no attempt is made to consider whether multiple accounts have been combined.

Nontaxable Distributions

If any portion of the dividend was nontaxable, you must reduce your basis in the stock by the amount of distribution. (Likewise, any nontaxable dividends should be eliminated from the total dividends reported.) Nontaxable distributions reduce the tax gains of your investment; and if the total distributions received exceed your cost basis, you must report the balance as capital gain.

Taxable Refunds of State and Local Income Taxes (Line 11)

State income tax refunds of $10 or more are reported by the state to the IRS. If you itemized your deductions last year and received a state tax refund, that amount is taxable as income on your 1987 return. Where a taxpayer recovers a previously deducted state income tax, any refund is excluded from income only to the extent that the amount did not reduce taxable income.

Alimony Received (Line 12)

Report any alimony payments received.

Business Income or Loss (Line 13)

See Chapter 4 (and Schedule C) for instructions.

Capital Gain or Loss (Line 14)

If you received a capital gain or loss from sale or exchange of property, you must report the transaction on Schedule D.

As a general rule, you will be notified by the payor company if any portion of a dividend qualifies as long-term capital gain (to be excluded from dividend income and reported on Schedule D). See Chapter 5.

Other Gains or Losses (Line 15)

Complete and attach Form 4797, Supplemental Schedule of Gains and Losses if you sold any business assets during the year.

Pensions, IRA Distributions, and Annuities (Lines 16a and 16b)

Pensions and Annuities

Plans involving nondeductible employee contributions have new basis recovery rules on money distributions. For pension distributions received after the annuity starting date, the 3-year basis recovery rule is eliminated, which means that part of each payment would be considered income; the remainder, a recovery of employee contributions.

For pension distributions paid before the annuity starting date, employee contributions would be recovered pro rata; e.g., if an employee has contributed $12,000 to his pension and the total benefits are valued at $60,000, one-fifth of the withdrawal would be treated as a recovery of employee contributions—the balance would be fully taxable as income.

Pensions—Premature Distributions

In the case of pension distributions before age 59½, disability, or separation from service, there is a 15 percent premature withdrawal penalty, except for (1) distributions in the form of single life (or joint and survivor annuity); (2) distributions following early retirement after age 55; and (3) distributions in the case of unforeseen hardship.

Retirement Payout Options: Taxpayers who reached age 50 before January 1, 1986, may choose between 10-year or the new 5-year averaging on lump-sum distributions. Government and private sector workers who retired after June 30, 1986, and contributed to their pension start paying tax immediately on their benefits.

If you received a widow's/widower's award from your spouse's company, the first $5,000 you received is tax-free. Tax is paid only on sums in excess of that amount.

Rents, Royalties, Partnerships, Estates, Trusts, etc. (Line 17)

See Chapter 6 (and Schedule E) for instructions.

Farm Income or Loss (Line 18)

Complete and attach Schedule F.

Unemployment Compensation Benefits (Line 19)

Beginning this year, the full amount of unemployment compensation benefits is taxable.

Social Security Benefits (Lines 20a and 20b)

Up to 50 percent of Social Security benefits may be taxable, depending upon your income bracket. The taxable amount is the lesser of:

1. One-half of an amount determined by subtracting a base amount from the total of modified adjusted gross income added to one-half the Social Security benefits received
2. One-half the Social Security benefits received during the year.

Determining Base Amount

Single	$25,000
Married filing jointly	$32,000
Married filing separately	-0-

Add back Medicare premiums deducted when totaling Social Security benefits.

Determining Modified Adjusted Gross Income

Modified adjusted gross income is adjusted gross income (without Social Security benefits) plus these add-backs:

1. Income received from foreign sources and U.S. possessions
2. Tax-free interest income.

Examples

	Example 1 (Single)	Example 2 (Married)	Example 3 (Married)
Social Security benefits	$7,000	$10,000	$12,000
Adjusted gross income	$25,000	$30,000	$35,000
Add back: tax-free income	2,000	4,000	5,000
Total modified adjusted gross income	$27,000	$34,000	$40,000
Add back: one-half Social Security benefits	3,500	5,000	6,000
Total	$30,500	$39,000	$46,000
Less: base amount	25,000	32,000	32,000
Excess over base	$ 5,500	$ 7,000	$14,000
Taxable amount (half of excess)	$ 2,750	$ 3,500	$ 6,000*

* Due to limit of one-half of Social Security benefits received.

Additional Considerations for Computing Social Security

● Single senior citizens living together can earn as much as $50,000 before paying income tax on their Social Security income. If they are married, the combined figure is $32,000.

● When figuring estimated tax for next year, don't forget estimated tax on any (taxable) Social Security benefits as well as on the alternative minimum tax. Two ways to get around an underpayment of estimated tax penalty are to: (1) prepay 90 percent of next year's tax based on your total 1987 tax liability; or (2) pay in at least 100 percent of your total 1987 tax.

● Tax-free interest income must be figured into the computations of your taxable Social Security benefits.

● Dividends that are return of capital do not increase the tax base in computing taxable Social Security.

Social Security Benefits (and Tier 1 Railroad Retirement Benefits) Worksheet
(Keep for your records)

Check box A, B, C, or D below, whichever applies to you. Check only one box. Then go on to line 1 of the worksheet below.

- ☐ A. Single—enter $25,000 on line 8 below.
- ☐ B. Married filing a joint return—enter $32,000 on line 8 below.
- ☐ C. Married not filing a joint return and lived with your spouse at any time during the year —enter -0- on line 8 below.
- ☐ D. Married not filing a joint return and *did not* live with your spouse at any time during the year—enter $25,000 on line 8 below.

1. Enter the total amount from Box 5 of *all* your Forms SSA-1099 and Forms RRB-1099 (if applicable) .... _____

Note: *If line 1 is zero or less, stop here; none of your benefits are taxable. Otherwise, go on to line 2.*

2. Divide the amount on line 1 by 2 .... _____
3. Add the amounts on Form 1040, lines 7 through 21. Do not include here any amounts from Box 5 of Forms SSA-1099 or RRB-1099 ..... _____
4. If you received any interest income in 1987 that was not taxable, enter the amount of the nontaxable interest on this line. In the space to the left of line 9 show the amount of this interest, but *do not* include this interest on line 20a .... _____

5. Add lines 2, 3, and 4 .... _____
6. Add the amounts on Form 1040, lines 23 through 28. Also enter on this line any write-in amount included on line 29 (other than the foreign housing deduction). .... _____
7. Subtract line 6 from line 5 .... _____
8. Enter $25,000 if you checked box A or D, or $32,000 if you checked box B, or -0- if you checked box C _____
9. Subtract line 8 from line 7 .... _____

Note: *If line 9 is zero or less, stop here. Do not enter any amounts on line 20b because none of your benefits are taxable. Otherwise, go on to line 10.*

10. Divide the amount on line 9 by 2 .... _____
11. Taxable social security benefits.
    - First, enter on Form 1040, line 20a, the amount from line 1 above.
    - Then, compare amounts on lines 2 and 10 above, and enter the smaller of the two amounts on this line and also on Form 1040, line 20b .... _____

Line	Tax Law	Pay Less Tax Legally
Line 21	**Income Other Than Wages, Dividends, and Interest** All income other than that reported on lines 7–20 is reported on line 21. The sources of this income are to be reported both on the appropriate line as well as on the additional form to which you are referred. ***Prizes, Awards, and Premiums*** If you win a contest (raffle, door prize, sales contest), the value of that prize is taxable. ***Gambling Winnings*** While gambling winnings are fully taxed as income, you may deduct gambling losses only up to the amount of gambling winnings. In effect, this means that you get no deductible gambling loss on your tax return. The deduction must be itemized. For example, if you win $500 at the racetrack but spend $1,000 for losing tickets, you may write off only $500 in losses —and only if you itemize. ***Exclusions from Income*** The value of meals and lodging furnished to an employee is not considered income under certain conditions: 1. When the meals are furnished on the business premises 2. When lodging is furnished on the business premises and is a condition of employment. Gifts from your employer of up to $400 in total value and linked to the safety or productivity on the job are tax-free. You can receive a tax-free gift of $1,600 if you were the recipient of an awards plan that did not favor highly paid employees	• If you win a noncash prize, determine how much that item would cost at a discount store (or the lowest possible retail price) and list that lower value as income. • Keep an up-to-date diary of gambling losses; save ticket stubs so that you will have provable losses to offset winnings. In a recent case the court ruled that a diary was reliable because it contained winnings, as well as additional non-racetrack winnings the taxpayer didn't think he had to report. • Reduce the tax on lottery winnings by sharing ownership of tickets with those with whom you intend to share winnings (Be sure that your agreement is set up prior to the drawings). • Your employer can provide you with tax-free baby-sitting for your children, either by paying for such care directly or by providing the baby-sitter. However, this benefit must be part of a written plan that does not discriminate in favor of highly paid owner-employees.

Line	Tax Law	Pay Less Tax Legally
	and if the average award was at least $400. ***Foreign Income*** Americans working overseas may exclude the first $70,000 from income earned abroad. In addition, Americans abroad may overlook any reimbursement for housing expenses over $6,350 (or may deduct expenses over that amount). In order to qualify, a taxpayer must live abroad for either the entire year or for 330 days in any consecutive 12-month period. Form 1040 must be filed even if no taxes are to be paid.	

REPORTING BUSINESS INCOME OR LOSS: SCHEDULE C

If you operate a business as a sole proprietor (as opposed to a partnership or corporation) or are a self-employed professional, you must report income or loss on Schedule C. If you operate more than one business, you must file a separate Schedule C for each. If you operate as a sole proprietor and your net income is more than $400, you must file Schedule SE and pay the resulting Social Security self-employment tax (see page 211).

If you have a small business, you can reduce your Social Security tax liability by lowering your net profit. Pay out more in tax-free fringe benefits, e.g., health insurance premiums and employer contributions to qualified retirement plans.

Dividends, interest, rental, and royalty income are not subject to Social Security tax. Neither are pension benefits, including IRA and Keogh distributions. Other income that is not subject to Social Security tax include: profits from an S corporation, long-term capital gains, gifts, inheritances, and income from investment partnerships. Retirees who live off these passive types of income pay no Social Security tax.

Fill in the questions on Schedule C, Part I and Part II. Cost of sales should be reported at Part III of Schedule C, or attach a separate computation if you feel it would explain your situation more clearly. Line 29 is a catch-all for listing business expenses that do not fit elsewhere on the form.

Actors and Actresses

A new Schedule C deduction has been allowed under the Tax Reform Act for business expenses of performing actors and actresses. Under the new law, the expenses must exceed 20 percent of wages earned in the business and must be incurred in connection with services rendered.

In order to qualify for this deduction, the actor, actress, or artist (1) must have worked for more than one employer as an actor or artist during the year, and (2) must have earned less than $16,000 before expenses.

Although filling out Schedule C is quite easy, you should be aware of the opportunity for tax savings at every step of the way—tax savings that are discussed throughout this chapter. You should also note that the IRS recently announced a policy of increased audit activity for small, unincorporated businesses.

Your net profit or loss is determined by deducting all business expenses from income and entering the net income gain or loss from line 31, Schedule C to both line 13, Form 1040, and line 2, Schedule SE.

Schedule C

Schedule C (Profit or Loss from Business or Profession) has been revised slightly to reflect the limitations on the deduction of certain losses covered by Tax Reform.

SCHEDULE C (Form 1040)

Department of the Treasury
Internal Revenue Service

Profit or (Loss) From Business or Profession
(Sole Proprietorship)

Partnerships, Joint Ventures, etc., Must File Form 1065.

▶ Attach to Form 1040, Form 1041, or Form 1041S. ▶ See Instructions for Schedule C (Form 1040).

OMB No. 1545-0074

1987

Attachment Sequence No. 09

Name of proprietor: DOUGM

Social security number (SSN): 004 19 7912

A Principal business or profession, including product or service (see Instructions): TRAVEL AGENT

B Principal business code (from Part IV) ▶ 6635

C Business name and address ▶ FAYE'S TRAVEL

D Employer ID number (Not SSN):

E Method(s) used to value closing inventory:
(1) ☐ Cost   (2) ☒ Lower of cost or market   (3) ☐ Other (attach explanation)

F Accounting method: (1) ☒ Cash   (2) ☐ Accrual   (3) ☐ Other (specify) ▶

	Yes	No
G Was there any change in determining quantities, costs, or valuations between opening and closing inventory? (If "Yes," attach explanation.)		X
H Are you deducting expenses for an office in your home?		X
I Did you file **Form 941** for this business for any quarter in 1987?		X
J Did you "materially participate" in the operation of this business during 1987? (If "No," see Instructions for limitations on losses.)	X	
K Was this business in operation at the end of 1987?	X	
L How many months was this business in operation during 1987? ▶ 12		

M If this schedule includes a loss, credit, deduction, income, or other tax benefit relating to a tax shelter required to be registered, check here . . ▶ ☐
If you check this box, you **MUST** attach **Form 8271**.

Part I Income

1a	Gross receipts or sales	1a	7600
b	Less: Returns and allowances	1b	
c	Subtract line 1b from line 1a and enter the balance here	1c	7600
2	Cost of goods sold and/or operations (from Part III, line 8)	2	
3	Subtract line 2 from line 1c and enter the **gross profit** here	3	7600
4	Other income (including windfall profit tax credit or refund received in 1987)	4	
5	Add lines 3 and 4. This is the **gross income** ▶	5	7600

Part II Deductions

6	Advertising			23	Repairs		360
7	Bad debts from sales or services (Cash method taxpayers, see Instructions.)			24	Supplies (not included in Part III)		50
				25	Taxes		45
8	Bank service charges			26	Travel, meals, and entertainment:		
9	Car and truck expenses		2415	a	Travel		1405
10	Commissions			b	Total meals and entertainment	950	
11	Depletion						
12	Depreciation and section 179 deduction from Form 4562 (not included in Part III)		600	c	Enter 20% of line 26b subject to limitations (see Instructions)	190	
13	Dues and publications						
14	Employee benefit programs			d	Subtract line 26c from 26b		760
15	Freight (not included in Part III)			27	Utilities and telephone		160
16	Insurance		100	28a	Wages		
17	Interest:			b	Jobs credit		
a	Mortgage (paid to financial institutions)			c	Subtract line 28b from 28a		
b	Other			29	Other expenses (list type and amount): MISC		100
18	Laundry and cleaning		75				
19	Legal and professional services		25				
20	Office expense						
21	Pension and profit-sharing plans						
22	Rent on business property		300				
30	Add amounts in columns for lines 6 through 29. These are the **total deductions** ▶			30			6395
31	**Net profit or (loss).** Subtract line 30 from line 5. If a profit, enter here and on Form 1040, line 13, and on Schedule SE, line 2 (or line 5 of Form 1041 or 1041S). If a loss, you **MUST** go on to line 32			31			1205

32 If you have a loss, you **MUST** answer this question: "Do you have amounts for which you are not at risk in this business?" (See Instructions.) ☐ Yes ☐ No
If "Yes," you **MUST** attach **Form 6198**. If "No," enter the loss on Form 1040, line 13, and on Schedule SE, line 2 (or line 5 of Form 1041 or Form 1041S).

Schedule C (Form 1040) 1987 — Page 2

Part III Cost of Goods Sold and/or Operations (See Schedule C Instructions for Part III)

1	Inventory at beginning of year. (If different from last year's closing inventory, attach explanation.)	1
2	Purchases less cost of items withdrawn for personal use	2
3	Cost of labor. (Do not include salary paid to yourself.)	3
4	Materials and supplies	4
5	Other costs	5
6	Add lines 1 through 5	6
7	Less: Inventory at end of year	7
8	**Cost of goods sold and/or operations.** Subtract line 7 from line 6. Enter here and in Part I, line 2	8

The One-Minute Taxman: Business Expenses

Look over this checklist of deductible business expenses. It should serve as a worksheet to help you in preparing Schedule C. It is important that you consider stipulations as explained in the chapter before claiming deductions on your tax forms.

Business Expenses	Amount	*Business Expenses*	Amount
☐ Advertising	_____	☐ Interest, business	_____
☐ Answering machine or answering service	_____	☐ Legal and accounting fees	_____
☐ Attaché case	_____	☐ License fees, related to business or profession	_____
☐ Auto expenses (mileage or actual)	_____	☐ Newspapers, if business-related	_____
☐ Bad debts	_____	☐ Office expenses	_____
☐ Banking charges	_____	☐ Parking, tolls	_____
☐ Books and periodicals	_____	☐ Petty cash	_____
☐ Calculator, cost of	_____	☐ Postage	_____
☐ Christmas presents and greeting cards	_____	☐ Professional organizations (dues)	_____
☐ Commissions	_____	☐ Rent	_____
☐ Computer costs	_____	☐ Repairs	_____
☐ Credit card fees	_____	☐ Salaries	_____
☐ Decorations, home office	_____	☐ Secretarial supplies	_____
☐ Depreciation, professional equipment	_____	☐ Subscriptions	_____
☐ Dry cleaning (while traveling)	_____	☐ Supplies	_____
☐ Entertainment (only 80%)	_____	☐ Tape recorder	_____
☐ Equipment (purchase and maintenance)	_____	☐ Tax preparation fees	_____
☐ Freight	_____	☐ Telephone (office telephone and calls from pay phones)	_____
☐ Gifts ($25 or less)	_____	☐ Travel	_____
☐ Home office	_____	☐ Typewriter (purchase and maintenance)	_____
☐ Insurance, auto and business	_____	☐ Utilities	_____
		Total	_____

Net Operating Losses

If your business operates at a loss for the year, you may have the basis for a net operating loss that will affect other years. With certain modifications, your business loss is carried back 3 years; if any unused loss remains, it can be carried forward for the next 15 years. You can elect to carry net operating losses forward only. You will need either Form 1045 or Form 1040X.

To compute your net operating loss, deduct the following from your taxable income:

1. Any operating loss from other years
2. Any capital loss deducted on your return
3. Your deduction for personal exemptions
4. The excess of nonbusiness deductions (itemized deductions) over nonbusiness income (interest, dividends) for the year.

Line	Tax Law	Pay Less Tax Legally
Line F	**Method of Accounting—Cash or Accrual Basis** There are 2 methods of reporting income: *accrual basis* and *cash basis.* If you need inventories in order to operate your business, you should file on the accrual basis. In this case you must record charge sales regardless of whether you collected the money during the tax year or not. You can also deduct expenses before they are paid. If inventories are not material to the operation of your business (as in a service business), you have the option of reporting income on either the cash or accrual basis. Under the cash basis, income is reported when you actually receive the cash. In both cases, save sales invoices, register tapes, bank statements, deposit tickets, and daily or weekly income worksheets for your records. **Income**	• If you receive money to apply to future services, that money is usually taxable in the year it is received. However, if you take the money with the understanding that it is a refundable deposit (it will apply to the balance due), you can forestall paying tax on the money until the year you actually render the service. Make sure you maintain a separate bank account for deposits.
Part I Line 1	**Gross Receipts** Using either method of accounting, re-	

Line	Tax Law	Pay Less Tax Legally
	cord your total gross receipts less any returns and allowances.	
Line 2	**Cost of Goods Sold and/or Operations** In order to arrive at a figure for gross profit, fill out Part III and deduct your costs from your gross receipts.	
Part II Lines 6–8	## Deductions Enter amount.	
Line 9	**Car and Travel Expenses** If you use your car for business purposes, there are 2 methods of deducting expenses. You are permitted to use the method that will result in the largest tax deduction and may change methods from year to year. *Optional Expense Method* Deduct 22.5¢ per mile for the first 15,000 miles of business use per year and 11¢ per mile for every mile in excess of 15,000. In addition to this basic allowance, you are permitted to deduct tolls and parking. *Actual Expense Method* Add all the expenses of operating the car, including depreciation, gas and oil, rustproofing, tires, and car washes. For full discussion of writing off business autos, see page 87.	• Generally, owners of older cars (4 years or older) should use the *optional expense method;* new car owners should use the *actual expense method.* • You can write off the amount of tires and tubes from the purchase price of a new car or truck immediately instead of including it with the total cost of the car or truck and taking depreciation. • If you often go out of town on business, get into the habit of going to your office first, and return to the office before going home. You will get a bigger tax deduction. Be sure to keep accurate documentation.
Line 12	**Depreciation and Section 179 Deduction** You can deduct an extra $10,000 of the cost of business equipment, fixtures, or machinery, or $2,560 for a business car, with the balance subject to regular depreciation. You must fill in the top of Form	• One way to write off a business car is to set up a corporation to receive employment or consulting income and have the corporation buy and use the car. The corporation may pay tax at a lower rate. After the first year of operation, you may want to elect S Corporation status.

Line	Tax Law	Pay Less Tax Legally
	4562 (see page 120), specifying to which items the election applies. Any future gain on the sale of these expensed assets is treated as ordinary income (to the extent of the amount expensed). For a full discussion of depreciation, see page 116.	• Consider becoming an independent contractor for your present company. You may lose certain company fringe benefits, including hospitalization insurance, but you could more than make up for the loss by being able to claim home office and auto expenses (or not having to pass a company physical exam when you know you can't).
Lines 13–16	Enter amount.	
Line 17	**Mortgage Interest Paid to Financial Institution** Form 1098 (to be provided by financial institutions) will have all names of persons listed on the mortgage but will be sent to the "main" person on the mortgage. The "main" person should attach a statement to Form 1098 listing names and addresses of others named in the mortgage.	
Lines 18–21	Enter amount.	
Line 22	**Rent on Business Property** Enter the full amount of rent paid during the year. If you had to give a security deposit during the year, that amount is not deductible as rent (unless it is used to pay the last month's rental).	
	Home Office Deductions You can only deduct a home office if it is used exclusively for business and on a regular basis and is your principal place of business for seeing patients, customers, or clients. As an employee, you must also be able to prove that the office is maintained in your home at the request and for the convenience of your employer. In order to meet the use test as an employee, it would be best to have a letter from your employer to the effect that you could not do your job without taking work	• A college professor was permitted to write off a home office where he did most of the research and writing required to keep his position. The court felt that the focal point of the teacher's business activities was in the home and that the maintenance of a home office was a convenience to the employer, since it spared the school the necessity of providing suitable office space. • In a recent case, a doctor who worked

Line	Tax Law	Pay Less Tax Legally

	home on a regular and consistent basis. If a taxpayer meets these tests, he may deduct the costs of using the home as an office. This means that an employee may have a full-time job as well as a sideline business operating out of his home, and home office expenses may be tax-deductible. For a full discussion of home offices, see page 264.
	
	The amount of the deduction is limited to the income derived from the business less mortgage interest and real estate taxes. The IRS interprets gross income as gross receipts less the expenditures required for the activity but has recently lost an important case in this area.
	
	To compute a home office deduction consider this example: A taxpayer is an art teacher and a self-employed artist operating out of his home. His studio is used exclusively and on a regular basis for painting and occupies one-fourth of the house. During the year, $1,500 worth of paintings were sold that were produced at the home studio. The mortgage interest for the year was $2,500; real estate taxes, $1,500; and other home expenses, $4,000. The deduction for the home studio would be $500, computed as follows:
	
	    Total income generated
	      by home studio $1,500
	    Less: one-fourth of real-
	      estate taxes and
	      interest (¼ × $4,000) 1,000
	    Limit on other expenses $ 500
	
	Even though one-fourth of the expenses amounted to $1,000, the taxpayer would be limited to a deduction of $500 as a home office expense and the full amount of the real estate taxes and interest as itemized deductions.
	
	A deduction can be claimed for a home office only if clients visit the premises, unless the home office is the taxpayer's
		full-time in a hospital managed 6 rental properties and deducted one bedroom in his home as an office. The court felt that the doctor's management activities were of a nature to constitute a business even though he had a full-time job. But the owner of a hotdog stand could not write off a home office since the hotdog sales were made at the stand—not at home.
		
		• The Tax Court has held that a portion of a room can qualify as part of a dwelling unit for purposes of the exclusive-use test. Arrange your furniture in such a way as to create a separate work area within the room.
		
		• Another way to compute home office rent is on the basis of square feet. For example, if the room used exclusively for business measures 200 square feet and the total home measures 2,000 square feet, the allowable deduction is a corresponding 10 percent of eligible expenses.
		
		• If you maintain a home office, you may be able to write off additional auto expenses. Since your home is your place

Line	Tax Law	Pay Less Tax Legally
	principal place of business or the office is located in a separate structure not attached to the home. Telephone contacts alone are not enough to meet the "dealing with clients" requirement of the deductibility.	of work, your first trip is spent traveling between places of business. • A musician was entitled to deduct for a home practice room on the grounds that the room constituted the principal place of his business. The court noted that the place of performance was immaterial as long as the musician was well prepared and the preparation took place at home. • As long as you're consistent, you can choose an arbitrarily low amount—for example, $100—under which an expenditure would constitute a repair; anything over that amount would be subject to depreciation.
Line 23	**Repairs** A repair is any expenditure that brings an asset up to proper operating standards (rather than improving it or extending its useful life). If a repair is actually an improvement that will last more than one year, it should be depreciated over its assigned life rather than deducted as an expense in one year. See page 88.	
Lines 24–25	Enter amount.	
Line 26	**Entertainment Expenses** If a meal is considered lavish or extravagant, only the nonlavish portion of the cost is taken into account. Eighty percent of that portion is allowed as a business meal deduction. If the meal is eaten during the course of luxury water travel (which is subject to per diem limits), the percentage reduction is applied before the application of the per diem limitation. Getting a deduction allowed for business entertainment expenses depends to a large extent on how good your records are. Rules are very specific, and every item must be verified by the proper records. If you entertain people with whom you have business relationships, you should keep a diary and enter: 1. Name of the person you entertained 2. Business relationship 3. Business purpose 4. Date 5. Amount spent on each occasion.	• Only 80 percent of expenses for business meals and entertainment is deductible, with these exceptions: 1. The full cost of the meals and entertainment is deductible if taxed as compensation to the recipient or if treated as a tax-free fringe benefit—an employee cafeteria, for example. 2. Meals at certain banquets are still deductible in full. 3. Sample and promotional activities made available to the general public. 4. Traditional recreational expenses for employees (e.g, holiday parties, summer outings) are fully deductible. For more information about writing off meals and entertainment, see page 131. • IRS agents are trained to look at the travel and entertainment deduction in relation to the size and nature of the business, and to determine if any such

Line	Tax Law	Pay Less Tax Legally
	Any restaurant that does not have distracting entertainment will be assumed to be a businesslike setting. You do have to record the business purpose of the meeting, but you do not have to discuss business directly for the expense to be considered a valid business deduction. As of 1987, only 80 percent of the cost of business meals and entertainment is deductible. For full discussion, see page 131. ***Limitations on Entertainment Expenses*** No longer deductible are the costs associated with buying and operating yachts, fishing camps, bowling alleys, hunting lodges, or swimming pools. Tennis club dues are also not deductible. However, specific expenses of entertaining at any of these places would be deductible. Also, country club dues and fees are deductible if the taxpayer can show a direct relationship to business. The cost of tickets to theatrical and sporting events is also deductible. The cost of home entertaining may be deductible if: 1. The dinners were not too frequent 2. Small groups were invited (facilitating discussion of business) 3. You can point to other social entertaining that was not deducted.	expenses might be "buried" elsewhere on the return (for example, in advertising). The agent will analyze the situation as to whether personal expenses could be included with business costs, whether the taxpayer keeps adequate records, and whether business was generated from the expenditure. • Cab fares and parking expenses in connection with entertainment are deductible. • If a bill exceeds $25, save the receipt. For amounts under $25, an entry in a diary will suffice to document the expense. • If you are audited, the agent will want to see an up-to-date diary. If restaurants are involved, the agent will want to see the bill; if home entertainment is involved, the agent will want to determine if the occasion was for business or pleasure; where sporting events are concerned, the agent will look to see if there was a bona fide business meeting either immediately before or after the event. • A dentist was recently involved in a Tax Court battle with the IRS over his club expenses. The Tax Court held that a professional person cannot deduct entertainment expenses solely because they provide social contacts that could lead to future business. An incidental business benefit is not enough to warrant the deduction. • If you own a boat, airplane, or recreational vehicle and want to write it off, consider converting it for rental purposes—find a charter company to lease it out to others and split rentals. You would be entitled to depreciation without necessarily having to eliminate your own use. Be sure to report the income on the lease. • Food and liquor used in entertaining business associates at home are deductible. Save all bills. Record the names of guests in a notebook.

Line	Tax Law	Pay Less Tax Legally
	Gifts The maximum deductible gift is $25 per business associate per year. Keep records of recipients' names and keep receipts if the gift cost more than $4. **Supper Money** Supper money for employees who work overtime is not taxable income for the employee and is tax-deductible for the employer.	• The cost of cigars has been held to be deductible as a business expense. The taxpayer was a nonsmoker who gave the cigars to customers.

Travel Expenses

There are new rules for deducting meals and entertainment expenses. See page 131 for a complete explanation.

IRS rules on deductible travel expenses are very specific, and every item must be substantiated by proper records. Travel expenses are deductible if incurred in connection with business or investment, and include air, rail, and bus fares, baggage charges, taxis to and from the terminal, meals, lodging, and tips, cleaning and laundry, local transportation, the cost of transporting display materials, renting sample rooms, and hiring a public stenographer. You are not considered traveling away from home unless you are away from your tax home at least overnight, or long enough to require rest or sleep. However, your residence is not necessarily home for tax purposes. According to the IRS, your home is your place of business or post of duty regardless of where your family may reside. If both income earned and time spent are greater at one location, that location will generally be considered your tax home even though your residence may be at the other location. If you work more than one job during the year, your tax home is the area where your principal employment (or business) is located.

As a general rule, you can deduct travel to brokers' offices but not to attend stockholders' meetings. Investors cannot deduct travel expenses while looking for rental or other income-producing property. Travel and transportation expenses in determining a location for a new business are not deductible but must be added to the cost of the new property. However, travel expenses in connection with an unsuccessful attempt to buy a specific operating business are deductible.

Transportation and travel expenses in looking for a new position in the same field of employment are deductible. Reimbursement from a prospective employer for travel or transportation expenses to the interview is income only to the extent that it exceeds expenses.

The IRS looks at the following criteria in determining your principal place of employment:

1. Total time spent in each area
2. Amount of business derived from each area
3. Amount of money earned from each respective location.

The cost of meals and lodging en route to and from the secondary place of employment are tax-deductible. A salesman working out of his home is generally permitted to deduct all travel expenses from the residence to the territory and back home again.

Temporary assignment. If you find it necessary to work at another location on a temporary basis, you are considered away from home for the entire temporary period, and your expenses are fully deductible. The IRS considers a position temporary if the assignment is expected to last for more than one year but less than 2 years.

In a temporary assignment, all travel expenses incurred while you're going to the new location, meals and lodging at the temporary place of assignment (even for weekends), and expenses for return trips home are tax-deductible.

Indefinite assignment. If you are assigned to a new location for an indefinite period of time (you cannot foresee the end of work within a fixed reasonably short period of time), the new location becomes your new tax home, and none of your expenses is deductible.

Whether an assignment is temporary or indefinite is usually determined when the work begins; however, a series of jobs at the same location, each of which may only last a short period of time (but combine to cover a long assignment), may be considered "indefinite."

Line	Tax Law	Pay Less Tax Legally
	Foreign Convention Travel Only coach or economy travel is deductible. At least one-half the trip days must be devoted to business, or the deduction is limited to a percentage of the costs that is equal to the percentage of the trip days devoted to business. Meals and lodging are currently deductible up to the federal per diem rate. An attendance record signed by the sponsor of the convention must accompany the tax return, and no more than 2 foreign conventions may be claimed per year unless the employer includes the expenses in the employee's income.	● For a full discussion of travel-expense deductions, see page 129. ● Keep an accurate log of time and expenses, and instead of limiting yourself to a half-day, try to attend two-thirds of all scheduled activities.
Lines 27–28a	Enter amount.	
Line 28b	**Targeted-Jobs Credit** If as an employer you hire persons from certain groups, you can claim a tax credit of up to 40 percent of the first $6000 of qualified first-year wages. The employee	● Amounts paid by self-employed handicapped persons for travel, meals, or lodging of helpers who help on business trips are deductible. Also, the payments a blind

Line	Tax Law	Pay Less Tax Legally
	must work a minimum of 90 days or 120 hours.	person makes to his reader are deductible.
		• The costs of removing barriers to the handicapped are deductible. A taxpayer who incurs expenses to remove architectural and transportation barriers to the handicapped or elderly may deduct them on his return, limited to a maximum deduction of $35,000.
Line 29	**Other Business Expenses**	
	List all other business deductions on the appropriate lines on Part II.	• See "The One-Minute Taxman," page 133, for more deductible business expenses.
	Start-up Expenses	
	Taxpayers can elect to write off business start-up expenditures over a period of not less than 60 months after the business was begun, or these expenditures will be viewed as nondeductible capital items. If a business is sold or disposed of before the end of the 60-month period, the balance of start-up expenses may be deducted as an investment expense.	• Looking for a new business to get into? If you zero in on a particular business, your expenses would be deductible, even if the deal fell through. However, you must pinpoint a particular business; looking at businesses in general doesn't count.
		• If you have a business that goes bankrupt and you start a new business, you may deduct your prior losses.
	Losses of Business Property	
	If you have a theft loss, you are permitted a deduction for any amount not reimbursed by the insurance company. Keep all police reports, insurance claim forms, photographs, and invoices.	• You are permitted to deduct the cost of rewards paid to locate stolen business property.
	If you have a casualty loss (from fire, flood, or wind damage), the amount of your deductible loss depends on whether the property was partially or completely destroyed. Business casualty and theft losses are filed on Form 4797 rather than on Schedule C.	• A fire at your plant causes extensive damage to your roof. The building had originally cost $19,000; you have taken $9,000 depreciation to date, bringing your adjusted basis to $10,000. The value of the building before the fire was $26,000; after the fire it was $22,000 ($3,000 insurance recovery). The deductible loss is $1,000:
	Measuring a Partial Loss. A partial loss is measured by the difference between what the item was worth before the casualty and what it was worth afterward, less any insurance recoveries. This loss is limited to the original cost of the asset less the accumulated depreciation to the date of the casualty (the "adjusted basis").	Value before fire $26,000 Value after fire −22,000 Loss in value $ 4,000 Minus insurance recovery − 3,000 Net deductible loss $ 1,000

Line	Tax Law	Pay Less Tax Legally
	Calculating a Complete Loss. In the case of a complete loss, ignore market values and take a deduction for the adjusted basis of the property (minus any insurance recovery).	• All business losses are limited to the adjusted basis of the property. In the above case, $10,000 would be the maximum loss. • Using the same facts in the example above, except that the building was completely destroyed, your deductible loss is $7,000: Adjusted basis $10,000 Insurance recovery -3,000 Net deductible loss $ 7,000
	Employing Family Members If you have children or grandchildren capable of helping out in the business, consider putting them on the payroll, if only during the summer months. In this way they will be working for their allowance, and you will be getting a tax deduction. Also, you will not be paying Social Security or unemployment taxes for your minor children. List these salaries on line 29 as "casual labor." However, make sure their rate of pay is the same as you would pay a nonfamily member, and have someone other than a relative keep records of the working hours and work accomplished. **Hiring Your Spouse.** Consider paying money that would otherwise be paid to an outsider to your spouse. Wages paid to a spouse are not subject to Social Security tax when the business is run as a sole proprietorship, and the spouse's salary can possibly be used to fund an IRA. Your spouse must be covered by all federal programs and local laws, e.g., workman's compensation and unemployment insurance. In addition, you can take out a hospitalization insurance policy for your employees, covering your spouse. If you have a position that needs to be filled and you hire an outsider, you'll incur those costs anyway. You can come out ahead by hiring your spouse.	• If you have a sole proprietorship or partnership, you can pay your spouse a salary and ignore payroll taxes. Your business net income must be less than $43,800 to save money. • The owner of a sole proprietorship is not considered an employee and cannot pay his family medical insurance premiums out of the business. But if your spouse is active in the business and you put him or her on the payroll, you can transfer the policy into his or her name and deduct the cost as a business expense.

Line	Tax Law	Pay Less Tax Legally
Line 31	**Net Profit or Loss** *Deducting Hobby Losses* If you collect coins or stamps, or have other hobbies, gain on a sale is taxable, but losses are deductible only if you are involved in the hobby for profit. If you can show a profit in any 3 or more years within a 5-year period, your losses from the venture will be tax-deductible. Even if you have not shown a profit in any of the 5 years, your losses would still be tax deductible if you could show a profit motive. Here are the factors the IRS looks for in determining the profit motive: 1. Your history of income or losses in the business. 2. Your expertise in operating the business—can you ever break even? 3. Your past successes or failures in operating other businesses. 4. How much time you actually devote to the business—are you working in a full-time job as well? 5. Are you keeping proper records? 6. Can you make money in the business? 7. How much in income and losses have you generated to date? In the absence of a trade or business, you still may be able to deduct a capital loss. If the property was held for less than 6 months and no other capital losses were recognized during the tax year, the entire loss would be deductible.	● John bought a coin collection from Nancy for $2,000, thinking he could sell it at a profit. He actually sold it for $1,500, a loss of $500. The IRS disallowed the loss on the grounds that he was not involved in coin collecting as a business; the loss was a hobby loss and therefore not deductible. ● If you held collector's items (e.g., comic books or stamps) for more than 6 months before you sold them, the profit is considered long-term capital gain; however, you can deduct related expenses up to the full 100 percent of your profit, including insurance premiums, appraisal fees, and safe deposit box rental. ● In the absence of a trade or business, you still may be able to deduct a capital loss. If the property was held for less than 6 months and no other capital losses were recognized during the tax year, the entire loss would be deductible.
Part III Line 1	**Cost of Goods Sold and/or Operations** *Inventories* If inventories are a major income-producing factor in your business, you must account for them with a physical inventory	● On a columnar sheet, list all items on hand as of the end of the year. Look up your most recent invoice for the latest

Line	Tax Law	Pay Less Tax Legally
	at both the beginning and the end of your tax year. You may choose your method of costing the inventory, but the 2 most common are actual cost and market value. Choose the lower of the 2 figures, but whichever method is used must be consistently followed from year to year.	price paid, and multiply your quantities by their unit costs. Total these extensions and you have a total inventory. If you have items in your ending inventory that are damaged or obsolete or have no value, they should be valued at bona fide selling price, but not less than scrap value.
Line 2	**Purchases Less Cost of Items Withdrawn for Personal Use** If you are using the cash basis, report only the amount of cash spent during the year for merchandise. If you file on the accrual basis, add your cash purchases to accounts payable at the end of the year to arrive at total deductible purchases. If inventory is a material income-producing item, the purchases must be reported on the accrual basis of accounting, which means taking accounts payable into consideration.	• Merchandise taken out of a business for personal use is not deductible. Keep records on everything taken out of the business for personal use.

Depreciation

The rules that prevented property acquired before 1981 from being depreciated under ACRS (Accelerated Cost Recovery System) still apply to property originally placed in service before January 1, 1980.

For example, if a car is purchased in 1979 but not put into business use until 1982, it must be depreciated under pre-ACRS rules (based on the date of purchase). If a car is bought in 1985 but put into business use in 1987, it must be depreciated under MACRS (Modified Accelerated Cost Recovery System—new rules), the rules in effect at the time the car was converted to business use.

Business Autos

If you are planning to buy a business auto this year, you can time your purchase to get a larger depreciation writeoff. If you buy the car before October 1, you can depreciate it under a half-year convention. An auto bought during the last quarter of the year on or after October 1 will be depreciable under a mid-quarter convention, which has the effect of cutting your depreciation in half.

Example

You buy a car in April for $18,000 and use it 100 percent for business. Your first-year depreciation writeoff is $2,560. Here's why: You are permitted to claim as depreciation the lower of (1) 20 percent of the cost (using the half-year convention rate) or (2) $2,560 (the maximum first year writeoff) if you buy before October 1.

However, if you buy the car after September 30, you must use the mid-quarter rate; this means depreciation of 5 percent of the $18,000 cost, or $900. If at all possible, try to buy the car earlier in the year.

If you purchase other business equipment during the year, the mid-quarter rules will apply to the car purchase only if the cost of all equipment bought during the last quarter—including the car—is over 40 percent of the total cost of all equipment placed in service during the year.

Depreciation of a Business Auto

Autos placed in service in 1987 (and in later years) are in a 5-year ACRS class but are depreciated over a 6-year period due to the mid-year or mid-quarter rule. The ACRS rate is based on 200 percent declining balance method with a switch to straight-line depreciation, but the full amount is now allowed because of these limits.

Year	Annual Limit	Year	Annual Limit
1	$2,560	4	$1,475
2	4,100	5	1,475
3	2,450	6	1,475

These limits are combined with the depreciation rates on the original basis of the auto, and your annual deduction will be as follows under the mid-year convention:

Year	Lower of	Year	Lower of
1	10% of cost of auto or $2,560	4	11.52% of cost of auto or $1,475
2	32% of cost of auto or $4,100	5	11.52% of cost of auto or $1,475
3	19.20% of cost of auto or $2,450	6	5.76% of cost of auto or $1,475

New Depreciation Rules

The cost of property placed in service after July 31, 1986, and before January 1, 1987, may be covered under the new rules at the election of the taxpayer, on an asset-by-asset basis. Up to $10,000 can be expensed annually, not to exceed taxable income from active trade or business. For every dollar of investment over $200,000, the $10,000 ceiling is reduced by $1. This rule applies to all property placed in service after 1986.

Accelerated Cost Recovery System

ACRS has been modified to provide classes making reference to asset depreciation range (ADR) midpoints:

3-Year Class. ADR midpoints of 4 years or less, excluding autos and light trucks, including horses.

5-Year Class. ADR midpoints of more than 4 years and less than ten, adding autos, light trucks, computer-based telephone central-office switching equipment, qualified technological equipment, experimentation property, biomass properties that constitute qualifying small power production facilities, and geothermal, ocean thermal, solar, and wind energy properties.

7-Year Class. ADR midpoints of 10 years and less than 16, adding property with no ADR midpoint that is not classified elsewhere; also adding single-purpose agricultural or horticultural structures.

10-Year Class. ADR midpoints of 16 years and less than 20.

15-Year Class. ADR midpoints of 20 years and less than 25, adding telephone distribution plant and comparable equipment used for two-way exchange of voice and data communications, and municipal wastewater treatment plants.

20-Year Class. ADR midpoints of 25 years or more, adding municipal sewers, and excluding Section 1250 real property with an ADR midpoint of 27.5 years or more.

27.5-Year Class. Residential rental property (including manufactured homes that are residential rental property, and including elevators and escalators). Straight-line only.

31.5-Year Class. Nonresidential real property (Section 1250 real property that is not residential rental property and either does not have an ADR midpoint or whose ADR midpoint is 27.5 years or more, including elevators and escalators). Straight-line only.

Special Types of Property. New ADR midpoints are assigned to certain special types of property.

Luxury Cars (cost over $12,060). Fixed limitations on deductions conform to the new recovery period, so the price range of cars is unaffected. Limitations are: $2,560 for first recovery year; $4,100 for second; $2,450 for third; and $1,475 for each succeeding taxable year in the recovery period. These fixed limitations apply to all depreciation deductions, not just accelerated depreciation.

Alternative Cost Recovery System

This system applies to property used predominantly outside the United States and for property leased to a tax-exempt entity, for minimum tax purposes, and for computing earnings and profits of a domestic corporation.

Taxpayers may elect this system or the straight-line method over the ACRS recovery period for property that does not require the alternative system.

Lessee Leasehold Improvements

A lessee follows general rules for recovering capital costs. To determine the amortization period for lease acquisition costs, the term of lease is determined by including all renewal options and any period for which the parties reasonably expect to be renewed.

Accounting Conventions

On personal property, both first and last depreciation allowances reflect the half-year convention. A mid-quarter convention applies to taxpayers who place more than 40 percent of their property in service during the last quarter of the taxable year.

5

CAPITAL GAINS AND LOSSES AND RECONCILIATION OF FORM 1099-B: SCHEDULE D

Schedule D is the gathering place for stock transactions, sale of a home or business property, and capital-gain distributions. The form is divided into 2 distinct sections—short-term gains and losses (held for 6 months or less) and long-term gains and losses (held for more than 6 months).

It's the date of sale (not the date payment is received for stock) that counts in determining long- or short-term treatment. If you sell stock after 5 months 29 days, it's still considered short-term.

Part I of Schedule D requires that you report the amount from Forms 1099B (sale of stocks and bonds). If you received bartering income, you must also complete Part VII.

Although short-term gains are treated the same as ordinary income, a special provision in the tax law permits the taxing of only 28 percent of long-term capital gains. If you had a loss on your capital transactions during the year, 100 percent of your long-term losses is deductible, to a maximum of $3,000 in any given year. Your net capital gain or loss is determined on Schedule D and then entered on Form 1040, line 14. Sales of business property are computed on Form 4797, not Schedule D; gain on sale of a home is computed on Form 2119. Schedule D has been revised to reflect the maximum 28 percent tax rate on long-term capital gains (Part IV).

Forms of Ownership

Consider these factors in deciding which family member should be the owner of your real estate and stock. The 3 types of ownership for most personal property are:

1. Individual property—property held in your name alone. In many states, property held by one person is treated as if it were owned jointly with a spouse.
2. Tenancy-in-common—property owned by 2 or more people; each person's share is considered individual property.
3. Joint tenancy—joint tenancy differs from tenancy-in-common only in the right of survivorship: when a co-owner dies, his or her shares automatically pass to the other owner.

Tax-Planning Checklist: Assets and Investments

- If you rent out a home for less than 2 weeks, the income is tax-free.

- Tax-exempt interest can save you money in the higher tax brackets. Look for bonds that are tax-free for state purposes as well.

- An Individual Retirement Account is the easiest way to shelter income tax-free, whatever your tax bracket, but be aware of new limitations (page 132).

- Accelerated depreciation allows larger deductions in early years, generally resulting in tax savings. The deductions decline in subsequent years.

- Oil and gas investments offer continued opportunity to shelter income, since intangible drilling-cost deductions are still available. However, depletion may be subject to the Alternative Minimum Tax, and intangible drilling costs may be subject to recapture upon disposition of the investment.

- Consider investing in companies that pay tax-free dividends, but remember to reduce the cost of your stock by the amount of the tax-free dividend.

- Consider investing in companies that pay stock dividends, since stock dividends are not generally taxable income.

- The purchase of Series E bonds gives you the opportunity to defer tax liability.

- The income from municipal bonds, including general obligation and revenue bonds, is exempt from tax.

- Bond premiums and payments in excess of face value are deductible in certain cases.

- The amount of loss you can take in any tax-sheltered investment other than real estate cannot exceed the amount you have "at risk" in such activity. (See page 106 for new rules.)

- Interest and dividend income for a deferred annuity accumulates tax-free until earnings are withdrawn.

- Home improvements (building a new kitchen, remodeling a basement, planting shrubbery) should be added to your basis to minimize future capital-gain liability. Keep all bills in a separate file.

Securities, Stocks, and Bonds

Market discounts on bonds and other debt instruments are taxed as ordinary income (not capital gains) upon sale or redemption at maturity. A pro rata share of the market discount is treated as ordinary income. Deductions of interest on loans used to buy or hold discount bonds are limited; a portion of the interest paid is deferred until the bonds are sold or redeemed. Interest on tax-exempt bonds issued below par value is added to the cost of the bonds in the same way that interest on taxable bonds is added.

Capital Assets

A capital asset is anything of value except inventory, accounts or notes receivable, business property, copyrights in the possession of the writer, and certain U.S. govern-

SCHEDULE D (Form 1040)

Capital Gains and Losses and Reconciliation of Forms 1099-B

Department of the Treasury
Internal Revenue Service

▶ Attach to Form 1040. ▶ See Instructions for Schedule D (Form 1040).
For Paperwork Reduction Act Notice, see Form 1040 Instructions.

OMB No. 1545-0074

1987
Attachment Sequence No. 12

Name(s) as shown on Form 1040: **DOUGH**

Your social security number: **329 04 1040**

1. Report here, the total sales of stocks, bonds, etc., reported for 1987 by your broker to you on Form(s) 1099-B or an equivalent substitute statement(s) . . . . **1 | 4250**

If this amount differs from the total of lines 2b and 9b, column (d), attach a statement explaining the difference. See the Instructions for line 1 for examples.

Do not include real estate transactions reported to you on a Form 1099-B on this line.

Part I — Short-term Capital Gains and Losses—Assets Held Six Months or Less

(a) Description of property (Example, 100 shares 7% preferred of "Z" Co.)	(b) Date acquired (Mo., day, yr.)	(c) Date sold (Mo., day, yr.)	(d) Sales price (see Instructions)	(e) Cost or other basis (see Instructions)	(f) LOSS If (e) is more than (d), subtract (d) from (e)	(g) GAIN If (d) is more than (e), subtract (e) from (d)

2a Form 1099-B Transactions (Sales of Stocks, Bonds, etc.): (Report real estate transactions reported on a Form 1099-B on line 2c.)

2b Total (add column (d)) ▶

2c Other Transactions:

3. Short-term gain from sale or exchange of a principal residence from Form 2119, lines 8 or 14 — **3**
4. Short-term gain from installment sales from Form 6252, lines 23 or 31 — **4**
5. Net short-term gain or (loss) from partnerships, S corporations, and fiduciaries — **5**
6. Short-term capital loss carryover — **6**
7. Add all of the transactions on lines 2a and 2c and lines 3 through 6 in columns (f) and (g) — **7** ( )
8. Net short-term gain or (loss), combine columns (f) and (g) of line 7 — **8**

Part II — Long-term Capital Gains and Losses—Assets Held More Than Six Months

9a Form 1099-B Transactions (Sales of Stocks, Bonds, etc.): (Report real estate transactions reported on a Form 1099-B on line 9c.)

FIRSTAX	1982	1987	4250	1250		3000

9b Total (add column (d)) ▶ **4250**

9c Other Transactions:

10. Long-term gain from sale or exchange of a principal residence from Form 2119, lines 8, 10, or 14 — **10**
11. Long-term gain from installment sales from Form 6252, lines 23 or 31 — **11**
12. Net long-term gain or (loss) from partnerships, S corporations, and fiduciaries — **12**
13. Capital gain distributions — **13**
14. Enter gain from Form 4797, line 7 or 9 — **14**
15. Long-term capital loss carryover — **15**
16. Add all of the transactions on lines 9a and 9c and lines 10 through 15 in columns (f) and (g) — **16** ( ) **3000**
17. Net long-term gain or (loss), combine columns (f) and (g) of line 16 — **17 | 3000**

Proof of May 18, 1987

Page 2

Name(s) as shown on Form 1040. (Do not enter name and social security number if shown on other side.)
Dough

Your social security number
329:04:1040

Part III — Summary of Parts I and II

18	Combine lines 8 and 17, and enter the net gain or (loss) here. If result is a gain, also enter the gain on Form 1040, line 14. **Note:** If lines 17 and 18 are net gains and your taxable income is taxed over the 28% tax rate, you should use Part IV below to figure your tax.	18	3000
19	If line 18 is a loss, enter here and as a loss on Form 1040, line 14, the **smaller** of: a The amount on line 18; **or** b $3,000 ($1,500 if married filing a separate return)	19	

Part IV — Alternative Tax Computation

(You will have to complete Form 1040 in order to figure your taxable income for purposes of line 20.)

Use Part IV if both lines 17 and 18 show net gains, **AND**:

You checked filing status box:	AND	Form 1040, line 36 is over:	You checked filing status box:	AND	Form 1040, line 36 is over:
1		$27,000	3		$22,500
2 or 5		45,000	4		38,000

20	Enter amount from Form 1040, line 36	20	
21	Enter the smaller of the gain on line 18 or the gain on line 17	21	
22	Subtract line 21 from 20 and enter the result	22	
23	Enter: **a** $16,800 if you checked filing status box 1; **b** $28,000 if you checked filing status box 2 or 5; **c** $14,000 if you checked filing status box 3; **or d** $23,000 if you checked filing status box 4	23	
24	Enter the **greater** of line 22 or line 23	24	
25	Subtract line 24 from line 20	25	
26	Figure the amount of tax on line 24. (See Instructions.)	26	
27	Multiply line 25 by 28% (.28) and enter the result	27	
28	Add lines 26 and 27. Enter the result here and on Form 1040, line 37 and check the box for Schedule D	28	

Part V — Computation of Capital Loss Carryovers From 1987 to 1988

(Complete this part if the loss on line 18 is more than the loss on line 19.)

29	Enter the loss shown on line 8; if none, enter zero and skip lines 30 through 33	29	
30	Enter gain shown on line 17. If that line is blank or shows a loss, enter zero	30	
31	Subtract line 30 from line 29	31	
32	Enter the smaller of line 19 or 31	32	
33	Subtract line 32 from line 31. This is your **short-term capital loss carryover from 1987 to 1988**	33	
34	Enter loss from line 17; if none, enter zero and skip lines 35 through 38	34	
35	Enter gain shown on line 8. If that line is blank or shows a loss, enter zero	35	
36	Subtract line 35 from line 34	36	
37	Subtract line 32 from line 19. (**Note:** If you skipped lines 30 through 33, enter the amount from line 19.)	37	
38	Subtract line 37 from line 36. This is your **long-term capital loss carryover from 1987 to 1988**	38	

Part VI — Complete This Part Only If You Elect Out of the Installment Method and Report a Note or Other Obligation at Less Than Full Face Value

39	Check here if you elect out of the installment method ▶ ☐
40	Enter the face amount of the note or other obligation ▶
41	Enter the percentage of valuation of the note or other obligation ▶

Part VII — Reconciliation of Forms 1099-B for Bartering Transactions

Complete this part if you received one or more Form(s) 1099-B or an equivalent substitute statement(s) reporting bartering income.

Amount of bartering income from Form 1099-B or equivalent statement included on:

42	Form 1040, line 21	42	
43	Schedule C (Form 1040)	43	
44	Schedule D (Form 1040)	44	
45	Schedule E (Form 1040)	45	
46	Schedule F (Form 1040)	46	
47	Other (identify) (if not taxable, indicate reason—attach additional sheets if necessary) ▶	47	
48	Total (add lines 42 through 47)	48	

Note: The amount on line 48 should be the same as the total bartering income on all Forms 1099-B or equivalent statements received.

ment obligations. Capital assets include stocks, bonds, homes, and automobiles. Although the gain on the sale of a home is treated as a capital gain, a loss on home sale is considered personal in nature and generally not deductible.

Save all your broker's advice, statements, and stock records until 3 years after the return reporting the sale was filed.

Long-Term vs. Short-Term Gains and Losses

Although the tax rates on capital gain and ordinary income are the same, that doesn't mean that the distinction between the two types of income has disappeared; e.g., a new long-term installment can absorb a long-term loss that must otherwise be carried over. If you sold stock this year, make a list showing gains and losses to date. Determine the status of gains and losses, noting date of purchase, purchase price, and sell date and price. Paying special attention to dates, consider which securities could bring sizable short- or long-term gains or losses if sold. Noting any capital-loss carryover that you may have had in previous years, you are now in a position to plan what you need to do for the remainder of the year for tax purposes. If you own shares purchased on different dates and at different prices, you must be able to pinpoint exactly which group of shares you want to sell. If you cannot identify the shares, you must use the "first-in, first-out" method: the shares purchased first will be considered sold first.

Line	Tax Law	Pay Less Tax Legally
Part I	**Short-Term Gains and Losses** Short-term gains are fully taxable. Losses are fully deductible up to $3,000.	• You can sell borrowed shares now and replace them with your own shares next year, thereby locking in gains on the date of the transaction while deferring the tax until next year. When you use your shares to replace the borrowed ones, the transaction is closed for tax purposes. However, this "short sales against the box" will make your gain short-term regardless of how long the short sale is open.
	Nonbusiness Bad Debt If you lend money to an individual and find the amount to be uncollectable, you have the basis of a deductible short-term capital loss, limited to $3,000 per year against ordinary income. An uncollectable loan to a company to protect an investment as a stockbroker is treated as a	• The IRS often considers loans between friends, family members, and close business associates as little more than nondeductible gifts. If you intend to make a loan (or guarantee one), require the borrower to sign a note indicating the amount borrowed, interest rate, and repayment date.

Line	Tax Law	Pay Less Tax Legally
	short-term capital loss. Capital gains and up to $3,000 of remaining loss can be offset against ordinary income in the year that the loan becomes uncollectable; additional losses can be carried forward. A personal bad debt is deductible in the year the loan becomes uncollectable, but you must be able to prove worthlessness—there is no deduction for partial bad debts. As proof, the IRS will accept a debtor's failure to respond to demand for payment, bankruptcy, or insolvency, or the disappearance of the debtor. You do not have to take the debtor to court; if you can show that the debtor had no assets and that a lawsuit would have been a waste of attorneys' fees, the IRS will be satisfied. ***Writing Off Bad Family Loans*** If you plan wisely, you can deduct bad debts from loans to family members. In the year the loan becomes totally worthless, you can deduct the bad debt as a short-term capital loss. You will have to keep proper documents to prove that you (and your relative) intended to create a true debtor-creditor relationship, and that you intend to pursue legal channels if he or she does not repay the loan. Have the borrower sign a promissory note showing principal, interest rate, and date payable. Be sure to establish the loan just as you would with a stranger. Lending money to relatives can cause problems; but with careful planning, you will at least be able to deduct any losses. ***Business Bad Debt*** Business bad debts are entered on Schedule C. See Chapter 4.	You can then write off a partially worthless bad debt by selling the note at a loss. However, when a taxpayer has a loss arising from the guarantee of a loan, he is treated as if he had made the loan, and credit for loss will depend on his motivation for the guarantee. If it arose from the taxpayer's trade or business, it is deductible as a business expense; if the guarantee was part of a transaction entered into for profit, a loss is treated as a nonbusiness bad debt and deductible as a short-term capital loss; if the guarantee does not fit into either of the above situations, there is no deductible loss. ● Frequently, an owner of a small company will lend money to his corporation. If

Line	Tax Law	Pay Less Tax Legally
		the loan becomes worthless, the bad-debt deduction may be hard to prove. • Keep some evidence of having made a loan in the first place (e.g., a promissory note), as well as evidence to show that you unsuccessfully attempted to collect the debt.
	How to Handle Dividend Reinvestment Plan Stock If you hold stock purchased through a dividend reinvestment plan, the rules limiting sales within a year still apply, and the 6-month holding period for capital gains will not help. The proceeds from sales of dividend reinvested stock (up to a year after the last tax-free reinvestment) are taxed as ordinary income (to the total of untaxed dividends reinvestment within that period).	
Part II	**Long-Term Capital Gains and Losses** You can get long-term capital gain treatment on an option if you exercise the option to keep the property for more than 6 months before selling.	• If the value of property is high and you have held an option for more than 6 months, consider selling the option. If the value of the property is low, exercise the option and hold the property until it increases in value.
	Sale of Inherited Property If you sell inherited property, your basis in the property is either the value placed on it at the date of death or the value 6 months after death. Check with the executor to find out which valuation was used.	• When Mr. J. died, he left certain property to his son that had cost $20,000 but was worth $50,000 at the date of death; if the son were to sell the property for $50,000, he would have neither a gain nor a loss.
	Sale of Inherited Rental Property If you inherit rental property and ultimately sell it at a loss, that loss is deductible on your return, even if the property is used for personal purposes for a period of time.	• Under his deceased wife's will, Mr. W. inherited a house that he had lived in for 11 years. He sold the house at a $10,000 loss. The Tax Court allowed him to take the loss as a tax deduction.

Line	Tax Law	Pay Less Tax Legally
	Sale of a Patent An inventor or investor in either a patent or patent application can get long-term capital-gain treatment on the sale of the patent or application without regard to the 6-month holding period or how the payments were made, if substantially all rights to the invention are transferred at the time of sale. In addition, inventors are permitted to deduct any and all research and development expenses paid during the year. A statement on the return that expenses are being deducted currently instead of being capitalized is necessary.	*Example 1* Long-term loss of $7,400 for 1986 (current deduction of $3,000). The long-term capital loss carryover to 1987 is $1,400 (double the $3,000 deduction and subtract from $7,400). *Example 2* Long-term loss of $6,400, short-term loss of $200, current deduction of $3,000. The long-term capital-loss carryover is $800: deduct the $200 short-term loss from $3,000 ($2,800); double the $2,800 ($5,600); and subtract from $6,400. The capital-loss carryover for 1987 is $800. • Bondholders may be better off selling bonds at a tax loss and replacing them with others of similar yield, as long as the same bonds are not repurchased within 30 days of the sale date.

Part III: Summary of Parts I and II

Combine lines 8 and 17 and enter the net gain or loss on line 18. If the result is a gain, enter that gain on Form 1040, line 14.

If you have long-term capital gains and your taxable income is taxed over the 28 percent rate, use Part IV to figure your tax.

If line 18 is a loss, enter on line 19 and on Form 1040 line 14 the smaller of (1) the amount on line 18 or (2) $3,000 ($1,500 if married filing separately).

Alternative Tax Computation (Part IV)

The alternative tax calculation on the new Schedule D is computed as follows:

1. Enter your taxable income. $_____
2. Subtract your net capital gain (net long-term capital gain less net short-term capital loss). $_____
3. Taxable income without net capital gain. $_____
4. Enter $16,800 if you are single;
   $28,000 if you use joint rates;
   $23,000 if head of household;
   $14,000 if married filing separately. $_____
5. Enter the greater of line 3 or line 4. $_____
6. Subtract line 5 from line 1. $_____
7. Figure the amount of tax on line 5. $_____
8. Multiply line 6 by 28 percent and enter the result. $_____
9. Add lines 7 and 8. This is your tax for 1987. $_____

SAVE MONEY NOW

Example:

You file a joint return showing a taxable income of $60,000, including a net capital gain of $15,000. Your 1987 tax is $13,040, as follows:

1. Taxable income	$60,000
2. Net capital gain	15,000
3. Taxable income without net capital gain	45,000
4. Starting point for 28% tax rate (joint return)	28,000
5. Greater of line 3 or 4	45,000
6. Net capital gain subject to ceiling	15,000
7. Tax before adding capital gain tax	8,840
8. 28% of $15,000 on line 6	4,200
9. Add lines 7 and 8. This is the alternative tax for 1987.	$13,040

Without the alternative tax, the tax on $60,000 would be $14,090. The alternative tax provides a tax savings of $1,050 for the $15,000 of net capital gain that would otherwise be taxed at 35%. The amount of saving is the 7 percent difference between the 28 percent ceiling and the 35 percent regular rate, of $1,050 (7 percent of $15,000).

Avoiding Gain on Condemnation

If you have a gain on condemnation, you can defer the tax by replacing the property within 3 years after the close of the first taxable year in which any part of the gain is realized. This 3-year replacement period applies only to condemnations of real property. Replacement of condemnations of personal property, and theft and casualty losses of all other property, must occur within 2 years.

Capital Losses (Part V)

Beginning this year, the full amount of long-term capital losses is tax deductible. However, only $3,000 of ordinary income (e.g., salary) can be offset by capital losses in any one year. Unused losses can be carried over into future years. (Under the old law, only half of net long-term capital losses were deductible.) Excess long-term losses are no longer subject to a 50 percent scale-down.

Line	Tax Law	Pay Less Tax Legally
Part VI	**Sale on the Installment Method** In an installment sale, you can elect to have all of your gain taxed in the year of sale. The amount of wraparound mortgages is treated as payments to the seller,	• If you are going to sell nondepreciable property (i.e., real estate, art, stock) at a large profit, sell it on a deferred-payment basis. In this way, you only have to report

Line	Tax Law	Pay Less Tax Legally
	which has the effect of increasing the gain in the year of sale—but only to the extent that the wraparound mortgage exceeds the seller's cost. Installment treatment is no longer available for sales of marketable securities. If you are reporting the discounted value of notes in an election to be taxed on your full gain in one year, you must enter the amount on the appropriate lines of Schedule D. If you want to avoid installment sales tax treatment, list the total sales price as income, including the face value of any notes. The repeal of the capital gain deduction affects all capital gain income, even if it was received as part of a contract entered into before 1987. This means that a taxpayer receiving installment payments from the sale of a capital asset is required to treat the payments as ordinary income. **Nontaxable Exchanges** You can exchange real estate held for rental or investment property without recognizing any gain or loss on the exchange. An apartment building may be exchanged for another building or a store, a farm for city property, or a vacant lot for improved land. The asset received takes on the same basis as the property disposed of in the trade, increased by any cash that may have changed hands in the trade. However, gain may be recognized to the extent of any cash received.	profits on the principal as you receive the payments. Installment sales apply regardless of how much (or how little) cash you receive in the year of sale; you could sell property at a gain this year even if full payment is due next year. • An investor who sold stock for cash and 2 notes (pledged as collateral on a real estate deal) was permitted to report his stock gain on the installment method. • In a recent case, both husband and wife were upper-income professionals, and each had stocks. The wife sold some stock to her spouse and reported the gain on the installment method. Since it was a bona fide sale, it held up in the courts. • If you want to sell one piece of property and invest the proceeds in another, consider exchanging properties. If your property has decreased in value, it may be better to sell (and get the benefit of a deductible loss). If the property has increased in value, you may be better off exchanging. • An investor wanted to sell an apartment building and purchase some land. A realtor bought the land and traded it for her building, which the realtor promptly sold simultaneously, with each sale contingent on the next. The IRS claimed it was a sale—not a tax-free exchange. The Tax Court felt otherwise and sided with the taxpayer.

Recapture Rules

When you sell a depreciated asset for more than its adjusted basis (original cost less depreciation claimed), part of the profit is taxed as ordinary income; this add-back is called "recapture." Recapture is the difference between the fast depreciation claimed and the straight-line depreciation over a longer life. For machinery, equipment, and nonresidential buildings, all depreciation is recaptured. However, depreciation on residential buildings is recaptured only to the extent that it exceeds the amount that would have been deducted under the straight-line method.

Line	Tax Law	Pay Less Tax Legally
Form 2119	**Sale or Exchange of Principal Residence**	
	If you sell your home for less than it cost (including improvements), your loss is not deductible; if you sell it at a gain, that gain is taxable at long-term capital-gain rates. However, you can escape any gain on the sale if you reinvest the sales price of the house into a second residence within 24 months before or after the date of sale of the first house. Use must also begin within 2 years after the sale in the case of new construction.	• A member of the Armed Forces stationed outside the United States or required to reside in government quarters may have the 2-year period on the gain on the sale of a residence extended to the later of (1) 4 years after the sale of the residence or, (2) one year after the taxpayer is no longer stationed outside the United States or is no longer required to reside in government quarters.
	If you sell a replacement home within 2 years of sale of a former home, you may be taxed on the deferred gain on the first home plus profit on the second home. The basis of each new residence in multiple rollovers must be reduced by the deferred gain on the preceding sale.	• A yacht is considered a replacement residence if it becomes your home and costs as much as or more than the home that you sold. • Sold more than one home in the 2-year period? You can defer both gains if the sales were in connection with work at a new location and the moves were more than 35 miles in distance.
	Adjusted sales price is the selling price of a house less any fixing-up expenses (such as repairs or decorating) and selling expenses (commissions and legal fees) incurred within 90 days before the sale and paid within 30 days after the sales date. For example, suppose you bought your home in 1973 for $29,000 and have since spent $800 for central air conditioning and $1,200 for a garage, bringing your total investment to $31,000. In July, you spent an additional $2,000 to decorate (paying the bill immediately). The house was sold in August for $66,000 less com-	• Save all bills, canceled checks, and receipts on home improvements; they are used in determining the adjusted sales price. • If you sell your home and the sales price includes some furnishings, be sure to reduce the adjusted sales price by their value. • Homeowners who sell their home and an adjacent lot can also defer the gain on the lot if the proceeds go into another house.

Form 2119 — Sale or Exchange of Principal Residence

Department of the Treasury — Internal Revenue Service (X)

OMB No. 1545-0072
Attachment Sequence No. 21

▶ See instructions on back.
▶ Attach to Form 1040 for year of sale (see instruction B).

Name(s) as shown on Form 1040: **DOUGH**
Your social security number: **329 04 1040**

Do not include expenses that you deduct as moving expenses.

1 a Date former residence sold ▶ **7-1-87**
b Enter the face amount of any mortgage, note (for example, second trust), or other financial instrument on which you will receive periodic payments of principal or interest from this sale ▶

2 a If you bought or built a new residence, enter date you occupied it; otherwise enter "None" ▶
b Are any rooms in either residence rented out or used for business for which a deduction is allowed? (If "Yes," see instructions) — **No**

3 a Were you 55 or over on date of sale? — **No**
b Was your spouse 55 or over on date of sale? — **No**
If you answered "No" to 3a and 3b, do not complete 3c through 3f and Part II.
c Did the person who answered "Yes" to 3a or 3b own and use the property sold as his or her principal residence for a total of at least 3 years (except for short absences) of the 5-year period before the sale?
d If you answered "Yes" to 3c, do you elect to take the once in a lifetime exclusion of the gain on the sale?
e At time of sale, was the residence owned by: ☐ you, ☐ your spouse, ☒ both of you?
f Social security number of spouse, at time of sale, if different from number on Form 1040 ▶ (Enter "None" if you were not married at time of sale.)

Part I — Computation of Gain

4	Selling price of residence less expense of sale. (Do not include personal property items.)	**175,000**
5	Basis of residence sold	**100,000**
6	Gain on sale (subtract line 5 from line 4). If zero or less, enter zero and do not complete the rest of form. Enter the gain from this line on Schedule D, line 3 or 10*, unless you bought another principal residence or checked "Yes" to 3d. Then continue with this form	**75,000**

If you haven't replaced your residence, do you plan to do so within the replacement period? ☐ Yes ☐ No
(If "Yes" see instruction B.)

Part II — Age 55 or Over One-Time Exclusion

Complete this part only if you checked "yes" to 3(d) to elect the once in a lifetime exclusion; otherwise, skip to Part III.

7	Enter the smaller of line 6 or $125,000 ($62,500, if married filing separate return)	
8	Gain (subtract line 7 from line 6). If zero, do not complete rest of form. Enter the gain from this line on Schedule D, line 10*, unless you bought another principal residence. Then continue with this form	

Part III — Gain To Be Postponed and Adjusted Basis of New Residence

Complete this part if you bought another principal residence.

9	Fixing-up expenses (see instructions for time limits)	**2500**
10	Adjusted sales price (subtract line 9 from line 4)	**172500**
11	Cost of new residence	**180,000**
12	Gain taxable this year (subtract line 11 plus line 7 (if applicable) from line 10). If result is zero or less, enter zero. Do not enter more than line 6 or line 8 (if applicable). Enter the gain from this line on Schedule D, line 3 or 10*.	**0**
13	Gain to be postponed (subtract line 12 from line 6. However, if Part II applies, subtract line 12 from line 8)	**75000**
14	Adjusted basis of new residence (subtract line 13 from line 11)	**105,000**

*****Caution:** If you completed Form 6252 for the residence in 1a, do not enter your taxable gain from Form 2119 on Schedule D.

The One-Minute Taxman: Buying or Selling Homes

Special tax breaks for home ownership (including condos and co-ops) include deductions for the points paid at purchase, plus interest and real estate taxes (in most cases enabling you to itemize your deductions and save even more). Your home goes up in value, and you pay no tax. When you sell your home—usually at a profit—you are given 2 years to reinvest the money into a more expensive home and defer the tax; or, if you or your spouse is at least age 55 as of the date of sale, you may overlook the first $125,000 of profit on the sale of the home. However, loss on a sale is not deductible.

Total all home-purchase and selling expenses and enter the figures in the appropriate sections on Form 2119. Use your closing statement to obtain exact figures.

Home Purchase Costs	Amount	Home Selling Costs	Amount
☐ Attorneys' fees	_____	☐ Credit report	_____
☐ Credit report	_____	☐ Decorating expenses for the purpose of making a sale	_____
☐ Escrow fees	_____	☐ Escrow fees	_____
☐ Forwarding fees	_____	☐ FHA points	_____
☐ Insurance fees	_____	☐ Loan fees	_____
☐ Loan service charges	_____	☐ Notary	_____
☐ Realtor commissions	_____	☐ Recording fees	_____
☐ Recording fees	_____	☐ Repair expenses, for the purpose of making a sale	_____
☐ Tax stamps	_____	☐ State transfer tax	_____
☐ Termite inspection	_____	☐ Survey	_____
☐ Title insurance	_____	☐ Tax stamps	_____
Total	_____	☐ Termite inspection	_____
		☐ Title costs	_____
		☐ Title insurance	_____
		☐ Title registration	_____
		Total	_____

Home Selling Costs	Amount
☐ Abstract	_____
☐ Advertising	_____
☐ Appraisal fees	_____
☐ Attorneys' fees	_____
☐ Broker's commission	_____

Home Improvement Costs

Any home improvement costs are added to the cost basis of property and result in a smaller gain (and less tax) upon sale.

Home Improvement Costs	Amount	Home Improvement Costs	Amount
☐ Acreage or lots	_____	☐ Barbeque grill built-in	_____
☐ Additions, including garage, supports, partitions, breezeway, shed, patio, siding, porch, wings	_____	☐ Bookcases, if permanently installed	_____
		☐ Cabinets	_____
		☐ Carpeting	_____
		☐ Ceilings	_____

Home Improvement Costs	Amount	Home Improvement Costs	Amount
☐ Chimes	_____	☐ Landscaping: trees, bushes	_____
☐ Closets	_____	☐ Laundry: washer and dryer	_____
☐ Cupboards	_____	☐ Mailbox	_____
☐ Driveway: paving, black-topping	_____	☐ Mirrors	_____
☐ Electrical: circuit breaker, new wiring, lightning rods, outlets	_____	☐ Patios	_____
		☐ Playground equipment	_____
☐ Fences and posts	_____	☐ Plumbing: pipes, drains	_____
☐ Fire-alarm systems	_____	☐ Prefabricated wall unit	_____
☐ Fireplace	_____	☐ Retaining walls	_____
☐ Flooring	_____	☐ Roofing	_____
☐ Foundation work	_____	☐ Room additions	_____
☐ Garage: electric door opener	_____	☐ Sauna	_____
		☐ Screens	_____
☐ Gardening: trees, shrubs, sod, grading, pumps	_____	☐ Security system and burglar bars	_____
☐ Gutters and drainpipes	_____	☐ Storm windows or doors	_____
☐ Hardware, furnace repair	_____	☐ Surveying	_____
☐ Heating/air conditioning: portable units, central air-conditioning, heat pump, hot-water heater, permanent space heater	_____	☐ Swimming pool	_____
		☐ Telephone outlets	_____
		☐ Terraces	_____
		☐ Tuckpointing	_____
		☐ Venetian blinds	_____
☐ Hot tub, if permanently installed	_____	☐ Ventilators	_____
		☐ Walkways	_____
☐ Insulation: ceiling, floor, walls	_____	☐ Waterproofing	_____
		☐ Water softener	_____
☐ Intercom system	_____	☐ Windows, replacement	_____
☐ Kitchen: remodeling, counters, cabinets, dishwasher, disposal, range, built-in microwave or grille	_____	☐ Window shades	_____
		☐ Workshop	_____
		Total	_____

Tax Law

missions of $6,600. In October, you bought a house for $57,000. Your long-term capital gain on the sale is $400.

Sale price	$66,000
Less: commissions and decorating expenses	8,600
Adjusted sales price	$57,400
Replacement home cost	57,000
Gain to be reported	$ 400

However, your actual gain on the sale is $28,400:

Sale price	$66,000
Less: commissions	6,600
Net sales price	$59,400
Cost of first home	31,000
Gain on sale	$28,400
Taxable gain	400
Nontaxable gain	$28,000

The nontaxable gain of $28,000 reduces your basis in the new house; the cost basis of the new home is $29,000 ($57,000 less $28,000). The gain is reported as a long-term gain; if there had been a loss on the sale, the loss would not have been deductible.

Conversion to Rental Property

The basis for taking depreciation in a conversion of a home rental property is the value of the house as of the date of the conversion, provided that it is not greater than the original cost. If, for example, you originally paid $25,000 for your house (excluding land) and it was worth $75,000 as of the date rented, your base for computing depreciation is $25,000 (using the straight-line method only).

If you rent out a former residence, you can have the benefit of a tax loss when you finally sell it, provided the property was actually rented out and not merely advertised for sale or rent.

Pay Less Tax Legally

- Realtors may find it easier to report long-term capital gains on sales of privately held property. In a recent case, a realtor owned his own firm and was an investor in other land deals. The properties sold were held for relatively long periods of time, no improvements were made, and he did not advertise them for sale in the normal course of his business; he merely accepted unsolicited offers for sale. Since he was able to keep his investments separate from his realty business, he was permitted to report the gain as long-term capital gain.

- If you want to sell your home and not reinvest the proceeds, you can make a gift of the property to your children, pay the resulting gift tax, and let them sell.

- If you sell your home, your home office may be treated as a business property and not as part of a (tax-deferred) sale of a personal residence. However, even if you may have claimed a home office deduction in previous years, a house is considered a residential property if you do not claim a home office in the year of sale.

- A loss on the sale of a personal residence may be deductible. A taxpayer who was building his own home had a change of plans and decided to live elsewhere. He altered the building plans, finished the house, and sold it at a loss. Since he had decided not to live there, the house was not considered a personal residence, and the deduction was allowed.

- A couple moved to another city but did not advertise their home for sale immediately in case their new jobs did not work out. However, because the first home was sold within 12 months, they were able to defer paying tax on the gain. Another couple that was transferred could not sell their home because of the poor real estate market and, out of financial necessity, had to rent the home periodically.

Line	Tax Law	Pay Less Tax Legally
Part II	**55-or-Older Exclusion** If you are at least 55 years of age as of the date of sale of your home and have lived in the home as the principal place of residence for at least 3 of the past 5 years, you can overlook the first $125,000 profit (or $62,500 for married persons filing separately). Generally, a taxpayer cannot total the use of 2 residences to meet the necessary time requirements. However, if the home was destroyed (e.g., by fire) and replaced with a second home, the occupancy period of the first residence may be added to the second one. **Special Rules on $125,000 Exclusion** 1. There is only one lifetime exclusion for married taxpayers. If either of the 2 parties has made an election before marriage, there will be no recapture of income. 2. If couples divorce after taking the exclusion, there are no further elections available to them (or to their new spouses if they remarry). 3. If only one spouse is age 55 as of the date of sale, both qualify. 4. If one of the spouses is deceased, the remaining spouse must be at least age 55 to qualify. **Lump-Sum Distributions** Lump-sum distributions from a pension or profit-sharing plan are not reported on Schedule D, but rather on Form 4792. You may qualify for 5- or 10-year averaging. See page 194 for new tax law.	Since the rentals were necessary, no gain was recognized on the sale. But in another case, where the previous residence was rented for more than 2 years, the IRS would not permit a tax deferral. ● Mr. S. abandoned his home in August because of a change of jobs. He attempted to rent his home but could not find a tenant, and he finally sold the house the following year at a loss. Because the home was never actually rented, he was allowed only a deduction for maintenance, depreciation, and the advertising necessary to attract a tenant. ● Let's assume that you intended to reoccupy your home at some time in the future but circumstances beyond your control made the return impossible. If a replacement home has already been purchased, renting out the original home for a short period of time does not necessarily change the character of the home from a personal property to a business property, especially if you can show that you tried to sell. ● Although you need to have lived in your home for 3 out of 5 years, you need not have actually owned it for 3 years. You could have been a tenant for 2 years, then bought the home and lived there during one of the next 3 years. ● A couple over 55 years of age were permitted to exclude the gain on sale of a residence even though they did not live in the home during the winter. ● A brother and sister can each exclude $125,000 on their jointly owned home. Two exclusions are also allowed for an elderly parent living with a child age 55 or older: if the home you share with an elderly parent has appreciated by more than $125,000, make the parent a co-owner at least 3 years before the intended date of sale.

6

SUPPLEMENTAL INCOME: SCHEDULE E

If you received rental income during the year, you are required to complete Schedule E. You are asked to describe the property, answer question 2 of Part I concerning personal use of the property, include the total income received during the year, and deduct depreciation (which can be computed on Form 4562) and any rental expenses. The resulting figure is totaled on line 29 and entered on Form 1040, line 17.

If you own rental property, don't forget to take depreciation (see page 116), and be sure to list each property separately. If you need more room to list expenses than is provided on Schedule E, attach your additional notes to the form, but be sure to state: *See Schedule Attached.*

If you have royalty income, report the amount on Part I of Schedule E; do not forget to claim depletion.

If you received income from partnerships, estates, trusts, small business corporations, or real estate mortgage conduits, report the details on Parts II to IV of Schedule E. These entities act as a conduit for income, and you may be entitled to certain deductions that "pass through" to your tax return—for example, additional first-year depreciation.

Passive Losses and Credits

You can deduct up to $25,000 in losses from real estate rentals and other existing investments in which you actively participate. If you are engaged in non-real estate rentals and satisfy a "significant services" test, you can offset current income with losses from the activity. Also, you may deduct your suspended losses when you dispose of your passive investments.

If you have at least a 10 percent interest in the activity and actively participate (that is, make management decisions), you can avoid the limit imposed on passive losses and may claim up to $25,000 in losses from the activity against *any* type of income. This $25,000 is phased out as adjusted gross income exceeds $100,000 and is eliminated when AGI reaches $150,000.

The $25,000 limit applies to losses and tax credits combined. Low-income housing and rehabilitation investment tax credits can be used as part of the $25,000 even if you don't actively participate in the rental real estate activity involved.

First, calculate the net income (or loss) from all your rental real estate activities in which you actively participate. If there is a net loss for the year, net passive income is then applied against it from other activities to determine how much is eligible for the loss allowance.

The $25,000 maximum is reduced by 50 percent of the amount by which your income exceeds $100,000 and is completely phased out when your income reaches

$150,000. AGI is calculated without considering IRA deductions, passive activity losses, and taxable Social Security benefits.

A married taxpayer filing separately and living apart cannot claim more than $12,500 of the losses, further reduced by 50 percent of the amount by which AGI exceeds $50,000. A married taxpayer living with his spouse for the entire year and filing separately has the $25,000 maximum loss reduced to zero.

For rehabilitation credit and low-income housing credit, the phase-out for offsetting tax on up to $25,000 nonpassive income is between $200,000 and $250,000 adjusted gross income. The phase-out applies first to the passive activity loss, second to credits other than rehabilitation and low-income housing, and last to the deduction equivalents of rehab and housing credits.

Portfolio income is not treated as passive activity income, so passive losses (and credits) cannot be used as an offset. The term "portfolio income" includes:

1. Interest, dividends, annuities, and royalties received (other than in the ordinary course of business)
2. Gains or losses from the sale of property held for investment purposes and not used in a passive activity, and from property that normally yields interest, dividend, annuity, or royalty income
3. Dividends from corporation stock, interest on debts, royalties from licensing property, and real estate investment trusts or regulated investment companies.

If your adjusted gross income is over $100,000 (before subtracting rental or other passive losses), the $25,000 deduction phases out, being reduced by 50 percent of the amount of AGI over $100,000; at $150,000, the deduction becomes zero. The levels are cut in half for married couples filing separately.

The new passive loss rule will be phased in gradually. In 1987 you may still deduct 65 percent of losses from rental properties considered to be passive, 40 percent in 1988, 20 percent in 1989, and 10 percent in 1990.

Any losses you can't take due to the adjusted gross income limitation (or phase-in rules) may be carried forward and deducted in a future year, if you have enough passive income in that year to cover the deduction.

You may deduct the loss when you dispose of your real estate investment.

Example

You have rental property that shows a loss in 1987 of $40,000. Your AGI is $95,000. You write off the $25,000 active participation loss plus 65 percent of the additional $15,000 loss, or $9,750, as allowed under the phase-in rules for total deductible losses of $34,750. The remaining $5,250 can be carried forward as a passive loss in a future year.

Passive Income/Losses

Before Tax Reform, if you earned $100,000 in salary and lost $20,000 on investments, you could reduce your reportable income to $80,000. Under Tax Reform, you can only deduct passive losses from passive earnings on other investments. You may not deduct passive losses against income from "other sources," e.g., interest, dividends, or portfolio income.

However, you may use tax shelter losses to offset income from other sources when you dispose of the investment (or when it ceases operation), and you may carry forward your unused losses to offset income from tax shelters in future years.

SCHEDULE E (Form 1040)
Department of the Treasury
Internal Revenue Service

Supplemental Income Schedule
(From rents, royalties, partnerships, estates, trusts, REMICs, etc.)
▶ Attach to Form 1040, Form 1041, or Form 1041S.
▶ See Instructions for Schedule E (Form 1040).

OMB No. 1545-0074
1987
Attachment Sequence No. 13

Name(s) as shown on Form 1040: DOUGH

Your social security number: 329:04:1040

Part I — Rental and Royalty Income or (Loss)
Caution: Your rental loss may be limited. See Instructions.

1. In the space provided below, show the kind and location of each rental property.
2. For each property listed, did you or a member of your family use for personal purposes any of the properties for more than the greater of 14 days or 10% of the total days rented at fair rental value during the tax year? Yes / No
3. For each rental real estate property listed, did you actively participate in the operation of the activity during the tax year? (See Instructions.) Yes / No

- Property A: TWO APT BLDG — No: X — Yes: X
- Property B:
- Property C:

Rental and Royalty Income	A	B	C	Totals (Add columns A, B, and C)
4 Rents received	2400			4: 2400
5 Royalties received				5:

Rental and Royalty Expenses

		A	B	C	Totals
6	Advertising				
7	Auto and travel				
8	Cleaning and maintenance				
9	Commissions				
10	Insurance	101			
11	Legal and other professional fees				
12	Mortgage interest paid to financial institutions (see Instructions)	902			12: 902
13	Other interest				
14	Repairs	817			
15	Supplies				
16	Taxes (Do not include windfall profit tax here. See Part V, line 40.)	712			
17	Utilities	615			
18	Wages and salaries				
19	Other (list) ▶ MISC	102			
20	Total expenses other than depreciation and depletion. Add lines 6 through 19	3249			20: 3249
21	Depreciation expense (see Instructions), or depletion (see Publication 535)	800			21: 800
22	Total. Add lines 20 and 21	4049			
23	Income or (loss) from rental or royalty properties. Subtract line 22 from line 4 (rents) or 5 (royalties)	⟨1649⟩			
24	**Deductible rental loss. Caution:** Your rental loss on line 23 may be limited. See Instructions to determine if you must file **Form 8582**, Passive Activity Loss Limitations	⟨1649⟩			

25. Profits. Add rental and royalty profits from line 23, and enter the total profits here 25:
26. Losses. Add royalty losses from line 23 and rental losses from line 24, and enter the total (losses) here 26: (1649)
27. Combine amounts on lines 25 and 26, and enter the net profit or (loss) here .... 27: ⟨1649⟩
28. Net farm rental profit or (loss) from Form 4835, line 34. (Also complete Part VI, line 43.) 28:
29. Total rental or royalty income or (loss). Combine amounts on lines 27 and 28, and enter the total here. If Parts II, III, IV, and V on page 2 do not apply to you, enter the amount from line 29 on Form 1040, line 17. Otherwise, include the amount from line 29 in line 42 on page 2 of Schedule E .... 29: ⟨1649⟩

Proof of August 13, 1987

Page 2

Name(s) as shown on Form 1040. (Do not enter name and social security number if shown on other side.)
DOUMA

Your social security number
329:04:1040

Part II Income or (Loss) from Partnerships and S Corporations

If you report a loss below and have amounts invested in that activity for which you are not at risk, you MUST check "Yes" in column (e) and attach Form 6198. Otherwise, you must check "No." See instructions.

	(a) Name	(b) Enter P for partnership; S for S Corporation	(c) Check if foreign partnership	(d) Employer identification number	(e) At-Risk: Yes / No
A	FIRSTAX INC	S		36-1279430	Y
B					
C					
D					
E					

Passive Activities | **Nonpassive Activities**

	(f) Passive loss allowed from Form 8582	(g) Passive income from Schedule K-1	(h) Nonpassive loss from Schedule K-1	(i) Section 179 deduction	(j) Nonpassive income from Schedule K-1
A			⟨200⟩		
B					
C					
D					
E					
30a Totals					
b Totals			⟨200⟩		

31 Add amounts in columns (g) and (j), line 30a. Enter total income here ... **31** ⟨200⟩
32 Add amounts in columns (f), (h), and (i), line 30b. Enter total here ... **32** (⟨200⟩)
33 Total partnership and S corporation income or (loss). Combine amounts on lines 31 and 32. Enter the total here and include in line 42 below ... **33** ⟨200⟩

Part III Income or (Loss) from Estates and Trusts

	(a) Name	(b) Employer identification number
A		
B		
C		

Passive Activities | **Nonpassive Activities**

	(c) Passive loss allowed from Form 8582	(d) Passive income from Schedule K-1	(e) Other portfolio loss from Schedule K-1	(f) Other portfolio income from Schedule K-1
A				
B				
C				
34a Totals				
b Totals				

35 Add amounts in columns (d) and (f), line 34a. Enter total income here ... **35**
36 Add amounts in columns (c) and (e), line 34b. Enter total (loss) here ... **36** ( )
37 Total estate and trust income or (loss). Combine amounts on lines 35 and 36. Enter the total here and include in line 42 below ... **37**

Part IV Income or (Loss) from Real Estate Mortgage Investment Conduits (REMICs)—Residual Holder

(a) Name	(b) Employer identification number	(c) Excess inclusion from Schedules Q, line 2c (see Instructions)	(d) Taxable income (net loss) from Schedules Q, line 1b	(e) Income from Schedules Q, line 3b

38 Combine columns (d) and (e) only. Enter the total here and include in line 42 below ... **38**

Part V Windfall Profit Tax Summary

39 Windfall profit tax credit or refund received in 1987 (see Instructions) ... **39**
40 Windfall profit tax withheld in 1987 (see Instructions) ... **40** ( )
41 Combine amounts on lines 39 and 40. Enter the total here and include in line 42 below ... **41**

Part VI Summary

42 TOTAL income or (loss). Combine lines 29, 33, 37, 38, and 41. Enter total here and on Form 1040, line 17 ▶ **42** ⟨1849⟩
43 Farmers and fishermen: Enter your share of GROSS FARMING AND FISHING INCOME applicable to Parts I, II, and III (see Instructions) ... **43**

Real Estate Investments

Under Tax Reform, holding real estate is regarded the same way as other investment activities. At-risk rules limit your deductible losses to the combined total of the following items:

1. Your cash contributions
2. The adjusted basis of your property contributions
3. The amount you borrowed (only to the extent that you have personal liability or pledge other personal assets as security).

There is an exception for "qualified nonrecourse financing" (financing secured only by the property itself). In order to qualify, the nonrecourse financing must be:

1. Secured only by the real property
2. An actual debt (not disguised equity)
3. Obtained from a qualified lender (bank, savings and loan, or a related party such as the seller of the investment, if it is commercially reasonable and similar to loans made to unrelated parties).

Passive Loss Rules

1. Rental activities are considered passive regardless of the participation of the taxpayer, except that up to $25,000 in losses is allowed if there is active participation.

    Losses are treated as allowed before credits. If more than one property is involved, the allocation over all loss properties is done on a pro rata basis with respect to losses (or credits) for each.

    For example, if you have losses of $12,000 from one activity and losses of $48,000 from another, under the pro rata allocation rule (using the full $25,000 allowed), $5,000 (20 percent of $25,000) would be applied to the first activity and $20,000 (80 percent of $25,000) to the second, against income from passive activities.

    To begin, determine whether an allocation is required by determining net income and loss from all rental activities involving active participation. If there is a net loss, net passive income from other activities is applied against the loss first to determine the amount eligible for the $25,000 allowance.

    The bottom line is that if you have a gain in one rental activity of $15,000 and a loss in another of $15,000, simply offset the two, and you have no further loss against the $25,000 allowance.

    If you have losses from nonrental passive activities, and the losses from all combined passive activities exceeds income from the passive activities, no part of the $25,000 allowance may be used.
2. Losses and credits from nonrental activities are not deductible in excess of income unless you materially participate in the activity. Involvement throughout the year must be regular, continuous, and substantial.
3. Losses disallowed may be claimed in full in the year an activity is sold or disposed of. If an abandonment results in a fully taxable loss, it is treated as a disposition.

    Suspended losses connected with an installment sale are allowed in the ratio that the gain realized each year has to the total gain on the sale.
4. Payments to a retiring partner (even a limited one) that represent payment for

Supplemental Income: Schedule E   111

services (current or prior) are not considered passive income, and may not be used to offset losses and credits from passive activities.

Form 8582 (Passive Activity Loss Limitations)

If you invested in limited partnerships and other tax shelters you will be required to use Form 8582 to calculate any losses you may deduct in connection with your investment. (This form is also for estates, trusts, and personal service corporations that have passive activity losses.) A passive activity is one in which you did not materially participate which involves the conduct of a trade, business, or a real estate business that is presumptively passive.

A working interest in oil and gas property is not a passive activity whether you participated or not. See page 156 with regard to interest on your residence, page 211 regarding low-income housing, page 106 regarding rental activities, and other information throughout this book pertaining to passive activity losses in particular, to determine which activities would be applicable to this Form 8582.

This form may affect various other forms, such as Schedule A (Itemized Deductions), Schedule C (Profit or Loss from Business or Profession), Schedule D (Capital Gains and Losses), Schedule F (Farm Income and Expenses), Form 4797 (Sales or Exchanges of Assets), Form 4935 (Farm Rental Income and Expenses), Form 4952 (Investment Interest Expense Deduction), Form 6198 (Computation of Deductible Loss), Form 6251 (Alternative Minimum Tax), and Form 6252 (Installment Sale Income Computation).

Form 8582—Part I

You only need to complete this part thru line 1g if you participate actively in rental real estate activities. Use the worksheet before completing Part I.

Worksheet for lines 1a, 1b, 1d, and 1e (Keep for your records)

Name of Activity	Form or Schedule To be Reported on	Activities acquired before 10-23-86		Activities acquired after 10-22-86	
		(a) Income line 1a	(b) (Loss) line 1b	(c) Income line 1d	(d) (Loss) line 1e
Totals. Enter on lines 1a, 1b, 1d and 1e of Form 8582 .. ▶					

Lines 2a, 2b, 2d, and 2e.—These lines are used for rental real estate activities without active participation, other rental activities, and all other passive activities such as a trade or business in which you did not materially participate. Lines 2a and 2b are used for activities acquired before 10-23-86 and lines 2d and 2e are used for activities acquired after 10-22-86.

Enter the total in columns (a) through (d) on the corresponding lines of Form 8582 and then complete lines 2c, 2f, and 2g.

Worksheet 2 for lines 2a, 2b, 2d, and 2e (Keep for your records)

Name of Activity	Form or Schedule To be Reported on	Activities acquired before 10-23-86		Activities acquired after 10-22-86	
		(a) Income line 2a	(b) (Loss) line 2b	(c) Income line 2d	(d) (Loss) line 2e
Totals. Enter on lines 2a, 2b, 2d and 2e of Form 8582 .. ▶					

Under Part I, lines 1a (net income) and 1b (net loss) are for activities acquired before 10-23-86. Line 1c is the combination of these two amounts.

Lines 1d (income) and 1e (loss) are for activities acquired after 10-22-86. Line 1c is the combination of these two amounts.

Line 1g: Combine lines 1c and 1f and enter the result here.

You need to complete Part I, lines 1a through 1g only if you have rental real estate activities *without* active participation or any other passive activities in which you did not materially participate.

Lines 2a (income) and 2b (loss) pertain to activities acquired before 10-23-86. Combine these two amounts and put the result on line 2c.

Lines 2d (income) and 2e (loss) are for activities acquired after 10-22-86. Combine these two amounts and put the result on line 2f.

Line 2g is the combination of lines 2c and 2f.

On line 3 enter the result of combining lines 1g and 2g. If this figure is net income, add losses from lines 1b, 1e, 2b, and 2e, and enter the result on line 19. All passive losses are allowed.

You may report the amount of each individual loss entered on the two worksheets in columns 1b, 1d, 2b, and 2d on the form or schedule you usually use to report them.

If line 3 is a *loss,* and line 1g is a loss, complete Part II (line 4). If line 3 and line 1g are not both losses, place a zero on line 9 and go to line 10 (skip over Part II).

Part II

Enter the amount from line 1g or from line 3, whichever is smaller (loss), on line 4.

On line 5 enter $150,000 (or $75,000 if married filing separately).

Calculate for line 6: In order to arrive at your modified adjusted gross income, you start with your adjusted gross income and include net income or loss other than those from passive activities, and not including taxable Social Security and railroad retirement payments, deductible contributions to IRA's or employee pension plans, or any amount not allowable as a deduction in computing adjusted gross income. When you arrive at your modified adjusted gross income, put the resulting figure on line 6.

If line 6 is equal to or more than line 5, enter a zero on line 9 and proceed to line 10. If line 6 is less than line 5, subtract line 6 from line 5 and put the result on line 7.

Multiply line 7 by 50 percent.

Place the resulting figure on line 8 *but not over* $25,000 (not over $12,500 if married filing separately and lived apart for the entire year).

On line 9 put the figure from line 4 or line 8, whichever is smaller.

Part III

Line 10. Combine lines 1c and 2c and enter the result on line 10. If the result is net income or zero, skip to line 16. If the result is net loss, continue to line 11.

Line 11a. If line 9 is zero, enter zero here and go to line 12. Otherwise, make no entry on this line.

Line 11b. If line 1c either has income, no entry, or is a zero, put zero on line 11b and go to line 12. If none of these apply, enter on 11b the smaller of line 1c or line 8.

Line 12. Subtract line 11 from line 10 and put the amount here.

Line 13. Subtract line 9 from line 3 and place the amount here.

Line 14. Enter line 12 or line 13, whichever is smaller.

Line 15. Multiply line 14 by 65 percent and enter the result on line 15.

Form 8582 — Passive Activity Loss Limitations

Form 8582
Department of the Treasury
Internal Revenue Service

▶ See separate instructions.
▶ Attach to Forms 1040, 1041, 1041S, or 1120 (Personal service corporation).

OMB No. 1545-xxxx
1987
Attachment Sequence No. 88

Name(s) as shown on return: DOUGH

Identifying number: 329 04 1040

Part I — Computation of 1987 Passive Activity Loss
Caution: See the worksheets on page 4 of the instructions before completing Part I.

Rental Real Estate Activities With Active Participation (See the definition of active participation under **Rental Activities** on page 1 of the instructions.)

Activities acquired before 10-23-86:
- **1a** Activities with net income
- **1b** Activities with net loss
- **1c** Combine lines 1a and 1b

Activities acquired after 10-22-86:
- **1d** Activities with net income
- **1e** Activities with net loss
- **1f** Combine lines 1d and 1e
- **1g** Net Income or (loss). Combine lines 1c and 1f

All Other Passive Activities (See **All Other Passive Activities** on page 3 of the instructions.)

Activities acquired before 10-23-86:
- **2a** Activities with net income
- **2b** Activities with net loss
- **2c** Combine lines 2a and 2b

Activities acquired after 10-22-86:
- **2d** Activities with net income
- **2e** Activities with net loss
- **2f** Combine lines 2d and 2e
- **2g** Net income or (loss). Combine lines 2c and 2f

3 Combine lines 1g and 2g. If the result is net income, see the instructions for line 3. If this line and line 1g are both losses, go to line 4; otherwise, enter -0- on line 9 and go to line 10

Part II — Computation of the Special Allowance for Rental Real Estate With Active Participation
Note: See page 4 of the instructions for how to treat numbers as if they were all positive in Parts II and III.

4 Enter the smaller of the loss on line 1g or the loss on line 3

5 Enter $150,000 ($75,000 if married filing separately and you lived apart for the entire year)

6 Enter modified adjusted gross income, but not less than -0-, (see instructions). If line 6 is equal to or greater than line 5, skip lines 7 and 8, enter -0- on line 9, and then go to line 10. Otherwise, go to line 7.

7 Subtract line 6 from line 5

8 Multiply line 7 by 50% (.5). Do not enter more than $25,000 ($12,500 if married filing separately and you lived apart for the entire year)

9 Enter the smaller of line 4 or line 8

Part III — Computation of Passive Activity Loss Allowed

10 Combine lines 1c and 2c and enter the result. If the result is -0- or net income, skip to line 16

11a If line 9 is -0-, enter -0- and go to line 12.

11b If line 1c shows income, has no entry or shows -0-, enter -0- and go to line 12; otherwise, enter the smaller of line 1c or line 8

12 Subtract line 11 from line 10. (See instructions.)

13 Subtract line 9 from line 3. (See instructions.)

14 Enter the smaller of line 12 or line 13

15 Multiply line 14 by 65% (.65) and enter the result

16 Enter the amount from line 9

17 **Passive Activity Loss Allowed for 1987.** Add lines 15 and 16

18 Add the income, if any, on lines 1a, 1d, 2a, and 2d and enter the result

19 **Total losses allowed from all passive activities for 1987.** Add lines 17 and 18. See page 4 of the instructions to see how to report the losses on your tax return

Proof of August 13, 1987

Line 16. Enter the amount from line 9 on line 16.

Line 17. Add lines 15 and 16 and this is your Passive Activity Loss Allowed for 1987.

Line 18. If there is income on lines 1a, 1d, 2a, and 2d, add the income together and enter the result on line 18.

Line 19. Add line 78 to line 18 and enter the result on line 19. If only one activity with a loss is shown on Form 8582, the amount on line 19 will be the actual loss allowed for the year. Enter this amount on the form on which you normally report it, such as Schedule C or E.

The unallowed amount is the loss shown on lines 1b, 1e, 2b, or 2e minus the amount on line 19. Keep a record of this amount and the activity to which it belongs so you can take the loss when it becomes deductible in a future year.

Line	Tax Law	Pay Less Tax Legally
Part I Lines 4, 5	**Rent and Royalty Income or Loss** If you have rental property, you must report the total rents but may then deduct depreciation and property expenses. If you have a personal apartment in a building that you also rent to others, you are allowed to deduct only the building expenses applicable to the rental portion. You may not deduct the personal expenses of your own apartment.	• If you receive security deposits that will be refunded at the end of the lease and do not apply to the last month's rental, those deposits are not taxable and should be deposited in a separate bank account. • If your royalties were from the sale of a patent or invention, you may be entitled to long-term capital-gain treatment. See page 97.
Lines 6–11	Enter amount. If one spouse manages rental property, the other spouse may pay him or her a salary (free of Social Security), which may be sheltered in an IRA.	• See page 211 for a discussion of the credit on oil royalties. • See page 135 for limitations on IRA contributions.
Line 12	**Mortgage Interest Paid to Financial Institution** Form 1098 (to be provided by financial institutions) will have all names of persons listed on the mortgage but will be sent to the "main" person on the mortgage. That "main" person should then attach a statement to Form 1098 listing names and addresses of others named in the mortgage.	

Line	Tax Law	Pay Less Tax Legally
Lines 13–19	**Rental Expenses** If you own rental property, you are entitled to deduct all rental expenses, including interest, real estate taxes, insurance, utilities, and repairs. If 2 people own the same residence and one makes rent payments to the other, the second person can deduct depreciation and expenses, provided: 1. The tenant (owner) lives at the property full-time (as a principal residence) 2. A fair rental is charged for the use of half the residence. **Repairs versus Improvements?** Repairs are treated differently under ACRS guidelines than they were previously. A distinction between a repair and a capital improvement must be made in considering the deductibility of an item, and any amounts qualified as capital expenditures must be written off under the ACRS guidelines. The determination as to deductibility is based upon the nature of the repair and the expected length of service. If the cost of a repair is large in proportion to the value of the property, it may be considered a capital improvement.	• If you convert your home into a rental unit, you may claim depreciation and perhaps a loss on the sale. • In one case, a taxpayer bought a house in a resort area. He rented it out at a $9,000 loss each year, hoping to make up for the loss in appreciation. The IRS said that because he did not intend to make a profit on rentals, no claim of loss could be made. The courts felt otherwise: they allowed the expenses of maintaining investment property for future income. However, in another case, a couple could not sell their former home and rented it out on a month-to-month basis for 8 months until it was sold. Since there was no profit motive, no deduction was allowed for depreciation or other operating expenses. See page 294 for further discussion. • A factory building had a leaky roof that resulted from a structural defect and cost $20,000 to repair. The Tax Court noted that since the work merely restored the building to normal operating conditions, the cost was a repair and fully deductible. • The cost of fixing up an apartment for rent is deductible, even if the apartment is never rented. An owner who showed an apartment in a high-crime neighborhood and had no success in finding a tenant was still allowed the deduction for redecorating. • If you have children doing janitorial or repair work on rental property, keep detailed records. Pay them and take a tax deduction as casual labor.

Line	Tax Law	Pay Less Tax Legally
	Renting to a Relative If you rent property to relatives who pay a fair rental (up to 20 percent less than the market rate), all deductions (including depreciation) are allowed. Large gifts made to the related tenant to pay the rent are the only exception. The property does not have to be the relatives' principal residence. The Tax Court feels that relatives make better tenants and relieve you from having to pay a realtor to manage the property.	• In one case, parents lived on one side of a duplex and rented the other side to their daughter. Expenses and depreciation amounted to twice the fair rental the daughter paid. The courts nevertheless felt that a profit motive existed—that the property would increase in value over the long run—and allowed the parents to deduct expenses. • Married couples living apart, take note. If the wife lives in the jointly owned home and pays rent to the husband for half of the home, the husband can depreciate the home over 27½ years and write off all property expenses—even if they file jointly.

Depreciation (Line 21)

Depreciation is the recovery of the cost of an asset over an assigned period. Any asset that will be in existence after one year must be depreciated rather than expensed in the year purchased. Land will presumably always be in existence and is not subject to depreciation, so any land values must be removed from the cost of property before any depreciation is figured. Use Form 4562 to compute depreciation.

New Depreciation Rules under Tax Reform

The 19-year accelerated depreciation is replaced by 31.5-year life (for commercial property) and 27.5-year life (residential) straight-line depreciation (a 66 percent increase for

15-Year Depreciation Tables
(For property placed in service before March 15, 1984)

15-year real property low-income housing—

Year	\multicolumn{12}{c}{Use the column for the month of taxable year placed in service}
	1	2	3	4	5	6	7	8	9	10	11	12
1st	13%	12%	11%	10%	9%	8%	7%	6%	4%	3%	2%	1%
2nd	12%	12%	12%	12%	12%	12%	12%	13%	13%	13%	13%	13%
3rd	10%	10%	10%	10%	11%	11%	11%	11%	11%	11%	11%	11%
4th	9%	9%	9%	9%	9%	9%	9%	9%	10%	10%	10%	10%

15-year real property other than low-income housing—

Year	\multicolumn{12}{c}{Use the column for the month of taxable year placed in service}
	1	2	3	4	5	6	7	8	9	10	11	12
1st	12%	11%	10%	9%	8%	7%	6%	5%	4%	3%	2%	1%
2nd	10%	10%	11%	11%	11%	11%	11%	11%	11%	11%	11%	12%
3rd	9%	9%	9%	9%	10%	10%	10%	10%	10%	10%	10%	10%
4th	8%	8%	8%	8%	8%	8%	9%	9%	9%	9%	9%	9%

The One-Minute Taxman: Rental Income and Expenses

A variety of rental expenses, including depreciation, can be used to offset rental property income—and perhaps turn rental income into a tax loss.

Look over the checklist of deductible rental expenses and place a check in the box for each expense that you incurred last year. Enter specific dollar amounts from your canceled checks and receipts.

Total all deductible rental expenses from this worksheet and enter that figure on Schedule E.

Rental Expenses	Amount	Rental Expenses	Amount
☐ Abandonment losses	____	☐ Insurance	____
☐ Accounting and legal fees	____	☐ Interest on mortgage	____
☐ Advertising (to attract tenants)	____	☐ Lawn and landscaping	____
		☐ Legal fees	____
☐ Alterations (not capital repairs)	____	☐ Losses	____
		☐ Maintenance expenses	____
☐ Appliances, repairs to	____	☐ Management costs	____
☐ Auto expenses (visiting property; running errands)	____	☐ Moving of equipment	____
		☐ Night security	____
		☐ Office supplies	____
☐ Banking charges	____	☐ Painting and decorating	____
☐ Bookkeeping	____	☐ Plumbing repairs	____
☐ Cleaning supplies and services	____	☐ Reconditioning	____
		☐ Record-keeping	____
☐ Collection fees	____	☐ Redecorating	____
☐ Damages to property	____	☐ Refuse and scavenger services	____
☐ Depreciation on property	____		
☐ Destruction, casualty losses	____	☐ Repairs (maintenance)	____
		☐ Safe-deposit box rental	____
☐ Electricity, cost of	____	☐ Salaries	____
☐ Excavating	____	☐ Security systems	____
☐ Fire extinguishers (cost and inspection of)	____	☐ Sprinkler system	____
		☐ Stationery and postage	____
☐ Furniture	____	☐ Storage	____
☐ Gardening, lawn mower, plants	____	☐ Taxes (real estate and personal property)	____
☐ Gas, cost of	____	☐ Telephone calls	____
☐ Hauling	____	☐ Water and sewer	____
☐ Heating, cost of	____	Total	____
☐ Hot-water heater (to be depreciated)	____		

18-Year Real Estate Depreciation Tables
(For property placed in service between March 15, 1984, and May 8, 1985)

18-year real property—(no mid-month convention)

Year	Use the column for the month of taxable year placed in service

Year	1	2	3	4	5	6	7	8	9	10	11	12
1st	10%	9%	8%	7%	6%	6%	5%	4%	3%	2%	2%	1%
2nd	9%	9%	9%	9%	9%	9%	9%	9%	9%	10%	10%	10%
3rd	8%	8%	8%	8%	8%	8%	8%	8%	9%	9%	9%	9%

18-year real property—(mid-month convention)

Year	1	2	3	4	5	6	7	8	9	10	11	12
1st	9%	9%	8%	7%	6%	5%	4%	4%	3%	2%	1%	0.4%
2nd	9%	9%	9%	9%	9%	9%	9%	9%	9%	10%	10%	10%
3rd	8%	8%	8%	8%	8%	8%	8%	8%	9%	9%	9%	9%

19-Year Real Estate Depreciation Tables
(For property placed in service between May 8, 1985, and December 31, 1986)

19-year real property—(no mid-month convention)

Year	1	2	3	4	5	6	7	8	9	10	11	12
1st	8.8%	8.1%	7.3%	6.5%	5.8%	5.0%	4.2%	3.5%	2.7%	1.9%	1.1%	0.4%
2nd	8.4%	8.5%	8.5%	8.6%	8.7%	8.8%	8.8%	8.9%	9.0%	9.0%	9.1%	9.2%
3rd	7.6%	7.7%	7.7%	7.8%	7.9%	7.9%	8.0%	8.1%	8.1%	8.2%	8.3%	8.3%
4th	6.9%	7.0%	7.0%	7.1%	7.1%	7.2%	7.3%	7.3%	7.4%	7.4%	7.5%	7.6%
5th	6.3%	6.3%	6.4%	6.4%	6.5%	6.5%	6.6%	6.6%	6.7%	6.8%	6.8%	6.9%

commercial and 45 percent for residential). These new rules cover property acquired after 1986.

If you have been claiming depreciation over 15, 18, or 19 years on existing property, continue using those tables. The 27½- and 31½-year lives affect only property purchased after January 1, 1987. (As of the date of publication, the IRS had not released the 27½- and 31½-year tables. Please contact the IRS for these tables.)

Depletion (Line 21)

If you have investments in assets such as oil or gas, you are permitted to recover your cost through the depletion method, either through cost depletion or percentage depletion. However, percentage depletion is not allowed for purchased producing properties, while a developed property (one currently in production) is eligible.

You can change depletion methods from year to year to get the largest possible tax deduction. It is usually best to use cost depletion until you recover your cost, then switch to percentage depletion.

Cost Depletion

To recover your costs through the cost-depletion method, divide your original cost in the property by the estimated number of units to be produced (in the case of oil, state units in terms of barrels). Divide your cost by the number of units in order to arrive at a per-unit cost, and multiply this per-unit cost by the number of units removed during the year. For example: You paid $10,000 for an interest in an oil well, and the geologist estimates that 100,000 barrels remain. During the year, 20,000 barrels are taken out. Your depletion deduction is $2,000 ($10,000 ÷ 100,000 = 10¢ per barrel; 10¢ × 20,000 barrels = $2,000).

If you have oil investments, find out if any amounts were spent for intangible drilling costs (they are deductible). However, if the oil or gas property was disposed of, a portion of the intangible drilling costs may have to be recaptured as income.

Percentage Depletion

The alternative to cost depletion is percentage depletion: a fixed percentage of royalty income is taken for the particular mineral. For example, during the year you received $1,000 from a producing oil well, your depletion deduction would be $220 (22 percent of $1,000).

The current depletion rates are:

Oil and gas	15% or 22% (see explanation below)
Sulfur and uranium	22%
Asbestos, zinc, lead, nickel	22%
Metallic and other minerals	14%
Domestic gold, silver, oil, shale, copper, iron ore	15%

The depletion rate for regulated natural gas sold under fixed contract is 22 percent; the rate for independent producers and royalty owners, with limitations based on average daily production of 1,000 barrels of oil and 6 million cubic feet of gas, is 15 percent. Advance royalties paid on gas and oil leases are not eligible for percentage depletion except to the extent that oil or gas is produced during the year the royalty is paid. Oil and gas lease bonuses are not eligible for percentage depletion, since they are not paid for out of deductions.

Form 4562 — Depreciation and Amortization

Form **4562**
Department of the Treasury
Internal Revenue Service (3)

OMB No. 1545-0172
Attachment Sequence No. **67**

▶ See separate instructions.
▶ Attach this form to your return.

Name(s) as shown on return: DOUGH
Identifying number: 329-04-1040

Business or activity to which this form relates:

Part I — Depreciation
(Do not use this part for automobiles, certain other vehicles, computers, and property used for entertainment, recreation, or amusement. Instead, use Part III.)
See instructions under Items You Should Note for new rules for certain assets placed in service after July 31, 1986.

Section A.—Election To Expense Recovery Property (Section 179)

(a) Class of property	(b) Cost	(c) Expense deduction
1		

2 Listed property—Enter total from Part III, Section A, column (h).

3 Total (see instructions for limitations). (Partnerships or S corporations—see the Schedule K and Schedule K-1 Instructions of Form 1065 or 1120S)

Section B.—Depreciation of Recovery Property

(a) Class of property	(b) Date placed in service	(c) Basis for depreciation (Business use only—see instructions)	(d) Recovery period	(e) Method of figuring depreciation	(f) Deduction

4 Accelerated Cost Recovery System (ACRS) (see instructions): *For assets placed in service ONLY during tax year beginning in 1986*

a 3-year property
b 5-year property
c 10-year property
d 15-year public utility property
e Low-income housing
f 15-year real property
g 18-year real property
h 19-year real property

5 Listed property—Enter total from Part III, Section A, column (g).

6 ACRS deduction for assets placed in service prior to 1986 (see instructions) .... **800 (E)**

Section C.—Depreciation of Nonrecovery Property

7 Property subject to section 168(e)(2) election (see instructions).

8 Other depreciation (see instructions) .... **600 (C)**

Section D.—Summary

9 Depreciation from Form 4562A (see instructions).

10 Total (add deductions on lines 3 through 9). Enter here and on the Depreciation line of your return (Partnerships and S corporations—Do NOT include any amounts entered on line 3.) **1400**

Part II — Amortization

(a) Description of property	(b) Date acquired	(c) Cost or other basis	(d) Code section	(e) Amortization period or percentage	(f) Amortization for this year

1 Amortization for property placed in service **only** during tax year beginning in 1986

2 Amortization for property placed in service prior to 1986.

3 Total. Enter here and on Other Deductions or Other Expenses line of your return.

Part III — Automobiles, Certain Other Vehicles, Computers, and Property Used for Entertainment, Recreation, or Amusement (Listed Property).

If you are using the standard mileage rate or deducting vehicle lease expense, complete columns (a) through (d) of Section A, all of Section B, and Section C if applicable.

Section A.—Depreciation (If automobiles and other listed property placed in service after June 18, 1984, are used 50% or less in a trade or business, the Section 179 deduction is not allowed and depreciation must be taken using the straight line method over 5 years. For other limitations, see instructions.)

Do you have evidence to support the business use claimed? ☐ Yes ☐ No   If yes, is the evidence written? ☐ Yes ☐ No

(a) Type of property (list vehicles first)	(b) Date placed in service	(c) Business use percentage (%)	(d) Cost or other basis (see instructions for leased property)	(e) Basis for depreciation (Business use only—see instructions)	(f) Depreciation method and recovery period	(g) Depreciation deduction	(h) Section 179 expense

Total (Enter here and on line 2, page 1.) . . . .

Total (Enter here and on line 5, page 1.) . . . .

Section B.—Information Regarding Use of Vehicles

Complete this section as follows, if you deduct expenses for vehicles:

- Always complete this section for vehicles used by a sole proprietor, partner, or other more than 5% owner or related person.
- If you provided vehicles to employees, first answer the questions in Section C to see if you meet an exception to completing this section for those items.

	Vehicle 1	Vehicle 2	Vehicle 3	Vehicle 4	Vehicle 5	Vehicle 6
1 Total miles driven during the year . . .						
2 Total business miles driven during the year						
3 Total commuting miles driven during the year.						
4 Total other personal (noncommuting) miles driven						

	Yes	No	Yes	No	Yes	No	Yes	No	Yes	No	Yes	No
5 Was the vehicle available for personal use during off-duty hours? . . .												
6 Was the vehicle used primarily by a more than 5% owner or related person? . . .												
7 Is another vehicle available for personal use?. . .												

Section C.—Questions for Employers Who Provide Vehicles for Use by Employees.

*(Answer these questions to determine if you meet an exception to completing Section B. **Note:** Section B must always be completed for vehicles used by sole proprietors, partners, or other more than 5% owners or related persons.)*

	Yes	No
8 Do you maintain a written policy statement that prohibits all personal use of vehicles, including commuting, by your employees?		
9 Do you maintain a written policy statement that prohibits personal use of vehicles, except commuting, by your employees? (See instructions for vehicles used by corporate officers, directors, or 1% or more owners.)		
10 Do you treat all use of vehicles by employees as personal use?		
11 Do you provide more than five vehicles to your employees and retain the information received from your employees concerning the use of the vehicles? . .		
12 Do you meet the requirements concerning fleet vehicles or qualified automobile demonstration use (see instructions)?		

Note: *If your answer to 8, 9, 10, 11, or 12 is "Yes," you need not complete Section B for the covered vehicles.*

7

ADJUSTMENTS TO INCOME
- **REIMBURSED EMPLOYEE BUSINESS EXPENSES**
- **IRA DEDUCTION**
- **SELF-EMPLOYED HEALTH INSURANCE DEDUCTION**
- **KEOGH RETIREMENT PLAN AND SELF-EMPLOYED SEP DEDUCTION**
- **PENALTY ON EARLY WITHDRAWAL OF SAVINGS**
- **ALIMONY PAID**

After you combine your total income from all sources, you are permitted to take a tax deduction for certain expenses regardless of whether or not you itemize your deductions. (See lines 23–28 on Form 1040).

1. *Reimbursed Business Expenses* (line 23): An employee is permitted to deduct expenses under a reimbursement or other expense allowance arrangement on Form 2106. All other unreimbursed employee business expenses must be claimed as an itemized deduction subject to the 2 percent floor. See page 184 for a complete discussion.
2. *Your IRA Deduction* (line 24a) and *Spouse's IRA Deduction* (line 24b): You are permitted to deduct an IRA if you are not covered under a company plan or have income below certain levels. See page 132 for a complete explanation.
3. *Self-Employed Health Insurance Deduction* (line 25): For the first time, self-employeds are permitted to deduct 25 percent of their health insurance premiums without having to lump them in with other medical expenses.
4. *Keogh Retirement Plan and Self-Employed SEP Deduction* (line 26): Enter any contributions to the plan.
5. *Penalty on Early Withdrawal of Savings* (line 27): If you incur a penalty on early withdrawal of a certificate, enter that amount.
6. *Alimony Paid* (line 28): Be sure to enter recipient's last name and Social Security number. For a complete discussion of alimony deductions under Tax Reform, see page 146.

Form 2106

Changes on Form 2106

Only reimbursed travel and entertainment will remain fully deductible on Form 2106. All other expenses—including those incurred by outside salesmen—must be itemized as miscellaneous expenses subject to a 2 percent floor on line 20 of Schedule A.

Entertainment and meal expenses must be separately reported in Column B. If an employee wishes to deduct those expenses, he or she must take into account employer reimbursements and the 20 percent of business meals and entertainment that are considered personal and nondeductible.

Report any excess reimbursement as wages on Form 1040, line 7.

Reimbursed employee business expenses from Form 2106 are to be claimed as an adjustment to income on page 1, line 23 (but only to the extent of the reimbursement).

Any unreimbursed business expenses from Form 2106 are to be treated as miscellaneous itemized deductions on line 20, Schedule A, and are subject to the 2 percent floor.

Form 2106: *Line-by-Line Instructions*

Complete Part II (self-explanatory) first and enter the resulting amount in Part I, Step 1. In Part I there are two columns: one for meals and entertainment and the other for vehicle expenses, parking, tolls, travel, and other business expenses.

List expenses as itemized on lines 1–5, and enter the total on line 6. If you were not reimbursed for any of these expenses, skip lines 7 through 13 and enter the amount from line 6 on line 14.

In Step 2, list reimbursements for expenses in Step I. Subtract line 7 from line 6 and enter the result on line 10. If line 7 is greater than line 6, you must report excess reimbursements on Form 1040, line 7. Line 11 is for reimbursements shown on Form W-2 (or Form 1099). On line 12, list whichever is smaller, line 10 or 11. Be sure to use both columns as you go through the form line by line.

Add line 12 from Column A to line 12 of Column B, and enter the total on line 13 and on Form 1040. This amount represents your fully deductible reimbursed expenses.

Step 4 deals with miscellaneous deductions subject to the 2 percent limitation. Subtract line 12 from line 10 and enter the result on line 14. If the result is zero in both columns of line 14, stop here. If not, multiply line 14 by 20 percent (Column B) and subtract line 15 from 14 and enter the result on line 16. Add the two columns on line 16 and enter the resulting amount on line 17 and on Schedule A, Form 1040, line 20 as a miscellaneous deduction (subject to the 2 percent limitation along with other miscellaneous deductions).

Line	Tax Law	Pay Less Tax Legally
Part I Lines 1–5	**Employee Business Expenses** If, as an employee, you incurred expenses other than reimbursed auto or travel, you must itemize in order to claim the expense. You may deduct $2,560 of the cost of a business car and up to $10,000 for equipment, fixtures, or machinery, with the balance subject to regular depreciation. You must fill in the top of Form 4562, specifying to which items the election ap-	• See page 184 for a discussion of educational expenses and other nonreimbursed business expenses. • Form 2106 now contains a check-off box asking if you have complied with record-keeping regulations. If you check "no," you may lose your deduction; if you check "yes" but fail to keep records, you

Form 2106 — Employee Business Expenses

Form 2106
Department of the Treasury
Internal Revenue Service

Employee Business Expenses
► See separate instructions.
► Attach to Form 1040.

OMB No. 1545-0139
1987
Attachment Sequence No. 54

Your name: DOUGH
Social security number: 329:04:1040
Occupation in which expenses were incurred: EXECUTIVE - SALES

Part I — Employee Business Expenses

STEP 1 — Enter Your Expenses

		Column A — Other than Meals and Entertainment	Column B — Meals and Entertainment
1	Vehicle expense from Part II, line 15 or line 22	3682	
2	Parking fees, tolls, and local transportation, including train, bus, etc.	260	
3	Travel expense while away from home, including lodging, airplane, car rental, etc. Do not include meals and entertainment	384	
4	Business expenses not included in lines 1 through 3. Do not include meals and entertainment	618	
5	Meals and entertainment expenses. See Instructions		381
6	Add lines 1 through 5 and enter the total expenses here	4944	381

Note: If you were not reimbursed for any expenses in step 1, skip lines 7 through 13 and enter the amount from line 6 on line 14.

STEP 2 — Figure Any Excess Reimbursements to Report in Income

7 Reimbursements for the expenses listed in step 1 that your employer did not report to you on Form W-2 or Form 1099

Note: If, in **both columns**, line 6 is more than line 7, skip lines 8 and 9 and go to line 10. You do not have excess reimbursements.

8 Subtract line 6 from line 7. If zero or less, enter zero
9 Add the amounts on line 8 of both columns and enter the total here. Also add this amount to any shown on Form 1040, line 7. This is an **excess reimbursement** reportable as income ▶

STEP 3 — Figure Fully Deductible Reimbursed Expenses

10 Subtract line 7 from line 6. If zero or less, enter zero
11 Reimbursements for the expenses listed in step 1 that your employer separately identified to you as a reimbursement on Form W-2 or Form 1099

Note: The amount entered on line 11 should also have been reported as income on Form 1040, line 7.

12 Enter the smaller of line 10 or line 11
13 Add the amounts on line 12 of both columns. Enter here and on Form 1040, line 23. This is your **fully deductible reimbursed expenses** ▶

STEP 4 — Figure Expenses to Deduct as an Itemized Deduction on Schedule A (Form 1040)

		Col A	Col B
14	Subtract line 12 from line 10. If zero or less, enter zero	4944	381
15	Enter 20% of line 14, Column B		76
16	Subtract line 15 from line 14	4944	305
17	Add the amounts on line 16 of both columns and enter the total here. Also enter the total on Schedule A (Form 1040), line 20. This is the amount to deduct as a **miscellaneous itemized deduction**, subject to a 2% limitation ▶		5249

Note: If **both columns** of line 14 contain a zero, **do not complete the rest of Part I.**

Proof of August 13, 1987

Page 2

Part II — Vehicle Expenses (Use either your actual expenses or the standard mileage rate.)

Section A. — General Information

		Vehicle 1	Vehicle 2
1	Enter the date vehicle was placed in service	1/1/86	/ /
2	Total mileage vehicle was used during 1987	19775 miles	miles
3	Miles included on line 2 that vehicle was used for business	17797 miles	miles
4	Percent of business use (divide line 3 by line 2)	90 %	%
5	Average daily round trip commuting distance	miles	miles
6	Miles included on line 2 that vehicle was used for commuting	miles	miles
7	Other personal mileage (subtract line 6 plus line 3 from line 2)	1978 miles	miles

8 Do you (or your spouse) have another vehicle available for personal purposes? ... ☒ Yes ☐ No

9 If your employer provided you with a vehicle, is personal use during off duty hours permitted? ... ☐ Yes ☐ No ☒ Not applicable

10 Do you have evidence to support your deduction? ☒ Yes ☐ No. If yes, is the evidence written? ☒ Yes ☐ No

Section B. — Standard Mileage Rate (Do not use this section unless you own the vehicle.)

11	Enter the smaller of Part II, line 3 or 15,000 miles	11	15000 miles
12	Subtract line 11 from Part II, line 3	12	2797 miles
13	Multiply line 11 by 22.5¢ (.21) (see instructions for a fully depreciated vehicle)	13	3375
14	Multiply line 12 by 11¢ (.11)	14	307
15	Add lines 13 and 14. Enter total here and on Part I, line 1	15	3682

Section C. — Actual Expenses

		Vehicle 1	Vehicle 2
16	Gasoline, oil, repairs, vehicle insurance, etc.		
17	Vehicle rentals		
18	Value of employer-provided vehicle (applies only if included on Form W-2 at 100% fair rental value, see instructions)		
19	Add lines 16 through 18		
20	Multiply line 19 by the percentage on Part II, line 4		
21	Depreciation from Section D, column (f) (see instructions)		
22	Add lines 20 and 21. Enter total here and on Part I, line 1		

Section D. — Depreciation of Vehicles
(Depreciation can only be claimed for a vehicle you own. If a vehicle is used 50 percent or less in a trade or business, the Section 179 deduction is not allowed and depreciation must be taken using the straight line method over 5 years. For other limitations, see instructions.)

	Cost or other basis (a)	Basis for depreciation (Business use only—see instructions) (b)	Method of figuring depreciation (c)	Depreciation deduction (d)	Section 179 expense (e)	Total column (d) + column (e) (enter in Section C, line 21) (f)
Vehicle 1						
Vehicle 2						

Proof of August 13, 1987

Line	Tax Law	Pay Less Tax Legally
	plies. Any future gain on the sale of these expensed assets is treated as ordinary income (to the extent of the amount expensed). Outside salesmen are permitted to deduct only reimbursed business expenses from gross income in much the same way as someone who owns his own business and files Schedule C. Reimbursed expenses are treated as itemized deductions and are subject to a 2 percent floor.	may be charged with penalties in case of an audit. ● One who is not an outside salesman but still incurs business expenses (e.g., teachers, musicians) is expected to deduct only reimbursed travel expenses from gross income; any other business expenses must be deducted as miscellaneous itemized deductions subject to the 2 percent floor.
	Temporary Away-from-Home Deductions It has been generally accepted that a stay away from your tax home for less than one year is temporary, and a longer stay is classified as indefinite. The IRS is now looking more at facts and circumstances when the assignment is more than one year and less than 2 years in determining a travel expense deduction. If a taxpayer expects the employment to last a year or more and it does, the IRS considers the employment indefinite and does not allow an away-from-home deduction. If the employment is expected to last one year but less than 2 years (and it does), this second year can be reexamined by the IRS. In determining the deductions for this second year, the IRS requires that the taxpayer prove that he expected to return to his tax home in less than 2 years, when the job terminated. In order to claim a tax home away from home, there are three factors to be considered: 1. The taxpayer used the claimed tax home for lodging while working in the vicinity immediately prior to the	● In a recent case, a taxpayer had a job for 3 years that was supposed to have lasted less than 6 months. The courts held that the employment was in fact temporary because the taxpayer had to prove himself on the job before he could receive any future assignments. The taxpayer was therefore able to deduct all living expenses away from home. ● A teacher on sabbatical worked in Washington, D.C., for a year before going home. Since the teacher was away from his tax home, all expenses were deductible. ● Students who work part-time on campus during the year and summers in their hometown can deduct their living expenses during the summer and the cost of round-trip travel.

Line	Tax Law	Pay Less Tax Legally
	temporary assignment away from home, and continues to maintain work contacts in that area during the temporary employment. 2. Living expenses at the claimed tax home are duplicated due to the job away from home. 3. Whether taxpayer has family members living in the tax home or currently uses it frequently for his own lodging. If a taxpayer demonstrates the realistic-expectation-to-stay standard but fails to satisfy at least 2 of these 3 factors, the IRS will consider the employment indefinite and will not allow a deduction for the second year's living expenses. *Automobile Deductions* If you are not reimbursed by your employer or if you are self-employed, you can deduct depreciation, oil, gas, insurance, and other actual expenses to the extent a car is used for business, provided you keep records of expenses. Or you may calculate deductions by using the optional method: you are entitled to a deduction of 22.5¢ a mile for the first 15,000 miles of business use and 11¢ for every mile thereafter, plus parking fees and tolls incurred in business use. The 22.5¢ per mile rate on depreciating business autos is deductible to a maximum of 60,000 miles, after which point the IRS considers the car fully depreciated. The standard mileage rate is then limited to 11¢ per mile, but only if the straight-line method is used in computing depreciation. The optional method cannot be used with the accelerated method of depreciation. You are permitted to change from year to year between the optional and actual methods. For a complete discussion of writing off autos, see page 87.	● Because of the rising costs of fuel and repairs, it may be to your advantage to itemize your auto expenses (i.e., the actual expense method). ● You must use your own car to deduct the standard mileage rates. In a recent case, an auto salesman using a company car tried to deduct the mileage. The courts disallowed the claim. Only owners are entitled to depreciation, and they alone can claim the 22.5¢ per mile. All others are limited to deducting gas and oil only. ● If you bought a new car during the year, it is usually to your advantage to itemize your automobile expenses (because of the large depreciation factor). After 5 years, when the car is fully depreciated (or longer in the case of an expensive auto), change to the optional method to continue getting tax deductions. ● Tradesmen carrying bulky tools are limited to a deduction only for the additional costs incurred transporting those tools to work (e.g., trailer rental). But tradesmen

Line	Tax Law	Pay Less Tax Legally
	Proper records must be maintained to claim deductions for automobile expenses. Record the number of business miles driven and the business purpose of the travel. **Commuting Costs.** There is no deduction for the cost of going to and from work in the morning and evening. Driving expenses from one job to a second job are deductible. In this instance, the travel from home to the first job and the return home are nondeductible. Attorneys, accountants, and salespeople, who often stop to see a customer or a client on the way to the office, or a doctor who drives from his home to the hospital on the way to his office, cannot deduct commuting expenses. **Deducting Commuting When You Have a Home Office.** An anesthetist used her home office as a primary place of business, since the hospital did not provide her with an office. She kept surgery records and books there, took hospital-related phone calls, and wrote the hospital's anesthesia manual. She deducted 90 percent of the cost of driving between her home and the hospital and was allowed a commuting deduction by the Tax Court. A salesman working out of his home was allowed to write off the cost of his daily sales trips, since the cost of traveling between two places of business is deductible. A policeman working in New York City was required to carry a gun in the city. The quickest way to work was through New Jersey, but he took a longer route because he could not legally carry a gun	going to more than one job in the course of the day would be allowed to write off mileage from the first to the second job. Musicians carrying instruments are restricted to the same rules. ● Good records will make or break your deduction. A long-haul trucker lost his deduction because his logbook failed to make entries listing the nature and amount of each expenditure. ● Accountant S drives from his home to his office. He uses his car to see clients, return to the office, and to go home in the evening. With the exception of traveling from his home to his office and from his office to his home, all his driving expenses are deductible. If his office were in his home, all the auto expenses would be tax-deductible. ● In order to improve his skills, Lawyer K takes special courses after working hours. His tuition, fees, and the cost of books are deductible, and so are the transportation costs. Home to work is commuting, work to school is deductible, school to home is commuting. ● An engineer working out of town on a temporary assignment sleeps in a hotel during his stay. Going to work in the morning appears to be regular commuting, but the engineer can deduct the cost of his daily round trips between his temporary position and the hotel. ● A court recently allowed a tax deduction for daily commuting costs for 3 years. The case involved a construction worker who expected a winter layoff at a distant site. According to the court, the possibility of a layoff made the job temporary and the commuting expenses therefore deductible. ● As a general rule, a spouse's travel expenses are considered personal and nondeductible, even if the spouse performs

Line	Tax Law	Pay Less Tax Legally
	through New Jersey. No deduction was allowed for commuting since the extra expense resulted from where he lived and not the demands of his job.	incidental business services (answering the telephone, typing). However, if you can show that your spouse's presence was essential to the purpose of the trip, his or her expenses may be deductible; for example, if a spouse is fluent in a foreign language and accompanies an executive on a business trip abroad, or if the taxpayer has a specific medical problem and it is necessary to have the spouse present in case of possible medical emergency.

Charitable and Educational Travel Costs, Cruises

Tax Reform has applied the following limits to certain kinds of travel:

1. *Educational Travel:* No deduction is allowed if the travel is claimed as a form of education; however, if the travel qualifies as a business expense, it will be allowed. For example, a teacher who travels abroad to do research that cannot be done at home may deduct unreimbursed travel costs (subject to the 2 percent AGI floor, as an itemized deduction). Meals expenses are subject to the 80 percent limit.
2. *Luxury-Water Transportation:* Cruise costs that are deductible are limited to twice the highest federal per diem for travel in the United States times the number of days you are en route.

    If you keep meals and entertainment costs separate, you may count 80 percent of these; otherwise, the double per-diem rule applies to expenses without consideration of the 80 percent limit.

    Cruise ship convention costs are deductible up to $2,000 a year, if all ports of call are in the United States (or U.S. possessions) and if the ship is registered in the United States.
3. *Charitable Travel:* You must prove that there is *no* significant element of personal pleasure or vacation in travel away from home in order to claim a deduction for charitable travel expenses. Trips organized by educational groups as research studies in vacation and exotic areas forced Congress to come up with this limitation.

Employee Travel Expenses

Travel abroad for conventions or business usually comes under close scrutiny by the IRS, which tends to view such travel as being little more than a tax-deductible vacation. If a trip was primarily a vacation, you may deduct business expenses incurred during the vacation. If a trip was primarily for business, or to attend a seminar (and the time spent attending classes was substantial), transportation to and from the destination is also deductible. A complete discussion of deductible and nondeductible travel expenses may be found in Chapter 4, Reporting Business Income or Loss. For a full discussion of travel expenses, see page 133.

Foreign Travel Allowance

Here are the updated maximum per diem allowances for travel abroad. These amounts include meals, lodging, laundry, dry cleaning, taxes, and tips.

If as an employee traveling abroad you receive a daily reimbursement of less than $44/day (or the maximum per diem per location—see table below), and your travel expenses are substantiated to your employer, you won't have to make a further accounting to IRS.

Maximum Daily Foreign Travel Allowances

Location	Allowance	Location	Allowance
Amsterdam, Netherlands	$ 85	Munich, West Germany	78
Brussels, Belgium	96	Paris, France	125
Edinburgh, Scotland	101	Rome, Italy	105
Lisbon, Portugal	70	Stockholm, Sweden	142
London, England	138	Tokyo, Japan	147
Melbourne, Australia	96	Zurich, Switzerland	100

Business Travel

Although meal and entertainment expenses are subject to the 80 percent limit, the travel and lodging costs are not. In the case of room service, it is necessary to break down the charges so that the meals can reflect the 80 percent limit. It may be best to get an itemized bill from the hotel or motel.

If a hotel room has one or more meals included in the cost of the room, a portion will have to be designated as meal expenses in order to be subject to the 80 percent limitation.

Meal and Entertainment Expenses (Line 5)

These expenses are limited to 80 percent of cost. Combining this with the reduction in tax rates raises the after-tax cost of meals and entertainment considerably.

When an employee deducts moving expenses, related meals are subject to the 80 percent limit on the employee's tax return. If the employer reimburses the employee, the *employer* is subject to the 80 percent limit unless the reimbursement is treated as compensation to the employee.

Employees should try to negotiate a reimbursement arrangement with their employers not only because of the 80 percent limit but because of the 2 percent AGI floor on unreimbursed meals and entertainment expenses.

There is a banquet exception, which exempts meals at qualified meetings from the 80 percent limit in 1987 and 1988. This applies to meals at seminars, annual meetings, and conventions only if: (1) there are at least 40 participants, (2) at least 50 percent of the attendees are away from home, (3) there is a speaker presentation, and (4) the cost of the meal is not stated separately.

Meals furnished at functions such as company picnics for ordinary employees are not subject to the 80 percent limit. Neither are meals that are treated as fringe benefits—e.g., in the company cafeteria.

Meals—Limitations

The meal expenses must be directly related to the active conduct of business. Unless business is discussed before, during, or after the meal (a bona fide, substantial business discussion), no business deduction is allowed. (There are a few exceptions, which apply to the business-connection requirement for entertainment expenses.) A specific deal does not have to be discussed, however. The cost of business meals must be reasonable and substantiated adequately in an up-to-date diary.

Your diary should clearly show:

1. Name, title, and business connection of the person(s) you entertained
2. Date
3. Business purpose and a simple explanation of the business discussion that took place
4. Amount spent on each separate part of the entertainment
5. Where you went, including the address of the restaurant, theater, or sporting event.

Parking near the restaurant is *not* 100 percent deductible. Only 80 percent is deductible as part of the meal or entertainment. The new rules apply to meals at all types of restaurants, including fast-food places.

Entertainment—Limitations

When tickets to shows and sporting events are used for business entertaining, the 80 percent limit applies to the face value of the ticket. Additional amounts paid to agents or scalpers are not deductible.

The full cost of the ticket is allowed (without the 80 percent limit and including ticket agent costs) if: (1) the event is manned by volunteers, (2) it is organized primarily to benefit a charitable organization, and (3) 100 percent of the net proceeds go to that organization.

Travel and Entertainment

Here are some examples of the types of expenses deductible under the Tax Reform Act:

	Percent Deductible
1. Lunch with client, *if* business is discussed before, during, or after meal	80%
2. Cab fare to the restaurant	100%
3. Tickets to charity event manned by volunteers	100%
4. Treating client to golf: green fees, food, beverages, carts, *if* business is discussed	80%
5. Airfare to investment seminar	None
Lodging at investment seminar	None
6. Airfare to call on client out of town	100%
Lodging out of town	100%
Meals out of town; no business discussed	80% of your meal; none for client's

132 SAVE MONEY NOW

	Percent Deductible
7. Airfare to attend medical convention	100%
Meals in town of medical convention	80%
8. Sporting event: tickets, food and drink, (*business discussed*), taxpayer and client	80%
Cab fare to sporting event	100%

Business Meals While Traveling

IRS will allow $14 a day for business meals without a receipt. But if you use this $14 deduction once, you must use it for each day you eat while on the road. You probably will spend more than $14 per day, so you may be better off using actual receipts and forgetting the deduction for the few missing receipts.

Line	Tax Law	Pay Less Tax Legally
Form 1040 Lines 24a, b	**Individual Retirement Accounts** If you or your spouse are covered by a company pension plan and your AGI is greater than $50,000 ($35,000 if single), you cannot deduct IRA contributions; however, you are still allowed up to $2,000 of *nondeductible* contributions. When you withdraw money from your IRA, the IRS lumps all your IRAs together and treats it as combined deductible and nondeductible contributions. If you keep detailed records of all your IRA contributions, a portion of every withdrawal will be taxable and a portion will be tax-free. The deferred earnings on IRAs are taxed at withdrawal, so each withdrawal has to be broken down into three parts in order to calculate the amount of tax: 1. Earnings on the IRA (100 percent taxed regardless of whether the contributions were deductible or nondeductible) 2. Return of a deductible contribution (those made before 1987), taxed at withdrawal because it hasn't been taxed before 3. Return of a nondeductible contribution (those made in or after 1987),	• Beginning this year, alimony income may be tax-sheltered with an Individual Retirement Account. • *IRA and Keogh Contributions:* You may open an IRA as late as April 15 and have the deduction retroactive to last year's return. When an IRA contribution is mailed to a bank, the envelope showing the cancellation mark by the post office must be dated prior to April 15. In the case of a Keogh contribution, you have up to the due date of the return plus extensions. As a general rule, the post office has been considered the agent, and the postmark has been accepted as evidence. If you intend to make a last-minute IRA or Keogh contribution, use registered (or certified) mail so that you will have a record of your mailing date. • *Tax Saving with IRAs:* IRA money must be deposited by April 15 to be deductible on this year's return. File your return early, claiming the deduction for your IRA, and use your tax refund to fund the IRA contribution. (Filing by February 15 is almost certain to result in a refund by April 15.)

# The One-Minute Taxman: Employee Business Travel Expenses

You may deduct ordinary and necessary travel expenses while away from your tax home. These expenses are deducted before arriving at adjusted gross income; you need not itemize to claim them. Enter unreimbursed travel expenses on Form 2106. All unreimbursed travel expenses are treated as miscellaneous itemized deductions and are subject to the 2 percent floor.

Where Is Your Tax Home?

Your tax home is your principal place of business, regardless of where you may reside. If you regularly work in 2 different locations, your tax home is determined by applying the following tests:

1. How much time did you spend in each area performing your duties?
2. How much time did you spend in each area for personal purposes?
3. How much income did you earn in each area?

Deducting Foreign Travel

If your entire trip is business-related, all expenses are deductible. If your trip combines both business and pleasure, you must allocate expenses. The nondeductible portion is the ratio of nonbusiness days to total days away from home. If you travel to a foreign convention and can show that attendance was a condition of employment, expenses would be deductible.

Travel Expenses of Your Spouse

You must be able to show a bona fide business purpose to deduct your spouse's travel expenses. If your spouse's presence was essential (typing notes and helping with the entertaining, for example, do not count) his or her expenses would be deductible as well.

	Amount		Amount
☐ Air, rail, and bus fares	_____	☐ Office supplies	_____
☐ Airport limousine	_____	☐ Parking	_____
☐ Attaché and briefcases	_____	☐ Photocopying	_____
☐ Auto expenses	_____	☐ Secretarial and typing services	_____
☐ Baggage handling	_____		
☐ Calculator	_____	☐ Shoeshines	_____
☐ Cleaning and laundry	_____	☐ Taxi	_____
☐ Entertainment	_____	☐ Telephone and telegraph	_____
☐ Gifts	_____	☐ Traveler's checks	_____
☐ Job hunting	_____	☐ Tips	_____
☐ Liquor consumed at airport	_____	☐ Valet	_____
☐ Luggage costs	_____		Total _____
☐ Newspapers and magazines	_____		

Line	Tax Law	Pay Less Tax Legally
	not taxed at withdrawal because it has already been taxed on your return for the year it was contributed. Income earned by an IRA is not taxed until withdrawal. Generally, you cannot withdraw the money for retirement before the age of 59½ or later than April 1 of the year after you reach age 70½, without substantial penalty; when you do receive funds from the plan, you must report those funds as fully taxable income. You may deduct a contribution to a spousal IRA even though the spouse may be over 70½ at the time of the contribution. If an individual dies before receiving all the funds in the account, the remainder must be distributed to his beneficiaries within 5 years or be used to purchase an annuity within that time.	Don't wait until April 15 to get an IRA deduction. Contribute IRA dollars during the year to take advantage of tax-free compounding. ● Borrow the money to make your IRA contribution. Although the interest paid out may no longer be deductible, interest earned by the IRA is still tax-deferred. ● An IRA contribution may be a good idea even if a taxpayer is critically ill, since the IRA can be used to provide survivor's benefits to a spouse or other family member. The contributions must be made before the taxpayer dies; any contributions made after the death are not deductible. ● Taxpayers who invest in IRAs paying high rates of interest while maintaining a separate account paying little or no interest in the same financial institution might find their IRAs disallowed by the IRS. (These tandem IRAs have only been offered by a few savings and loan associations in the Midwest.) ● Be on guard for large service charges—both loan charges and commissions—that can reduce your investment value. As your IRA grows, fees will become larger and therefore more important. ● Self-directed IRAs with a discount broker or a bank offering brokerage services allow you to invest in stocks, government securities, and corporate bonds; you can even write covered call options. Interest and dividends are automatically invested in a money-market fund, and fees are low compared to similar accounts with full-service brokers. A typical discount broker has no setup, maintenance, or termination charges; there is no required minimum contribution, and the commissions on stocks, bonds, and mutual-fund transactions are low.

IRA Under Tax Reform

Tax Reform placed new restrictions on the deductions of higher-paid employees participating in company-sponsored IRA plans.

A ceiling has been placed on AGI: $50,000 (before subtracting IRA contributions) for marrieds filing jointly and $35,000 for singles. Over this ceiling, you may not deduct IRA contributions if either you or your spouse is covered by a company plan.

If your AGI is less than $25,000 a year ($40,000 for marrieds filing jointly) you may make deductible IRA contributions whether you or your spouse is covered by a company-sponsored retirement plan or not.

Between $25,000 and $35,000 AGI for singles or between $40,000 and $50,000 AGI for marrieds are allowed a partial deduction.

Company-sponsored retirement plans (which will preclude your having an IRA) are defined as:

1. Qualified pension, profit-sharing, or stock bonus plans, including 401(k)
2. Qualified annuity plans
3. Simplified employee pension plans (SEP's)
4. Retirement plans for state or local government employees
5. Certain union pension trusts (Section 501(c) (18) plans)
6. Tax-sheltered annuities for employees of non-profit organizations.

In the final analysis, put away as much as you can for retirement. Don't get sidetracked with what is deductible and what isn't on your tax return. Whether it's deductible or not, you'll be glad you saved the money.

Deductible and Nondeductible IRAs

A fully deductible $2,000 IRA is only available to singles earning $25,000 or less, those filing jointly earning $40,000 or less, and workers not covered by a company pension plan. However, you can't get a $2,000 IRA if you don't earn $2,000.

If you are covered by a company pension plan and your income is above those levels, you may make a nondeductible contribution (up to $2,000 per year) deferring tax on the interest earned until withdrawal. To claim a nondeductible IRA, you must file the new Form 8606.

Form 8606: Line-by-Line Instructions

If you are unable to claim deductions for contributions to an IRA because of high income, you must report any nondeductible contributions on new Form 8606, which is also used to compute the basis in your IRA and the nontaxable portion of IRA distributions made in 1987.

Even if you don't file Form 1040, you must still file Form 8606. If you are married filing jointly, each spouse must list his or her own IRAs on a separate Form 8606.

You should receive a statement by the first of February showing the value of each IRA on December 31. Use these year-end values in filling out Form 8606.

Line 1. List all your IRAs and their year-end values regardless of whether your IRA contributions were deductible or not.

Line 2. Enter the total values as of December 31.

Line 3. If you were covered by a retirement plan at work, complete Worksheet 2. On line

3 of Form 8606, enter the nondeductible contributions shown on line 8 from the worksheet. (Your spouse files a separate Form 8606 and the amount from Line 17 of the worksheet.) You cannot enter more than $2,000 (or $2,250) for your Form 8606, and your IRA contribution cannot exceed earned income.

Worksheet 2

Use this worksheet only if: You (or your spouse who is employed, if you file jointly) were

IRA Worksheet 2 (keep for your records)

1. Enter: $35,000 if your filing status is single or head of household;
   $50,000 if your filing status is married filing a joint return;
   $10,000 if your filing status is married filing a separate return. **1.**

2. Enter the amount from Form 1040A, line 10. (If this amount is equal to or larger than the amount on line 1, none of your IRA contributions are deductible. Stop here; see Form 8606.) **2.**

3. Subtract the amount on line 2 from the amount on line 1. Enter the result. If the result is $10,000 or more, stop here; complete Worksheet 1. **3.**

4. Multiply the amount on line 3 by 20% (.20). Enter the result. If it is not a multiple of $10, round it up to the next multiple of $10 (for example, round $490.30 to $500). However, if the result is less than $200, enter $200 on line 4. Go to line 5. **4.**

	(a) Your IRA	(b) Your working spouse's IRA
Deductible IRA contributions		
5. Enter your wages, salaries, and tips. **5.**		**5.**
6. Enter IRA contributions you made for 1987, but **do not** enter more than $2,000. **6.**		**6.**
7. Enter your IRA deduction. Compare the amounts on lines 4, 5, and 6, and enter the **smallest** of the three amounts on line 7. Enter on Form 1040A, line 11a, the amount from line 7, column (a); and, if applicable, enter on Form 1040A, line 11b, the amount from line 7, column (b). (If the amount on line 6 is more than the amount on line 7 and you want to make a nondeductible IRA contribution, go on to line 8.) **7.**		**7.**
Nondeductible IRA contributions		
8. Subtract the amount on line 7 from the amount on line 4 or line 6, whichever is **smaller**, and enter the result. Enter the amount from line 8, column (a), on your Form 8606, line 3; and, if applicable, enter the amount from line 8, column (b), on your spouse's Form 8606. (This amount cannot be more than $2,000 for each.) **8.**		**8.**

If contributions were made to an IRA for your nonworking spouse (as defined on page 17) and you file a joint return, complete lines 9 through 17.

Deductible IRA contributions for nonworking spouse

9. Enter the **smaller** of $2,250 or the amount from line 5.   9.

10. Add the amounts on lines 7 and 8, column (a), and enter the result.   10.

11. Subtract the amount on line 10 from the amount on line 9. Enter the result. If zero or less, stop here; you cannot make deductible or nondeductible IRA contributions for your nonworking spouse.   11.

12. Enter the **smallest** of: (a) IRA contributions you made for 1987 that are for your nonworking spouse; (b) $2,000; or (c) the amount on line 11.   12.

13. Multiply the amount on line 5 by 22.5% (.225). Enter the result. If it is not a multiple of $10, round it up to the next multiple of $10. However, if the result is less than $200, enter $200 on line 13.   13.

14. Enter the amount from line 7, column (a).   14.

15. Subtract the amount on line 14 from the amount on line 13. Enter the result, but **not more** than the amount on line 12.   15.

16. Nonworking spouse's IRA deduction. Compare the amounts on lines 4, 5, and 15, and enter the **smallest** of the three amounts on line 16. Also enter this amount on Form 1040A, line 11b. (If you want to make a nondeductible IRA contribution for your nonworking spouse, go on to line 17.)   16.

Nondeductible IRA contributions for nonworking spouse

17. Subtract the amount on line 16 from the amount on line 12 and enter the result. Enter the amount from line 17 on line 3 of the Form 8606 for your nonworking spouse.   17.

covered by a retirement plan at work *and* your income is (1) $25,000–$35,000 single (2) $40,000–$50,000 married filing jointly, or (3) 0–$10,000 married filing separately.

Just follow the worksheet instructions line by line. The amounts determined on lines 16 and 17 will be transferred to your Form 1040 or 1040A, and the new Form 8606.

The line-by-line instructions printed on the worksheets are easy to follow one line at a time, but be sure to use the separate columns for you and your spouse.

Remember: The figure you end up with will be entered on Form 1040 or 1040A, and will be used in working up the new Form 8606.

Form **8606**	**Nondeductible IRA Contributions,**	OMB No. 1545-XXXX
Department of the Treasury Internal Revenue Service	**IRA Basis, and Nontaxable IRA Distributions** ▶ Attach to Form 1040, Form 1040A, or Form 1040NR.	**1987** Attachment Sequence No. **86**

Name: Doubu

Your social security number: 329-04-1040

Present home address (number and street) (or P.O. Box number if mail is not delivered to street address)

City, town or post office, state, and ZIP code

---

1. Enter name of trustee and value of all your IRAs—

   Name of trustee — Value on 12/31/87

   a. _____ 1a
   b. _____ 1b
   c. _____ 1c

2. Total value of all IRAs. Add lines 1a through 1c 2

3. Enter your designated nondeductible contributions for 1987 (see instructions) 3

4. Enter designated nondeductible contributions for 1987 made in 1988 by April 15, 1988 4

5. Subtract the amount on line 4 from the amount on line 3. Enter the result (but not less than zero) . 5

6. Adjustments (see instructions) 6

7. Combine lines 5 and 6 and enter the result. If you did not receive any IRA distributions in 1987, skip lines 8 through 12 and enter the amount from line 7 on line 13. 7

8. Enter the value of all your IRAs as of 12/31/87 (from line 2). Include any outstanding rollovers 8

9. Enter total IRA distributions received during 1987. Do not include amounts rolled over before 1/1/88 9

10. Add amounts on lines 8 and 9 and enter the total 10

11. Divide the amount on line 7 by the amount on line 10 and enter the result . 11 × .

12. Multiply the amount on line 9 by the percentage on line 11. Enter the result. This is the amount of your nontaxable distributions for 1987 . . . . ▶ 12

13. Subtract the amount on line 12 from the amount on line 7. Enter the result. This is your basis in your IRA(s) as of 1/1/88 . . . . ▶ 13

Please Sign Here ▶ Under penalties of perjury, I declare that I have examined this form, and to the best of my knowledge and belief, it is true, correct, and complete.

Your signature ▶ Date

Proof for August 13, 1987

IRA Worksheet 1 (keep for your records)

		(a) Your IRA	(b) Your working spouse's IRA
1.	Enter IRA contributions you made for 1987, but **do not** enter more than $2,000.	1.	1.
2.	Enter your wages, salaries, and tips.	2.	2.
3.	Enter your IRA deduction. Compare the amounts on lines 1 and 2, and enter the **smaller** of the two amounts on line 3. Enter on Form 1040A, line 11a, the amount from line 3, column (a); and, if applicable, enter on Form 1040A, line 11b, the amount from line 3, column (b). If you are married and made contributions to an IRA for your nonworking spouse, go on to line 4.	3.	3.
Complete lines 4 through 8 only if contributions were made to an IRA for your nonworking spouse (as defined on page 17) and you file a joint return.			
4.	Enter the **smaller** of $2,250 or the amount from line 2.	4.	
5.	Enter the amount from line 3.	5.	
6.	Subtract amount on line 5 from amount on line 4.	6.	
7.	Enter IRA contributions made for 1987 for your nonworking spouse, but **not more than** $2,000.	7.	
8.	Enter nonworking spouse's IRA deduction. Compare the amounts on lines 2, 6, and 7, and enter the **smallest** of the three amounts on line 8. Also enter this amount on Form 1040A, line 11b.	8.	

Worksheet 1

Use this worksheet if:

1. You (and spouse if you file jointly) were not covered by a retirement plan at work; *or*
2. You (and spouse if jointly) *were* covered by a plan at work and your income is $25,000 or less if single or head of household, or $40,000 married filing jointly.

On line 3 of worksheet I is the amount of IRAs you may deduct. Enter on Line 3 of Form 8606 the difference between the amount of IRA contributions you are deducting and the amount on Line 3 of Worksheet 1.

Line 8 of Worksheet 1 is the allowable deduction for a nonworking spouse's IRA. You may designate all or part of that amount as nondeductible. Enter on Line 3 of your spouse's Form 8606 the difference between the amount deducted and the amount on Line 8 of Worksheet 1.

Continuing with Form 8606:
Line 4. Enter nondeductible contributions made by April 15, 1988, applied toward 1987 on Line 3. This amount will be figured in your 1988 basis.
Line 5. Subtract Line 4 from Line 3 and enter the amount (not less than zero).
Line 6. If you decided to change a nondeductible contribution on a prior year's return to a deductible one or vice versa, you must file an amended tax return (Form 1040X) and show the change in designation on Line 6 of Form 8606.

Line 7. Add line 6 to line 5 and enter the total on line 7. List this amount on line 13 and skip lines 8 thru 12 if you received no distributions this year.
Line 8. Enter the total value of all IRAs as of December 31 (from Line 2), including any outstanding rollovers. (See page 141 for explanation of rollovers.)
Line 9. Line 9 does not include any distributions received in 1987 that you rolled over to another IRA by December 31, 1987.
Line 10. Add line 9 to line 8 and enter the total here.
Line 11. Take the amount on line 7 and divide it by the amount on Line 10, and enter the resulting figure as a percentage.
Line 12. Multiply the amount on Line 9 by the percentage on line 11. Show the amount on line 12 as your amount of nontaxable distributions for the year.
Line 13. Subtract line 12 from line 7 and enter the amount here. This is your basis in IRA's as of year end.

Inherited IRAs

IRA distributions in the case of death are subject to estate tax and federal income tax. If the surviving spouse is also the IRA beneficiary and rolls the distribution over into his or her IRA within 60 days of receipt, payment of tax will be deferred until the money is withdrawn. Other beneficiaries, however, may not roll over IRA distributions and must pay tax in the year they receive the distribution.

A taxpayer who is the beneficiary of a parent's IRA may be allowed to transfer the IRA to a new trustee, if no distributions had been made to the parent prior to his or her death and the new trustee maintains the IRA in the parent's name.

If you borrow money from the plan or use the funds as collateral for a loan, you may have to report the total plan assets as income on that year's return, and you will also have to pay a 15 percent penalty.

If you deposited too much money into your IRA, you have until April 15 to remove any excess contribution—or the IRS can impose a penalty. If you took an excess contribution in a prior year, you may reduce your deduction in the current year.

Once each year you can make a tax-free (and penalty-free) withdrawal of your IRA funds; however, the entire amount borrowed must be reinvested (rolled over) within 60 days, or you'll be subject to a 15 percent withdrawal penalty (if you are under 59½ years of age), in addition to having to report the money as income. If you are 59½ or over, you may withdraw IRA funds without being penalized.

Where to Invest Funds

IRA funds can no longer be invested in collectibles or precious metals, and either an insurance company or a financial institution must act as custodian.

You can invest pension money in real estate, bonds, stock, annuities, CDs, bond mutual funds and zero coupon bonds; or you can buy an IRA annuity from an insurance company or invest in real estate.

Adjustments to Income 141

Line	Tax Law	Pay Less Tax Legally
	Tax-Free Rollovers There are 3 types of tax-free rollovers from one retirement plan to another. 1. *Funding Medium Change* You are permitted to change the funding medium of an account without triggering a premature distribution within 60 days after receipt, but you can perform this type of rollover only once every year. 2. *Lump-Sum Distributions* A lump-sum distribution received from a qualified annuity, pension, or profit-sharing plan may be contributed tax-free to another plan (or to another IRA). A distribution from an IRA can be rolled over tax-free to a qualified plan if the assets came solely from a qualified plan. The full amount need not be rolled over, but you will be taxed on any amount not transferred. 3. *Partial Distribution* A partial distribution may be rolled over on the same basis as a lump-sum distribution if (a) the amount is at least half of the account balance, (b) the distribution is not part of a series of periodic payments, and (c) the transfer occurs within 60 days after receipt of the distribution. Subsequent distributions from the same plan are eligible for neither the 10-year averaging nor long-term capital-gains treatment. In a partial rollover, the maximum amount to be rolled over may not exceed the taxable portion of the distribution. In addition, IRAs may not be rolled over to a qualified pension plan (or to a tax-sheltered annuity contract) if part of the balance in the IRA consists of a rollover of a partial distribution.	● There are no tax-free rollovers for amounts received by an individual from an inherited IRA, but an IRA received by a surviving spouse of the original owner will still be permitted rollover treatment. ● If you receive bonds under a qualified bond-purchase plan, you may roll over the proceeds (in excess of your contribution) within 60 days after the redemption. ● Larry, a participant in a company pension plan, retired on March 11, when the balance in the plan was $20,000. He received $12,000 as a lump-sum distribution, with the balance to be paid at a later date. He rolled over the $12,000 to his existing IRA within a few days. The rollover is tax-free, since the $12,000 distribution was at least half of the balance in his plan and was not part of a series of periodic payments. ● The proceeds of a tax-sheltered annuity can be rolled over into an Individual Retirement Account, but the entire amount in the annuity must be rolled over within 60 days of the payout. The total amount of the distribution need not be transferred into the IRA. ● If you shift IRAs more than once in a year (and receive the funds yourself each time) you will be taxed on the second rollover, even if you properly roll over the money within 60 days. Here's the hitch: While you can have as many trustee-to-trustee switches as you want in the course of the year, you are permitted to handle the money yourself only once during a 12-month period. ● There are limits on IRA withdrawals: $750,000 for lump sums qualifying for averaging; $150,000 for all other types of distributions. If you exceed these limits,

Line	Tax Law	Pay Less Tax Legally
	IRA Early Withdrawals

The Tax Reform Act has not changed the early withdrawal penalty. Withdrawal of deductible contributions for any reason before age 59½ (or in case of death or disability) will cost you an extra 10 percent penalty. (IRA contributions that were subtracted from taxable income when made plus earnings accumulated on those amounts during the years, are "deductible contributions," which will be penalized if withdrawn early.) No penalty applies to nondeductible IRA contributions; however, the distribution of earnings attributable to these non-deductible contributions is subject to the 10 percent penalty.

Exception: If the distributions are made in the form of an annuity or periodic payments over your lifetime, you may withdraw the funds early. To qualify, payments must be based on your life expectancy (or the joint life expectancies of you and your beneficiary) and must be equal (or nearly equal) amounts made at least annually.

Example: You contributed to an IRA for the past 5 years and are only 49 years old. The account balance is about $13,000. You may not withdraw the money without paying the 10 percent penalty *unless* you instruct your IRA trustee to pay the funds in regular periodic payments based on your life expectancy.

IRA Rollovers

It is now easier to treat withdrawals from a qualified plan as a partial distribution eligible for rollover to an IRA, which should avoid tax completely. For the distribution to qualify as a rollover, it must be at least 50 percent of the plan's account balance, determined just before the distribution.

After-tax contributions may be | you will be subject to a 15 percent penalty on the excess withdrawal.

The following distributions are not affected by these limits:

1. Distributions from a qualified plan rolled over to an IRA
2. Distributions equal to your after-tax contributions to a plan or your investment in an annuity contract
3. Distributions received by the beneficiary of a deceased individual
4. Distributions to a former spouse ordered by a domestic relations court. (The former spouse takes the distribution into account in determining whether the penalty applies.)

Special 1987 and 1988 Election

You may elect to exempt from penalty benefits accrued as of August 1, 1986, subject to certain IRS guidelines.

Surviving spouses may roll over funds from the IRA of a deceased spouse into another IRA, but other beneficiaries may not make a rollover. Other beneficiaries than the surviving spouse must make withdrawals from the IRA.

If the deceased IRA owner was receiving payments on a specified schedule, the beneficiary must receive distributions at the same pace. If the deceased had not begun receiving distributions, the entire account must be distributed to the beneficiary within five years. Exception: a beneficiary may delay payments. If payments begin within one year of the owner's death, a designated beneficiary may spread distributions over the life expectancy of the beneficiary.

If the beneficiary is not receiving immediate distribution of the entire account, he or she may make investment changes during the payout period (e.g., transfer the account to a different IRA trustee, provided the IRA is kept in the name of the deceased IRA owner). |

Line	Tax Law	Pay Less Tax Legally

	included for purposes of determining the 50 percent, but these amounts are not eligible for rollover.
	
	    Partial rollovers are permitted only in the case of death, disability, or separation from service. The new Tax Reform Act permits the rollover of a partial distribution that is one in a series of periodic payments, but the old law did not.
	
	    And, last but not least, amounts rolled over to an IRA escape the 10 percent tax on distributions both before and after age 59½.
		Tax Reform created a way to withdraw money from your IRA before you reach age 59½ without paying a penalty: Convert the account to an annuity and receive a scheduled series of equal payments over your lifetime.

Line 25	**Self-Employed Health Insurance Deductions**
	
	Self-employeds may deduct one-half the cost of health insurance premiums in a nondiscriminatory plan. Self-employeds who pay their family's (and their own) health insurance may deduct 25 percent of this cost directly from their gross income for tax years through 1989. This deduction may not be used, however, to reduce self-employment income in figuring self-employment tax. The remaining 75 percent is added to all other medical expenses, which total must exceed 7.5 percent of your adjusted gross income.
	
	    In order to qualify for this writeoff, taxpayers must cover all their employees in all unincorporated businesses of which they own at least 5 percent, and the taxpayer must not be eligible under a health insurance plan of an employer.
	
	    If the 25 percent deduction exceeds your AGI from the activity, you may claim it to the extent of your AGI. If you have a loss from your unincorporated business, for example, you may not write off the 25 percent as well to result in a larger loss.	

Adjustments to Income   143

Line	Tax Law	Pay Less Tax Legally
Line 26	**Self-Employed Retirement Plans** ***Keogh Retirement Plan and Self-Employed (SEP) Deduction*** If you are self-employed, you can contribute toward retirement the lesser of (1) $30,000 or (2) 25 percent of net earnings from self-employment into a Keogh Plan. You are permitted to contribute an additional 10 percent of your self-employment earnings to your Keogh plan over and above your maximum 25 percent or $30,000. This is a voluntary contribution and not deductible. The additional interest income your contribution earns is tax-free. You may have both an IRA and a Keogh plan at the same time. Your retirement contribution is treated as an adjustment to income, which means that you may still claim the standard deduction amount on your return. You cannot withdraw the money before age 59½ unless you are disabled. If, however, you own 10 percent or less of a unincorporated business, you can borrow up to $50,000 from your Keogh. The loan must be repaid within 5 years at a reasonable rate of interest. There are 2 basic types of Keogh plans—defined benefit and defined contribution. A defined benefit plan is a retirement plan, which establishes pension amounts to be paid upon retirement. Under a defined benefit plan, retirement benefits are expressed in terms of annuity payments (e.g., $500 per month), as well as total benefits to be paid out. Maximum annual benefits may not exceed the lesser of $90,000 or 100 percent of the participant's average earnings for the highest 3 years. Total benefits will usually be higher than those that would be received from a defined contribution plan, taxes will be lower during the working years, and the	• Self-employed individuals making contributions under Keogh plans are permitted to wait until the due date of the return before they have to make any contribution to the plan—provided they had a bona fide plan in existence as of the end of the year. They can then treat the contribution as having been made the previous year. Thus, an individual can make his contribution to his plan on or before the due date of his return—April 15 (or later, if he obtains an extension). • Even if your business is just beginning to grow, it may be worthwhile for you to start a Keogh plan now. • In the case of a defined contribution plan, self-employed persons may deduct 20 percent of the net self-employment income. The definition of net earnings from self-employment has been revised to exclude the amount of the Keogh plan contribution. Multiply business net profit by 20 percent to arrive at the maximum allowable contribution. For example, a taxpayer with self-employment gross income of $40,000 and deductible business expenses of $20,000 will have a net business income of $20,000. To calculate his maximum Keogh contributions, he must multiply 20 percent by the $20,000 net profit and will arrive at a figure of

Adjustments to Income   145

Line	Tax Law	Pay Less Tax Legally
	taxpayer will have the benefit of advance information concerning future retirement benefits. Under the new law, defined benefit plans would be geared to Social Security benefits and either age 60 or age 65. Defined benefit plans are more complex to administer and fund than defined contribution plans. The contributions needed to fund the plan must be determined by actuarial tables, and the self-employed person must calculate the amount of the retirement benefits that will be available. **Simplified Employee Pension (SEP) Plans** An alternative to the Keogh plan is the SEP plan. Check with your broker for details. If you have a Keogh plan, you must file an annual report Form 5500, even if you are the only participant in the plan.	$4,000. In order to show that the $4,000 is the correct amount, he must make the following computation: Gross business income $40,000 Less business expenses $20,000 Less Keogh plan 4,000 Total deductions −$24,000 Net income $16,000 ● With a self-employed retirement plan, the employer makes contributions to the IRAs of its employees rather than maintaining its own pension plan, and the employer may deduct its contributions. The employer's contributions are included in the employee's gross income, but the employee also takes a deduction in the same amount, so the two offset each other. Under Tax Reform, many employees may make elective deferrals to the SEP, but they are subject to a $7,000 cap.

Tax-Planning Checklist: Retirement

● If you are a corporate employee, a company qualified pension or profit-sharing plan enables you to accumulate retirement funds on a tax-free basis.

● Employee contributions to qualified pension and profit-sharing plans are tax-deductible.

● Under a deferred compensation arrangement, income is postponed to retirement (when you are likely to be in a lower tax bracket).

● The monthly retirement benefit paid to a retired employee under a deferred compensation plan is deductible by the company and taxable to the employee as income.

● Every individual earning $2,000 or more per year and *not* covered by a company plan may establish a tax-favored Individual Retirement Account (IRA).

● A self-employed businessman or professional may establish a Keogh retirement plan or SEP plan in addition to an IRA.

● Social Security benefits may be taxable. See page 69.

Line	Tax Law	Pay Less Tax Legally
Line 27	**Penalty on Early Withdrawal of Savings** If you paid a penalty on a premature withdrawal of a savings certificate, that penalty is deductible on line 27.	
Line 28	**Alimony Paid** If you are either divorced or separated under a written agreement, periodic payments made to your former spouse as alimony are deductible. The name and Social Security number of the spouse receiving the alimony must be reported. The distinction between alimony and property settlements has been eliminated. Once the new definition of alimony is met, payments will be taxable to the recipient and deductible by the payor, regardless of how the payments are characterized by local law. If the parties decide by written agreement to designate otherwise qualified payments as excludable by the recipient and nondeductible by the payor, their wishes will be followed. Payments need no longer arise out of the marital obligation of support or be periodic. The payments will qualify as deductible alimony or separate maintenance (if the divorce is not final) if they meet these requirements: 1. They are made in cash (not property) to a spouse or former spouse. 2. They are made pursuant to a divorce or separation decree or agreement. 3. They do not extend beyond the death of the recipient. 4. They extend for at least a 3-year time period (but they may stop with death or remarriage), and the alimony payments in any calendar year exceed $10,000. 5. They are not between spouses who	● If you and your spouse separate without a court decree and you agree to pay alimony, put the agreement in writing and continue to live apart, and don't file a joint return for the year. ● You don't have to be physically separated to deduct alimony. One couple still lived in the same house while getting a divorce. The court ordered the husband to pay temporary support to the wife, which was later deductible as alimony. ● If you fall behind in alimony payments and have to settle the amount in one lump sum, that amount is deductible. For example, a man agreed to pay $500 per month alimony but fell $8,000 in arrears. His former wife agreed to take $6,000 in full settlement of any past and all future claims. The entire amount is deductible when paid because he was acting under a legal obligation. ● Back alimony is deductible in the year paid; consider whether paying back alimony would generate more tax savings next year than now. However, you cannot prepay next year's alimony and deduct it this year, unless acting under a legal obligation. ● Alimony deductions are taken into consideration in determining withholding exemptions; be sure your withholding exemptions are current. ● Although child-support payments are not deductible, you may still be able to

Adjustments to Income   147

Line	Tax Law	Pay Less Tax Legally
	file jointly or live in the same household.	claim the children as exemptions (see page 59).
	If any amount specified in a divorce or separation decree or agreement is to be reduced upon the happening of an event —e.g., the child's reaching a specific age, marrying, or graduating—the amount of the reduction will be considered child support and will be ineligible as alimony. The rules apply to all payments made under divorce or separation instruments executed after 1984. The old rules apply to payments made under agreements entered into before 1985 (unless the instrument was changed after 1984 and the changes specifically made the new rules apply). In addition, any payor of alimony is required to report the spouse's Social Security number on his or her tax return; there is a penalty for failure to comply.	● For tax planning tips on divorce, see page 251.
	Alimony received by divorced spouses may be sheltered with an IRA. To qualify, the taxpayer must satisfy all other IRA rules.	
	Legal Fees	
	Legal fees incurred in obtaining a divorce or collecting child support payments are not deductible. There are, however, certain instances in which a portion of the legal fees may be deductible: (1) the legal fees paid to get alimony (and to make sure that payments are kept up) are deductible to the spouse collecting the alimony; (2) legal fees paid for tax advice are deductible; and (3) legal fees paid to protect income-producing assets are deductible.	● Legal fees incurred in collecting alimony are deductible. In a recent case, an ex-wife paid her attorneys 10 percent of all alimony received, and the amount was found to be deductible.
● Ask your attorney for a separate bill for charges on income, estate, or gift tax planning incurred in the process of obtaining a divorce.

Alimony and Tax Reform

Tax Reform repealed the requirement for a provision in divorce or separation instruments that payments terminate upon the death of the payee. It also repealed the 6-year minimum term recapture rule, replacing it with a 3-year rule.

Under Tax Reform, alimony payments must be included in the gross income of the recipient and may be deducted by the payor-spouse, provided these requirements are met:

1. Payments are made in cash (or check).
2. Payments are received by (or on behalf of) a spouse under a divorce or separation instrument.
3. The instrument does not designate the payment as one that is *not* taxable by the recipient spouse or is nondeductible by the payor.
4. Spouses legally separated under a divorce decree (or separate maintenance agreement) must not be living together in the same household at the time the payment is made.
5. Payments must terminate upon death of the recipient-spouse, and there must be no liability to make any payment, in cash or in property, as a substitute for such payments.
6. The parties must not file a joint return (with each other).
7. The payment must not be for child support.

Instead of 6 years, the new rule provides for the recapture of excess amounts of alimony during a 3-year period. Excess amounts that have been treated as alimony (either during the calendar year in which the payments began or in the next calendar year) are to be recaptured in the payor-spouse's third post-separation year by requiring the payor to include any excess as income. During this third year the recipient may deduct the amount from gross income.

Here is a formula for calculating the excess alimony payments: For the first recapture year, the excess payment is (a) the total alimony paid in the first post-separation year over (b) the sum of $15,000, (c) the average of the amount paid in the second post-separation year (less any excess payments for that year) and (d) the amount of alimony paid in the third post-separation year.

In simpler terms:

1. Start with alimony payments made in the second year.
2. Deduct excess payments made in that year from that amount.
3. Add alimony paid in the third year.
4. Divide the total by 2 (for an average of the 2 years).
5. Subtract this figure and $15,000 from the amount of alimony paid in the first year.
6. The result equals excess payments for the first year.

In order to determine the excess payments for the second year, add alimony paid in the third year to $15,000 and deduct this figure from alimony paid in the second year. The result is excess payments for the second year.

After you determine the excess for the first and second years, add these two figures to determine the amount to be recaptured in the third post-separation year.

ITEMIZING YOUR DEDUCTIONS

- MEDICAL AND DENTAL EXPENSES
- TAXES
- INTEREST EXPENSE
- CONTRIBUTIONS
- CASUALTY LOSSES
- MOVING EXPENSES
- MISCELLANEOUS DEDUCTIONS

In order to itemize your deductions, you must complete Schedule A; however, before you concern yourself with itemizing, you should have arrived at a figure that includes your total income less any adjustments to income and entered that calculation on line 33a.

To determine whether it is to your advantage to itemize or to claim the standard deduction amount, you must first total your deductions by category: medicine and drugs and other medical expenses; taxes; interest paid; contributions given by check, cash, or merchandise; losses incurred during the year; and other deductible items as discussed in this chapter. If it is to your advantage to itemize, complete Schedule A and transfer the total from line 26 to Form 1040, line 33a. After you have entered a figure on line 33a, or have decided not to itemize, turn to page 192.

Itemize or Claim the New Standard Deduction?

Beginning in 1987, you can claim the new standard deduction or total itemized deductions, whichever is greater. The standard deduction amounts are:

$3,760—married filing jointly or surviving spouse
$2,540—single or head of household
$1,880—married filing separately

For taxpayers who are blind *or* elderly, the standard deduction amounts are:

$5,000—married filing jointly or surviving spouse
$3,000—single
$4,400—head of household
$2,500—married filing separately

A married taxpayer filing jointly who is both elderly and blind may claim an additional $600; if both spouses are elderly and blind, they may claim a total of $1,200 in addition to the $5,000 standard deduction.

A taxpayer who files as single or head of household and is either blind or elderly may claim an additional $750; if he or she is elderly *and* blind, he or she may deduct an additional $1,500 in addition to the $3,000 or $4,400 standard deduction.

Changes in Schedule A—Itemized Deductions

Note that the Schedule A—Itemized Deductions section has been changed to reflect the following:
1. *Medical expenses* (line 2). They must top 7½ percent of adjusted gross income (up from 5 percent).
2. Sales taxes are no longer deductible.
3. *Interest paid* (lines 9a and 9b). There are new rules on mortgage loans incurred after August 16, 1986.
4. *Interest paid on consumer loans* (lines 12a and 12b). Only 65 percent of consumer interest is tax deductible.
5. *Moving Expenses* (line 19). Moving expenses must now be treated as an itemized deduction but are not subject to the 2 percent floor.
6. *Miscellaneous deductions* (lines 20–25). Certain miscellaneous deductions to be entered on lines 20 and 21 are subject to a 2 percent AGI limit, whereas entries on line 25 are not. (See page 184 for complete explanation.)

Line	Tax Law	Pay Less Tax Legally

Schedule A Lines 1–4	**Medical and Dental Expenses**
	
	You are permitted a deduction for medical expenses paid for yourself, your family, and your dependents. Either divorced parent is entitled to deduct medical expenses paid on behalf of a child, whether or not that child is claimed as an exemption. See page 58 for a discussion of who is a dependent.
	
	Only expenditures for prescription drugs and insulin are deductible. Other medical expenses are deductible only if they exceed 7.5 percent of adjusted gross income. For example, assume that a taxpayer who itemizes and has an adjusted gross income of $20,000 has unreimbursed medical expenses of $2,000:
	
	Other medical expenses $1,000
	Insurance 750
	Insulin/drugs 250
	  Total $2,000
	Less 7.5% of income 1,500
	  Net deduction $ 500
		• A taxpayer may deduct as medical expenses amounts paid to maintain a dependent in a therapeutic center for drug addicts. The deduction includes the cost of the dependent's meal and lodging.
		
		• A son paid his parents' medical expenses even though they had enough money in the bank. The courts allowed him not only the medical deduction but the parents' exemptions, and head-of-household rates as well.
		
		• If hospitalization or medical-insurance premiums are deducted from pay, save pay statements as proof.
		
		• Hospitalization insurance required by your child's after-school activity group, summer camp, and school can be claimed as part of your medical insurance deduction.
		
		• Senior citizens may include Medicare payments in computing their medical insurance payments.

SCHEDULES A&B (Form 1040)

Schedule A—Itemized Deductions
(Schedule B is on back)

Department of the Treasury — Internal Revenue Service
▶ Attach to Form 1040. ▶ See Instructions for Schedules A and B (Form 1040).

OMB No. 1545-0074
1987
Attachment Sequence No. 07

Name(s) as shown on Form 1040: DOUGH
Your social security number: 329:04:1040

Medical and Dental Expenses
(Do not include expenses reimbursed or paid by others.)
(See Instructions on page 21.)

- **1a** Prescription medicines and drugs, insulin, doctors, dentists, nurses, hospitals, insurance premiums you paid for medical and dental care, etc. — **1a** 2756
- **b** Transportation and lodging — **1b** 150
- **c** Other (list—include hearing aids, dentures, eyeglasses, etc.) ▶ .... — **1c**
- **2** Add lines 1a through 1c, and enter the total here. — **2** 2906
- **3** Multiply the amount on Form 1040, line 31, by 7.5% (.075). — **3** 4312
- **4** Subtract line 3 from line 2. If zero or less, enter -0-. Total medical and dental ▶ **4** 0

Taxes You Paid
(See Instructions on page 21.)

Note: Sales taxes are no longer deductible.
- **5** State and local income taxes — **5** 1930
- **6** Real estate taxes — **6** 2414
- **7** Other taxes (list—include personal property taxes) .... — **7**
- **8** Add the amounts on lines 5 through 7. Enter the total here. Total taxes ▶ **8** 4344

Interest You Paid
(See Instructions on page 22.)

Caution: If your home mortgage interest includes interest on a loan taken out **after August 16, 1986**, and if the loan proceeds were **not used to buy** your home, attach Form 8598 and check here. ▶ ☐

- **9a** Deductible home mortgage interest you paid to financial institutions (report deductible points on line 10) — **9a** 6003
- **b** Deductible home mortgage interest you paid to individuals (show that person's name and address) ▶ .... — **9b**
- **10** Deductible points — **10**
- **11** Deductible investment interest — **11** 611
- **12a** Personal interest you paid (see page 22) **12a** 1915
- **b** Multiply the amount on line 12a by 65% (.65). Enter the result — **12b** 1244
- **13** Add the amounts on lines 9a through 11, and 12b. Enter the total here. Total interest ▶ **13** 7858

Contributions You Made
(See Instructions on page 22.)

- **14a** Cash contributions. (If you gave $3,000 or more to any one organization, report those contributions on line 14b.) — **14a** 840
- **b** Cash contributions totaling $3,000 or more to any one organization. (Show to whom you gave and how much you gave.) ▶ — **14b**
- **15** Other than cash. (You must attach Form 8283 if over $500.) — **15** 315
- **16** Carryover from prior year — **16**
- **17** Add the amounts on lines 14a through 16. Enter the total here. Total contributions ▶ **17** 1155

Casualty and Theft Losses
- **18** Casualty or theft loss(es) (attach Form 4684). (See page 23 of the Instructions.) ▶ **18** 0

Moving Expenses
- **19** Moving expenses (attach Form 3903 or 3903F). (See page 23 of the Instructions.) ▶ **19** 5100

Miscellaneous Deductions Subject to 2% AGI Limit
(See Instructions on page 23.)

- **20** Unreimbursed employee business expenses (attach Form 2106) — **20** 5249
- **21** Other expenses (list type and amount) ▶ NON REIMB. ENTERTAINMENT — **21** 600
- **22** Add the amounts on lines 20 and 21. Enter the total. — **22** 5849
- **23** Multiply the amount on Form 1040, line 31, by 2% (.02). Enter the result here — **23** 1150
- **24** Subtract line 23 from line 22. Enter the result (but not less than zero) ▶ **24** 4699

Other Miscellaneous Deductions
- **25** Miscellaneous deductions not subject to 2% AGI limit (see page 23). (List type and amount.) ▶ .... ▶ **25**

Total Itemized Deductions
- **26** Add the amounts on lines 4, 8, 13, 17, 18, 19, 24, and 25. Enter the total here and on Form 1040, line 33a. ▶ **26** 23156

The One-Minute Taxman: Medical Expenses

The IRS defines medical expenses as monies paid for the diagnosis, cure, mitigation, treatment, or prevention of disease, for the purpose of affecting any structure or function of the body, or for insurance coverage that pays for all or part of the medical care needed by you or your family. In order to be deductible, your medical expenses must exceed 7.5 percent of adjusted gross income.

Medical Expenses	Amount	*Medical Expenses*	Amount
☐ Abortions	_____	☐ Christian Science practitioner's fees	_____
☐ Acupuncture	_____	☐ Computer data bank membership	_____
☐ Air conditioner, air filtration system if required by a physician	_____	☐ Contact lenses	_____
☐ Alcohol and drug addiction clinics; Alcoholics Anonymous membership fees	_____	☐ Contact lens insurance premiums	_____
		☐ Contact lens solutions and appliances; distilled water	_____
☐ Ambulance, cost of rental	_____	☐ Cosmetic surgery, even if only to improve personal appearance	_____
☐ Anesthesiologist	_____		
☐ Arch supports	_____	☐ Crutches	_____
☐ Arthritic appliances and aids	_____	☐ Deaf: guide dog or cat; hearing aids, cost and maintenance; audio equipment	_____
☐ Auto, especially equipped for the disabled	_____		
☐ Back supports, special mattress, and wood boards for severe back problems	_____	☐ Dental expenses: fluoride, cleaning, X-rays, fillings, bridgework	_____
		☐ Dermatologist	_____
☐ Bathroom: special facilities for handicapped	_____	☐ Diagnostic services	_____
		☐ Diathermy	_____
☐ Blind: cost of guide dog; tape recorder; special typewriter; lenses; braille books and magazines	_____	☐ Elastic stockings	_____
		☐ Electroshock therapy	_____
		☐ Eye exams and treatment	_____
☐ Blood transfusions	_____	☐ Eyeglasses	_____
☐ Braces	_____	☐ Fluoridation treatments at home	_____
☑ Capital improvements: swimming pools, hydrotherapy whirlpools (if prescribed by physician), ramps	_____		
		☐ Guide dog for blind and deaf	_____
		☐ Gynecologist	_____
☐ Chiropodist	_____		
☐ Chiropractor	_____		

(Continued)

Medical Expenses	Amount	Medical Expenses	Amount
☐ Hair transplant	_____	☐ Optician	_____
☐ Healing services	_____	☐ Optometrist	_____
☐ Health club fees (if prescribed by doctor)	_____	☐ Organ transplant	_____
		☐ Orthodontist	_____
☐ Hospitalization and institutionalization costs	_____	☐ Orthopedic shoes	_____
		☐ Orthopedist	_____
☐ Hospitalization insurance premiums	_____	☐ Osteopath	_____
		☐ Oxygen	_____
☐ Hydrotherapy	_____	☐ Pacemaker	_____
☐ Injections	_____	☐ Periodontist	_____
☐ Insulin	_____	☐ Physical exam	_____
☐ Intercom for disabled	_____	☐ Preadoption medical expenses	_____
☐ Invalid, special chair	_____		
☐ Iron lung	_____	☐ Prosthesis	_____
☐ Jacuzzi (if prescribed by doctor)	_____	☐ Psychiatrist	_____
		☐ Psychotherapist	_____
☐ Kidney dialysis	_____	☐ Radiologist	_____
☐ Lab fees, including blood tests and x-rays	_____	☐ Reclining chair, on advice of physician	_____
☐ Legal fees, guardianship	_____	☐ Remedial reading for child with dyslexia	_____
☐ Lip reading and signing instruction	_____	☐ Sacroiliac belt	_____
		☐ School for mentally retarded	_____
☐ Long-distance phone calls to physicians	_____		
		☐ Speech therapy	_____
☐ Medical insurance premiums	_____	☐ Splints	_____
		☐ Training for handicapped	_____
☐ Midwife expenses	_____	☐ Travel to physician, hospital, pharmacy	_____
☐ Mobile telephone, for patient required to keep in touch with doctor	_____		
		☐ Trusses	_____
		☐ Wheelchair	_____
☐ Neurologist fees	_____	☐ Wig, if prescribed by doctor	_____
☐ Nursing attendants in home	_____		
☐ Obstetrician	_____		Total _____
☐ Oncologist	_____		
☐ Ophthalmologist	_____		

Line	Tax Law	Pay Less Tax Legally
	Transportation for medical care is deductible to the extent of 9¢ per mile or actual expenses (gasoline, parking, tolls) to and from the doctor, pharmacy, or hospital, or the amount of any cab, train, or bus fares. The cost of travel out of town to see a doctor in connection with a specific ailment is also deductible. If a spouse or parent is required to accompany a patient or visit, those expenses would be deductible as part of the total medical expenses. Medical deductions may include up to $50 per day per person for lodging away from home while an outpatient at a hospital or clinic. Meal costs are nondeductible if outside a hospital setting.	• One taxpayer made an annual pilgrimage from Los Angeles to New York to be examined by his family doctor. Since the primary purpose of the trip was to visit the doctor, the travel costs were deductible. • When treatment by doctors in the United States was not productive, a taxpayer traveled to a foreign country for treatment. Since the primary purpose of the travel was of a medical nature, the travel expenses were deductible. • Substantiate all medical deductions by keeping canceled checks and statements. • For other medical deduction saving tips, see "Save Money Later," page 275. • The full costs of home improvements for physically handicapped persons now qualify as medical expenses, including widening hallways and doorways, ramps, railings, and adjustments to cabinets to make them more accessible.
Lines 5–8	**Taxes as Deductions** The IRS permits deductions for taxes in these categories: real estate tax; personal property tax; and state, local, or foreign income tax. For a tax to be deductible, it must be imposed on the individual claiming the deduction. (Real estate taxes, for example, are deductible only to the owner of the property.) In addition, the tax must be paid during the tax year in order to get a tax writeoff for that year. Income taxes paid to a foreign country may be deducted as either an itemized deduction or a tax credit against your income tax.	• Look at W-2s for amounts withheld by the state and/or city. These amounts are deductible if you itemize. • Even though it is no longer deductible, sales tax will be added to the original cost of property, which reduces taxable profit when you sell. Keep a record of sales tax paid when you buy investment property.
Line 5	**State and Local Income Taxes** Any income tax withheld by the state or city during the year is deductible on your federal return, as well as payments made this year for last year's taxes—including	

Line	Tax Law	Pay Less Tax Legally
	estimated tax and amounts sent in with an extension of time to file. If a refund was received in 1987 for overpayments on 1986 state and/or city income tax, that refund must be reported as income on Form 1040, Line 11 if you deducted the state or city tax in a prior year.	
Line 6	**Real Estate Taxes**	
	Real estate taxes are deductible in the year paid.	• Your lending institution will most likely send a year-end form to advise you of real estate taxes paid (if you have an escrow account).
	Real-estate taxes must be split between the buyer and the seller of the property, based on the number of days each held the property. As a general rule, real estate taxes are imposed on the seller up to but not including the date of the sale.	• Check your closing statement for the prorations.
	Condominium special assessments are usually not deductible because they tend to increase the value of property.	• If the purpose of an assessment was for maintenance or repair, or to meet interest charges with respect to such benefits, the assessment may be deductible.
Line 7	**Other Taxes, Including Personal Property Tax**	
	You are permitted to deduct personal property tax, but only if you can itemize. Where a state fee on autos is based on value, it is deductible as a personal property tax.	

Interest Expense (Lines 9a–9b)

Interest: Is It Deductible?

Beginning this year, 2 things are important: timing and records. Most interest will no longer be deductible (other than home mortgages). If you do borrow for a qualifying purpose (stock investments or running a small business, for example), the IRS will assume that your first expenditure after borrowing the money was funded by the loan, which can result in a presumption that you spent it for a qualifying purpose. In the first 15 days the law gives you an opportunity to choose between disbursements made during the period. For example, a person borrows $10,000 and first pays down a loan related to a passive property by $10,000 and then repays a qualified home equity loan by $10,000, both within the 15 days of the initial borrowing. The general rule would result in the allocation of interest on the new loan to a passive activity since the repayment of the passive loan occurred before the equity loan paydown. When a taxpayer has net losses from passive activities, the interest expense may provide no current tax benefit. However, since the equity loan was also paid within 15 days of the new loan, you may consider the equity loan to have been paid with the new loan proceeds and, voila, you have deductible home mortgage interest!

Home Mortgage Interest

On mortgages obtained after August 16, 1986, interest expense may no longer be deducted on loans over the original price of the home plus improvements, except when the loan is used for medical or education expenses.

Try to keep extremely accurate records of home improvements, medical expenses, and educational expenses if you take out a mortgage for more than the cost of your home.

Form 8598 - Computation of Deductible Home Mortgage Interest

With all the changes and limits on interest deductions under the new Tax Reform law, you may find it necessary to complete Form 8598 this year. If you took out a home equity loan since August 16, 1986, and used the mortgage to finance the purchase of a second home, you will not need to complete Form 8598. Also, if your loan was taken out before August 17, 1986, you will not need to complete Form 8598 unless the loan amount exceeded the fair market value of the home at the time the loan was taken out.

You *will* need to complete Form 8598 if you took out a home equity loan or other financing secured by your home and did not use the money to buy the home, but only if you itemize your deductions.

If you refinanced an old mortgage or borrowed additional sums on your home (e.g., a home-equity line of credit) after August 16, 1986, you will have to complete Form 8598.

Form 8598: Line-by-Line Instructions

Part I

Line 1. You may compute the average daily balance in one of 5 ways, which follow. Place the resulting figure on line 1.

Method 1—Average balance reported by lender. You may not use this method if the debt was outstanding at any time that the home was not a qualified home. You may use the average balance reported to you by the lender in 1987 if the debt was outstanding during the entire time that the property was a qualified home. If the debt was not owed for all of the time that the home was qualified, multiply the average balance reported by the lender by the number of days the debt was owed during 1987. Divide that result by the number of days during 1987 that the property was a qualified home.

Method 2—Average daily balance. To figure the average daily balance:

1. Add the principal balance of the debt on each day in 1987 that the home was qualified and enter the total .... _____
2. Divide the amount on line 1 by the number of days the home was qualified. Enter the result. This is the average balance of the debt ... _____

The debt is treated as having a zero balance on any day during that period in which the debt was not yet incurred or was no longer owed.

Itemizing Your Deductions **157**

Method 3—Interest paid divided by interest rate. You may use this method if the following conditions are met:

- All accrued interest was paid at least monthly; and

- At all times in 1987 that the debt was owed, the debt was secured by your home.

To use this method, complete the following worksheet:

1. Enter the interest paid or accrued during 1987 . . . . _____
2. Enter the interest rate on the debt stated on an annual basis. (If the interest rate varied during 1987, use the lowest rate for the year.) . . . _____
3. Divide the amount on line 1 by the amount on line 2. If the home was qualified all of 1987, stop here; this is the average balance of the debt. However, if the home was not qualified all of 1987, go to line 4 . _____
4. Enter the percentage of the year that the home was qualified . . . . _____
5. Divide the amount on line 3 by the percentage on line 4. Enter the result. This is the average balance of the debt . . . . _____

Example. Mr. Blue had a line-of-credit loan secured by his principal home all of 1987. The interest rate on the line-of-credit loan was 9 percent throughout the year. The principal balance of the line-of-credit changed throughout 1987. He paid accrued interest of $2,500. His average balance using this method is $27,777 ($2,500/.09).

Method 4—Average of first and last balance. You may use this method if all three of the following conditions apply:

1. The debt was owed all of 1987, or if the home was qualified for less than the whole year, for the part of 1987 that the home was qualified; and
2. The principal balance of the debt did not increase in 1987; and
3. The debt required level payments in 1987 and the payments were made neither more frequently nor less frequently than required. The payments will be treated as being level-payment even if they may be adjusted from time to time because of changes in the interest rate.

To figure the average balance by this method, if the home was qualified ALL of 1987, complete the following worksheet:

1. Enter the balance of the debt as of January 1, 1987 . . . . _____
2. Enter the balance of the debt as of December 31, 1987 . . . . _____
3. Add amount on lines 1 and 2 . . . . _____
4. Divide the amount on line 3 by 2. Enter the result. This is the average balance of the debt . . . . _____

If the home was not qualified all year, use the principal balance as of the first day of the year that the home was qualified and the principal balance as of the last day of the year that the home was qualified.

Example: Mr. Brown is required to make level monthly payments of principal and interest to pay off, over 20 years, a loan of $10,000 secured by a second mortgage on his principal home. The balance of his second mortgage on January 1, 1987, was $9,652, and on December 31 of the same year it was $9,450. His average balance using this method is: $9,551 (the sum of $9,652 plus $9,450 divided by 2).

Method 5—Average of monthly balance method.—To figure the average balance using this method, either (1) add the average monthly balance of the debt and divide that total

Form **8598**
Department of the Treasury
Internal Revenue Service

Computation of Deductible Home Mortgage Interest
▶ Attach to Form 1040.
▶ See Separate Instructions.

OMB No. 1545-XXXX
1987
Attachment Sequence No. **85**

Name(s) as shown on Form 1040: Dough

Your social security number: 329 04 1040

Note: Complete a separate Form 8598 if you have two qualified homes. See the separate instructions.

Am I Required To Complete and File This Form? — Complete this form to figure your deductible home mortgage interest if:
- You took out a mortgage on your home (or other debt secured by your home) after August 16, 1986, and
- You took out the mortgage for a purpose **other than** to buy the home.

You **do not** have to complete this form if:
- You took out only one mortgage on your home and that mortgage was to buy your home, or
- You took out all mortgages on your home before August 17, 1986, and you did not refinance any of these mortgages or borrow additional amounts on any of these mortgages after August 16, 1986. However, if the mortgages were above the fair market value of the home at the time you took them out, then you must file this form.

If you have to complete this form, attach it to Form 1040.

How Much of My Home Mortgage Interest May I Deduct? — In general, you may still deduct all interest you paid on any mortgage you took out to buy your home. However, you may not be able to deduct all of your home mortgage interest if the cost of the home (including the cost of improvements you made) is less than the "average balance" of your mortgage(s). "Average balance" means the average principal amount you owed for 1987 on your mortgage, or the total of the average principal amount you owed for 1987 on each mortgage if you had more than one.

Any part of the interest you cannot deduct as home mortgage interest will usually be treated as personal interest. For 1987, only 65% of personal interest is deductible.

Which Parts of the Form Do I Complete? — You must complete Part I to see if you can deduct all interest paid on the home mortgages. If you find that you may deduct all of the mortgage interest, then stop after completing Part I. However, if after you complete Part I you find that not all of your interest on the mortgages is deductible, then read on to see if you should complete Part II or Part III to figure the amount of home mortgage interest you may deduct.

You should read the additional separate instructions carefully before you begin to complete Part I. These instructions explain what is meant by cost plus improvements to your home and when you can use an amount higher than cost plus improvements if you had a mortgage on your home before August 17, 1986. These instructions also explain in detail how to determine the average balance of each mortgage.

We have provided several methods you may be able to choose from to figure the average balance of each mortgage. You may be able to use more than one method for each mortgage or different methods for different mortgages.

Note: In some instances you must use Part III. Or, in other situations, using Part III instead of Part II may result in a larger deduction.

You must use the special method in Part III instead of Part II if you used any of the proceeds of any mortgage or other debt secured by your home in your trade or business.

You may use the special method in Part III if you used any part of the proceeds of any debt secured by the home to pay for:
a. any qualified medical or educational expenses, or
b. any investment property or expenses, or
c. any passive activity property or expenses.

In Part III, you figure the amount of deductible home mortgage interest separately for each mortgage. By using Part III, you may increase your cost plus improvements to the home by the amount of certain medical or educational expenses and thereby qualify more interest as deductible home mortgage interest. In addition, if you use Part III, the part that is not deductible home mortgage interest may be deducted as investment interest or passive activity interest if applicable.

Part I — Complete To Decide If You Can Deduct All Home Mortgage Interest

1. Figure the average balance for 1987 of each mortgage on your home, and enter the sum of the average balances. See the separate instructions **1**

2. Enter the cost of the home plus the cost of any improvements. See the separate instructions **2**

3. If you had any mortgage on your home that you incurred before August 17, 1986, add the amount of the pre-August 17 debt as determined in the separate instructions for line 3 and enter the total . . . **3**

   Note: If the home was personal property, such as a boat, see the separate instructions.

4. Enter the **larger of: a)** the amount on line 2, or **b)** the amount on line 3 . . . . **4**

   - If line 4 is **equal to or more than** line 1, **STOP HERE** and enter on Schedule A (Form 1040), line 9a or 9b, as applicable, ALL interest paid on the mortgages included on line 1. If you have deductible points, or the mortgage was used other than for personal purposes, see the separate instructions for Part III, lines 15 and 16.
   - If line 4 is **less than** line 1, you cannot deduct all interest paid on the mortgages included on line 1. To figure deductible home mortgage interest you should complete Part II. However, see the **Note** above to determine if you should use Part III.

Part II — Regular Method To Figure Deductible Home Mortgage Interest

5. Enter the total interest paid for 1987 on the mortgages included on line 1. See the separate instructions . . **5**

6. Divide the amount on line 4 by the amount on line 1 and enter the percentage . . . . **6** × .

7. Multiply the amount on line 5 by the percentage on line 6 and enter the result. Also, enter this amount on Schedule A (Form 1040), line 9a or 9b, as applicable, as **home mortgage interest.** If you have deductible points, see the separate instructions **7**

8. Subtract the amount on line 7 from the amount on line 5, and enter the result. Also, enter this amount on Schedule A (Form 1040), line 12a, as **personal interest** **8**

Form 8598 (1987) — Page 2

Part III — Special Method To Figure Deductible Home Mortgage Interest

Note: *Complete one full column at a time starting with the earliest debt in Column A. If you have more than three debts complete a separate Column C, Form 8598 for each additional debt. See separate instructions.*

Complete Column A first — Enter the earliest debt first

		A	B	C
		(mo., yr.)	(mo., yr.)	(mo., yr.)
1	Enter the date on which you secured the debt with your home. See the separate instructions	/	/	/
2	Enter the **average balance** of the debt. See the separate instructions			
3	Enter the amount from Part I, line 4. See the separate instructions			
4a	Enter the amount, if any, from the worksheet in the separate instructions for medical or educational expenses			
4b	Enter the amount, if any, from line 4a of the **previous** column	-0-		
4c	Add amounts on lines 4a and 4b			
5	Add amounts on lines 3 and 4c			
6	Enter the **smaller of**: a. the amount on line 5, or b. the fair market value of the home at the time the debt was secured by the home. See the separate instructions			
7	Enter the amount from line 9 of the **previous** column	-0-	-0-	
8	Enter the **smaller of**: a. line 2 of the **previous** column, or b. line 10 of the **previous** column	-0-		
9	Add amounts on lines 7 and 8, and enter the total	-0-		
10	Subtract the amount on line 9 from the amount on line 6 and enter the result			
11	Enter the **total interest** for 1987 that applies to the debt. See the instructions			
	• If line 10 is **equal to or more than** line 2, skip line 12. Then enter the amount from line 11 on line 13.			
	• If line 10 is **less than** line 2, go to line 12.			
	• If line 10 is **zero**, skip lines 12 and 13. Then enter the amount from line 11 on line 14.			
12	Divide the amount on line 10 by the amount on line 2. Enter the percentage	× .	× .	× .
13	Multiply the amount on line 11 by the percentage on line 12. Enter the result			
14	Subtract the amount on line 13 from the amount on line 11. Enter the result			
15	Add the amounts in the columns on line 13 and enter the total. Also enter this amount on Schedule A (Form 1040), line 9a or line 9b, as applicable. If this total includes deductible points, see the separate instructions. This is the amount you can deduct as **home mortgage interest**			
16	Add the amounts in the columns on line 14 and enter the total. See the separate instructions to figure how much, if any, of the total amount of interest on this line may be deducted elsewhere on your tax return			

Proof of August 13, 1987

by 12, or (2) add the principal balance of the debt as of the end of each calendar month, and divide that total by 12.

If the home was not qualified all of 1987, use either the average monthly balance or the principal balance as of the end of each calendar month that the home was qualified and divide by the number of months that the home was qualified. For this purpose, the home is presumed to be qualified for the entire month if it was qualified for more than 15 days during the month.

Line 2. Total original purchase price plus costs of any improvements to the home through December 31, 1987, and enter the total on line 2.

Line 3. This is for any mortgage on your home (other than to buy the home) incurred before August 17, 1986.

Line 4. Enter either the amount on line 2 or the amount on line 3, whichever is larger. If the resulting figure on line 4 is equal to (or larger) than the figure on line 1, stop here. Enter on Schedule A of Form 1040, line 9a or 9b, ALL interest paid on your mortgages as totaled on line 1 of Form 8598. If the figure on line 4 is *smaller* than that on line 1, you must continue, and complete Part II or Part III of Form 8598.

If any part of the loan was used to pay for (1) medical or educational expenses, (2) investment property or expenses, or (3) passive activity property of expenses, you may prefer to use Part III in order to get a larger interest deduction.

In completeing Part II, part of your interest paid will be treated as deductible home mortgage interest and part as personal interest.

Part II

Line 5. Enter here the total interest paid in 1987 on all debts secured by your home.
Line 6. Divide line 4 (Part I) by line 1 and enter the percentage on line 6.
Line 7. Multiply line 5 by the percentage on line 6 and enter the result on line 7 *and* on Schedule A, Form 1040, line 9a or 9b.
Line 8. Subtract line 7 from line 5 and enter the result on line 8 *and* on line 12a of Form 1040, Schedule A as personal interest.

Part III

If you took out a second mortgage (or other secured debt) to pay for (1) certain medical or educational expenses, (2) investment property or expenses, or (3) passive activity property or expenses, Part III will enable you to deduct more interest by identifying these items.

There are 3 columns. Use column A for the earliest loan, B for the next, and C for the most recent. If more than 3 loans are involved, complete an additional column C on a separate Form 8598 for each additional loan. (Column A is usually the actual first mortgage on the home used to purchase the home.)

Line 1. Enter the date of the loan.
Line 2. Enter the average balance of the debt (using one of the same 5 methods allowed in Part I, line 1, for calculating the average balance).
Line 3. Enter the amount shown in Part I on line 4 (the adjusted cost of the home).
Line 4a. If you secured a loan after August 16, 1986, and used the money for (1) medical expenses for you, your spouse, or a dependent that were not reimbursed by insurance or for (2) educational expenses for you, your spouse, or a dependent, you will need to determine the amount to enter on line 4a by use of the following worksheet:

1. Enter the average balance of this loan from Part III, line 1. If you used at least 95 percent of the loan proceeds for medical or educational

expenses, enter this amount on line 4a and stop here. If not, continue to step 2.

2. Enter the amount of this loan used to pay these expenses as of 12-31-87. _____
3. Enter the total paid on the principal of the debt through 12-31-86 (not including repayments if they exceeded the amount used to pay for these expenses at time repayment was made). _____
4. Subtract line 3 from line 2 and enter the result here. _____
5. Enter either the amount on line 1 (of this worksheet) or line 4, whichever is smaller, on this line, *and* on line 4a of Part III in the column for this debt. _____

A separate worksheet must be completed for each loan involving medical or educational expenses, and the result entered in a separate column for that particular debt.

Line 4b. Enter in column B the amount on line 4a for column A, and enter in column C the amount on line 4b for Column B. (and so on, for any additional columns C)

Line 4c. Add the figures in 4a and 4b and enter the total on line 4c.

Line 5. Add line 3 to line 4c and place result on line 5.

Line 6. Determine the fair market value of your home at the time the money was borrowed. Enter on line 6 either this value or the amount from line 5, whichever is smaller.

Lines 7, 8, 9. Follow Form.

Line 10. Subtract line 9 from line 6 and enter the result on line 10.

Line 11. Enter the total amount of interest which applies to the debt for 1987.

If line 10 equals or is more than line 1, enter the amount on line 11 on line 13 (skip 12).

If line 10 is less than line 2, go to line 12.

If line 10 is zero, skip lines 12 and 13 and enter the line 11 amount on line 14.

Line 12. Divide the amount on line 10 by line 2 and enter the percentage on line 12.

Line 13. Multiply line 11 by the percentage on line 12 and enter the result on line 13.

Line 14. Subtract line 13 from line 11 and enter the result on line 14.

Line 15. Add all amounts in the columns from line 13 and enter the total on line 15. Also enter this figure on Schedule A, Form 1040, line 9a or 9b. This is your deductible home mortgage interest.

Line 16. Add all columns on line 14 and enter the total on line 16. This is your nondeductible home mortgage interest.

Qualified Residence Interest

Qualified residence interest means interest on a loan obtained by a primary or second residence (e.g., a vacation home that is being treated as a qualified residence).

The temporary regulations on interest expense allocation specifically say that the asset securing a loan is not the basis upon which to allocate interest expense on that loan. Tracing of the disbursement of loan proceeds is determinative.

Line	Tax Law	Pay Less Tax Legally
	Mortgage Interest as a Deduction Under Tax Reform, you can deduct the amount of interest payments on the basic cost of your home plus any improvements, if the improvements are intended to be permanent. Because mortgage interest is fully deductible (and consumer interest is being eliminated as a writeoff), it is very important to keep accurate records on home improvements. Do not confuse improvements with repairs; there is a fine line that divides the two. Although painting a room for the first time would be an improvement, the second painting of the room would be considered a repair. A rule of thumb is: If the item cannot be removed when the home is sold—e.g., a built-in bookcase—it is an improvement. Here is a list of items that generally are included in the home improvements category: 1. *Appliances* (freezer, washing machine, air conditioner)—*if* they will not be removed when the house is sold 2. *Bathroom fixtures*—medicine cabinet, towel racks, sliding doors for the tub 3. *Building improvements*—screen doors, tool shed, waterproofing, termite inspection, mantel, fireplace, drainpipes 4. *Communications systems*—intercoms, permanent telephone outlets, fire alarms, burglar alarms 5. *Flooring*—wood floors, wall-to-wall carpeting 6. *Furniture and fixtures*—built-in cabinets, closet shelves, drapery (*if* not removed when the house is sold) 7. *Garden, grounds*—birdbath, terraces, trees, sprinkler system, fence and gate, barbecue pit, pool, landscaping	● Zero-rate mortgages can give rise to interest deduction. In one case, buyers of a no-interest home were in fact paying interest as part of the purchase price. They were allowed to deduct 22 percent of payments on a 5-year loan as interest and 30 percent of payments on a 7-year loan. ● Be wary of prepaying your mortgage at a discount since you may have taxable income to the extent of the discount. Putting the money into your business, tuition, buying a car, or fixing up the mortgaged property is still permitted, but if you use the money to buy tax-exempt bonds, your deduction is lost. Payment of loan service charges is deductible only if it increases the lender's rate of interest. For a full discussion of limits on interest deduction, see page 165. ● If as a home buyer you are obligated to pay a fixed amount per year as ground rent, those payments are deductible as interest. In most cases, a redeemable ground rent is an agreement in which there is a right to redeem upon payment of a specified sum. If the lease period is for more than 15 years, including renewal periods, and the leaseholder has a present or future right in the property, the land is considered redeemable. Payment on nonredeemable ground rent is not deductible unless the property is used in business or for rental purposes. ● According to the IRS, if you refinance your home mortgage, you must claim a deduction evenly over the life of the new mortgage. However, if the owner dies (or the home is sold), the balance (not written off) becomes fully deductible in the year of either death or sale.

Line	Tax Law	Pay Less Tax Legally
	8. *Kitchen*—garbage disposal, countertops 9. *Laundry*—laundry chute, laundry tub 10. *Lighting/electricity*—rooftop TV antenna and wiring, fuses replaced with circuit breakers, floodlights 11. *Mechanical*—attic fan, hot water heater, central air 12. *Paving*—driveway, cement walk 13. *Plumbing*—septic system, water pipes, copper tubing 14. *Renovation*—converting the attic into a bedroom or the basement into a family room 15. *Walls and ceilings*—insulation, wood paneling 16. *Windows and doors*—storm windows and doors, weather-stripping. For more information, see The One-Minute Taxman on Buying and Selling Homes, page 102. Interest on loans for home improvement is fully deductible; however, the cost of the addition is not deductible. It must be added to the cost basis in the home to determine the ultimate gain or loss upon sale. Prepayment penalties and late payment charges are also deductible. If you paid an individual $600 or more of mortgage interest, you must file a Form 1099. Form 1098 (to be provided by financial institutions) will have all names of persons listed on the mortgage but will be sent to the "main" person on the mortgage, who should then attach a statement to Form 1098 listing the names and addresses of others named in the mortgage. **Contingent Interest** Contingent interest is interest equal to a specified percentage of increase in value	

Line	Tax Law	Pay Less Tax Legally
	of a residence over the term of a Shared Appreciation Mortgage (SAM) and is payable upon termination of the SAM. A cash-basis taxpayer who finances the purchase of his home with a SAM (in which he is obligated to pay contingent interest as well as fixed-rate interest) may deduct the contingent interest on the mortgage loan. A SAM normally ends at the earliest of (1) prepayment of the entire SAM balance, (2) transfer of ownership of the residence, or (3) 10 years from the date of the SAM loan. The taxpayer may deduct the full amount of the contingent interest if: (1) he has sold the mortgaged residence and used a portion of the proceeds to pay the contingent interest, or (2) he has prepaid the SAM. If there is a refinancing agreement with the original lender and contingent interest is paid over the term of the second mortgage, it is deductible as interest when paid. ***Points Charged by Banks*** When you buy your principal home, points are fully deductible in the year paid. The points must be paid separately, not deducted from the loan proceeds. (Write a check separately for the points.) The points cannot be fees for specific services provided by the lender—e.g., notary charges, mortgage preparation costs, or appraisal fees. Points paid for refinancing are not deductible in one year, but must be amortized over the life of the loan. The refinance of a refinanced loan may trigger the current deduction of points on the first refinanced loan. ***Consumer Interest*** Interest on tax deficiencies of federal, state, or local income taxes is considered personal (consumer) interest. This includes interest on a tax deficiency attributable to a business disallowance.	• John and Jane Taxpayer bought a home in June for $100,000. According to their closing statement, they paid the following amounts: Points on loan $3,000 Notary fee 5 Stamp tax 20 Termite inspection 100 Credit reporting 10 Title charges 150 Total $3,285 Of this amount, the only deductible is for the points, or $3,000. The remaining $285 is an addition to the cost of the property. • If a seller pays the buyer points to help make a sale, the amount paid may not be deducted as interest. But any amount paid by seller for points reduces the sales price and any taxable gain.

Line	Tax Law	Pay Less Tax Legally
Line 12a	**_Other Deductible Forms of Interest_** Other types of deductible interest include interest paid on vacant land, interest paid on personal loans (but only if there is true indebtedness), interest paid on insurance loans, interest paid on bank loans to finance automobiles, and interest paid to a broker for margin accounts (only in the year paid). For 1987, only 65 percent of consumer interest is deductible. **_Interest Deductions_** For purposes of interest writeoffs, the type of interest involved will be determined according to the use of the loan proceeds. In the case of a taxpayer (other than a corporation) the deduction for investment interest expense is limited to net investment income (after a 5-year phase-in). In addition, no deduction is allowed for personal interest paid during the tax year (after a 5-year phase-in). Personal interest is any interest other than investment interest, home mortgage interest, interest on deferred tax payments, and interest incurred in connection with a trade or business (other than as an employee). When the proceeds of a loan are used solely to buy an interest in a passive activity, they will be taken into account when computing the income (or loss) from the passive activity. When the proceeds are used solely to make personal expenditures, they will be treated as consumer interest. Interest on student loans is deductible, but a parent must be personally liable on the loan in order to take a deduction in the interim. If both you and the child are liable, you may deduct interest that you paid. Where a guarantor of a loan (not necessarily a corporate one) is called	● _Guaranteed Loans:_ A taxpayer who guarantees a loan for a corporation that subsequently declares bankruptcy may deduct interest paid on the note. This is not true when a guarantor pays his principal's debt without a bankruptcy discharge. ● _Paying Interest on Life Insurance Loans:_ Insurance companies usually offer below-market interest rates on loans, and merely add the interest charges to the outstanding loan balance. Since you must actually pay interest in order to deduct it, send the insurance company a check before December 31 (to cover interest due through that date) and take a deduction (even if it includes interest on the loan for previous years).

Line	Tax Law	Pay Less Tax Legally
	upon by the lender to pay interest on a defaulted loan, the guarantor is allowed an interest deduction.	
	If you are a tenant in a housing co-op, you are permitted a tax writeoff for your portion of the payment.	
	If you paid interest on a tax deficiency, that interest is tax-deductible, even though the tax itself may not be.	
	Life Insurance Policyholder Loans. When a life insurance policy covers the life of an officer, employee, or person financially interested in any trade or business carried on by the taxpayer, interest expense on any policy loan is disallowed to the extent that the debt exceeds $50,000. This rule applies to contracts purchased after June 20, 1986.	
	Limitation on Interest Deduction	
	Prepaid interest is deductible only over the term of a loan—not all in the year paid. Loan service charges (not home-mortgage points) must therefore be pro-rated.	• If you borrow money at a discount, interest is deducted immediately and you receive the net amount. You must then repay the face amount (and are in fact paying back interest with each payment). The rule of 78s, used by banks to compute interest, can no longer be used in figuring your interest deduction.
	Investment Interest	

	Under the Tax Reform Act, interest paid on investments (e.g., stock margin account) is still deductible, but only to the extent of net investment income. The $10,000 of investment interest in excess of investment income that was available under the old law is to be phased out. Therefore, if you purchase investment property on credit and have no net investment income for that year, you may not deduct any of your interest payments for the year. However, you are still permitted to carry the excess forward into a future year.	• Here is an example of how to compute deductible interest: You borrow $7,500 from Northwest Bank to finance a new car. The loan is a 12 percent discount over 3 years; your deduction is $900.
		
		Amount borrowed $7,500
		Interest rate: 12 percent
		  of $7,500
		  = $900
		  $900 × 3 = <u>2,700</u>
		The bank gives you <u>$4,800</u>
		
		Interest expense, $2,700 ÷ number of payments, 36 = $75 per payment. $75 × 12 = $900, interest deduction.

	Investment income will now include long-term capital gains and income or loss	

Line	Tax Law	Pay Less Tax Legally
	from certain working oil and gas interests. It will not include income from any passive activity. Investment interest expense also will not include interest on purchasing a passive activity. (For 1988 through 1990, some passive activity losses may be included.) When computing investment expenses, first apply the 2 percent floor on miscellaneous itemized deductions; this will possibly increase your net investment income. However, noninvestment expenses in the miscellaneous category are considered offset first by the 2 percent AGI floor. The $10,000 allowance on excess investment interest will be phased out from 1987 through 1990. During this time disallowed investment interest will be computed as if the new law were fully in effect, except that losses from passive activities that are deductible (under the phase-in provisions) are deducted in computing net investment income (except for the type eligible for $25,000 real estate rental passive loss allowance). The actual amount disallowed during the transition period (1987 to 1990) equals the applicable percentage (as shown on following chart) on the first $10,000 ($5,000 for married filing separately) of the disallowed interest deduction, plus 100 percent of the amount of investment interest above $10,000, which is disallowed. All disallowed investment interest during the transition period may be carried forward. This is the way the transition period breaks down: Year Percentage of First $10,000 Tentative Disallowance 1987 35% 1988 60% 1989 80% 1990 90% After 1990 New law is fully in effect	

Line	Tax Law	Pay Less Tax Legally
	More changes from Congress are expected. You may be able to avoid the investment interest limitation by reorganizing personal investment debts through a mortgage on your first or second home. Or try paying cash whenever possible. Although points paid to originate a mortgage in connection with the purchase of a principal residence are fully deductible in the year they are paid as interest expense, it is the IRS's position that points paid in connection with a refinance are amortized evenly. However, to the extent that some of the refinance proceeds are used to improve the residence, that portion of the points is immediately deductible. ***Part of Mortgage Loan Used for Home Improvements*** When you use a portion of the funds from a refinanced mortgage to pay off an existing mortgage and a portion for home improvements, the points paid for the improvements may be fully deductible. For the part of refinancing not used for home improvements, the points are treated the same as points not paid at the time of the loan. Withholding points from the loan proceeds (rather than paying them separately) does not constitute payment, and the IRS will allow the points to be deducted ratably only over the term of the loan, not deducted all in one year. In calculating the points for each year, divide the total points charged by the number of payments due (exclude the portion applicable to home improvements), then multiply by the sum of payments during the year (including those due during this year but made last year).	

Line	Tax Law	Pay Less Tax Legally
	Interest on Loans to Finance IRA Payments If you borrow money to create (or fund) an IRA, the interest is considered investment interest and is deductible up to the amount of your investment income. ***Car Loans*** In 1987 only 65 percent of the interest on car loans is deductible because it is consumer interest. The phase-out will be completed by 1991. Unfortunately, some employees have incorrectly assumed that they could take some of the interest on a car used for business expense. This interest is considered personal interest and is *not* deductible (except for the 5-year phase-out). ***Margin Interest Limited*** Deductions of margin interest on short-term debts (issued by governments and banks with a maturity of a year or less) are limited. In the past, short-term debts have been purchased on margin to give the buyer current interest writeoffs coupled with deferred interest income. Interest writeoffs are now deductible when the interest income is taxable. You may include interest income as it accrues or elect to delay deductions until receipt of income. ## Contributions	 • If a brokerage firm charges interest on your margin account by debiting your account, you cannot deduct this charged-but-not-paid interest. • If you need an interest writeoff, be sure there is enough money in your account to cover the interest charges during the year. If you want to shift the margin interest deduction into next year, keep a low balance in your margin account until that time.
Lines 14a-b	***Cash Contributions*** You are entitled to deduct contributions made to certain charitable organizations. (The contributions may be charged to a bank credit card.) In order to get a tax deduction, the contribution must have	• Most people give small cash contributions during the year but fail to keep records. Estimate the amount and take a deduction.

Line	Tax Law	Pay Less Tax Legally
	been given during the year—not merely pledged. You must keep written documentation for every charitable contribution of money. If you do not have a canceled check or receipt, you will need a letter from the recipient acknowledging receipt of the contribution and indicating dates and amounts. If any contribution totals more than $3,000 annually to any one organization, you will need the name of the organization on your tax form. As a general rule, the deduction for charitable contributions is limited to 50 percent of adjusted gross income (30 percent on contributions to fraternal organizations, public cemeteries, and private nonoperating foundations).	• If you attend a benefit performance, you are entitled to a tax deduction for the amount of the ticket in excess of the regular ticket price. Save ticket stubs. • If you don't have canceled checks, record in a notebook how much you donate in cash to the church collection box. New IRS rules require that you keep records of such donations, including the name of the charity, the date, and the amount of the donation. • A contribution to a foreign charity may be deductible if the donations were made to a domestic charity organized in the United States that used the funds in a foreign country. • Contributions made by credit card are deductible when the charge is made.
Line 15	**Noncash Contributions** If you contribute items to a charitable organization, you are allowed a deduction for the value of the item as of the date of the gift. If the gift has a value of more than $500, you must attach Form 8283 to your return showing: (1) the name and address of the organization; (2) the date the gift was given; (3) a description of the contribution; (4) the fair market value on the date given; (5) your original cost; (6) how and when you originally acquired it; and (7) the amount you are claiming as a deduction this year. Additional written records must also be kept for a property contribution over $500; i.e., you must attach to your return Form 8283 indicating the above information, as well as a statement as to how the value was computed and whether the donated property is ordinary income or capital-gain property. If you donate property other than securities and the value is over $5,000, Form 8283 must be filed. An authorized official of the charity must acknowledge receipt of the property on the form. An appraiser must provide a complete	• An appraisal will not withstand an audit "if the donor had knowledge of facts which would cause an appraiser falsely to overstate the value of the donated property. . . ." • When considering a sizable contribution, give appreciated property that will result in long-term capital gain. You will get a tax deduction for the full value of the property but avoid tax on the appreciation in value. • If you are active in a charity operation you are entitled to deduct any out-of-pocket expenses incurred on behalf of the charity, including the cost of any snacks, meals, and entertainment for meetings—even those held at your house. If you use your car for charitable work, you can deduct 12¢ per mile or actual costs. • Books donated to charity may be deducted at fair market value (even though they may have been purchased at a discount).

Line	Tax Law	Pay Less Tax Legally
	description of the property given, including the date and manner of the original purchase, the adjusted basis for the property, and the fair market value on the date of donation.	• If you are contributing old clothes or furniture to an organization, ask the charity to pick up the merchandise at your home. Ask for an itemized receipt and take a tax deduction for the fair market value of the items. If the charity will not pick up, send your appraisal of the items and ask the charity for acknowledgment in writing.
	Charitable Contributions	
	Unrelated-use tangible personal property (or any appreciated property donated to certain private nonoperating foundations) is limited in its deductibility to the donor's basis in the property. (In the past, the deduction was increased by any long-term capital gain that would have been realized if the property were sold rather than donated.)	
	Deducting the Cost of Private School	
	As a general rule, voluntary payments that cover the cost of a tuition-free school are not deductible; however, the IRS has provided a list of factors that change that conclusion.	
	A free school (to members) is one that receives most of its operating funds from contributions to the church. If contributions come from members (without children) and nonmembers are required to pay tuition to send their children to the school, those amounts are tax deductible. If a private school (that charges tuition) seeks additional gifts from parents during the year, those amounts are deductible as contributions. But if there is a contract by which the taxpayer agrees to make the contributions (and there are provisions ensuring the admission of the child), the charitable deduction is lost.	
Line 18	**Casualty and Theft Gains and Losses**	
	A casualty is an unexpected and sudden disaster that occurs without gross negligence on your part.	• Vandalism to property has the necessary attributes of suddenness and unexpectedness to be deductible as a casualty

Itemizing Your Deductions

Form **8283**
(Rev. October 1986)
Department of the Treasury
Internal Revenue Service

Noncash Charitable Contributions

▶ Attach to your Federal income tax return if the total claimed value of all property contributed exceeds $500.

OMB No. 1545-0908
Expires 9-30-88

Attachment Sequence No. **55**

Name(s) as shown on your income tax return: DOUGH

Identification number: 329-04-1040

Section A   Include in Section A **only** items (or groups of similar items) which have a claimed value of $5,000 or less per item or group and certain publicly traded securities (see instructions).

Part I   Information on Donated Property

1	(a) Name and address of the donee organization	(b) Description of donated property (attach a separate sheet if more space is needed)
A		
B		
C		
D		
E		

Note: Columns (d), (e), and (f) do not have to be completed for items with a value of $500 or less.

	(c) Date of the contribution	(d) Date acquired by donor (mo., yr.)	(e) How acquired by donor	(f) Donor's cost or adjusted basis	(g) Fair market value	(h) Method used to determine the fair market value
A						
B						
C						
D						
E						

Part II   Other Information—Complete questions 2 and 3 only if you gave less than the entire interest in property or if restrictions were attached to the contribution.

2   If less than the entire interest in the property is contributed during the year, complete the following:

   (a) Enter letter from Part I which identifies the property _____. (Attach a separate statement if Part II applies to more than one property.)

   (b) Total amount claimed as a deduction for the property listed in Part I for this tax year _____;
for any prior tax year(s) _____.

   (c) Name and address of each organization to which any such contribution was made in a prior year (complete only if different from the donee organization above).

Charitable organization (donee) name

Number and street

City or town, state, and ZIP code

   (d) The place where any tangible property is located or kept. _____
   (e) Name of any person, other than the donee organization, having actual possession of the property. _____

3   If conditions were attached to the contribution, answer the following questions: Yes | No

   (a) Is there a restriction either temporarily or permanently on the donee's right to use or dispose of the donated property? .

   (b) Did you give to anyone (other than the donee organization or another organization participating with the donee organization in cooperative fundraising) the right to the income from the donated property or to the possession of the property, including the right to vote donated securities, to acquire the property by purchase or otherwise, or to designate the person having such income, possession, or right to acquire? . . . .

   (c) Is there a restriction limiting the donated property for a particular use? . . . .

Page 2

income tax return. (Do not enter name and identification number if shown on the other side.)

Identification number
329-04-1040

isal Summary—Include in Section B only items (or groups of similar items) which have a claimed value of han $5,000 per item or group. *(Report contributions of certain publicly traded securities only in Section A.)*

cknowledgment *(To be completed by the charitable organization.)*

organization acknowledges that it is a qualified organization under section 170(c) and that it received the donated property as described in Part II on _____ .
(Date)

Furthermore, this organization affirms that in the event it sells, exchanges, or otherwise disposes of the property (or any portion thereof) within two years after the date of receipt, it will file an information return (**Form 8282,** Donee Information Return) with the IRS and furnish the donor a copy of that return. This acknowledgment does not represent concurrence in the claimed fair market value.

Charitable organization (donee) name	Employer identification number
Number and street	City or town, state, and ZIP code
Authorized signature	Title	Date

Part II — Information on Donated Property *(To be completed by the taxpayer and/or appraiser.)*

2 Check type of property:
☐ Art* ☐ Real Estate ☐ Gems/Jewelry
☐ Stamp Collections ☐ Coin Collections ☐ Books ☐ Other

*Art includes paintings, sculpture, watercolors, prints, drawings, ceramics, antique furniture, decorative arts, textiles, carpets, silver, rare manuscripts, historical memorabilia, and other similar objects.

3	(a) Description of donated property (attach a separate sheet if more space is needed)	(b) Date acquired by donor (mo., yr.)	(c) How acquired by donor	(d) Donor's cost or adjusted basis	(e) Appraised fair market value
A					
B					
C					
D					

4 If tangible property was donated, write a brief summary of the overall physical condition of the property at the time of the gift.

Part III — Taxpayer (Donor) Statement *(To be completed for items listed in Section B, Part II, with appraised value of $500 or less per item.)*

I declare that item(s) (enter letter(s) identifying property) _____ listed in Part II above has (have) to the best of my knowledge and belief an appraised value of not more than $500 (per item).

Signature of taxpayer (donor) ▶   Date ▶

Part IV — Certification of Appraiser *(To be completed by the appraiser of the above donated property.)*

I declare that I am not the donor, the donee, a party to the transaction in which the donor acquired the property, employed by or related to any of the foregoing persons, or a person whose relationship to any of the foregoing persons would cause a reasonable person to question my independence as an appraiser.

Also, I declare that I hold myself out to the public as an appraiser and that because of my qualifications as described in the appraisal, I am qualified to make appraisals of the type of property being valued. I certify the appraisal fees were not based upon a percentage of the appraised property value. Furthermore, I understand that a false or fraudulent overstatement of the property value as described in the qualified appraisal or this appraisal summary may subject me to the civil penalty under section 6701(a) (aiding and abetting the understatement of tax liability). I affirm that I have not been barred from presenting evidence or testimony by the Director of Practice.

Please Sign Here
Signature ▶   Title ▶   Date of appraisal ▶
Business address   Identification number

City or town, state, and ZIP code

… SAVE MONEY NOW

The One-Minute Taxman: Contributions

You are entitled to deduct contributions made to certain qualified charitable organizations. These organizations include churches, civic groups, and not-for-profit charities. If you are in doubt about the status of a given organization, check with the organization directly.

Qualified Charitable Contributions	*Amount*	*Qualified Charitable Contributions*	*Amount*
☐ Admission charges: art museums, natural history museums, planetariums	_____	☐ Foster-home care	_____
		☐ Fund-raising expenses	_____
		☐ Health research foundations	_____
☐ Amateur athletic associations	_____	☐ Hospitals, research or nonprofit	_____
☐ Artworks, at fair market value; if you created the work, your deduction is limited to out-of-pocket expenses	_____	☐ Land, based on fair market value	_____
		☐ Library funds	_____
		☐ Paramedic funds	_____
		☐ Pet shelters and similar funds	_____
☐ Benefit performances	_____	☐ Small cash contributions	_____
☐ Charity balls	_____	☐ Stock, at fair market value	_____
☐ Churches	_____	☐ Synagogues	_____
☐ Civil defense	_____	☐ United Fund payroll deductions	_____
☐ Clothing and furniture, limited to a percentage of fair market value	_____	☐ Volunteer expenses: clothing and uniforms, food, legal fees, telephone calls, travel expenses at 12¢ per mile, stamps, photocopying	_____
☐ Community Chest	_____		
☐ Domestic fraternal organizations	_____		
☐ Donations of clothing and other merchandise to qualified organizations	_____		
☐ Fire companies	_____	Total	_____

Itemizing Your Deductions 175

Line	Tax Law	Pay Less Tax Legally

	Gradual deterioration of property does not constitute casualty loss, no matter how quickly the final loss occurred.
	
	Insured Casualty Losses
	
	Under the Tax Reform Act, if you sustain a loss you will be able to deduct that loss only if you file a timely insurance claim with respect to damage to the property.
	
	The deduction for casualty losses is limited to any excess loss after deducting $100 plus 10 percent of adjusted gross income. Gains and losses from personal thefts and casualties are separately netted. If the gains on the casualty exceed the losses, such gains are treated as capital gains. The $100 floor is deducted from each loss before the netting. If losses exceed gains (after the netting), all losses will be ordinary. Losses to the extent of gains are deductible in full, but losses in excess of gains must exceed 10 percent of adjusted gross income. Any insurance recoveries reduce the deductible loss.
	
	Casualty losses and theft losses are deductible in the earlier of: (1) the year the loss was discovered or (2) the year sustained. Calculations are made on Form 4684 and entered on Schedule A, line 18.
	
	You must be able to show the following proof in order to claim a casualty loss:
	
	1. The nature of the casualty and when it occurred
	2. Actual ownership of the property in question
	3. Value of the property, before and after the casualty
	4. That the loss was the direct result of the casualty
	5. Depreciation allowed or allowable (if the property is depreciable)
	6. Salvage value
	7. Cost of the property, purchase con-
		loss. You may take the lesser of (1) economic loss—the value before less the value after—or (2) actual cost of the property damaged, further reduced by insurance proceeds, the $100 casualty loss floor, and 10 percent of adjusted gross income.
		
		• A casualty-loss deduction was allowed for loss incurred when a cement driveway cracked over a 4-month period because of heavy rain and unusual cold.
		
		• Here's an example of a casualty-loss calculation. Assume an adjusted gross income of $30,000. A hurricane destroyed your roof (loss of $4,000), someone stole your wallet ($100), and your car was in an accident ($350). Your deduction would be $1,150.
		
		   Hurricane $4,000
		     Less: 100 $3,900
		   Theft $ 100
		     Less: 100 0
		
		   Auto $ 350
		     Less: 100 250
		
		   Total loss $4,150
		     less 10 percent of $30,000 3,000
		   Deductible loss $1,150
		
		• Joe reports an adjusted gross income of $60,000, a $27,000 casualty loss (after the $100 floor), and a $17,000 casualty gain. His allowable casualty loss would be $21,000. (Add the $17,000—loss to the extent of gain—plus $6,000 of the remaining $10,000—balance of loss less 10 percent of $60,000 adjusted gross income.)
		
		• John reports a $40,000 adjusted gross income (without considering casualty gains or losses), a $15,000 gain from a casualty, and a $7,000 casualty loss. He can treat both the gain and loss as a capital gain and loss without having to take the 10 percent floor into account.

Form **4684**	**Casualties and Thefts**	OMB No. 1545-0177
Department of the Treasury Internal Revenue Service	▶ See separate instructions. ▶ To be filed with Form 1040, 1041, 1065, 1120, etc. Use a separate Form 4684 for each different casualty or theft.	Attachment Sequence No.: **35**
Name(s) as shown on tax return Doobn		Identifying number 329-04-1040

SECTION A.—Personal Use Property *(Casualties and thefts to property **not** used in a trade or business or for income-producing purposes.)*

1 Description of Properties (Show kind, location, and date of purchase for each)
Property A ......
Property B ......
Property C ......
Property D ......

	Properties (Use a separate column for each property lost or damaged from one casualty or theft.)			
	A	B	C	D
2 Cost or other basis of each property				
3 Insurance or other reimbursement you received or expect to receive for each property **Note:** *If line 2 is more than line 3, skip line 4*				
4 Gain from casualty or theft. If line 3 is more than line 2, enter difference here and skip lines 5 through 13				
5 Fair market value before casualty or theft				
6 Fair market value after casualty or theft				
7 Subtract line 6 from line 5				
8 Enter smaller of line 2 or line 7				
9 Subtract line 3 from line 8				

10 Casualty or theft loss. Add amounts from line 9 for all columns . . . .

11 Enter the amount from line 10 or $100, whichever is smaller . . . .

12 Subtract line 11 from line 10 . . . .
Caution: *Use only one Form 4684 for lines 13 through 18.*

13 Add the line 12 amounts from all Forms 4684, Section A . . . .

14 Add the line 4 amounts from all Forms 4684, Section A . . . .

15 If line 14 is more than line 13, enter difference here and on Schedule D, and do not complete the rest of form (see instructions). Otherwise, enter zero and complete lines 16 through 18. If line 14 is equal to line 13, do not complete the rest of form . . . .

16 If line 13 is more than line 14, enter difference . . . .

17 Enter 10% of adjusted gross income (Form 1040, line 33). Estates and trusts, see instructions

18 Subtract line 17 from line 16. If zero or less, enter zero. Enter on Schedule A (Form 1040), line 19. Estates and trusts, enter on the "other deductions" line of your tax return . . . .

Name(s) as shown on tax return (Do not enter name and identifying number if shown on other side) | Identifying number

Page **2**

SECTION B.—Business and Income-Producing Property
(Casualties and thefts to property used in a trade or business or for income-producing purposes.)

Part I — Casualty or Theft Gain or Loss (Use a separate Part I for each different casualty or theft.)

1. Description of Properties (Show kind, location, and date of purchase for each)
   Property A ....
   Property B ....
   Property C ....
   Property D ....

Properties (Use a separate column for each property lost or damaged from one casualty or theft.)

	A	B	C	D

2. Cost or adjusted basis of each property . . . .
3. Insurance or other reimbursement you received or expect to receive for each property . . . .
   Note: *If line 2 is more than line 3, skip line 4*
4. Gain from casualty or theft. If line 3 is more than line 2, enter difference here and on line 11 or 16, column (c). However, see instructions for line 15. Also, skip lines 5 through 10 . . . .
5. Fair market value before casualty or theft . .
6. Fair market value after casualty or theft . .
7. Subtract line 6 from line 5 . . . .
8. Enter smaller of line 2 or line 7 . . . . . .
   Note: *If the property was totally destroyed by a casualty, or lost from theft, enter on line 8, in each column, the amount from line 2.*
9. Subtract line 3 from line 8 . . . .
10. Casualty or theft loss. Add amounts from line 9 for all columns. Enter here and on line 11 or 16 . . . . .

Part II — Summary of Gains and Losses (From separate Parts I)

(a) Identify casualty or theft	(b) Losses from casualties or thefts		(c) Gains from casualties or thefts includible in income
	(i) Trade, business, rental or royalty property	(ii) Income-producing property	

Casualty or Theft of Property Held 6 Months or Less

11. _____

12. Totals. Add amounts on line 11 for each column . . . . . .
13. Combine line 12, columns (b)(i) and (c). Enter the net gain or (loss) here and on Form 4797, Part II, line 13. (If Form 4797 is not otherwise required, see instructions.) . . . .
14. Enter the amount from line 12, column (b)(ii) here and on Schedule A (Form 1040), line 19. Partnerships, S Corporations, Estates and Trusts, see instructions . . . .

Casualty or Theft of Property Held More Than 6 Months

15. Casualty or theft gains from Form 4797, Part III, line 31 . . . .
16. _____

17. Total losses. Add amounts on line 16, columns (b)(i) and (b)(ii) . . .
18. Total gains. Add lines 15 and 16, column (c) . . . .
19. Add amounts on line 17, columns (b)(i) and (b)(ii) . . . .
    Partnerships, enter the amount from line 20 or line 21 on your Schedule K-1, line 7. S Corporations, enter the amount from line 20 on your Schedule K-1, line 6.
20. If the loss on line 19 is more than the gain on line 18:
    a Combine line 17, column (b)(i) and line 18. Enter the net gain or (loss) here and on Form 4797, Part II, line 13. (If Form 4797 is not otherwise required, see instructions.) . . . .
    b Enter the amount from line 17, column (b)(ii) here and on Schedule A (Form 1040), line 19. Estates and Trusts, enter on the "other deductions" line of your tax return . . . . . .
21. If the loss on line 19 is equal to or smaller than the gain on line 18, combine these lines and enter here and on Form 4797, Part I, line 2 . . . .

The One-Minute Taxman: Casualty Losses

A casualty loss is the difference between the fair market value of an item before and after the casualty, limited to the original cost. In order to get a tax writeoff for casualty losses, you must absorb the first $100 floor and then exceed 10 percent of adjusted gross income.

You must be able to substantiate your casualty loss with canceled checks, receipts, and blue book values, if requested. If you have insurance, you must file a timely claim with the company before you can claim a deductible casualty loss.

Loss	Amount	Loss	Amount
☐ Accidents, including any loss, theft, or destruction of personal property	_____	☐ Embezzlement losses	_____
		☐ Extortion, losses from	_____
		☐ Flood damage	_____
☐ Appraisal fees, as part of determining amount of casualty-loss deduction	_____	☐ Forest fire, losses from	_____
		☐ Fraud and false representation	_____
☐ Beetle infestation	_____	☐ Freezing damage	_____
☐ Blackmail payments	_____	☐ Hail and icestorms	_____
☐ Blackouts, damage caused by, including vandalism	_____	☐ Kidnapping payments	_____
		☐ Landslide damage	_____
		☐ Larceny	_____
☐ Blasting damage	_____	☐ Lawn damage	_____
☐ Blizzard losses	_____	☐ Lightning, losses from	_____
☐ Breakage, during sudden event	_____	☐ Rain	_____
		☐ Shipwreck	_____
☐ Broken water pipes, hot-water heater	_____	☐ Smog damage	_____
		☐ Snow damage	_____
☐ Burglary losses	_____	☐ Sonic-boom breakage	_____
☐ Contractor, default of	_____	☐ Storm damage	_____
☐ Disaster: damage from avalanche, earthquake, tornado, flood, hurricane, volcano	_____	☐ Theft and burglary	_____
		☐ Tornado	_____
		☐ Vandalism and riots	_____
		☐ Water damage	_____
☐ Drought losses, if declared drought disaster area	_____	☐ Wind destruction	_____
☐ Dust storm damage	_____	Total	_____

Line	Tax Law	Pay Less Tax Legally
	tract, deed, and canceled checks and receipts showing improvement costs 8. Insurance or compensation received (or recoverable), including value of clean-up, restoration, and repairs provided by disaster-relief agencies. If your home was judged unsafe as a result of a disaster that warranted federal aid (regardless of whether your home was physically damaged) and you were ordered to demolish or relocate, you can claim a casualty-loss deduction, provided: (1) you were ordered by state or local government not later than 120 days after presidential determination to demolish or relocate the residence, and (2) your residence was rendered unsafe because of the disaster.	• You must be the owner of the property in order to deduct a casualty loss. In a recent case, a taxpayer paid $1,300 to a rental car company for damage to a rented car. Since he was not the owner of the vehicle, no tax deduction was allowed. (If the car had been rented for a business purpose, the loss would have been deductible.) • Attorneys' fees and other costs of settling claims are treated as part of the casualty loss. • If your car is completely wrecked in an accident, the insurance company will pay blue book value and you will have no basis for a loss unless: (1) you protest the amount paid by the insurance company and start legal proceedings, or (2) you show that your car had special equipment that was not insured. • In all matters of theft or casualty loss, keep pertinent records (including police reports). If records have been destroyed, obtain an appraisal immediately. "Before and after" photographs are one of the best means of substantiating claims—for both your insurance company and IRS in case of an audit. • File insurance claims on all insured losses. Otherwise the IRS may argue that the loss arose not from the casualty but from failure to file a claim. • However, in a recent case a taxpayer had been paid 3 times in the previous 8 years for burglaries and was afraid that a fourth claim would cancel his insurance. The Tax Court permitted the casualty loss, stating that it was the thefts that caused the loss, not the inability to put in the claim. • Psychological damage does not count. A landslide destroyed all homes around a taxpayer's residence and future slides threatened to wipe out his home. Since

Line	Tax Law	Pay Less Tax Legally
		there was considerable buyer resistance to the property, he took a deduction for the estimated loss in value. The court ruled that there must be physical damage to support loss deduction and disallowed the deduction. • Theft loss due to misrepresentation may be deductible. Mrs. N contracted to have a swimming pool built on her property. The contractor represented that all subcontractors were being paid when in fact he had kept the money for his own purposes. Mrs. N was allowed a deduction for the loss. • A taxpayer stored her possessions in a home she had shared with her estranged husband. He threw them out, entitling her to a theft-loss deduction.
Line 19	**Moving Expenses** Moving expenses are now treated as an itemized deduction but are not subject to the 2 percent floor covering miscellaneous deductions. Eligible moving expenses include reasonable: (1) travel to the new location, (2) house-hunting trips before making the move, (3) moving household goods and personal effects, (4) selling the old home and buying the new one, and (5) temporary lodging at the new location. The new place of employment must be located at least 35 miles farther from the old residence than the old place of employment. If there *was* no old place of employment, the new work place must be at least 35 miles from the old residence. For the year following the move, the taxpayer must work full-time for at least 39 of the next 52 weeks. A self-employed taxpayer, in addition to working for 39 weeks of the first year, must work full-time for at least 39 weeks of the second year after the move.	• If your employer reimburses you in part for the move, you are permitted to deduct any additional expenses against your income. If you are reimbursed for more than your cost, that excess is taxable as income.

Itemizing Your Deductions **181**

Line	Tax Law	Pay Less Tax Legally
	To be deductible, moving expenses must be incurred within one year from the time the employee first reports to the new job or business. The move should be made by the shortest, most direct route. Expenses in excess of what is considered reasonable will not be allowed.	

Foreign Country

The limit for moving to a new job location outside the United States is $6,000, and no more than $4,500 of this limit may be for house-hunting trips and temporary quarters.

Members of the Armed Forces who receive any excess reimbursement over actual moving costs must report the excess reimbursement as income.

Form 3903—Moving Expenses

This form has been changed to reflect the 80 percent limitation on the deduction of certain meal expenses and breaks down into more specific categories such items as travel, pre-moving, and temporary living expenses.

If you had to move your home last year either because you were transferred by your company or because you found a job on your own in a new location, you are entitled to a tax deduction for the cost of the move if the distance between the new job and the old residence is at least 35 miles greater than the distance from the old job to the old residence.

Deductible moving expenses include:

1. The cost of moving household goods and personal effects (9¢ per mile if you drive).
2. Traveling from the old to the new home (including meals and lodging) for the employee and members of his household.

- Moving expenses rarely cause an audit, and estimates are often permitted. Keep a diary on the trip.

- Many legitimate moving expenses are overlooked. Once you have landed your new job, you can deduct the cost of trips to find a home near the job (includes transportation, meals, and lodging for yourself and family) even if you don't find a new home as a result of the trips.

Temporary living expenses near your new job location are deductible for up to 30 days after you get the job (includes meals and lodging for you and your family while looking for or waiting to move into a new home).

Your costs of selling an old home (and buying a new one) may be deducted: transfer taxes, loan service charges, title fees, escrow fees, real estate agent's commission, and appraisal fees.

Lease costs are deductible, including penalties or lost security deposits from

Form 3903

Moving Expenses

Department of the Treasury
Internal Revenue Service

▶ Attach to Form 1040.
▶ See separate Instructions.

OMB No. 1545-0062

1987

Attachment Sequence No. 62

Name(s) as shown on Form 1040: DOUGH

Your social security number: 329 04 1040

1	Enter the number of miles from your **old** residence to your **new** work place	1	425
2	Enter the number of miles from your **old** residence to your **old** work place	2	3
3	Subtract line 2 from line 1. If the result is 35 or more, enter here and complete the rest of this form ▶	3	422

If line 3 is less than 35, you may not deduct moving expenses. This rule does not apply to members of the armed forces.

Section A.—Transportation of Household Goods:

4	Enter here the actual cost of moving your household goods and personal effects	4	

Section B.—Expenses in Traveling From Old to New Residence:

5	Travel and lodging NOT including meals	5	340	
6	Total meals	6	100	
7	Enter reimbursements you received for the meals shown on line 6 on which no income tax was withheld. Do not enter more than the amount shown on line 6	7	—	
8	Subtract line 7 from line 6	8	100	
9	Multiply line 8 by 80% (.80)	9	80	
10	Add lines 5, 7, and 9			10	420

Section C.—Pre-move Expenses in Looking for New Residence:

11	Travel and lodging NOT including meals	11	225
12	Total meals (house hunting)	12	190
13	Enter reimbursements you received for the meals shown on line 12 on which no income tax was withheld. Do not enter more than the amount shown on line 12	13	50
14	Subtract line 13 from line 12	14	140
15	Multiply line 14 by 80% (.80)	15	112
16	Add lines 11, 13, and 15	16	387

Section D.—Temporary Living Expenses (for any 30 days in a row after getting your job):

17	Lodging expenses NOT including meals	17	1902
18	Total meals (temporary quarters)	18	670
19	Enter reimbursements you received for the meals shown on line 18 on which no income tax was withheld. Do not enter more than the amount shown on line 18	19	500
20	Subtract line 19 from line 18	20	170
21	Multiply line 20 by 80% (.80)	21	136
22	Add lines 17, 19, and 21	22	2538

Section E.—Qualified Real Estate Expenses:

23	Expenses of (check one): a ☐ selling or exchanging your old residence; or b ☐ if renting, settling an unexpired lease	23	5719
24	Expenses of (check one): a ☐ buying your new residence; or b ☐ if renting, getting a new lease	24	—

Section F.—Dollar Limitations:

25	Add lines 16 and 22	25	2925
26	Enter the smaller of line 25 or $1,500 ($750 if married, filing a separate return, and at the end of the tax year you lived with your spouse who also started work during the tax year)	26	1500
27	Add lines 23, 24, and 26	27	7219
28	Enter the smaller of line 27 or $3,000 ($1,500 if married, filing a separate return, and at the end of the tax year you lived with your spouse who also started work during the tax year)	28	3000

Note: Use any amount on line **23a** not deducted because of the $3,000 (or $1,500) limit to decrease the gain on the sale of your residence. Use any amount on **24a** not deducted because of the limit to increase the basis of your new residence. See **No Double Benefit** in the Instructions.

29	Add lines 4, 10, and 28. This is your moving expense deduction. Enter here and on Schedule A (Form 1040), line 19 ▶	29	5100

Note: If your employer paid for any part of your move (including the value of any services furnished in kind), report that amount on **Form 1040, line 7**. See **Reimbursements** in the Instructions.

Line	Tax Law	Pay Less Tax Legally
	3. The cost of house-hunting trips incurred after obtaining employment in the new area. 4. The cost of meals and lodging in temporary quarters at the new location for a period of up to 30 days. 5. The cost of selling the old residence and purchasing the new home, as well as the expenses of settling an old lease or the acquisition of a new one (broker's closing fees, attorneys' fees, and "points" to the extent not deducted as interest). A loss on the sale of the old home is not deductible. The limit on expenses (3), (4), and (5) combined is $3,000 ($6,000 for married couples if each spouse relocates to a new job in different cities), of which not more than $1,500 can be for house hunting and temporary living expenses. Married persons filing separate returns may each claim $3,000 in moving expenses provided that: 1. Only one spouse starts work at a new place of employment for which a deduction is allowable. 2. Both spouses begin work at new places of employment that are at least 35 miles apart, and they do not live together at the same residence during the taxable year. ***Moving Expenses Limited*** You are entitled to a deduction for moving expenses if you remain employed on a full-time basis in the new area for at least 39 out of the 52 weeks following the move. The 39-week requirement is waived in cases of death, disability, transfer to another location by your employer, or discharge (other than for willful misconduct); the taxpayer is a member of the armed forces and moved because of a permanent change of station; the tax-	breaking a lease due to the move. Any commission paid to get a lease on a new residence, legal fees, and any loss incurred in subletting your old apartment are deductible as moving expenses. Also, don't forget to add the cost of food and lodging for your family at a hotel the day *before* you move or the day you arrive at the new location (if packing and moving make it impossible to be at home on those days). ● To deduct the loss on a sale of a personal residence, rent it out—then sell. See page 104. ● Moving expenses must be incurred within one year before or after beginning a new position in order to be deductible. ● If you were unemployed and moved to a new area to look for work (and you meet all other requirements) your moving expenses may be deductible. ● A couple postponed moving for more than a year after the wife changed jobs. The wife commuted 120 miles a day. After they moved to a town near her job, her husband began commuting. Since more than a year had elapsed between the start of her job and the move, the moving expenses were no longer deductible. ● More than 2 years after starting a new job, a taxpayer moved his family from Los

Line	Tax Law	Pay Less Tax Legally
	payer returned to the United States as a survivor of a taxpayer who lived and worked outside the country. The moving expense deduction is limited to one trip per move; moving to the new location, back home, and back to the new site is not allowable. Certain moving-related expenses are not deductible—e.g., telephone, laundry, parking, and dry cleaning costs. **Self-Employed Persons** Self-employed persons may deduct moving expenses provided they continue to work in the new location (either as a self-employed person or as an employee) for at least 78 weeks during the first 24 months following the move, of which at least 39 weeks must be in the first 12 months.	Angeles to Chicago. In spite of the time interval between taking the job and moving, his costs were held to be deductible because the reason for the delay was to enable the child to finish junior high school. • If you have not satisfied the 39-week requirement by April 15 but intend to complete the 39-week period during the year, take the deduction this year or you may lose it completely. If you have a change of circumstances next year, the moving expenses will be taxable as income. • If you take a tax deduction for an office in the home and subsequently move more than 35 miles, you are still entitled to deduct a pro rata share of the moving expenses as a business expense.

Miscellaneous Deductions (Lines 20–25)

Employee Business Expenses

All unreimbursed employee business expenses are now included in miscellaneous itemized deductions, all of which are subject to a floor of 2 percent of adjusted gross income. This means that income is fully taxable but the expense deduction is affected by the 2 percent floor and the 20 percent limitation.

Only expenses incurred under a reimbursement or expense allowance arrangement with your employer will be fully deductible from your gross income. This includes travel expenses—transportation, meals, and entertainment. With regard to meals, an 80 percent limitation must be applied before the 2 percent floor. The net effect is that you must absorb 20 percent of the meal costs personally.

When entertainment expenses are reimbursed, the reimbursed amount is included in gross income, and the expenses (up to amount of reimbursement) are deducted from gross income. If expenses exceed reimbursements (unless the employee is an outside salesperson), the excess must be treated as an itemized deduction.

Expenses not reimbursed for outside salespersons must be itemized and subject to the 2 percent floor on miscellaneous deductions. Outside salesperson is defined as one who spends most of his or her time soliciting business for his or her employer while away from the place of business.

This 80 percent limitation applies to entertainment and meals that are business-related; in the case of meals, the excess over a reasonable amount must first be subtracted from the total cost of the meal.

There are several exceptions to this 80 percent limitation:

1. Meal and entertainment expenses that are reimbursed are not affected. The party doing the reimbursing (usually the employer) is limited to an 80 percent deduction.
2. If a meal is provided as a central part of a qualified banquet meeting, the full cost is deductible (in 1987 and 1988). In order to qualify, the meeting must be a convention, seminar, or similar program with at least 40 individuals in attendance, more than half of them away from home, a program that involves a speaker, and food/beverage expenses not separately stated in the total cost of the business meeting.
3. Expenses incurred in the bona fide sale of goods or services to customers are fully deductible.
4. If the cost of a meal or entertainment activity is taxed to the recipient as compensation, the value is fully deductible, regardless of whether the recipient of the meal (or entertainment) is an employee.
5. Ticket cost and related expenses for a sporting event are fully deductible if the event is organized to benefit a tax-exempt organization, volunteers perform nearly all the work for the event, and all net proceeds of the event are contributed to the organization. (High school and college athletic events usually are not covered by this exception, because coaches and referees are compensated.)
6. Expenses for certain traditional recreational activities provided for employees' benefit are fully deductible.
7. Costs of samples or promotional items made available to the general public are fully deductible—e.g., tickets offered as a prize or food samples at the supermarket.
8. Food and beverage expenses associated with benefits that are excludable from gross income as fringe benefits are fully deductible.

These expenses are deductible only to the extent that their combined *total* exceeds 2 percent of your adjusted gross income:

1. Safe deposit box rental
2. Work uniforms
3. Trust administration fees
4. Subscriptions to investment publications
5. Union or professional dues
6. Job-hunting expenses
7. Attorneys' fees incurred in collecting income
8. Investment advisory or management fees
9. Costs of pursuing a business considered a hobby by IRS
10. Continuing education courses
11. Tax preparation and counseling fees
12. Investment travel and entertainment expenses that exceed the 80 percent limitation
13. Home office expenses
14. Appraisal fees for casualty loss or charitable contributions

15. Unreimbursed employee business expenses
16. Subscriptions to professional journals

These expenses are not subject to the 2 percent floor:

1. Interest, taxes, casualty losses, medical costs, and charitable contributions that qualify as deductible items
2. Deductions for amortizable premiums on bonds
3. Deductible gambling losses (up to the amount of winnings)
4. Unreimbursed employee expenses of actors who earned less than $16,000 for the year
5. Impairment-related work expenses of handicapped employees (e.g., special tools)
6. Deduction for an unrecovered investment in a terminated annuity
7. Expenses of short sales (selling borrowed stocks or securities)
8. Deductions for estate taxes paid on income not subject to income taxes at the time of death of the decedent
9. Deductions under "claim of right" (when you receive income in one year and return some or all of it in a later year due to an error in the original payment).

Line	Tax Law	Pay Less Tax Legally
	Union and Professional Dues Any amounts paid as union dues are deductible. **Tax Return Preparation Fee** Fees paid to an accountant or tax preparer are tax-deductible, as is the cost of tax preparation books (including *Pay Less Tax Legally* for last year). When you get a bill from a professional, insist on a flat fee billing including expenses. This pushes the limitation problem on him and, to the extent that the fee is otherwise deductible, you preserve full deductibility.	• See "Save Money Later," page 293, for union-related costs that are deductible. • If legal fees are attributable to the tax aspects of estate planning, they are deductible. Have the attorney who draws up your will and estate plan itemize how much of the total fee is for deductible advice. • Stylish work clothes are not deductible. A manager of a fashion boutique tried to deduct the cost of her designer clothing. Since the clothes could also be worn after work, they were not deductible.
Line 25	**Other Miscellaneous Deductions** **Job-Hunting Expenses** Deductions for job hunting (in the same field) include the following expenses (whether you land the job or not): career counseling, payments to employment agencies, auto and travel, cost of résumés, meals and lodging (while away	• Business-related telephone calls from home (or pay phones) that are not reimbursed by your employer are deductible. • *Meals for Firefighters:* The IRS will allow an itemized deduction for the cost of mandatory in-house meals that department rules require firefighters to buy—even if the food is not eaten. However, the cost of contributing to a voluntary mess fund is not deductible.

The One-Minute Taxman: Miscellaneous Business and Professional Expenses

Line 20–25, Schedule A, is a catch-all of miscellaneous deductions. For suggestions specific to educational or investment expenses, see the following pages.

Miscellaneous Deductions	Amount	Miscellaneous Deductions	Amount
☐ Actor's expenses: special clothing, costumes, wigs	_____	☐ Job-hunting expenses (if in same trade or business)	_____
☐ Airline pilot: maps, plotters, uniforms, shoes, special equipment	_____	☐ Library, depreciation of professional	_____
☐ Arbitration fees and awards	_____	☐ Malpractice insurance	_____
☐ Armed services: uniforms and their maintenance; reservists' expenses	_____	☐ Manager: briefcase, home entertaining, telephone calls	_____
☐ Artist: materials and supplies, home office, travel	_____	☐ Meals, if out of town or required on the premises of employer	_____
☐ Author (unpublished): editing, typing services, research, supplies, travel	_____	☐ Musician: depreciation of equipment, music, scores, room in home if used to practice	_____
☐ Briefcase	_____	☐ Nurse: uniforms and maintenance, shoes, malpractice insurance	_____
☐ Carpenter: protective clothing	_____	☐ Periodicals and business-related publications	_____
☐ Coach: uniforms, shoes, stopwatch	_____	☐ Photographer: camera and supplies	_____
☐ Commissioned salesperson: use of car, nonreimbursed entertainment	_____	☐ Plumber: special gloves, tools	_____
☐ Credit-card renewal fees	_____	☐ Police: uniform maintenance, depreciation on weapon, targets, and rounds	_____
☐ Dental technician: uniforms and cleaning	_____	☐ Professional dues	_____
☐ Electrician: safety shoes, tools	_____	☐ Safety equipment and protective clothing	_____
☐ Equipment: typewriter, computer, calculator, adding machine, tape recorder, answering machine, percentage of home telephone if required by employer	_____	☐ Teacher: payment to substitutes, room supplies	_____
		☐ Telephone calls	_____
		☐ Tools of the trade: any equipment necessary to do your job	_____
☐ Executive search fees	_____	☐ Uniforms and their maintenance	_____
		Total	_____

Line	Tax Law	Pay Less Tax Legally
	from home overnight), phone calls to prospective employers, and advertising for a new job.	• Teachers making payments to substitutes while on sabbatical can deduct the payments if they itemize.
		• Job insurance may be deductible. An executive purchased a policy that would pay his salary if he lost his job due to the company's merger or bankruptcy. Since the benefits would have been taxable, the insurance was deductible.
	Educational Expenses You are allowed a deduction for nonreimbursed educational expenses if the education was to maintain or improve skills required by your present job (rather than to qualify you for a new position), or to meet the express requirements of the law, your employer, or employment regulations in order to keep your present employment and salary. Educational expenses include tuition, books and supplies, and lab fees. If you want a tax writeoff for the cost of schooling, don't stay away from work for more than a year. If your course of study maintains or improves existing job skills, you can deduct the cost of returning to school. If you quit to take full-time courses, your tuition and related expenses are deductible—but for one year only. After a year of schooling you must return to work in the same trade or business to preserve your tax writeoff.	• If your employer requires you to go to school, ask for a letter stating that changes in your field necessitated your going back to school. Attach a copy of the letter to your return. Save report cards, course books, class programs, and itemized bills for all books. • A licensed practical nurse wanted to become a physician's assistant, so she deducted the educational expenses. The courts disallowed the deduction. As a physician's assistant, she would be able to perform complete physicals and minor surgery, which would qualify her for a new trade or business.
	Investment Expenses If investments produce taxable income, you may deduct fees and expenses paid to a broker or bank to collect interest or dividends, rental of a safe deposit box to store securities, and subscriptions to investment advisory services or newsletters. In active management—i.e., real estate	• If a professional adviser (CPA, attorney, investment counselor) reviewed a prospectus you brought to his attention, any fee charged is deductible as tax-investment advice. However, if the adviser brought the matter to your attention, fees must be added to your investment cost.

Line	Tax Law	Pay Less Tax Legally
	properties requiring supervision, maintenance, collecting rents, and record-keeping—you are allowed to deduct office expenses (rent, clerical help, telephone, depreciation, bookkeeping services). Investors may claim a deduction for a home office if the exclusive-use test can be met.	• A recent IRS ruling declared that you may deduct a portion of the annual expense of maintaining a home security system (plus depreciation) if you conduct a business from your home. • If you attend an investment club convention or seminar, your expenses are considered to be for the production of income and therefore deductible. Document whom you spoke to at the seminar. A key factor in claiming the deduction would be whether or not the new information helped in subsequent investment decisions.
	You may deduct custodial fees charged by a bank for holding mutual funds or trust shares. Trustees' fees paid in connection with an IRA are deductible as an expense incurred for the production of income. Payment of such fees does not constitute a contribution to the IRA. Expenses incurred in purchasing tax-free investments (e.g., municipal bonds) are not deductible, and an annual fee paid to an adviser for managing tax-exempt bonds is also not deductible. You may not deduct commissions on securities purchased or sold; the charges are added to the purchase price when you buy and deducted from the sales price of securities when you sell. If you are a shareholder in a publicly held company, you may not deduct stockholder meeting expenses.	• If you are billed separately for custodial fees to manage your IRA, those fees are a writeoff as a miscellaneous deduction. • If you buy the *Wall Street Journal* and other financial publications on the newsstand or have subscriptions to newspapers, journals, or newsletters, keep a record of the amount spent and take a tax deduction as an investment expense. • Legal fees in connection with estate tax planning are deductible. Ask your attorney for a separate itemized bill. • The cost of a home safe (including installation costs) may be deductible over 5 years. You must show that the primary purpose of having a safe is the protection of investments (e.g., stocks and bonds).

The One-Minute Taxman: Educational Expenses

Refresher courses, correspondence courses, courses to improve management skills, and academic and vocational courses are tax-deductible provided they have been incurred in order to maintain or improve existing job skills required by your present employer, or to meet the express requirements of the law, your employer, or employment regulations in order to keep your present employment and salary.

Educational Expenses	Amount	Educational Expenses	Amount
☐ Books and supplies	_____	☐ Travel, including meals and lodging—but only to attend classes or do research. See page 291 for a full discussion.	_____
☐ Lab fees	_____		
☐ Photocopying and printing	_____		
☐ Research	_____		
☐ Secretarial and typing fees	_____	☐ Tuition	_____
☐ Transportation to class (22.5¢ per mile) if the school is beyond your principal business location, or one-way transportation between your place of business and school	_____	☐ Tutorial instruction	_____
		Total	_____

Example 1
Barry is an outside salesman who decides to go to law school in the evenings. His expenses would not be deductible because this educational expenditure would qualify him for a new trade or business.

Example 2
Faye teaches during the day and decides to go for a master's degree at a local university. Since she is improving existing skills, and there is more than a reasonable relationship between her present job and her courses, her expenses would be deductible.

The One-Minute Taxman: Other Miscellaneous Deductions

☐ Executor expenses	_____	☐ Guardian expenses, for collection (or production) of income for minor	_____
☐ Gambling losses, to the extent of gambling winnings	_____		
☐ Guarantor payment—only if liable on a loan	_____	Total	_____

The One-Minute Taxman: Investment Expenses

If you manage your own investment portfolio, you are entitled to deduct expenses for the production, conservation, or management of income-producing property.

If you own rental property or have stock, be sure to read this One-Minute Taxman.

Investment Expenses	Amount	Investment Expenses	Amount
☐ Accounting and legal fees	_____	☐ Interest paid	_____
☐ Advertising	_____	☐ Liability insurance	_____
☐ Auditing of financial statements	_____	☐ Literature, investment	_____
		☐ Loan service charges	_____
☐ Auto expenses, parking, and tolls	_____	☐ Losses, including forfeitures	_____
☐ Automatic dividend reinvestment fees	_____	☐ Management fees	_____
		☐ Night security services	_____
☐ Bad debts, uncollected loans	_____	☐ Points, over life of loan unless personal residence	_____
☐ Bank service charges	_____		
☐ Bond premium amortization	_____	☐ Postage and mailing costs	_____
		☐ Proxy expenses	_____
☐ Bookkeeping fees	_____	☐ Research	_____
☐ Collection fees, including court costs	_____	☐ Safe, cost of	_____
		☐ Safe deposit box rental	_____
☐ Commissions paid	_____	☐ Salaries paid clerical help	_____
☐ Computer: portion of cost dealing with investment, subject to depreciation; computer software	_____	☐ Service charges	_____
		☐ Stationery and printing	_____
		☐ Statistical services, including charting services	_____
☐ Custodial charges	_____	☐ Stock advisory services	_____
☐ Damages, including breach of contract	_____	☐ Taxes, stamp or stock transfer	_____
☐ Dividends paid, short sales	_____	☐ Telephone calls to broker, including long distance	_____
☐ Financial counseling	_____	Total	_____
☐ Franchise fees and taxes	_____		
☐ Insurance, for protection of income-producing property	_____		

9
PUTTING IT ALL TOGETHER

Computing Your Tax

After computing your total income (line 22), deducting any adjustments to income (line 29), arriving at adjusted gross income (line 30), and deducting itemized deductions (line 33a) or the standard deduction (line 33b) and exemptions, you have arrived at taxable income (line 36).

You are now going to compute your tax using one of 2 means:

1. Tax tables
2. Tax-rate schedules (if taxable income exceeds $50,000).

From your total tax, now deduct the credits for child and dependent care, credit for the elderly and for the permanently or totally disabled, general business credit, and foreign tax credit.

Then add any self-employment tax and other taxes (lines 48–52).

On lines 54–60, deduct the withholding tax deducted from your pay, as well as estimated tax payments and payments made with an extension of time to file, and the Social Security payments in excess of $3,131.

If what you paid during the year (line 61) exceeds the tax as computed (line 53), you have a refund coming. If line 53 exceeds line 61, *Uncle Sam* has a refund coming, which means you have to pay. If by some strange coincidence lines 53 and 61 are the same, you have broken even with the IRS.

Itemize or Claim the New Standard Deduction?

Beginning in 1987, you may claim the new standard deduction or total itemized deductions, whichever is greater. The standard deduction amounts are:

$3,760—married filing jointly or surviving spouse
$2,540—single or head of household
$1,880—married filing separately

For taxpayers who are blind *or* elderly, the standard deduction amounts are:

$5,000—married filing jointly or surviving spouse
$3,000—single
$4,400—head of household
$2,500—married filing separately

A married taxpayer filing jointly who is both elderly and blind may claim an additional $600; if both spouses are elderly and blind, they may claim a total of $1,200 in addition to the $5,000 standard deduction.

A taxpayer who files as single or head of household and is either blind or elderly may claim an additional $750; if he/she is elderly *and* blind, he/she may deduct an additional $1,500 in addition to the $3,000 or $4,400 standard deduction.

Married Persons Filing Separately

If you and your spouse file separate returns, you must decide either to itemize or to take the standard deduction: you must *both* take the same type of deduction. If one of you elects to itemize, the other must itemize. If one claims the standard deduction, the other must use it as well, with a maximum deduction of $1,880 on each return. Also, marrieds filing separately having capital losses are each limited to a maximum loss of $1,500, and neither spouse can use part of the other's loss.

Filing Returns for Dependent Children

If a dependent child has salary or other earned income but no unearned income (investments), a return has to be filed only if the earned income is more than $2,540 in 1987 (increasing to $3,000 in 1988). If earned and unearned income both are involved, the dependent child is allowed a $500 standard deduction, so he or she does not have to file if gross income is $500 or less.

If the dependent child's gross income is between $501 and $1,000, tax is computed by using the $500 standard deduction or itemized deductions, whichever is greater. Regardless of whether the child is age 14 or over, the child's tax bracket is used.

When gross income is over $1,000, it makes a difference if the child is over age 14 as well as whether the income is earned or unearned. Investment income over $1,000 is taxed to a child under age 14 at the parents' top marginal rate; however, if the child reaches age 14 by the end of the year, all income is taxed at the child's rate.

When the child is age 14 or over, after the standard deduction or itemized deductions are claimed, any remaining taxable income is taxed at the child's rate.

Do not confuse a personal exemption with the standard deduction. The $500 standard deduction is allowed, but the personal exemption is claimed by the parent for the dependent child (if applicable). See page 61 for more information.

Example

Assume the child is under the age of 14.

Child has dividend income of	$1,300	No earned income.
Subtract standard deduction	− 500	
Taxable income is	$ 800	
Only	$ 500	is taxed at child's rate.
The additional	$ 300	is taxed at parents' rate.

Tax Tables

If you can't itemize deductions, it may be somewhat more difficult to compute your tax: the standard deduction is no longer built into the tax tables if your taxable income is

SAVE MONEY NOW

$50,000 or less. If your taxable income exceeds $50,000, you have to make your computations using the tax-rate schedule.

If you itemize and are single, or if you claim unmarried head of household, total your itemized deductions or subtract $2,540 (the standard deduction); if married, total itemized deductions or subtract $3,760; if married filing separately, subtract $1,880.

Regardless of which method is used, always compare your itemized deductions with the standard deduction and file the return with the lowest total tax. The tax tables can be found on pages 315–20.

Computing Your Tax with the Tables

Example 1
Ben Long is single and earned $19,500 for the year. He has itemized deductions of $1,800. Since the standard deduction is $2,540, it would not make sense to itemize—he would simply look up $15,060 in the tax table for single persons.

Example 2
Ben Long has itemized deductions of $2,790. He would compute his tax as follows:

Adjusted gross income	$19,500
Less itemized deductions	$2,790
Total	$16,710
Less one exemption	1,900
Taxable income	$14,810

Tax-Rate Schedules

The tax-rate schedules (see page 321) are to be used by those who cannot use the tax tables if taxable income exceeds $50,000.

Example 1
Mitchell and Selma Taxman are married, have one child, and report income of $86,000 and itemized deductions of $10,000. They would compute their tax on taxable income of $70,300.

Adjusted gross income	$86,000
Less itemized deductions	$10,000
Total	$76,000
Less exemptions (3 @ $1,900 each)	5,700
Taxable income	$70,300

Lump-Sum Distributions

A lump-sum distribution occurs if there is a distribution from a qualified pension, profit-sharing, stock bonus plan, or a qualified annuity—a distribution of the entire amount in the plan paid to the recipient (1) after the employee reaches age 59½, (2) due to employee's separation from service, (3) after an employee becomes disabled, or (4) as a result of the employee's death.

These distributions may receive several tax advantages:
1. Optional long-term capital gain treatment for the part of the distribution that is attributable to pre-1974 plan participation
2. An exclusion for the net unrealized appreciation of distributed employer securities
3. The forward averaging of tax over a period of either 5 or 10 years on the ordinary income portion of the distribution.

Forward averaging is limited to an election by an individual who receives the lump-sum distribution on or after age 59½ (to discourage premature withdrawals of funds set aside for retirement).

One exception is a transitional rule providing that forward averaging (and the capital gain treatment) may be elected by anyone who reached age 50 by January 1, 1986.

Ten-year averaging applies to lump-sum distributions prior to 1987, and 5-year averaging applies to distributions after 1986. Under the age-50 transitional rule, 10-year averaging may be elected (at 1986 tax rates taking into account the prior law zero bracket amount) or 5-year averaging (at tax rates in effect for the tax year of the distribution).

The following steps are used to calculate the tax on the ordinary income portion of a lump-sum distribution:

1. Determine the adjusted total taxable amount. This includes ordinary income and capital gain portions of the distribution (amounts from Form 1099-R, boxes 2 and 3) and the current actuarial value of an annuity distribution, if any (amount from Form 1099-R, box 29). Subtract from this amount any employee death benefit exclusion.
2. Subtract a minimum distribution allowance (up to $10,000, to allow additional relief for low-income individuals receiving lump-sum distributions). For a distribution of $20,000 or less, the allowance is half of the distribution amount. If the distribution is between $20,000 and $70,000, the allowance is $10,000 less than one-fifth of the excess over $10,000. Over $70,000, no allowance is made.
3. Subtract federal estate tax.
4. If using 5-year averaging, multiply by 0.2. If 10-year averaging is used, multiply by 0.1 and add $2,480 (zero bracket amount).
5. Determine the initial separate tax. Take the amount calculated up to this point (steps 1 through 4 above) and apply tax from the Tax Rate Schedule X (single taxpayers) for the appropriate tax year. Multiply the tax by 5 (if you use 5-year averaging) by 10 (if you use 10-year averaging). If no portion of the lump-sum distribution is in the form of an annuity (and the recipient does not elect capital gain treatment for pre-1974 plan participation), the tax on the ordinary income portion equals the initial separate tax.
6. If a portion of the distribution is the current actuarial value of an annuity, the tax that would have been separately calculated on such value is subtracted from the initial separate tax. (The annuity will be taxed under ordinary annuity rules.)
7. If capital gain treatment is elected for part of the distribution, the portion taxed at the capital gain rate is subtracted from the initial separate tax.

Ten-Year Averaging

The old 10-year averaging method has been replaced by 5-year averaging. According to the Tax Reform Act, you may use only 5-year averaging once in a lifetime and *only* after having reached age 59½.

If you receive a lump-sum distribution before age 59½ (e.g., a job change), you now have only 2 choices as to what to do with the money: (1) roll it over into another retirement plan within 60 days of receipt; or (2) accept the full tax impact, including penalties for premature distributions.

Although the changes are effective for 1987, there is one transition rule that may reduce your tax burden. If you were at least age 50 on January 1, 1986, you may choose between the new 5-year averaging (using 1987 rates) or the old 10-year method, using 1986 rates. Calculate the alternatives and decide which is best. If you use the transition rules (before age 59½) you can never again use either 5-year or 10-year averaging, so be sure that the tax savings are substantial enough to warrant your decision.

Forward Averaging

The forward averaging computation must be calculated on Form 4972, but the following table consolidates steps 1 through 5. (Remember that the adjusted total taxable amount should exclude any death benefit exclusion.)

This table applies to distributions received in 1987. Using 10-year averaging is preferable to 5-year averaging until the adjusted total taxable amount reaches $741,600. At that level, the tax under either method is $255,336. Above $741,600, the 5-year method is more favorable.

FORWARD AVERAGING TABLE FOR 1987
(combining 10-year averaging computed at 1986 tax rates using prior law zero bracket amount and 5-year averaging at 1987 tax rates)

If the adjusted total taxable amount is:		The initial separate tax is:		
at least	but not over	this amount	plus this %	of the excess over
....	$ 20,000	Zero	5.5	Zero
$ 20,000	21,583	$ 1,100	13.2	$ 20,000
21,583	30,583	1,309	14.4	21,583
30,583	49,417	2,605	16.8	30,583
49,417	67,417	5,769	18.0	49,417
67,417	70,000	9,009	19.2	67,417
70,000	91,700	9,505	16.0	70,000
91,700	114,400	12,977	18.0	91,700
114,400	137,100	17,063	20.0	114,400
137,100	171,600	21,603	23.0	137,100
171,600	228,800	29,538	26.0	171,600
228,800	286,000	44,410	30.0	228,800
286,000	343,200	61,570	34.0	286,000
343,200	423,000	81,018	38.0	343,200
423,000	571,900	111,342	42.0	423,000
571,900	741,600	173,880	48.0	571,900
741,600	....	255,336	38.5	741,600

Only those receiving very large distributions in 1987 will find 5-year averaging better, but in 1988 the 5-year averaging will be a better choice for a greater number of taxpayers (because of lower tax rates in 1988). The following table is for 1988, 5-year averaging:

5-YEAR AVERAGING TABLE
(for lump-sum distributions received in 1988)

If the adjusted total taxable amount is:		the separate tax is:		
at least	but not over	this amount	plus this %	of the excess over
....	$ 20,000	Zero	7.5	Zero
$ 20,000	70,000	$ 1,500	18.0	$ 20,000
70,000	89,250	10,500	15.0	70,000
89,250	215,750	13,388	28.0	89,250
215,750	447,800	48,808	33.0	215,750
447,800	....	125,384	28.0	447,800

In 1988, 10-year averaging is still more favorable until the adjusted total taxable amount reaches $473,700, at which point the tax under either method is $132,636. Above that level 5-year averaging is much more favorable because of the lower top tax rate.

Capital Gain Option

Before Tax Reform, the part of a lump-sum distribution attributable to pre-1974 contributions was eligible for capital gain treatment, but Tax Reform repealed this provision subject to an age-50 transitional rule and a 5-year phase-out.

An employee who reached age 50 by January 1, 1986, may elect capital gain treatment (without regard to the phase-out). The capital gain portion is taxed at 20 percent.

Individuals under age 50 on January 1, 1986, are subject to the 5-year phase-out. They are ineligible for forward averaging until they become 59½ years of age, but they may still receive lump-sum treatment for the capital gain portion of the distribution. (An employee who is separated from service at age 49 and receives a lump-sum distribution will be taxed on the capital gain portion.)

Form 1099-R indicates the amount of a distribution that qualifies as long-term capital gain. It can be computed by means of this formula: multiply the total received by the ratio of (1) months of active participation in the plan before 1974 to (2) total months of active participation. Any part of a pre-1974 calendar year is counted as 12 months; any part of 1974 or later years is counted as one month.

Example

Jeanne King retires in December 1987 and receives a lump-sum distribution of $300,000. She has been a continuous participant in her company's qualified pension plan since 1960. She has 168 months of plan participation both before and after 1974. The amount of the distribution to be treated as capital gain is $300,000 × 168/336, or $150,000. According to the 10-year averaging table, if Jeanne does not elect capital gain treatment, the tax on the entire distribution is $66,330. If she does elect capital gain treatment, the tax will be $33,165, as follows: $66,330 divided by 2 plus $30,000 (150,000 × 20 percent).

The flat 20 percent tax rate has made it easier to make the decision about capital gain treatment. Any time the adjusted total taxable amount is taxed at a rate of more than 20 percent, the taxpayer benefits by electing capital gain treatment.

In the above example, the effective tax rate without capital gain treatment was 22 percent ($66,330 ÷ $300,000), so the capital gain election resulted in $3,000 less tax, equal to 2 percent (the difference in tax rates) × $150,000 (amount of capital gain).

Summary of Federal Tax Rules on Lump-Sum Distributions and Qualifying Partial Distributions

The Internal Revenue Code provides many complex rules relating to the taxation of the amounts you receive in a lump-sum or qualifying partial distribution.

Rollovers—60-Day Time Limit

The Internal Revenue Code permits you to avoid current taxation on any portion of the taxable amount of an eligible distribution by rolling over that portion into another qualified employer retirement plan that accepts rollover contributions or into an Individual Retirement Account (IRA). There are specific and technical qualifications and requirements set forth in Section 402 of the Internal Revenue Code that must be satisfied in order for your plan distribution to be eligible to be rolled over. Some of these are summarized below.

A tax-free rollover is accomplished by transferring the amount you are rolling over to the new plan or IRA *not later than 60 days* after you receive the amount from this plan and by notifying the trustee (or issuer) of the new plan or IRA that you are making a rollover contribution. If you receive a series of distributions from this plan within a single year that would be treated as a lump-sum distribution, the 60-day period does not expire until 60 days after the day you receive the last distribution in the series.

Not all plan distributions are eligible to be rolled over. A distribution must be either a "qualified total distribution" or a "partial distribution" in order to be rolled over. In general, a qualified total distribution is either a lump-sum distribution or a distribution due to a plan termination. In this context, a lump-sum distribution is the payment of all your benefits under a plan because of death or other separation from service, or after you reach age 59½. In general, a partial distribution is payment of at least 50 percent of your vested benefits from all like plans of the employer upon death or other separation from service after 5 years of plan participation. A partial distribution may be rolled over only into an IRA, not into another employer plan.

A rollover of any portion of a partial distribution will disqualify a subsequent distribution from this plan (or any other similar plan maintained by the company) for capital gains treatment and 10-year or 5-year averaging (described below). Also, if you are not fully vested when you receive the distribution that you roll over (other than a distribution of $3,500 or less made without your consent) and you are later rehired and gain additional vesting in the amounts you forfeited, neither capital gains treatment nor 10-year or 5-year averaging will be available for a subsequent distribution from this plan (or any similar plan maintained by the company).

If you do not or cannot roll over the taxable amount of your distribution, it is taxable as ordinary income. However, the amount of tax you pay may be reduced if the distribution qualifies for the special tax treatment described below.

Special Tax Treatment for Lump-Sum Distributions

If your distribution qualifies under Section 402(e) of the Internal Revenue Code as a lump-sum distribution (which is a technical legal term) you may qualify for special tax treatment as described below. In general, your distribution will qualify as a lump sum if you are receiving the total amount of your plan benefits due to separation from service and you participated in the plan for any part of each of at least 5 years before the year of distribution. (The 5-year participation requirement does not apply to a distribution received by a beneficiary on account of the participant's death.)

Five-Year Averaging

You may elect to have your lump-sum distribution taxed under special 5-year averaging rules if no part of your distribution is rolled over. Use of this method will usually result in a lower tax than if your distribution were taxed as ordinary income. You cannot elect 5-year averaging unless you are at least age 59½ at the time of distribution, except as described under "Special Rules for Participants Born Before 1936" below.

Capital Gain

Any part of your lump-sum distribution that is attributable to plan participation prior to 1974 (your capital gain portion) may be treated as a long-term capital gain. The remainder may be taxed using 5-year averaging (if you qualify). Alternatively, you may be able to elect to have your entire distribution taxed under 5-year averaging (if you qualify). After 1987, only a percentage of the capital gain portion of your distribution can be treated as a long-term capital gain. That percentage is:

1988	95%
1989	75%
1990	50%
1991	25%

After 1991, no portion of your distribution may be treated as a long-term capital gain under these rules.

Special Rules for Participants Born Before 1936

If you were born before 1936, you may be able to have your lump-sum distribution taxed under two special rules, even if you are not age 59½ at distribution:

1. *10-Year Averaging.* You may elect special 10-year averaging (using 1986 tax rates) instead of 5-year averaging (using the tax rates of the year in which you receive your distribution). For smaller distributions, your tax will be lower if you use 10-year averaging.
2. *Capital Gain at 20 Percent Rate.* You may elect to have any capital gain portion of your distribution taxed at a flat 20 percent rate and the remainder taxed using 10-year or 5-year averaging. The capital gain phase-out described in "Capital Gain" above does not apply. Alternatively, you may elect to have your entire distribution taxed under 10-year or 5-year averaging.

One-Time Election

If you elect special tax treatment as described above for your lump-sum distribution in this year, you will not be able to make the election in any later year for any lump-sum distribution received from any other plan of any employer. If you elect special tax treatment and were not fully vested, and you then return to employment and gain additional vesting in the amounts you forfeited, you will have to repay the tax benefits you gained from your election. However, in this case, you will once again be able to elect special tax treatment on a future lump-sum distribution (if you qualify).

Effect of Participation in Other Plans

If you also participate in other qualified pension, profit-sharing, or stock bonus plans of your employer (or a different employer), more complex rules may apply, about which you should consult your tax adviser. These rules include the following:

1. If you have undistributed benefits under another plan of the employer that is of the same type as the plan making this distribution, you may not elect averaging or capital gain treatment for your distribution unless your entire vested benefit under that other plan is received in the same year.
2. Any election of 5-year or 10-year averaging must apply to all lump-sum distributions received in the same year from any plan of any employer.
3. If any distribution received from any other plan of any other employer is eligible for averaging and you roll over that distribution, you will not be able to elect averaging for any lump-sum distribution received during the same year from this plan.

Special Rule for Certain Participants Who Terminated Employment in 1986

If you terminated employment in 1986 and you received a lump-sum distribution before March 16, 1987, you may elect to treat it as though it were received in 1986 rather than in 1987. This means, for instance, that 10-year averaging and long-term capital gain treatment at 1986 tax rates may be available even if you were not born before 1936. Also, the additional taxes described in "Other Taxes" below will not apply. You must elect this special treatment by the due date (including extensions) of your tax return for 1987.

Other Taxes

Your distribution may be subject to taxes in addition to those described above.

Early Distribution Tax

In general, distributions received by individuals under age 59½ and not rolled over into an IRA or another qualified plan are subject to an additional 10 percent income tax. Distributions made on retirement after age 55 or because of death, disability, or a matrimonial- or parental-support court order, or received in a year that you have deductible medical expenses in excess of 7.5 percent of adjusted gross income, may be completely or partially exempt from this additional tax.

Excess Distribution Tax

Another possible tax is the 15 percent excise tax imposed on the amount by which the aggregate distributions an individual receives in a year from all retirement plans (whether or not the plans are sponsored by affiliated employers) and IRAs exceed a specified limit. In general, this limit is $150,000 for amounts received in 1987. Aggregate lump-sum distributions taxed under 5-year or 10-year averaging are subject to a separate limit of 5 times the otherwise applicable limit. For 1987, this separate limit is $750,000 (5 × $150,000). If the value of your benefits from all plans and IRAs exceeded $562,500 on August 1, 1986, you may be eligible to have your limit determined on a different basis. If you elect to do so, this election must be made on your tax return for a tax year before 1989.

Tax Credits

Tax credits have been reorganized, revised, and renumbered to simplify their structure. The credits are combined in 4 main categories. Three categories include nonrefundable credits; one applies to refundable credits.

Refundable Credits

Refundable credits can be claimed even though there may be no income tax against which they can be offset. These are:

1. Credit for withheld wages
2. Earned income credit
3. Tax withheld at source on nonresident aliens and foreign corporations
4. Gasoline and special fuels credit.

Nonrefundable Credits

Nonrefundable credits are allowed as an offset against tax liability and are claimed in the following order:

1. *The sum of the personal credits:* the total of the child and dependent care credit, and credit for the elderly and disabled
2. Foreign tax credit
3. Orphan drugs testing credit
4. Nonconventional source fuel credit
5. Research activities credit
6. General business credit (the sum of the investment credit on qualified rehabilitation expenses, alcohol fuels credit, and Employee Stock Ownership Plan [ESOP] credit).

Credits are claimed in the prescribed order, and each is allowable as an offset against the tax less credits previously claimed. The general business credit is subject to a maximum tax liability limitation; any unused credit can be carried back 3 years and forward 15 years until used up.

Child and Dependent Care Credit (Form 2441)

If you pay a sitter to watch your children and other dependents while you go to work (or look for a job), you may be entitled to a credit against your tax of up to $1,440 per year. To be eligible, you must provide more than half the cost of operating a home that includes a dependent child under 15, a disabled dependent of any age, or a spouse who, because of a physical or mental condition, is unable to care for himself or herself. To qualify for the dependent care credit, the disability must be so severe as to require constant attention to prevent the disabled person from injuring himself or others, or to keep the individual from eating, dressing, or attending to personal hygiene without help. A person is also considered disabled if he or she has suicidal tendencies that require constant attention.

Employment-Related Expenses

If employment-related expenses involve a child who is your dependent and under age 15, the fees paid to a day-care center, nursery school, or summer camp are includable in the child care credit. Allowable expenses also include the salaries, meals, and lodging of a maid, baby-sitter, or nurse. You are allowed to pay a relative, including a grandparent, who is not your dependent. If the relative is your child, he or she must have been 19 or older by the end of the year. If you pay any employee more than $50 in any calendar quarter, you are liable for Social Security taxes and will have to file Form 941.

Expenses for out-of-home care for a disabled spouse or a dependent who spends at least 8 hours a day at home qualify for the child and dependent care credit. However, in one case a single parent who sent her son to military school was permitted a child care credit: the courts felt that the motive in sending the child to the school was to help the parent find and maintain a job.

Computing the Credit

If you earn $10,000 or less, the tax credit for baby-sitting and child care is 30 percent of the first $2,400 (maximum $720) for baby-sitting costs for one child, or 30 percent of the first $4,800 (maximum $1,440) for baby-sitting costs for 2 or more children. The credit is reduced by one percentage point for each $2,000 (or part of $2,000) of income over $10,000; for couples earning over $28,000, the maximum credit is 20 percent of $2,400 (maximum $480) for watching one child, and 20 percent of $4,800 (maximum $960) for 2 or more children.

Limitation on the Credit

The allowable expenses that may be taken into consideration as a base for the credit may not exceed earned income. In cases involving single parents, allowable expenses may not exceed earnings for the year. In two-income families, allowable expenses may not exceed the earnings of the parent with the lower earned income. Thus, if only one parent works, there are no allowable expenses on which to base the child care credit, and therefore, no credit can be claimed. However, there is a special rule for a nonworking spouse who is a full-time student for at least 5 months during the year, or mentally or

Form **2441**	**Credit for Child and Dependent Care Expenses**	OMB No. 1545-0068
Department of the Treasury Internal Revenue Service (X)	▶ Attach to Form 1040. ▶ See instructions below.	Attachment Sequence No. **23**

Name(s) as shown on Form 1040: Douben

Your social security number: 329 04 1040

Note: *If you paid cash wages of $50 or more in a calendar quarter to an individual for services performed in your home, you must file an employment tax return. Get **Form 942**, Employer's Quarterly Tax Return for Household Employees, for details.*

1. Enter the number of qualifying persons who were cared for in 1986. (See the instructions below for the definition of qualifying persons.) ▶ **1** | 2

2. Enter the amount of **qualified** expenses you incurred and actually paid in 1986 for the care of the qualifying person. (See **What Are Qualified Expenses** in the instructions.) **Do not** enter more than $2,400 ($4,800 if you paid for the care of two or more qualifying persons) . . . . . . **2** | 4800

3a. You **must** enter your earned income on line 3a. See the instructions for line 3 for the definition of earned income. . . . **3a** | 45000

 b. If you are married, filing a joint return for 1986, you must enter your spouse's earned income on line 3b . . . **3b** | 12000

 c. If you are married filing a joint return, compare the amounts on lines 3a and 3b, and enter the **smaller** of the two amounts on line 3c . . . **3c** | 12000

4. • If you were unmarried at the end of 1986, compare the amounts on lines 2 and 3a, and enter the **smaller** of the two amounts on line 4.
   • If you are married filing a joint return, compare the amounts on lines 2 and 3c, and enter the **smaller** of the two amounts on line 4. **4** | 4800

5. Enter the percentage from the table below that applies to the adjusted gross income on Form 1040, line 33 . . . **5** | 20

If line 33 is:		Percentage is:	If line 33 is:		Percentage is:
Over—	But not over—		Over—	But not over—	
$0	10,000	30% (.30)	$20,000	22,000	24% (.24)
10,000	12,000	29% (.29)	22,000	24,000	23% (.23)
12,000	14,000	28% (.28)	24,000	26,000	22% (.22)
14,000	16,000	27% (.27)	26,000	28,000	21% (.21)
16,000	18,000	26% (.26)	28,000		20% (.20)
18,000	20,000	25% (.25)			

6. Multiply the amount on line 4 by the percentage shown on line 5, and enter the result . . . **6** | 960

7. Multiply any child and dependent care expenses for 1985 that you paid in 1986 by the percentage that applies to the adjusted gross income on your 1985 Form 1040, line 33, or Form 1040A, line 15. Enter the result. (See line 7 instructions for the required statement.) . . . **7** |

8. Add amounts on lines 6 and 7. Enter the total here and on Form 1040, line 41. This is the maximum amount of your credit for child and dependent care expenses . . . **8** | 960

physically disabled. In those cases there is a presumption of earned income of $166 per month for each month that the parent is either a student or mentally or physically disabled. The other spouse, however, must be a qualified individual. The presumption of earned income increases to $333 if more than one individual qualifies. Consider, for example, a parent of 2 children, ages 3 and 5, married to a full-time student. He earns $15,000 for the year and incurs $5,000 of employment-related expenses for the children's nursery school. His student-wife has no earnings for the year, but because she attends school full-time, she is considered by the IRS to be gainfully employed. Since both are qualifying members, the earned-income limitation is $3,996 ($333 month × 12 months); the maximum credit would be $799 ($3,996 × 20 percent).

Credit for the Elderly and for the Permanently and Totally Disabled (Schedule R)

The credit for the elderly and disabled is designed to assist taxpayers who receive small amounts of Social Security, railroad retirement, and other pension, annuity, or disability benefits and have relatively small amounts of other income. Qualified individuals who are citizens or residents of the United States and who are age 65 or older (or those under 65 who have retired with a permanent and total disability) and who receive disability income from a public or private employer can claim a tax credit. An individual is considered to be both permanently and totally disabled if he can prove to the IRS that he is unable to engage in any "substantial gainful activity" by reason of a medically determinable illness (physical or mental) that can be expected to result in death or has lasted (or can be expected to last) for at least 12 consecutive months. Married individuals must file jointly to claim the elderly and disabled credit. The credit may be claimed by a married person filing separately if he or she has been living apart from the spouse for the entire tax year.

Each individual is allocated an "initial amount" for the purpose of determining the credit. This amount is reduced for those who receive nontaxable Social Security and railroad retirement benefits and certain other excludable pensions or annuities, or whose adjusted gross income exceeds certain amounts. The tax credit is an amount equal to 15 percent of a specified maximum.

Determining the Initial Amount

The initial amount for qualified individuals age 65 or over (and subject to the credit) depends on their filing status:

Single individuals	$5,000
Married individuals, joint return, one spouse eligible	$5,000
Married individuals, joint return, both spouses eligible	$7,500
Married individual, separate return	$3,750

If a qualified individual is under age 65, the initial amount is limited to whichever is lower, disability income or the applicable initial amount. If both spouses are under age 65 and file jointly, the initial amount cannot exceed the total of the spouses' combined disability income (maximum $7,500). If one spouse is age 65 (or older) at the end of the taxable year, the initial amount cannot exceed the sum of $5,000 plus the disability income (up to $2,500) of the spouse who has not reached age 65 before the end of the taxable year.

Reductions to the Initial Amount

The initial amount is reduced dollar-for-dollar for nontaxable railroad retirement, Social Security, or veteran's benefits, and by other pensions, annuities, and disability benefits (excludable from gross income). Workmen's compensation benefits that reduce the amount of disability benefits must be treated as Social Security for reduction purposes.

In the case of a married couple filing jointly, the combined benefits of both spouses must be taken into account in determining the reduction.

Example
Mr. J, a single person, age 62, has adjusted gross income of $7,000. He received $1,200 in Social Security and $4,000 in private disability benefits for 1987. Mr. J retired at age 61 on total disability. His credit is $420, computed as follows:

Initial amount for disabled taxpayer under age 65	$4,000
Less Social Security benefits	1,200
Amount subject to credit	$2,800
Credit (15% of $2,800)	$ 420

If the qualified taxpayer's adjusted gross income exceeds a specific amount, a further reduction is needed. To the extent that adjusted gross income exceeds the applicable level, the initial amount must be reduced by one-half of such excess. The adjusted gross income levels are as follows:

Single individual	$ 7,500
Married individuals filing joint return	$10,000
Married individuals filing separate returns	$ 5,000

Example 1
Joe, age 70, receives $3,000 in Social Security benefits. His wife, Bea, age 62, is permanently and totally disabled and receives $1,200 in disability benefits. Joe and Bea file jointly and report adjusted gross income of $13,000. Their credit for the elderly and disabled is $255, determined as follows:

Initial amount ($5,000 + $1,200)		$6,200
Less Social Security benefits	$3,000	
One-half of AGI in excess of $10,000	1,500	
Total reductions		4,500
Amount subject to credit		$1,700
Credit (15% of $1,700)		$ 255

Example 2
Molly, age 65 and single, has adjusted gross income of $9,500 and received $3,500 of nontaxable Social Security benefits for the year. The amount of her credit is $75, computed as follows:

Initial amount		$5,000
Less Social Security benefits	$3,500	
One-half of AGI in excess of $7,500	1,000	
Total		4,500
Amount subject to credit		$ 500
Credit (15% of $500)		$ 75

Schedule R
(Form 1040)
Department of the Treasury
Internal Revenue Service

Credit for the Elderly or for the Permanently and Totally Disabled
▶ For Paperwork Reduction Act Notice, see separate Instructions.
▶ Attach to Form 1040.   ▶ See separate Instructions for Schedule R.

OMB No. 1545-0074

1987

Attachment Sequence No. **17**

Name(s) as shown on Form 1040: DOUGH

Your social security number: 329 04 1040

You may be able to use Schedule R to reduce your tax if by the end of 1987:
- You were 65 or over, **OR**
- You were under 65, you retired on permanent and total disability, and you received taxable disability income.

Even if one of the situations described above applies to you, you must meet other tests to be able to take the credit on Schedule R. See the separate Schedule R Instructions for details.

Note: *IRS can figure this credit and your tax for you. See page 13 of the Form 1040 Instructions.*

Part I — Check the Box That Applies to Your Filing Status and Age (Check only one box)

If your filing status is:	And by the end of 1987:	Check box:
Single*	1 You were 65 or over	1 ☐
	2 You were under 65 and you retired on permanent and total disability	2 ☐

* Includes head of household and qualifying widow(er) with dependent child

Married filing a joint return	3 Both spouses were 65 or over	3 ☐
	4 Both spouses were under 65, but only one spouse retired on permanent and total disability	4 ☐
	5 Both spouses were under 65, and both retired on permanent and total disability	5 ☐
	6 One spouse was 65 or over, and the other spouse was under 65 and retired on permanent and total disability	6 ☐
	7 One spouse was 65 or over, and the other spouse was under 65 and **NOT** retired on permanent and total disability	7 ☐
Married filing a separate return	8 You were 65 or over, and you did not live with your spouse at any time in 1987	8 ☐
	9 You were under 65, you retired on permanent and total disability, and you did not live with your spouse at any time in 1987	9 ☐

Note: *If you checked the box on line 1, 3, 7, or 8, skip Part II and complete Part III. If you checked the box on line 2, 4, 5, 6, or 9, complete Parts II and III.*

Part II — Statement of Permanent and Total Disability (Complete only if you checked the box on line 2, 4, 5, 6, or 9 above)

IF: 1 You filed a physician's statement for this disability for 1983 or an earlier year, or you filed a statement for tax years after 1983 and your physician checked Box B on the statement, **AND**

2 Due to your continued disabled condition you were unable to engage in any substantial gainful activity in 1987, check this box. ▶ ☐

If you checked this box, you do not have to file another statement for 1987. If you did not check this box, have your physician complete the following statement:

Physician's Statement

I certify that _____
Name of disabled person

was permanently and totally disabled on January 1, 1976, or January 1, 1977, **OR** was permanently and totally disabled on the date he or she retired. Date retired if retired after December 31, 1976. ▶ _____

Physician: Sign your name on **either** line A or B below and check the box to the right of your signature.

A The disability has lasted, or can be expected to last, continuously for at least a year ....   A ☐

B There is no reasonable probability that the disabled condition will ever improve ....   B ☐

Physician's signature _____ Date _____

Physician's name _____   Physician's address _____

Instructions for Statement

Taxpayer

Enter in the space provided the date you retired if you retired after December 31, 1976.

Physician

A person is permanently and totally disabled when—
- He or she cannot engage in any substantial gainful activity because of a physical or mental condition; and

- A physician determines that the disability:
  1. has lasted, or can be expected to last, continuously for at least a year; or
  2. can be expected to lead to death.

(Continued on back)

Page **2**

Part III — Figure the Amount of Your Credit

10 Enter: $5,000 if you checked the box on line 1, 2, 4, or 7 in Part I, **OR**
$7,500 if you checked the box on line 3, 5, or 6 in Part I, **OR**
$3,750 if you checked the box on line 8 or 9 in Part I. **10**

Caution: *If you checked the box on line 2, 4, 5, 6, or 9 in Part I, you MUST complete line 11 below. Otherwise, skip line 11 and enter the amount from line 10 on line 12.*

11 Enter on this line your taxable disability income (and also your spouse's if you checked the box on line 5 in Part I) that you reported on Form 1040. However, if you checked the box on line 6 in Part I, enter on this line the taxable disability income of the spouse who was under age 65 **PLUS** $5,000. (For more details on what to include, see the Instructions.) **11**

12 If you completed line 11 above, compare the amounts on lines 10 and 11, and enter the **smaller** of the two amounts on this line. Otherwise, enter the amount from line 10 on this line **12**

13 Enter the following pensions, annuities, or disability income that you (and your spouse if you file a joint return) received in 1987:
  a Nontaxable part of social security benefits **13a**
  b Nontaxable part of railroad retirement benefits treated as social security; and
  Nontaxable veterans' pensions; and
  Any other pension, annuity, or disability benefit that is excluded from income under any other provision of law. . . . **13b**
  c Add lines 13a and 13b. (Even though these income items are not subject to income tax, they must be included to figure your credit.) If you did not receive any of the types of nontaxable income listed on line 13a or 13b, enter -0- on line 13c **13c**

14 Enter the amount from Form 1040, line 31. **14**

15 Enter: $7,500 if you checked the box on line 1 or 2 in Part I, **OR**
$10,000 if you checked the box on line 3, 4, 5, 6, or 7 in Part I, **OR**
$5,000 if you checked the box on line 8 or 9 in Part I **15**

16 Subtract line 15 from line 14. Enter the result. If line 15 is more than line 14, enter -0-. **16**

17 Divide the amount on line 16 by 2. Enter the result **17**

18 Add lines 13c and 17. Enter the total **18**

19 Subtract line 18 from line 12. Enter the result. If the result is zero or less, stop here; you **cannot** take the credit. Otherwise, go on to line 21 . . . . **19**

20 Percentage used to figure the credit **20** × .15

21 Multiply the amount on line 19 by the percentage (.15) on line 20 and enter the result. This is your **credit for the elderly or for the permanently and totally disabled.** Also enter this amount on Form 1040, line 41. . . . . **21**

General Business Credit

Investment tax credit on qualified rehabilitation expenses, targeted-jobs tax credit, alcohol fuels credit, and employee stock ownership credit are combined into one credit (the general business credit). Each of these 4 credits is computed separately, and the total becomes the general business credit. A discussion of the targeted-jobs tax credit may be found on page 83.

Determining the Maximum Tax Liability

The general business credit can reduce tax liability to the extent of 100 percent of the first $25,000 of net tax liability and 75 percent of the net tax liability over $25,000. For example:

> Barry has a tax liability before credits of $50,000 and the following credits: foreign tax credit, $2,500; research activities credit, $500; investment tax credit for qualified rehabilitation expenses, $40,000; targeted-jobs tax credit, $3,000; and employee stock ownership plans (ESOP) credit, $8,000, for a total of $54,000 in credits. His general business credit is $51,000 ($40,000 investment tax credit for qualified rehabilitation expenses plus $3,000 targeted-jobs credit and $8,000 ESOP credit). Barry's net tax liability is $47,000 ($50,000 tax liability minus $2,500 foreign tax credit and $500 research activities credit). Maximum general business credit: $41,500 ($25,000 plus 75 percent of tax liability over $25,000). Unused business credit: $12,500 ($54,000 total credits minus a $41,500 limitation).

Carry-Backs and Carry-Forwards of Unused Credits

If the general business credit exceeds the maximum tax limitation, any unused business credit may be carried back 3 years and carried forward 15 years. If the business credits carried to (or earned in) a particular year are not fully used up, each unused credit is carried to the next year.

Earlier credits are used up first; the order in which credits are carried forward or back is as follows:

1. Carry-forwards to that year, first year's first
2. Business credit earned in that year
3. Carry-backs to that year, first year's first.

Rehabilitation Tax Credits

There is a 10 percent tax credit for rehabilitation expenditures of non-residential buildings that were built before 1936. For investments made before tax reform, there is a phase-in: 65 percent of losses are deductible in 1987, 40 percent in 1988, 20 percent in 1989, 10 percent in 1990, and zero in 1991.

Rehabilitation of Historic Structures

The tax credit under the Tax Reform Act has decreased from 25 percent to 20 percent for rehabilitation expenses of historic structures. This rehabilitation credit may be used to offset tax on up to $25,000 of nonpassive income but is phased out for taxpayers between $200,000 and $250,000 adjusted gross income (without regard to net passive losses, taxable Social Security benefits, or IRA contributions).

Rehabilitating a historic structure with profit potential could be a worthwhile investment, since other tax shelters have been substantially changed.

Low-Income Rental Housing

Owners of residential rental property providing low-income housing may claim a new tax credit each year for a period of 10 years. The rates are equivalent to a credit with a present value of 70 percent for new construction and rehabilitation, and 30 percent of acquisition costs of existing housing to be used for low-income housing. Low-income renters geared to area median income must occupy certain specified percentages of the units in order to be eligible.

Investment Tax Credit

The regular Investment Tax Credit was repealed effective January 1, 1986. ITC carryovers and credits are reduced by 17½ percent of tentative credits.

Windfall Profits Tax Credits (Oil Royalties)

Each investor can exempt the windfall profits tax on 2 barrels per day. In order to claim the exemption, enter the credit on Schedule E (Supplemental Income Schedule), Part III, Windfall Profit Tax Summary.

Self-Employment Tax (Schedule SE)

If you are an employee, Social Security tax is taken out of your pay to provide retirement benefits, and that amount is matched by your employer. However, if you have income of $400 or more (net profit) from operating a business or profession as a sole proprietor, you are liable for self-employment tax and must pay both the employer and employee portion. The current tax rate is 12.3 percent on income up to $43,800, to a maximum of $5,387. Filers who are employees of electing churches (or church-controlled organizations) should not enter W-2 wages on line 2. The tax provides funds for Social Security and Medicare benefits.

Self-employment income does not include rentals and real estate, dividends, interest, or capital gains, but it is usually limited to net business income. It is based on the lower of (1) the net profit of the business, or (2) $43,800. If you worked as an employee and earned more than $43,800 during the year, you need not pay self-employment tax on additional income earned in a sideline business.

If you are a consultant hired by a former employer, you must pay self-employment tax on money received, including retainers, even if services are no longer performed. However, you can establish IRA and Keogh or SEP plans to reduce the tax bite. If you aren't covered under another plan or have income below set amounts, see page 132.

SCHEDULE SE (Form 1040)
Department of the Treasury
Internal Revenue Service

Computation of Social Security Self-Employment Tax

▶ See Instructions for Schedule SE (Form 1040).
▶ Attach to Form 1040.

OMB No. 1545-0074

1987

Attachment Sequence No. **18**

Name of person with **self-employment** income (as shown on social security card): **FAME DOUGH**

Social security number of person with **self-employment** income ▶ **004 : 19 : 7912**

A If your only self-employment income was from earnings as a minister, member of a religious order, or Christian Science practitioner, AND you filed Form 4361, then DO NOT file Schedule SE. Instead, write "Exempt-Form 4361" on Form 1040, line 48. However, if you filed Form 4361, but have $400 or more of other earnings subject to self-employment tax, continue with Part I and check here ▶ ☐

B If you filed Form 4029 and have received IRS approval, DO NOT file Schedule SE. Write "Exempt-Form 4029" on Form 1040, line 48.

C If you are not a minister or a member of a religious order and your only earnings subject to self-employment tax are wages from an electing church or church-controlled organization that is exempt from employer social security taxes, skip lines 1–8. Enter zero on line 9. Continue with line 11a.

Part I — Regular Computation of Net Earnings From Self-Employment

1	Net farm profit (or loss) from Schedule F (Form 1040), line 37, and farm partnerships, Schedule K-1 (Form 1065), line 14a	1	
2	Net profit (or loss) from Schedule C (Form 1040), line 31, and Schedule K-1 (Form 1065), line 14a (other than farming). (See Instructions for other income to report.) Employees of an electing church or church-controlled organization DO NOT enter your Form W-2 wages on line 2. See the Instructions	2	1205

Part II — Optional Computation of Net Earnings From Self-Employment (See "Who Can Use Schedule SE" in the Instructions.)

See Instructions for limitations. Generally, this part may be used **only** if you meet any of the following tests:

A Your **gross** farm income¹ was not more than $2,400; **or**
B Your **gross** farm income¹ was more than $2,400 and your **net** farm profits² were less than $1,600; **or**
C Your **net** nonfarm profits³ were less than $1,600 and your **net** nonfarm profits³ were also less than two-thirds (⅔) of your **gross** nonfarm income.⁴

Note: If line 2 above is two-thirds (⅔) or more of your gross nonfarm income⁴, or, if line 2 is $1,600 or more, you may **not** use the optional method.

¹From Schedule F (Form 1040), line 12, and Schedule K-1 (Form 1065), line 14b. ³From Schedule C (Form 1040), line 31, and Schedule K-1 (Form 1065), line 14a.
²From Schedule F (Form 1040), line 37, and Schedule K-1 (Form 1065), line 14a. ⁴From Schedule C (Form 1040), line 5, and Schedule K-1 (Form 1065), line 14c.

3	Maximum income for optional methods	3	$1,600 00
4	Farm Optional Method—If you meet test A or B above, enter the **smaller of**: two-thirds (⅔) of gross farm income from Schedule F (Form 1040), line 12, and farm partnerships, Schedule K-1 (Form 1065), line 14b; **or** $1,600	4	
5	Subtract line 4 from line 3	5	
6	Nonfarm Optional Method—If you meet test C above, enter the **smallest of**: two-thirds (⅔) of gross nonfarm income from Schedule C (Form 1040), line 5, and Schedule K-1 (Form 1065), line 14c (other than farming); **or** $1,600; **or**, if you elected the farm optional method, the amount on line 5	6	

Part III — Computation of Social Security Self-Employment Tax

7	Enter the amount from Part I, line 1, **or**, if you elected the farm optional method, Part II, line 4	7	
8	Enter the amount from Part I, line 2, **or**, if you elected the nonfarm optional method, Part II, line 6	8	1205
9	Add lines 7 and 8. If less than $400, do not file this schedule. (**Exception:** If you are an employee of an electing church or church-controlled organization, enter zero and complete the rest of this schedule.)	9	1205
10	The largest amount of combined wages and self-employment earnings subject to social security or railroad retirement tax (tier 1) for 1987 is	10	$43,800 00
11a	Total social security wages and tips from Forms W-2 and railroad retirement compensation (tier 1). **Note:** Medicare qualified government employees whose wages are only subject to the 1.45% medicare (hospital insurance benefits) tax and employees of certain church or church-controlled organizations should **not** include those wages on this line. (See Instructions.)	11a	12000
b	Unreported tips subject to social security tax from Form 4137, line 9, or to railroad retirement tax (tier 1)	11b	
c	Add lines 11a and 11b	11c	12000
12a	Subtract line 11c from line 10. (If zero or less, enter zero.)	12a	31800
b	Enter your medicare qualified government wages if you are required to use the worksheet in Part III of the Instructions . . 12b		
c	Enter your Form W-2 wages of $100 or more from an electing church or church-controlled organization . . 12c		
d	If line 9 is less than $400, enter the amount from 12c. If line 9 is $400 or more, enter the total of lines 9 and 12c	12d	1205
13	Enter the smaller of line 12a or line 12d	13	1205
	If line 13 is $43,800, enter $5,387.40 on line 14. Otherwise, multiply line 13 by .123 and enter the result on line 14		× .123
14	Self-employment tax. Enter this amount on Form 1040, line 48	14	148

Alternative Minimum Tax (Form 6251)

The alternative minimum tax was instituted to keep high-income taxpayers from paying no income tax at all. It may affect you if you had large losses from passive-loss adjustments. You have to pay the alternative minimum tax only if it is more than your regular income tax. You are taxed at 21 percent of taxable income over $40,000 (married filing jointly), $30,000 (singles), or $20,000 (married filing separately).

Under the old law, the alternative minimum tax was 20 percent; under Tax Reform, it's 21 percent. It's a flat tax applied to make more income because income isn't reduced by as many breaks.

A taxpayer who made a lot of money on long-term capital gains might pay much less income tax than a taxpayer who made the same amount in wages for the same year. In addition, taxpayers who invest in tax shelters (or claim large deductions or credits) may end up paying virtually no tax. It's for these people that the alternative minimum tax was devised, in an effort to make everyone pay his fair share of taxes.

The AMT is a flat tax of 21 percent; it is applied to more of your income than the regular income tax covers, because your income isn't reduced by as many deductions. You calculate the AMT separately and pay it only when it exceeds your regular income tax.

The new rules and computations are even more difficult to comprehend than the old ones, but it's worth understanding, especially if you can save money. More taxpayers than ever before will be subject to this tax, and the income base to which the rate applies is determined differently from under the old law.

The only way to know whether you are affected is to look at the numbers. Some of the changes that will affect more taxpayers include:

1. Losses from passive investments (tax shelters) during the phase-in period. The losses may be deductible for regular tax but must be added back to taxable income when you figure the AMT.
2. Less spread between regular rates and AMT rate. Beginning in 1988, the AMT rate is 75 percent of the top tax bracket (AMT rate of 21 percent divided by top rate of 28 percent).
3. More items to be added back to income when figuring the AMT.

In order to figure the amount of your income subject to the AMT, adjust your regular taxable income according to the different treatment of certain items:

1. Depreciation on real and personal property placed in service after 1986. Either increase or decrease your regular taxable income by the net difference between (1) depreciation using Accelerated Cost Recovery System and (2) depreciation using the alternative depreciation method.
2. Gain on the sale of assets depreciated differently for AMT purposes from regular tax purposes (only for assets placed in service after 1986).
3. Passive activity investment losses (e.g., tax shelters). For regular tax purposes, you can use a certain percentage of your passive activity (or tax shelter losses) to offset your earned income and portfolio income during the 4-year phase-in period beginning this year. But you can't use these losses to offset that income when you figure your AMT income. You may carry forward a passive activity loss as a deduction against AMT passive income in succeeding tax years.

In addition, when you dispose of your entire interest in a tax shelter, you may use any carryovers resulting from denial of phase-in loss to compute the AMT income.

You must also increase your regular taxable income for more common tax preference items, including the following:

1. Itemized deductions that are not deductible for AMT, including medical expenses under 10 percent of your AGI, state and local income taxes, real estate taxes, and miscellaneous deductions that exceed 2 percent of your adjusted gross income. Also, all interest expense except home mortgage interest and investment interest to the extent of investment income.

    The phase-in rule for investment interest for regular tax purposes does not apply to AMT purposes. If you refinance your home mortgage, the only interest allowed for AMT purposes is that on the refinanced mortgage equal to the debt before you refinanced.
2. When you exercise an incentive stock option (ISO), the excess of the fair market value over the purchase price becomes part of the stock's basis. When the stock is sold, the gain for AMT purposes will be less than the gain for regular tax purposes.
3. Excess intangible drilling costs incurred in connection with productive oil and gas wells over 65 percent of the net income from the well.
4. Excess of percentage depletion over the tax basis of the property generating the mineral deposit subject to depletion.
5. Excess of accelerated depreciation over straight-line depreciation on real or leased personal properties placed in service before 1987.
6. Interest on certain tax-exempt bonds generally issued after August 7, 1986. This applies only to nonessential bonds—meaning bonds issued by state or local governments from which the proceeds are used by private enterprise (such as those used by small businesses for building needs).
7. Excess research and experimentation expenditures over the amount deductible if amortized over 10 years.
8. In the case of property contributed to a charitable organization and deducted for regular tax purposes as an itemized deduction, the excess of the value over the cost of such property.

After you've made the adjustments to your regular taxable income and accounted for all tax preference items, the net sum is your AMT income. You now reduce it by the standard exclusion: $40,000 for taxpayers filing jointly, and $30,000 for singles.

If your AMT income exceeds $150,000 for marrieds ($112,500 for singles), your exclusion is reduced by 25 percent of the amount over $150,000 ($112,500 for singles) after considering the AMT exclusion of up to $40,000.

Now multiply your adjusted AMT income by 21 percent and subtract allowable foreign tax credits. The result is your tentative minimum tax (TMT).

Compare the TMT to your regular tax. If you find that the TMT is larger, you have to pay the excess as alternative minimum tax in addition to your regular tax.

Passive activities, tax shelter farming losses, and installment sales of rental property over $150,000 (and of dealer property) are disregarded for AMT purposes. However, if you incur AMT in 1987 and a regular tax in 1988, you may be able to deduct your 1987 AMT from your 1988 regular tax. This tax credit is meant to even out the differences between AMT and regular tax reporting so that income reporting does not favor the government over a period of time.

Example

Your AMT in 1987 is $7,000, and your regular tax is $6,000. You carry forward the credit of $1,000. In 1988, your regular tax is $9,000, and your AMT is $4,000. You apply the $1,000 credit against your regular tax.

The reduction of regular tax is based on a prior AMT incurred after 1986, and the carry-forward period is indefinite. No credit is allowed to the extent that the AMT was based on percentage depletion, charitable donations of appreciated property, and tax-exempt interest. The credit may not reduce your tax below the AMT for any given year.

Incentive Stock Options

The excess of fair market value of stock over exercise price is still a tax preference; however, for AMT, the basis of stock acquired through ISO after 1986 must equal the fair market value, which is considered when determining the amount of the preference.

Example

You pay $10 to buy stock with a fair market value of $15. The preference is $5. The basis is $10 for regular tax and $15 for minimum tax purposes. You sell for $20. The gain is $10 for regular tax and $15 for minimum tax purposes.

Earned Income Credit

An earned income tax credit is available for low-income workers who have dependent children living with them in a household they maintain (i.e., in which they pay over half the expenses), but only if income is less than $14,500. Nontaxable income earned in another country may not be excluded from the total.

The dependent must be age 19 or younger, or a student, or disabled (and earn less than $1,900 per year). A foster child, grandchild, niece, or nephew may also be claimed, but only if he or she lives in the household for the entire year. Married persons must file a joint return for the year in order to claim the credit; however, a married person whose spouse has not been part of the household for the entire year can still claim the credit.

The earned income credit is equal to 14 percent of the first $5,714 of earned income, for a maximum credit of $800. The earned income credit is scaled to zero as earnings increase from $6,500 to $14,500. The maximum $800 credit is reduced by an amount equal to 10 percent of the adjusted gross income over $6,500 and is eliminated completely at $14,500.

Beginning in 1988, the credit phase-out will begin at $9,000 adjusted gross income with a total phase-out at $17,000.

Claiming the Credit

No special form is available to compute the earned income credit, but a worksheet is included in the tax forms provided by the IRS. Even if no taxes were deducted from wages, or if income earned is not enough to file a tax return, a return should be filed anyway and the credit claimed; a refund of up to $800 may be available. An advance payment of the earned income credit may be obtained by filing a W-5 form with the employer, stating eligibility to claim the credit and that no other form is on file with another employer.

10
LAST-MINUTE FILING TIPS AND SPECIAL FILING SITUATIONS

Last-Minute Filing Tips

According to the IRS, the following mistakes in filing are the most common:

- Failure to attach W-2 forms.
- Failure to attach a check for tax due.
- Incorrect computation of the standard deduction.
- Using a wrong Social Security number.
- Forgetting to check off the proper box on a form.
- Failure of both spouses to sign the return.
- Entries placed on wrong lines.
- Failure to use peel-off label.
- Adding income incorrectly. One of the most frequent errors is incorrect addition on page 1 of Form 1040.
- Miscalculating medical and dental expenses. Since the medical deduction is based on 7.5 percent of adjusted gross income, be sure to recheck page 1 of Form 1040 before you calculate medical expenses.
- Entering the wrong amount of tax. Be sure to use the correct table, and select the proper amount. If you use the tax rate schedule, compute your tax a second time.
- Overlooking credits. Be sure to read all tax forms carefully and take all credits—e.g., earned income credit.
- Mistakes in calculation of child and dependent care expenses. Be sure to file Form 2441 and recheck all math.
- Taking the incorrect earned income credit. To avoid mistakes, use the worksheet in the instruction booklet.
- Confusion about federal income tax withheld. Read your W-2 carefully; don't use the FICA or state tax withholding figure by mistake.
- Errors in tax due. Many errors are made on the last few lines of the tax return, which determine whether a refund is due or the taxpayer owes additional tax. Recheck math carefully. Be sure that a refund is in fact a refund.

Last-Minute Tax Forms

If you are in need of tax forms at the last minute, contact your local library and ask to photocopy forms from Package X, a set of the most common tax forms.

Checking on Your Refund

You can check on the status of your refund by calling a special IRS telephone number that provides automated refund information. When you call, be ready with your Social Security number, filing status, and the amount of your expected refund. Don't call unless it has been at least 10 weeks since you filed. If you mailed your return before April 15 and your check wasn't sent out by the IRS before June 1, you are entitled to interest on your refund.

Here are the IRS regions and phone numbers:

Atlanta (404) 221-6572	Denver (303) 592-1118	Newark (201) 624-1223
Baltimore (301) 244-7306	Detroit (313) 961-4282	Oakland (415) 839-4245
Boston (617) 523-8602	Houston (713) 850-8801	Philadelphia (215) 592-8946
Brooklyn (718) 858-4461	Indianapolis (317) 634-1550	Phoenix (602) 261-3560
Buffalo (716) 856-9320	Jacksonville (904) 353-9579	Portland (503) 294-5363
Chicago (312) 886-9614	Los Angeles (213) 617-3177	Seattle (206) 343-7221
Cincinnati (513) 684-3531	Manhattan (212) 406-4080	St. Louis (314) 241-4700
Cleveland (216) 522-3037	Milwaukee (414) 291-1783	St. Paul (612) 224-4288
Dallas (214) 767-1792	Nashville (615) 242-1544	Washington (202) 628-2929

If You Don't Have the Money to Pay Your Taxes

If you owe money and don't have the cash to pay, file your tax return by the deadline but attach a note of explanation. This will eliminate an extra penalty for late filing, which can add up to 25 percent to your tax bill. You still will owe a penalty for late payment and interest, however.

Interest Rates

The IRS charges 9 percent interest on overdue taxes and the penalty for underpayment of estimated tax (but only pays 8 percent interest on late refunds). Instead of twice a year, the Tax Reform Act provides for rates to be reset each quarter.

Proper Postage

If the IRS gets your return without the correct postage, they may return it to you—possibly after April 15—and you will be charged a late filing penalty.

Special Filing Situations

Filing a Late Return

If you are not ready to file your tax return by April 15, you may get a 4-month extension by filing Form 4868 before that date. File Form 2688 for an additional 2-month extension.

Form 4868
Department of the Treasury
Internal Revenue Service (X)

Application for Automatic Extension of Time To File U.S. Individual Income Tax Return

OMB No. 1545-0188

Please Type or Print

Your first name and initial (if joint return, also give spouse's name and initial): **Barry R & Faye** Last name: **Dough**
Your social security number: **329 04 1040**

Present home address (number and street or rural route). (If you have a P.O. Box, see the instructions.): **1000 City Drive**
Spouse's social security no.: **004 19 7912**

City, town or post office, state, and ZIP code: **Anyplace USA 07942**

Note: File this form with the Internal Revenue Service Center where you must file your income tax return and pay the amount shown on line 6 below. **This is not an extension of time for payment of tax.** You will be charged a penalty for late payment of tax and late filing unless you show reasonable cause for not paying or filing on time (see instructions).

If you expect to file a gift tax return (Form 709 or Form 709-A) for 1986, generally due by April 15, 1987, check this box ▶ ☐

I request an automatic 4-month extension of time to August 17, 1987, to file Form 1040A or Form 1040 for the calendar year 1986 (or if a fiscal year Form 1040 to _____, 19____, for the tax year ending _____, 19____).

1	Total income tax liability for 1986. (You may estimate this amount.) **Note:** You *must* enter an amount on line 1. If you do not expect to owe tax, enter zero (0).	**1** 3000
2	Federal income tax withheld **2** 3000	
3	1986 estimated tax payments (include 1985 overpayment allowed as a credit) . **3**	
4	Other payments and credits you expect to show on Form 1040A or Form 1040 . **4**	
5	Add lines 2, 3, and 4	**5** 3000
6	Income tax balance due (subtract line 5 from line 1). Pay in full with this form. (If line 5 is more than line 1, enter zero (0).) ▶	**6** 0
7	Total gift tax and generation-skipping transfer tax you expect to owe for 1986 (see instructions) ▶	**7** 0

If you send only one check for income, gift, and generation-skipping transfer taxes due, attach a statement showing how much of the check applies to each type of tax.

Signature and Verification

Under penalties of perjury, I declare that I have examined this form, including accompanying schedules and statements, and to the best of my knowledge and belief, it is true, correct, and complete; and, if prepared by someone other than the taxpayer, that I am authorized to prepare this form.

Signature of taxpayer ▶ *Barry N Dough*   Date ▶ 4/12/88

Signature of spouse ▶ *Faye Dough*   Date ▶ 4/12/88
(If filing jointly, BOTH must sign even if only one had income)

Signature of preparer other than taxpayer ▶   Date ▶

If you are married filing jointly, and either spouse is out of the United States on April 15, there is a blanket extension to file until June 15; however, if you are married filing separately, the automatic extension will apply only to the spouse who is out of the country. You also get an extension of time to make your first quarter estimated tax payment when you are out of the country.

If you owe tax and file for an extension, you will avoid the penalty for failing to file your return on time (5 percent of the amount of tax due for each month you are late, up to a maximum of 25 percent). If you owe tax and you do not send a payment with the extension form, you are subject to a penalty and interest. The automatic extension applies only to filing, not to paying your taxes. If you fail to pay at least 90 percent of your ultimate tax liability with the extension, the extension will be denied, and you will be penalized. If you can prove extreme financial hardship, you may be granted up to 6 months to pay your taxes by filing Form 1127 for an extension of time to pay, but you will still have to pay interest. For a discussion on installment agreements as a means to pay back taxes, see page 219, "Problems Resolution Office."

If your accountant fails to file your return on time, you may be subject to the late filing penalty, but you may be able to avoid that penalty if you can explain on Form 2688 that the late filing was due to "circumstances beyond your control." The IRS will also give consideration to the following excuses as a reasonable cause for not filing on time:

1. Tax returns mailed on time but not received by deadline
2. Returns mailed on time but to the wrong IRS office
3. Returns delayed due to death or serious illness of a family member
4. Unavoidable absence, such as out-of-town travel required by your employer
5. Tax returns filed late because of incorrect information from IRS employees
6. Inability to file due to waiting for the proper tax form to be mailed by the IRS
7. Failure to file where taxpayer was told by an accountant that filing a return was not necessary, when in fact it was
8. Failure to obtain the necessary records—e.g., in the case of a divorce where the former spouse refuses to give up the tax records
9. Destruction of records due to fire, flood, or theft.

Filing Very Late

If you don't send in your return within 70 days of the due date (and you did not file an extension), you may have to pay a penalty of $100 or 100 percent of the tax due, whichever is less. In addition, you will be penalized for paying late and will be charged interest on any late taxes.

In extreme circumstances (e.g., death in the family or loss of your records) you can get a second extension (Form 2688), in which case you will have 2 more months (until October 15) to file your return.

Filing an Amended Return

At any time before April 15, 1988, you can still make a change on your 1984, 1985, or 1986 tax returns if you made an error in filing during one or more of those years. Changes are made by filing Form 1040X.

It is somewhat risky to file an amended return, since it will be looked over more carefully than a regular form. If you do file an amended return, be sure to give adequate explanations on the back of the page and attach supporting data. Filing an amended return *will not necessarily bring on an audit.*

Possible reasons for filing an amended tax return include:

1. To increase income previously reported. If you neglected to report an item of income, now is the time to make the correction.
2. To add to or decrease deductions previously reported. You may have claimed a deduction for something you now realize was improper, or you may have overlooked a legitimate tax deduction.
3. To claim additional exemptions you did not report or to reduce the number you claimed earlier.

4. To change the credits you claimed on an earlier return (for example, if you worked for more than one employer and forgot to take a credit for excess Social Security).
5. To correct errors you made because you used the wrong tax table or tax-rate schedule in computing your tax.
6. To recover taxes paid if you and your spouse originally filed separate returns and you now realize that you could have saved money by filing jointly.

IRS Interest Charges

Interest that accumulates on tax assessments due to IRS delay no longer has to be paid by the taxpayer. If the IRS is to blame, they can eliminate the extra interest charges. This is retroactive to payments made after 1978, so if you paid interest due to IRS error (or delay), claim a refund by filing an amended return (Form 1040X) immediately.

Problems Resolution Office

It's usually difficult dealing with the IRS, especially when you feel that the problem was theirs. For instance, when a refund check never arrives, when the IRS continues to bill for an amount already paid, or when an amended return is never acted upon, it can get very frustrating. The solution? Contact the IRS's Problems Resolution Office immediately. They have the job of resolving problems that cannot be settled otherwise. It's another name for trouble-shooting.

The Problems Resolution officer is supposed to stay with a problem until it is completely resolved. But before you take your problems to him, you must exhaust all normal channels (such as writing complaints to the Service Center). You should allow at least two weeks to elapse before calling Problems Resolution about your dilemma.

Here are some instances in which the Problems Resolution Office may get involved:

1. A question has not been answered within 45 days, and you must make a second request
2. A second inquiry into a missing refund is made 90 days or more after the filing of a return
3. Situations involving IRS error or whenever it is in the best interest of the IRS for the Problems Resolution Office to become involved
4. When the taxpayer was contacted by the IRS, but normal channels have not resolved the problem.

To get in touch with the Problems Resolution Office, simply write your local District Director (or call the local IRS office and ask for the Problems Resolution Office). You should be ready to state the facts clearly and describe how you have not been able to resolve the problem through normal channels. The greater the time delay since the initial IRS contact, the greater the chance is that the Problems Resolution Office will get involved.

If at least 10 weeks have passed since you filed your tax return and you have not received your refund, call the IRS Tele-Tax service (listed in the telephone directory under IRS—Tele-Tax Recorded Tax Information). If after 2 additional weeks you have still not received a refund, call the IRS Problems Resolution Office.

Form 1040X (Rev. October 1986)
Amended U.S. Individual Income Tax Return
Department of the Treasury—Internal Revenue Service
OMB No. 1545-0091 Expires 4-30-88

This return is for calendar year ▶ 1985, OR fiscal year ended ▶ , 19 .

Your first name and initial (if joint return, also give spouse's name and initial) / Last name: Barry R & Faye Dough

Your social security number: 329 04 1040

Present home address: 1000 City Drive

Spouse's social security number: 004 19 7912

City, town or post office, state, and ZIP code: Anyplace USA 07942

Telephone number (optional): ( )

Enter below name and address as shown on original return (if same as above, write "Same"). If changing from separate to joint return, enter names and addresses used on original returns. (Note: You cannot change from joint to separate returns after the due date has passed.)

Same

a Service center where original return was filed: Kansas City

b Has original return been changed or audited by IRS? ☐ Yes ☒ No
If "No," have you been notified that it will be? ☐ Yes ☒ No
If "Yes," identify IRS office ▶

c Are you amending your return to include any item (loss, credit, deduction, other tax benefit, or income) relating to a tax shelter required to be registered? ☐ Yes ☒ No
If "Yes," you MUST attach Form 8271, Investor Reporting of Tax Shelter Registration Number.

d Filing status claimed. (Note: You cannot change from joint to separate returns after the due date has passed.)
On original return ▶ ☐ Single ☒ Married filing joint return ☐ Married filing separate return ☐ Head of household ☐ Qualifying widow(er)
On this return ▶ ☐ Single ☒ Married filing joint return ☐ Married filing separate return ☐ Head of household ☐ Qualifying widow(er)

Income and Deductions

		A. As originally reported or as adjusted (see Instructions)	B. Net change—Increase or (Decrease)—explain on page 2	C. Correct amount
1	Total income (see Instructions)	12693		12693
2	Adjustments to income (see Instructions)	2744	1000	3744
3	Adjusted gross income (subtract line 2 from line 1)	9949	1000	8949
4	Deductions (see Instructions)			
5	Subtract line 4 from line 3	9949	1000	8949
6	Exemptions (see Instructions)	4160		4160
7	Taxable income (subtract line 6 from line 5)	5789	1000	4789

Tax Liability

8	Tax (see Instructions). (Method used in col. C Tables)	246	⟨110⟩	136
9	Credits (see Instructions)			
10	Subtract line 9 from line 8. Enter the result, but not less than zero	246	⟨110⟩	136
11	Other taxes (such as self-employment tax, alternative minimum tax)			
12	Total tax liability (add line 10 and line 11)	246	⟨110⟩	136

Payments

13	Federal income tax withheld and excess FICA and RRTA tax withheld	1200	1200
14	Estimated tax payments		
15	Earned income credit		
16	Credits for Federal tax on gasoline and special fuels, regulated investment company, etc.		
17	Amount paid with Form 4868, Form 2688, or Form 2350 (application for extension of time to file)		
18	Amount paid with original return, plus additional tax paid after it was filed		
19	Total of lines 13 through 18, column C		1200

Refund or Amount You Owe

20	Overpayment, if any, as shown on original return (or as previously adjusted by IRS)	954
21	Subtract line 20 from line 19 (see Instructions)	246
22	**AMOUNT YOU OWE.** If line 12, col. C, is more than line 21, enter difference. Please pay in full with this return.	
23	**REFUND** to be received. If line 12, column C, is less than line 21, enter difference.	110

Please Sign Here
Your signature: Barry R Dough Date: 9/1/87
Spouse's signature: Faye Dough Date: 9/1/87

Paid Preparer's Use Only
Preparer's signature / Date / Check if self-employed ☐ / Preparer's social security no.
Firm's name (or yours, if self-employed) and address / E.I. No. / ZIP code

BE SURE TO COMPLETE PAGE 2

Page 2

Part I — Exemptions (see Form 1040 or Form 1040A Instructions)
If claiming more exemptions, complete lines 1–9.
If claiming fewer exemptions, complete lines 1–6.

			A. Number originally reported	B. Net change	C. Correct number
1	Exemptions—yourself and spouse, 65 or over, blind	1			
2	Your dependent children who lived with you	2			
3	For tax years beginning after 1984, your dependent children who did not live with you	3			
4	Other dependents	4			
5	Total exemptions (add lines 1 through 4)	5			
6	Multiply $1,080 ($1,040, for tax year 1985; $1,000, for tax years beginning before 1985) by the number of exemptions claimed on line 5. Enter the result here and on page 1, line 6	6			

7 First names of your dependent children who lived with you and were not claimed on original return: **Enter number ▶** ☐

8 For tax years beginning after 1984, first names of your dependent children who did not live with you and were not claimed on original return (see Instructions). (If pre-1985 agreement, check here ☐.)   **Enter number ▶** ☐

9 Other dependents not claimed on original return:

(a) Name	(b) Relationship	(c) Number of months lived in your home	(d) Did dependent have income of at least $1,080 ($1,040, for tax year 1985; $1,000, for tax years beginning before 1985)?	(e) Did you provide more than one-half of dependent's support?

Enter number ▶ ☐

Part II — Explanation of Changes to Income, Deductions, and Credits

Enter the line number from page 1 for each item you are changing and give the reason for each change. Attach all supporting forms and schedules for items changed. Be sure to include your name and social security number on any attachments.

If the change pertains to a net operating loss carryback, a general business credit carryback, or for tax years beginning before 1986, a research credit carryback, attach the schedule or form that shows the year in which the loss or credit occurred. See the Instructions. Also, check here ▶ ☐

FORGOT TO DEDUCT $1000 OF UNREIMBURSED TRAVEL EXPENSES FOR 1985.

Part III — Presidential Election Campaign Fund
Checking below will not increase your tax or reduce your refund.

If you did not previously want to have $1 go to the fund, but now want to . . . . check here ▶ ☐
If joint return and your spouse did not previously want to have $1 go to the fund, but now wants to . . . . check here ▶ ☐

The Problems Resolution Office cannot help you resolve a problem if:

1. You should have used an established administrative (or formal) appeal procedure
2. You have already received an appropriate response from the IRS
3. Another federal, state, or local agency is responsible for resolving the problem
4. The problem involves a nontax matter
5. The matter involves a criminal investigation
6. The matter involves a frivolous tax protester issue
7. The tax is correctly assessed, but you cannot (or will not) pay it.

Back Taxes: Negotiating Installment Agreements

The Problems Resolutions Office can also help work out payment arrangements. Although it is not specifically mentioned in the Internal Revenue Code, it is IRS policy to consider payment of delinquent taxes through installment payments. An installment agreement is not a consideration that is extended automatically, however; it is a privilege, to be exercised at the discretion of the IRS. Before considering an installment agreement, the IRS requires the delinquent taxpayer to exhaust all other means of trying to pay the tax, including personal loans or sale of assets.

The delinquent taxpayer will be required to complete a Collection Information Statement (a combination balance sheet and statement of income and expenses—Form 433A for individuals, Form 433B for businesses). The Collection Information Statement is examined by the collection agent to determine whether the taxpayer has the assets or income to pay the tax immediately. Before being granted an installment agreement, the taxpayer should have filed all the necessary tax returns and should have correctly reported all income. Any returns that become due during the period of installment agreement must be filed and paid on time. If any delinquent taxes are incurred during the period of the installment agreement, they will cause the agreement to default and will probably result in immediate collection.

The taxpayer may be asked to adjust his or her withholding to ensure no future delinquencies. If the taxpayer is self-employed, he or she will be informed of the estimated tax payment procedure and advised to make the necessary payments. To keep from defaulting, the taxpayer must meet all future filing deadlines without owing any additional delinquent tax.

If the installment agreement covers a lengthy period of time, annual reviews will be made to evaluate the ability to pay, and an updated Collection Information Statement may be requested. If the delinquent taxpayer has the ability to increase the payments (or pay the tax in full), he or she will be so advised.

Paying Off the IRS

Often—too often—the IRS will file a tax lien on a home to get at the proceeds from the sale when money is due them. The IRS won't release the lien until they get their money, but the Catch-22 is that banks usually won't lend money as long as the tax lien is on the house.

If this happens to you, ask the IRS for a Certificate of Discharge of Property from Federal Tax Lien. The IRS will agree to release the lien at the same time the money owed is paid. Then the bank can give you money and register a mortgage that takes priority over all other creditors, including the IRS.

11
IRS AUDITS
(And How to Avoid Them)

Audits under Tax Reform

One of the best things about the Tax Reform Act is that there may be fewer audits because IRS employees will have to learn the new law from scratch. Unless the IRS audit staff increases greatly, there should be fewer audits. On the other hand, since taxpayers can be expected to make more errors, there is a possibility of the IRS conducting more audits.

Reporting All Your Income

One important thing has not changed, however: the critical importance of reporting *all* your income. Anyone who tries to pay less tax by reporting less income is playing with fire. If you want to avoid an audit, be scrupulous about reporting income. The reason why the IRS treats underreporters more harshly than overdeductors is that they are not given the opportunity to easily analyze unreported income while they can scrutinize excessive deductions.

Documenting Your Expenses

Another unchanged area of the law is in record-keeping. It is more important than ever to keep clear records of all expenses. If you take a deduction on your tax return, you must be prepared to prove that you are entitled to it if the Internal Revenue Service asks for documentation. Plan ahead *now* instead of having to reconstruct your records after you receive an audit notice so you will not lose any deductions you have attempted to take.

Answering Unreported Income Notices

If your return does not correspond with dividend or interest income reported to the IRS by banks and financial institutions, the IRS will send you a computer-generated notice with the tax due recalculated, adding interest charges and a negligence penalty. Here's how you respond:

1. Look over the notice to determine what items, if any, you failed to report. These should appear on a separate page of the correspondence.
2. Review your copy of the tax return and the 1099 forms used to prepare it, and figure out whether the IRS is correct. (The IRS is frequently wrong, so don't automatically send them a check.)

3. Answer within the 30-day time limit by writing to the address given in the notice, keeping a copy of all correspondence for your records. If the IRS is correct but you did not overlook an income item intentionally, pay the tax and interest but ask that the negligence penalty be waived. State your reason in an enclosed letter.

   If the IRS is incorrect and you did report the income (or the notice is wrong in some other aspect), figure out the cause of the problem and explain it in detail in your letter. Perhaps the IRS has an incorrect Form 1099 or you reported dividends as interest income. End your letter with "If there are any further questions, please contact me" and give them a daytime phone number.
4. If you receive a second notice that seems to ignore your reply, send a second letter enclosing copies of both notices from the IRS and a copy of your first letter. It usually takes the IRS 4 to 6 weeks to update their records.

Dealing with Audits

1. If you have a Schedule C (Income or Loss from Business or Profession), review all items and be sure you have supporting receipts for all deductions claimed, including auto expense, office expense, and entertainment and promotion. If you don't have receipts, record the expense items claimed in a log. Remember, however, that if the individual amount claimed exceeds $25 and you have no receipt, the IRS will try to disallow it.
2. If you have a home office in a portion of your home used *exclusively* for business and you have a profit, you could qualify for a home office deduction. If you have a loss, you cannot claim a home office to create that loss. Your record-keeping must be accurate, and you must prove that the area is *never* used for personal matters. Compute the area of the part of your home that serves as a home office as a percentage of the total square feet of the home; then claim as your deduction the pro rata portion of all the operating costs of the home.

   You must keep records of property taxes, interest, insurance, repairs, maintenance, and utilities. Keeping track of your home costs and all improvements since the date of purchase will allow you to compute depreciation properly.
3. Item #1 above also applies to rental property, and there are other items to be considered when rental income is very low. You do not have to show rental income, but you must show that you tried your best to rent the property. Heavy advertising and nonexclusive rental agreements with rental agents in the area where your property is located will convince the IRS. In order to take a deduction for expenses connected with searching for rental properties, you must already have established a rental business (have several operating rental properties) for the expenses to be considered deductible. Otherwise, start-up costs (e.g., property search expenses) must be amortized over a minimum 60-month period after operations begin. Keep a detailed log of your search activities and record all expenses, particularly in resort areas. Signed offer sheets for properties that you investigated will influence the IRS to believe you and to allow those search expenses even if you do not make a purchase. If you combine search activities with a vacation, you can deduct the pro rata share based on the amount of time actually spent on investigations.
4. The IRS spends a great deal of time investigating employee business expenses.

The most important thing you need to substantiate the deductibility of your business expenses is a letter from your employer describing the company's reimbursement policy. If your employer says it will reimburse all business expenses, you have to explain why you are entitled to further deductions.

One reason for this could be that your employer expects you to pay certain items directly (for example, club memberships) and has increased your salary accordingly. Another reason could be that reimbursement is limited to a certain amount provided for in a departmental budget and your claim to the employer contains items that are not reimbursable. Therefore, you may claim the amount as a deduction on your tax return.

Ask your employer for a new reimbursement letter every year so that your department head will be currently employed and will be able to support your claim. Their replacements might not be familiar with the circumstances of your employment.

5. Item #1 above applies to employee business expenses, except for auto expense and entertainment and promotion expenses. A deduction for the use of an automobile, computer, plane, or boat for business *must* be supported by *written* documentation. For auto use you must have written mileage logs showing all business miles, and you must have receipts for all vehicle operating costs that are individually over $25.

On Form 2106, Employee Business Expenses, the IRS has 2 questions: Do you have documentation to support your deduction? Is that evidence written? You are under oath to answer truthfully and are under penalty of perjury if you do not. If you fail to answer their questions, the IRS will probably "red-flag" your return for audit.

6. In order to claim entertainment and promotion expenses, you must keep a log showing each deduction's date, location, people involved, what business was discussed, and the amount that was spent. This log has to agree with your appointment book and the expense reports you filed with your employer. (The IRS will ask for both of these items if they audit you.) Every item over $25 must be supported by a receipt or canceled check or charge account voucher. Beware: If the IRS suspects that a receipt has been altered or exaggerated, your credibility is damaged and you can do little to restore it. Under no circumstances should you cheat, either on the original return or in accumulating the documentation to support your deductions.

7. In the case of charitable contributions, you must have receipts for all cash donations. For non-cash contributions, you must have receipts, usually signed or confirmed by the third-party recipient. If the non-cash contribution is over $500, you must attach details to your tax return to support the deduction. When a non-cash contribution exceeds $5,000 in value, you must attach to your return an independent appraisal (at your cost). If you don't do this, expect to be audited and the contribution to be disallowed. At that time, the audit will probably be expanded to include other areas, such as employee business expenses or Schedule C expenses.

Form W-2 is not the only source that the IRS has of knowing about your income. Dividends, commissions, royalties, interest, pension plan distributions, and profit-sharing plan distributions are all reported to the IRS, as are activities of estates and trusts and pro rata shares of income and losses from business activities (on Form K-1). In addition, sale of stock is reported to the IRS through brokerage houses. Every year all this information is sorted and compared to your tax returns, and any discrepancies are investigated. If the difference is significant, it may result in an audit, which usually expands to include rental properties income (Schedule E), employee business expenses (Form 2106), and sole proprietorship income (Schedule C).

The IRS assumes that if you do such a bad job of record-keeping on items well documented by these third parties, you must really be bad in other areas of tax reporting. The IRS receives millions of dollars through audits generated in this way, proving that their assumption is accurate.

About 90 percent of all tax audits begin with the IRS auditor's asking the taxpayer about previously unreported income. Don't forget such items as interest from savings accounts established for children but listing the parent's Social Security number on bank records, savings accounts, and interest-bearing checking accounts held jointly with older family members.

The IRS matches 1099 forms with returns to be sure you are honest as well as ensuring honest taxpayers errors from going undetected. A 1099 form must be submitted to the IRS when stock is sold, showing the resulting profit or loss; this is matched up with what you report on your return. A similar form for reporting the sale of a house must be filed by the person responsible for the sale (homeowner, title company, broker, or lawyer), and this too will be matched up with your return. The review can be expanded to cover additional areas on your return rather than apparently limiting the expanded review to certain specific areas.

All these changes in the system mean that the auditing process will be even more tedious and slower than ever before.

Random Auditing

As it does with most other things in life, luck plays a part in whether or not you are audited. Part of the IRS system is a selection process called TCMP (Taxpayer Compliance Measurement Program), by which a certain number of returns (only the IRS knows how many) are selected for audit entirely at random. If your return is chosen by this program, every item on it will be scrutinized, whereas only certain items are examined in a normal audit. The intention here is not just to torture taxpayers; the results of these audits also provide the IRS with typical tax returns to which they can compare others.

Red-Flagging Returns

The IRS has always had a formula for red-flagging returns to be audited. Under the new audit system, all returns are scanned, and the IRS's mission is to identify returns that might contain errors or other abuses, especially abusive tax shelters. As the returns are scanned, they are divided into 3 basic categories: those with income under $50,000, those with income between $50,000 and $100,000, and those with income over $100,000. Like any smart businessperson, the IRS wants to make its work as profitable as possible, so they audit the returns that are likely to yield the most revenue. Taxpayers earning less than $50,000 do get audited, but with much lower frequency than those who earn more.

Although the decision-making process for audits is a closely guarded IRS secret, past years give many indications of which items make a return more rather than less eligible for a red flag. Some of the danger areas are:

1. Unusually large refunds. Try to avoid these anyway—unless you enjoy giving the government interest-free loans!

2. Missing forms or schedules. Check all forms carefully and then staple them to your return after everything is accounted for.
3. Unusually large deductions in relation to your income.
4. Marrieds filing separately but claiming the same deductions.
5. Reporting the sale of stock that pays dividends but not reporting the dividend income itself.
6. Reporting the sale of property on installments but not reporting interest income.
7. Employee business expenses out of proportion to your income.
8. Nonbusiness bad debts.
9. Special medical expenses (e.g., a swimming pool for someone with a heart problem).
10. Casualty and theft loss deductions.
11. Deductions of mortgage loan points on refinancing.
12. Large donations of property to charity.
13. Home office deductions.
14. Unusually high travel and entertainment expenses.
15. Losses in pleasure-oriented activities (car racing and horse breeding, for example).

Keep in mind, though, that the prospect of being audited should not keep you from claiming tax advantages to which you are entitled. Just be sure that you can *prove* you're entitled to them.

The Basic Audit Process

Before the returns are scanned, the IRS randomly selects 50,000 of the returns that were audited under the Taxpayer Compliance Measurements Program (TCMP). They use those sample returns to come up with a formula whereby they give numerical values to such key items as deductions, number of exemptions claimed, and adjustments to income. Their findings represent a kind of measuring stick against which other returns may be evaluated.

For instance, if a lawyer filed a return claiming 10 percent of his gross income for rent. When his return is fed into the computer, his rental expenses are compared to those of other lawyers. If his 10 percent claim is very different from that of his colleagues, his return may well be flagged for an audit.

Whenever a return has audit potential, it is red-flagged by the computer. Then an IRS staff member examines the flagged return more closely and notifies the taxpayer by mail or phone that the IRS has some questions. He or she is usually asked to send in documents by mail or bring them to the IRS office. (The IRS sometimes conducts an audit in the taxpayer's home or office.)

After the audit takes place, the IRS auditor either is satisfied that the figures are correct or proposes a settlement of taxes due. The taxpayer either signs an agreement (and pays the taxes due) or disagrees, in which case he pleads his case to the examiner's supervisor. If the taxpayer is still dissatisfied after a meeting with the supervisor, he may go before the appeals division. It is very rare for a case to go beyond that point, but if a compromise has still not been reached, the next (and last) step is Tax Court.

Types of Audit

Correspondence Audits

Some audits are done through the mail. Thousands of taxpayers receive correspondence asking for verification of a particular deduction. When that happens, all they need do is mail the photocopies of documentation. Usually there is no further audit, and the IRS never knows if other potentially weak areas of the return should have been questioned. If you choose to ignore the correspondence and form letter, the IRS will propose adjustments (which become assessments if you fail to respond). Most computer-prepared adjustments are incorrect because they are based on a mechanical audit of your return. If you don't agree with the results of a correspondence audit, ask that your case be assigned to an auditor.

Office Audits

Some audits are handled at the local office. Unless fraud or gross errors are suspected, only one or two deductions will be questioned. The office audit is conducted by workers looking for documentation of specific items. Office auditors don't have the training to spot additional problem areas. As a general rule, the audit letter will be specific as to the items in question, so prepare your records only for those items.

Field Audits

Field audits are conducted by agents trained specifically to audit wealthy individuals, unusual deductions, and small businesses. Field agents could question income or deductions; their job is to spot areas that will bring in the maximum tax dollars. Don't attempt to handle a field audit without your accountant; unreported income or disallowed items will likely be uncovered.

TCMP Audits

The Taxpayer Compliance Measurement Program is the most thorough (and rarely performed) audit. TCMP audits are conducted for statistical sampling, and the results are used to reprogram the IRS computers for future selection of returns. Agents are required to make a comment on every item on the return—down to the spelling of your name. Bank accounts are carefully analyzed to determine unreported income. A TCMP audit is lengthy, and the odds are that adjustments will cost you a lot.

What Triggers an Audit

It is assumed that the IRS computers use predetermined averages to determine whether deductions are "out of line," so accountants place great importance on staying within the norm by checking the most recent tables released by the IRS. Keep in mind that the table below only reflects averages and that falling within the averages does not guarantee avoiding an audit. However, the likelihood of an audit may be statistically lower, depending on where you work or live. Here are examples of some recently published IRS averages:

PRELIMINARY AVERAGE ITEMIZED DEDUCTIONS FOR 1985
BY ADJUSTED GROSS INCOME RANGES

Adjusted Gross Income Ranges	Medical Expenses	Taxes	Contributions	Interest
under $5,000	$ 3,165	$ 640	$ 438	$ 3,425
$ 5,000 under $ 10,000	3,118	1,094	607	2,528
$ 10,000 under $ 15,000	2,393	1,259	787	2,757
$ 15,000 under $ 20,000	1,862	1,579	819	2,839
$ 20,000 under $ 25,000	1,713	1,830	809	3,220
$ 25,000 under $ 30,000	1,379	2,133	800	3,591
$ 30,000 under $ 40,000	1,639	2,696	891	4,121
$ 40,000 under $ 50,000	1,727	3,483	1,105	5,234
$ 50,000 under $ 75,000	2,799	4,750	1,575	6,730
$ 75,000 under $ 100,000	5,500	6,942	2,538	10,038
$ 100,000 under $ 200,000	8,500	11,034	4,237	14,419
$ 200,000 under $ 500,000	27,592	24,407	15,014	23,473
$ 500,000 under $1,000,000	43,258	55,646	45,696	43,705
$1,000,000 and more	58,435	162,463	140,071	100,620

Where the income is reported on a return can make a difference as to whether or not a taxpayer will get audited. For example, if freelance income is reported as "other income" (and its source is noted), there may be less chance of being audited than if the income was entered on Schedule C, Profit or Loss from Business.

If you file as late as possible (October 15), the chances of audit are reduced. The IRS schedules audits more than a year in advance, and the forecast requirements may be filled before an extended return arrives—and scheduling and budget problems may preclude a "second batch." Of course, the IRS is aware of this problem—and that *you* are aware—but it is still to your advantage to be part of the late-filing group.

Certain deductions seem to catch the IRS's eye and are often found on the returns of those taxpayers who can least afford a thorough examination. I would suggest that as you prepare your return, and before mailing it, you try to put yourself in the shoes of the IRS agent and look for items that seem to "jump off the return." For example:

• If you claim only modest business income but report unusually high business expenses, the agent is going to wonder how you can afford to live.

• Many tax shelters have been identified by the IRS as abusive shelters; steer clear of them and choose those which are "safe."

• Avoid "barter clubs" that trade goods and services on a cash basis; the IRS can demand membership lists. If they do, *all* members' returns will be examined.

• Do not leave any unanswered questions on the return; the computer will flag a blank line.

• Be sure to report all K-1 and 1099 Forms on your return.

• Try to be neat; if the return is written sloppily, the IRS may assume that the figures are careless as well.

- Instead of lumping everything into a "miscellaneous" category, try to place as many deductions as possible into their separate categories; otherwise, the IRS may feel that you just grabbed numbers.

- Be conservative about tax-sheltered investments. Keep a low profile. Avoid large round numbers, since they appear to the IRS to be guesses, not real figures from your records.

- Keep your return neat, and answer all questions (even if you have to put "not applicable"). Be careful in choosing your accountant (IRS has a "problem preparer" list—which includes the names of unscrupulous tax preparers. Occasionally they audit all clients of a problem preparer).

- Check for errors, such as a figure that was put on the wrong line. Make sure you and your spouse *sign* the return, and that your Social Security number(s) appear(s) on each form.

Chances of Being Audited

Your overall chances of being audited were 1.31 percent in 1985. Individuals with total positive income (income total with losses treated as zero) of $50,000 or more were audited at the rate of 3.53 percent.

Your chances of being audited may depend on where you live. Here is a list showing how the odds of audit vary according to district.

IRS District	Percentage of Returns Audited	IRS District	Percentage of Returns Audited
Anchorage	2.6	Jacksonville	1.4
Atlanta	1.5	Los Angeles	2.2
Baltimore	1.3	Manhattan	2.2
Boston	1.1	Milwaukee	0.9
Brooklyn	1.7	Newark	1.8
Chicago	1.5	Philadelphia	1.1
Cleveland	1.2	Pittsburgh	0.8
Dallas	1.3	Reno	2.6
Detroit	1.2	Richmond	1.2
Greensboro	1.3	San Francisco	1.9
Indianapolis	0.8	St. Louis	1.2

Some occupations and types of deductions seem to be targeted by the IRS more often than others. Doctors, dentists, and business owners are investigated most often. Agents also look closely at limited partnerships (which may involve abusive tax shelters).

Airline pilots, who tend both to put money in questionable tax shelters and to claim nondeductible commuting expenses such as business travel, often provoke an audit. Flight attendants also provoke audits because they usually claim deductions for the cost of pantyhose, cosmetics, and hairdos, as well as a high percentage of nondeductible travel expenses, even though the courts have consistently ruled against them.

A large number of nonreimbursed employee business expenses by an executive are likely to invite an audit. As a matter of fact, the higher the income, the greater probability of an audit.

Home office deductions are routinely disallowed when claimed by teachers and college professors. Poorly documented travel expenses and what may be padded entertainment expenses by salespeople are also sought for audit. Any occupation where tips are a major source of income is also a likely candidate. A priest, minister, or rabbi who has income from nonchurch activity is suspect by the IRS, which may look for involvement in a mail-order ministry.

Beware of using inaccurate job titles in order to bypass the IRS. If your return is chosen for audit, any effort to disguise your real occupation might hint that you really do have something to hide—and you will be in for a difficult audit.

Audit Tolerances

Amended returns are scrutinized less than in the past. If you discover an overlooked deduction, tax credit, or the applicability of income averaging in a previous return and decide to file Form 1040X, you are not likely to have the original return audited. If your 1040X asks for less than a $1,000 additional refund, the IRS won't even check your original return or necessarily verify your math.

The IRS used to send out penalty notices when errors in estimated tax payments were over $50 for individuals or $100 for businesses. The tolerance level has been increased recently to $100 for individuals and $200 for businesses.

A $500 charitable donation on a return with $50,000 in taxable income will not necessarily red-flag a return for audit, but a $5,000 contribution on a $25,000 return probably will. Claim everything that is due you but be prepared to back up your deductions with proof. Remember, deductions that are significant (tax-wise) are compared to your entire return, taken as a whole.

Cash donations over $3,000 and property contributions over $500 are likely to trigger an audit. If you exceed these amounts (or if your donations appear large in relation to your taxable income), attach an explanation to your return—or perhaps copies of canceled checks.

IRS Examination Guidelines

The priority examination areas (those items most in need of an IRS agent's attention) include:

1. Partnership and fiduciary returns
2. Identification and examination of U.S. citizens who are possibly using foreign entities to evade U.S. taxes
3. S corporation returns and the study of unreported tips
4. Schedule C—uncovering unreported self-employment income
5. Abusive tax shelters
6. Specialized programs relating to employment, windfall profit and excise taxes, coordinated examination programs, estate and gift taxes, and computer audits
7. Tax protesters, tax havens, foreign tax credit manipulations, abusive Forms W-4, unreported income projects, and returns with potential unreported income shown on foreign information documents.

Although the above-listed items are current IRS priorities, any tax return can be selected for the above—or any other—reason.

Where Will the IRS Be Concentrating This Year?

Charitable Contributions

Contributions will be compared to both your taxable and adjusted gross income, and an amount exceeding 10 percent of either may trigger an audit. Be sure you can prove your contributions with canceled checks, receipts, and itemized lists.

Contributions of Art

If you donate art, the IRS requires that you complete Form 8283 showing when you purchased the art and your original cost. If you claim a deduction for more than your original cost, you may trigger an audit. Get a qualified appraiser to show the market value on the date of the donation if you want to claim the appreciated value.

Large Gains and Losses

Transactions such as selling real estate are likely to trigger an audit if large gains or losses are involved. Be sure to keep all papers proving your original purchase price, selling price, and gain or loss. Otherwise, the IRS may make their own estimates.

Business Use of Car

You may trigger an audit by claiming a large business percentage of the use of your car. A daily record showing dates and destinations can't help but impress an agent. Small business owners must be especially careful. If your auto logs are not specific, the IRS can decide that the use of your car was not a business expense and treat it as taxable compensation.

Shareholder-Employee Loans

If you are a shareholder in a closely held business, a company loan made to you may trigger an audit. If the IRS feels that the loan is a disguised form of compensation, they may treat it as a reportable dividend, which is not deductible by the corporation. Sign a promissory note and set up a repayment schedule, make all payments when due, and save your canceled checks to prove that your intent was to make a loan.

Hobby Losses

Some experts expect that IRS agents will renew their attack on hobby losses claimed by businessmen and professionals now that Tax Reform has eliminated a lot of tax shelters. Some of the activities that agents are most likely to suspect as being disguises for deducting hobby expenses are sailing, horse racing, farming, dog breeding, and fishing. Be sure to keep accurate, detailed records and be able to prove that you operate in a businesslike manner with the intention of making a profit.

Casualty Losses

The IRS is particularly suspicious of casualty losses, especially thefts near year-end.

Report a theft to the police immediately, and file an insurance claim. Keep any papers connected with the item stolen (e.g., a sales receipt or a note referring to the gift).

Disaster Loss

Provide before-and-after pictures of a disaster to prove damage. Obtain evidence from a local real estate agent as to any decrease in your property value as a result of the casualty and deduct that amount as a casualty loss.

Travel and Entertainment Expenses

IRS particularly looks at business meals and travel to business seminars. Be sure you keep detailed records showing who was entertained, where, the amount spent, and what business was discussed. Agents prefer a written travel and entertainment diary used on the spot, as well as credit card receipts. If you entertain often, be especially careful about keeping good records. You'll have a lot to lose if your deductions are challenged.

Dealing with an Audit

Avoiding an Audit Altogether

Even after the IRS has informed you that your return has been selected for examination, you may avoid the audit by having your case transferred to another IRS district. If you work in another IRS district (or your accountant has an office there), you may be able to get the case transferred.

You can count on a delay in the transfer because of the workload (or rescheduling problems) in the new district. If all goes well, the second district may just decide that your return isn't worth being audited and close your case with no change.

Postponing Your Appointment

Agents are under departmental pressure to begin and finish audits within a specific time framework: the possibility exists that the audit may be canceled if an appointment can be postponed enough times. If you are notified about an audit more than a year after filing, and you cancel your appointments, the 3-year statute of limitations may run out. The best time to cancel an audit date is the day before the appointment—chances are good that the agent will not have any time available for a month or two. You may be able to avoid an audit entirely.

When You Should Ask for an Audit

Sometimes you would be wise to ask for an audit—for example, after a business closes and the personnel who could explain tax matters are no longer employed. In the event of a death, only the net amount after tax will be left to divide among the heirs; they would be wise to ask for an audit to settle tax matters as soon as possible. Heirs to an estate must act within 18 months. Form 4810 is used to request that the IRS conduct an audit; or you may state in a letter that the request is being made under Code Section 6501(d), which calls for a prompt assessment.

How to Conduct Yourself in an Audit

If your business is being audited, have the audit conducted at your accountant's office rather than your home or place of business, or, you can take your records to the IRS office. You don't want the auditor to see your standard of living or to hear an employee (or family member) say the wrong thing. The IRS believes that audits can be more productive if the agent confronts the taxpayer personally with questions, rather than through an accountant or lawyer. If the agent insists on talking with you personally, tell him firmly that you will answer all questions only after you have had a chance to review them with your accountant or attorney.

If your business is being audited and you have no accountant, be aware that you will be dealing with a field agent, who may choose to go over all your deductions.

Some time periods for an audit may be better (for your side) than others. For example, just before a long weekend an agent may be more interested in the holiday than the audit; at the end of the month, he may be anxious to close out cases to meet his quota. Requesting a 10:00 A.M. meeting may bring matters to a close at lunch time.

If you are selected for an audit, be well prepared. Accumulate all receipts for items in question and make a detailed list of all expenditures in that category. You should be ready to explain any cash expenditures. If you demonstrate that you made an effort to be honest and that you kept receipts as best you could, the auditor will find your stance easier to believe. Neatly organized records that are carefully reconciled with your return will often result in the agent's quickly finishing his review in your favor. On the other hand, if your records are disorganized and the figures don't agree, the agent will have to spend additional time getting you organized. This time must be justified to his supervisors, and it usually results in additional taxes.

If you are asked to prove travel and entertainment expenses, ask the auditor to select a period for examination as a sample check (for example, a 3-month period) or to limit the dollar amount of receipts to be reviewed (e.g., amounts over $100). You will not have to assemble as much documentation, and the agent will not be able to rummage through *all* your receipts.

Many agents will try to disallow expenses by not allowing you to use approximate figures in determining deductions. If you can prove that you legitimately incurred deductible expenses but that your records are incomplete, don't accept a compromise. In the case of overnight travel, gifts, or business entertainment, however, you must be able to document deductions.

If a revenue agent is examining the books of your small business, one area he is sure to examine is bank deposits. He will add all the deposits in all checking and savings accounts for the year and compare the total to income reported on your return, adjusting deposits for loans, transfers, and other nontaxable transactions. Do your own bank deposit analysis before you meet the revenue agent and be ready to explain all large and unusual items. If there are no discrepancies, the agent is likely to accept your reported income as accurate.

If the IRS wants to review your return, consider mailing in the information to avoid a personal meeting with an agent. In most cases, this satisfies the IRS. (Although one disadvantage is that you cannot influence the auditor's findings, the major advantage is that you can't be asked any questions that might open a "can of worms.")

Frequently the IRS agent will ask the taxpayer for a copy of a tax return for the year prior to the one being audited (as well as the return for the year following the audit) to make comparisons of both income and expenses. It's easier for the agent to get these returns from you than from the IRS, even though they are in the IRS's files—somewhere.

If this happens, ask the agent if you can give him copies of the returns *after* he has finished his examination and tells you which items are being adjusted. He'll probably agree. In this way you may prevent the agent from making comparisons that could be potentially costly.

IRS Service Centers

If you don't know whom to write to at the Service Center, address the letter to "Chief, Taxpayer Service." When responding to correspondence from the Service Center, put the stop number on the envelope. (This is the number after the zip code in the Service Center's address.) Your letter will be directed to the correct person.

If you feel that you're not being treated well by a lower-level IRS employee, contact the chief of the division in the local IRS district office. Recent hearings and need for legislation to protect taxpayers' rights by Congress have made higher-level personnel more responsive to irate taxpayers frustrated by the system.

Return Compliance Failures

Under the Tax Reform Act, greater penalties have been imposed for failure to comply with the tax laws. Taxpayers are subject to a $50 penalty for each return not filed and every statement not supplied to the IRS. The maximum for failure to file information has increased from $50,000 to $100,000 for a year.

If failure to file is intentional, the penalty is $100 per failure or a percentage of the total amounts not reported, whichever is greater. Failure to report exchanges of certain partnership interests or certain donated property is 5 percent of the unreported amount.

There is a $5 per return penalty (maximum of $20,000 per calendar year) for failing to include correct information. If the failure is deemed intentional, the $20,000 limit does not apply.

Failure to pay taxes shown (or required to be shown) on a return is penalized at 1 percent per month (previously ½ percent per month) effective December 1, 1986.

If a taxpayer fails to make a reasonable attempt to comply with the law, or is deemed careless, reckless (or in intentional disregard of the requirements), he is subject to a negligence penalty.

Returns with due dates after 1986 are subject to fraud penalties of 75 percent of the portion of the underpayment resulting from fraud plus 50 percent of the statutory interest beginning on the last day allowed for payment (no extensions considered) and ending on the date of tax assessment or payment, whichever is earlier.

Understating tax liability is penalized by 25 percent (up from 10 percent) for penalties assessed after October 21, 1986.

The penalty for failure to register a tax shelter is 1 percent of the aggregate amount invested in the tax shelter or $500, whichever is greater, effective after October 22, 1986. Failure to report the tax shelter I.D. number on the tax return will be penalized at $250 (up from $50) effective for returns filed after October 22, 1986.

Avoiding Penalties

Even if you are due a refund, if you don't file your return on time you may be subject to a 5 percent penalty. Unless you file by April 15 (or later, with a valid extension), your refund may be shorted by the 5 percent penalty.

The only way to avoid the penalty is to show that your failure to file was not due to intentional disregard of the rules or to negligence.

Avoiding the Fraud Penalty

Lying to an IRS employee and failing to report all your income are crimes.

A 5 percent negligence penalty is assessed for failing to report income deposited in a bank (deposits of nonreported income in an out-of-state bank are usually considered a fraudulent and willful attempt to conceal income). Agents are now making fraud referrals to special agents in charge of criminal investigations on cases that in the past would have simply called for a negligence penalty.

Who gets caught? About one in every 5 tax-fraud cases involves a professional or business executive, and the average amount of taxes owed is $70,000. The IRS does not care about spending $20,000 to prove an understatement of income: they are interested in keeping honest taxpayers nervous and nervous taxpayers honest. From the IRS's point of view, a "pillar of the community" is the ideal person to prosecute, since they are interested in the deterrent effect it will have on others.

To prove fraud, the IRS must show that there was a willful and intentional failure to file, understate income, or take unsubstantiated deductions. Fewer than 20 percent of the cases end in convictions. The other 80 percent are dropped, end in acquittal or dismissal, or the Justice Department refuses to prosecute.

Settling the Dispute

As a general rule, you are unlikely to get through an audit completely unscathed; just try to keep the dollar amount as low as possible. If you are adamant about certain proposed adjustments, the agent may back down. Be open to bargaining. Most agents just want to close your case and get on to the next one; take your cues from them. Be aware, though, that an auditor's training manual warns that "hasty agreements to adjustments and undue concern about immediate closing of the case" may indicate that a more thorough examination is needed, so don't come to terms too quickly with the auditor, or it may appear that you have more to hide. Protest any adjustments initially, then eventually show a willingness to compromise.

The best audit strategy may be persistence. Don't let an audit end until you are satisfied that the final outcome is both equitable and reasonable. You can usually wear the auditor down until he completely changes his mind or compromises to your point of view. On the negative side, too much stalling can result in the agent's issuing an unfavorable assessment.

If the agent asks a pointed question that you aren't sure how to answer, the best thing you can do is stall. Tell him that you'll need more time to give the question some thought, and that you will give him a satisfactory answer at your next meeting (if there is one). At that time you can give a truthful, well thought-out answer that won't damage your case. Or, if you really luck out, the agent may forget about the question altogether. Even if you give your accountant a power-of-attorney form, you may be asked to be present at the initial IRS interview.

After you agree on the amount of the total adjustment, call the following day and suggest one or two adjustments that you feel should be reduced or eliminated. The chances are that the agent will agree to some (or all) of your changes, but you are taking the chance that he will withdraw any concessions he may have originally made. If you arrange to pay back taxes and any new tax liability is incurred and remains unpaid, the agreement will be terminated. If you can't pay those additional taxes, ask the agent to keep a partial-payment agreement open until the audit is completed, so any tax deficiency can be added to the payment agreement.

If you reach an agreement with an agent to settle a tax dispute, don't consider the case closed. Until a superior (with final settlement authority) approves the matter, you are still liable for the entire amount.

And finally, if you receive notice for the third consecutive year that you are getting audited, heed this advice. If the audits for the past 2 years resulted in little (or no) change in your tax liability, you cannot be audited for the third consecutive year on the same issue, or that third audit would constitute harassment. If you receive a letter for a third year, call the IRS and request that they initiate their *repetitive audit procedure,* and enclose copies of IRS correspondence for the previous 2 years.

After the Audit

The first thing you hear from the IRS after your audit is the 30-day letter, which is a copy of the audit report showing proposed adjustments. (It got its name because you have to respond or request an extension within 30 days.) You must respond to the 30-day letter or you will receive a 90-day letter, which means you'll have to file a court petition; naturally, it's always best to try to settle out of court.

If you send a protest letter, your case will be moved from the audit division to the IRS appeals office, where the officers have more authority to settle a case than the IRS auditor. They can judge their chances of winning or losing in court.

At this point, it's a good idea to seek the help of a tax professional, to review your case and tell you what information to include in your protest letter. The protest letter should include:

1. The statement that you want to appeal the examiner's findings to the appeals office
2. Your name and address
3. The years or tax periods involved
4. The date and symbols from the IRS's letter to you that you are protesting
5. A statement outlining the authority (or law) on which you rely
6. An itemized list of the adjustments you do not agree with
7. A statement that what you have written is true under penalty of perjury.

The Appeals Conference

After you have protested the findings of an audit, you may have a 6-month to one-year wait, before your case is heard. You will be notified by the IRS when the appeals conference will take place. You can go alone, but it's better to be represented by a professional who has the necessary qualifications and experience in presenting your side to the IRS.

At this point, the majority of cases are settled out of court (although abusive tax shelter cases may be tested in court by the IRS in order to set a precedent). If you continue an appeal past this point, you should seek legal counsel. Prepare yourself for a costly fight.

In Tax Court you do not have to pay the tax until the trial is over. If you lose your right to go to Tax Court, you can always pay the tax first, then sue in District Court or Claims Court to get your money back.

Criminal Tax Cases

IRS Special Agents conducting criminal tax investigations will show up at your home or business without notice. They will read you your rights (the Miranda law): that you have the right to remain silent, that anything you say can and will be held against you in court, and that you do not have to answer any questions without an attorney present. The Special Agents may indicate that they will close their file if you cooperate, but this is not necessarily the case. They intend to prove that you made a willful error or omission in reporting your income—in other words, that you committed fraud.

Always ask to see your lawyer immediately. The Special Agents will press for answers before your lawyer arrives. You will be better off saying nothing than lying; giving false or misleading information to an IRS employee is a criminal offense. Many taxpayers are afraid that if they keep quiet, they will appear guilty, so they tend to tell all. Some of the questions that may be asked include:

1. Did you report all your income?
2. Did you have a large amount of cash on hand at the beginning of last year?
3. Do you gamble?
4. Where do you keep savings and checking accounts?
5. What procedure do you use to report sales in your business?
6. What kind of car do you drive?

One method frequently used to establish unreported income is to examine all deposits made into savings, checking, and brokerage accounts and to compare the total to an estimate of your net worth and the amount you reported as income on your return. The Special Agents will assume that you had a large increase in income to cause a large increase in assets. They will ask how much cash and property you had on hand at the beginning of the year; if you give a low figure, the IRS may claim that anything else acquired during the year should have been reported as income. (Adjustments are made for transfers between accounts, deposits of nontaxable income, and loans.) They can subpoena bank statements and canceled checks, and they may talk to your neighbors and business associates. Through an examination of public records they will learn about any real estate, cars, or boats you may own. By looking over insurance records, they will learn about ownership of jewelry and other expensive items. Examining passports may give clues about expensive overseas vacations you may have taken. While they can't legally open your mail, they may conduct surveillance on your mail, and they can tell who your customers and suppliers are by the return addresses. Be aware of indications that they may have already obtained information from third-party sources.

Your best maneuver is to make it difficult for the agents to establish your beginning net worth. The bulk of the information that the IRS obtains to build a fraud case comes from *you* as well as third parties; keeping as much information out of the hands of the IRS as is legally possible is the best strategy. Of course, seek the help of a professional immediately.

PART II
Save Money Later

An In-Depth Analysis,
Arranged Alphabetically
by Subject, of Tax-Planning
Opportunities That Will
Save You Hard-Earned Dollars
Both Now and Later On

Introduction

Attempting to find ways to save on last year's taxes between January 1 and April 15 is like closing the barn door after the horse has run out. Last year's tax bill is determined by what happened last year. Too many taxpayers mistakenly believe that real savings come from locating some mysterious new deduction or tax loophole.

Genuine tax savings result from adequate tax planning. The secret to cutting your tax bill comes from thinking about tax impact and consequences before entering into a personal or business transaction that may affect your taxes. There are many options and alternatives to choose from, each with varying degrees of tax impact.

Four Tax-Planning Strategies

The object of good tax planning is not to minimize taxes but to *maximize disposable income after taxes*. Frequently, you may be better off paying some extra taxes now in order to wind up with more after-tax income at a later date.

There are basically only 4 methods—4 tax-planning strategies—to consider. They all work. And the best time to start is now.

Strategy 1:
Generating Tax-Free Income

All income is not necessarily subject to tax. For instance, interest on municipal bonds is tax-exempt. (However, interest on arbitrage bonds issued by state or local governments after October 9, 1969, and interest on industrial development bonds issued after April 30, 1968, generally is taxable.) Fringe benefits are tax-exempt, and some types of payments to employees are free from payroll taxes. When a U.S. corporation receives dividends from another U.S. corporation, 80 percent of the dividends may be tax-free.

How much tax-free income you need depends largely on your tax bracket and the economics of the situation. For example, if you are in the 15 percent tax bracket, you would be better off to buy fully taxable bonds paying 15 percent interest than to buy tax-exempts paying 10 percent, because the taxable bonds will give you an after-tax yield of 12.75 percent. However, if you are in the 38.5 percent tax bracket, the after-tax yield on the 15 percent bonds would be only 9.22 percent; so the 10 percent tax-exempts would probably make the most sense.

Strategy 2:
Claiming Everything to Which You Are Entitled

This method is the one that receives the most attention during the tax-filing season. Deductions, exemptions, and tax credits are written into the tax law for various reasons. A number of loopholes in the law may be taken advantage of by wage earners.

For instance, you could be entitled to a deduction for the use of your car to visit the doctor, and in connection with volunteer activities; a partial deduction for a home office; a credit for fees paid a baby-sitter to watch the kids while you work; or a deduction for the cost of moving from one residence to another. If you don't think about them in advance, these and other deductions might be forgotten.

All the books and instructions that are written by the IRS for public use are carefully designed to tell you what you *can't* deduct. Getting the most out of the various deductions, exemptions, options, and credits that are permitted by law requires a positive frame of reference and a small amount of time to keep abreast of the latest in techniques. Hence, the value to you of *Pay Less Tax Legally*.

Strategy 3:
Lowering Your Tax Bracket

Income taxes are based on a somewhat graduated tax-rate system, and additional income can throw a taxpayer into a higher bracket. Although exemptions and deductions are a main concern to middle-income taxpayers, taxes can also be saved by dropping down a few tax brackets. Deferred compensation plans and proper use of tax-exempt income and corresponding deductions may also contribute to a lower marginal tax rate.

Strategy 4:
Deferring the Tax

Another basic strategy for tax planning is to defer paying the tax by holding off taxable income or by electing to deduct various items as quickly as possible. In some cases, deferring income will carry over from year to year, resulting in what is the equivalent of permanent tax savings.

Many tax shelters are simply devices to delay paying tax from year to year. Qualified pension plans, Individual Retirement Accounts, and Self-Employed Retirement Plans are among the most effective tax-deferral techniques available. No tax is paid on the income deposited in the plan, and earnings are currently exempt from tax. By removing the retirement income from current taxes you keep yourself out of a higher tax bracket and thus have more disposable income. The money allotted to a retirement plan is *not* tax-free, only tax-deferred: when you withdraw the money at the time of retirement, you have to pay the tax. However, you will have benefited by postponing the tax bite, and that tax bite will most likely be at a lower rate in your retirement years.

One good reason for delaying payment of the tax is that money has a present value. As the saying goes, "A bird in the hand is worth two in the bush." Businessmen and investors want to keep as much money working as long as possible—the primary reason for leasing business equipment, for example, instead of buying it outright. And, of course, the individual taxpayer, in whatever bracket, also appreciates having the expendable income now.

Combining Various Tax Strategies

Finding ways to receive tax-free income, to increase your deductions, to lower your tax bracket, and to defer income all have the identical result: reducing your effective tax rate. Converting taxable income into tax-free income, or deferring income, may increase your allowable medical deductions by reducing the 7.5 percent floor. Conversion of taxable income also enhances the 10 percent casualty loss deduction (although the allowable charitable contribution will be lowered since it is limited to a percentage of adjusted gross income).

Avoiding Tax Penalties

The tax law is very much like a booby-trapped battlefield, with land mines planted by the government. One would think the IRS is trying to protect the Treasury Department from what it considers to be the excessive generosity of Congress. For example, when Congress writes new tax laws, it usually permits the IRS to issue its own interpretations—called "regulations." The result is law replete with traps for the unwary taxpayer.

Avoiding the IRS traps is often the primary concern of many tax advisers—to the point where they can't see the forest for the trees. Trying to anticipate and get around all of the potential tax traps causes many accountants to take an extremely conservative position, a conservatism often inadvertently forced on them by clients who expect their tax advisers to be "godlike"—correct all the time.

A 1.000 batting average is impossible: aggressive tax planning involves taking some risks that can go sour. The worst thing that can happen: you may have to pay some money that you would have paid to start with if you had not tried, plus interest (and sometimes penalties). Current interest rates and penalties can, however, be considerable. The interest rate the government will charge you is pegged to the prime rate and adjusted at regular intervals.

How Much Does Tax Saving Cost?

They say there's no such thing as a free lunch, but the small cost of achieving substantial tax savings comes as close to a free lunch as anything I can think of. Your only cost consists of a little time set aside to get into the habit of tax planning all year long. You have a great deal to gain and nothing to lose by looking for tax-planning opportunities all year.

Accountants

Choosing an Accountant

In order to get the most out of your accountant:

1. Become familiar with and knowledgeable about the basic concepts of tax preparation. Ask intelligent questions.
2. Give your accountant all the information you can. Presenting correct information can open up a variety of deductions you didn't know you could claim.
3. Categorize your canceled checks for the entire year and summarize them for your accountant. Show him your diary so that he can tell you if it's up to IRS standards.
4. Organize your records and papers to save your accountant time. He should spend his time on tax planning, not bookkeeping.
5. Before you decide that something is not deductible, ask your accountant for his opinion.

6. Ask your accountant for financial planning advice and investment advice while all your records are in front of him. Find out what you can do to help cut your taxes for next year.

As a point of information, a recent study claims that accountants are more aggressive on tax returns than lawyers or nonprofessional return-preparers. The study also indicates that male accountants are more aggressive than their female counterparts, which may result in greater tax savings and more audits. Help your tax expert by informing him about deductions that are unusual and by bringing complete records to the interview. The better you prepare yourself, the more you save.

Here are some ideas for rating an accountant:

1. Did he tell you about new tax law changes, or did you have to ask? Did he appear to be up on the latest developments? Did he know the answers to your questions, or did he have to look them up? Were you impressed by his knowledge?
2. Did he offer suggestions and advice for planning the following year's return? Just putting numbers on forms is not enough; he should care about helping you boost your refund.
3. Did you get what you paid for? Did you get the most value for your money? How would his price compare with that charged by other accountants—for the same degree of service?
4. Will he represent you in case of an audit? He may charge extra for an audit, but he should be willing to go with you to the IRS.
5. The more thorough the interview, the more tax breaks you will get. He should go through records and discuss in depth with you any investment or changes from last year. Did he provide you with a worksheet before the appointment so you would be better prepared for the meeting?
6. Is he afraid of the IRS? If he does not know the law, he may be more concerned with not getting you audited than saving you money. If he doesn't know the ropes, you are wasting your money. He must be aggressive enough to get as much money for you as possible without needlessly exposing your return for audit.
7. Expect promptness and courtesy from a real professional. He should keep appointments with you, be prompt, return phone calls within a reasonable time, and finish your return when promised. He should have courteous and efficient employees in his office. If you get excuses—don't accept them.

Selecting the person to prepare your tax return can be a difficult decision. Usually the best route to take is a personal referral: Have a friend or colleague who is happy with the job done for him refer you to his taxman.

The majority of accountants are simply public accountants whose training and experience vary. The most qualified are certified public accountants (CPAs) who pass a series of accounting and tax tests to get their certificates. Fees vary depending on the size of the firm, quality of services offered, and competency.

Tax Preparers

About 15 million Americans will have their returns prepared by someone just in the business of preparing returns, who usually offers no tax planning advice. Some of them promise that they will accompany the taxpayer to an audit free of charge; unfortunately, most are neither licensed nor regulated. If you choose a tax preparer, find out how much training he or she has had, whether he or she is available year-round or just during the tax season, and what guarantee is offered regarding payment of penalties or interest in case of errors.

Enrolled Agents

These are tax specialists who have worked as revenue agents (for the IRS) or have passed the two-day written exam and are certified by the IRS. Enrolled agents have received certification after taking a test that demonstrates that they are knowledgeable about taxes. Many times enrolled agents make house calls, and their fees are typically much higher than those of tax preparers. If an enrolled agent represents you before the IRS, you will probably pay an hourly fee.

Attorneys

Lawyers are specialists, and so if you want advice on the tax implications of a particular transaction, consider hiring a lawyer. An attorney can also draft a will to reduce taxes. Generally, lawyers should not be hired to help you file a tax return. Attorneys are best at law; accountants are better at details and, accordingly, are better able to prepare returns.

Advertising People, Deductions for

If you are in the advertising profession, there is a whole host of deductible items that are considered miscellaneous deductions and subject to a 2 percent floor. These include:

- The cost of a videorecorder, TV set, camera (regular and video), personal computer, stereo, tapes, car stereo, tape recorder, and typewriter. The first $10,000 cost is deductible in full—and all in one year.

- Video Recorder rentals and membership dues.

- The cost of cable TV.

- The cost of your portfolio, including the cost of producing reels.

- Foul-weather gear for filming commercials on location.

- Tickets to the theater, movies, and sporting events that can be considered client research.

- Membership fees.

- Award show entry fees.

- Books, professional magazines, daily newspapers.

- Furniture, desk, file cabinets at home, pictures at the office.

- Country club and credit-card dues.

- Home telephone calls and cost of telephone answering machine.

- Home entertaining (limited to 80 percent of cost).

- Cost of cleaning formal wear; tux rental.
- Nonreimbursed business expenses: tips, dry cleaning on the road, upgrades on air flights, cost of drinks while waiting for a flight.
- Parking at the office (to have your car available for last-minute trips out of town or to pick up clients at the airport).
- All freelance and research expenses, including travel, résumés, meals out of town. Be sure to write and save thank-you letters.
- Business gifts, gifts to secretary—up to $25 per gift.

Audit Lottery

Until recently many taxpayers had never heard of the "audit lottery," a phrase former IRS Commissioner Jerome Kurtz made known to the general citizenry. Kurtz expressed his ire about the audit lottery that upper-bracket taxpayers play; but, instead of stopping the game, his interviews simply aroused taxpayers' curiosity.

Tax attorneys and accountants have been helping wealthy clients play the lottery since 1913, when the income tax was first instituted.

Understanding the Rules

Think of the audit lottery as Russian roulette, only with the revolver having about 50 chambers instead of 6—and it is you who will usually win. The odds are heavily stacked in favor of you, the taxpayer. A rule of the game is that you must play the lottery by the rules—fraud, cheating, or evasion will bring on serious penalties. However, the IRS players are permitted greater leniency by the scorekeepers (the courts) if they play dirty—probably because there are so few of them and so many of us.

The IRS computer is like a big raffle drum with tickets in it. The tickets have Social Security numbers on them, and one of the tickets no doubt belongs to you. When the IRS player pulls the winning (or losing) tickets, some players have their tax returns audited. The tickets differ in size, shape, and color; bigger tickets are worth more and are more likely to produce a "prize" than the tiny tickets, which may be overlooked completely; square tickets are for workers; and round tickets are for people in their own business, and they are worth more to the IRS. Black tickets indicate returns with low odds of owing tax, while red tickets indicate players with deductions that exceed the average.

How to Play

Like the blackjack dealer, the IRS plays the game by trying to better its odds. It instructs its computer to red-flag tax returns that will most likely have the largest audit potential—and dollar returns—for the time spent by the IRS agent-players.

Smart taxpayers play the lottery by trying to keep a low profile and looking like a low-paying ticket. Since the odds are stacked heavily in their favor, most taxpayers will usually win by not being audited. Another taxpayer strategy is to try to claim everything but the kitchen sink without getting thrown out of the game for engaging in fraud. Since aggressively playing the game by claiming big deductions is not consistent with maintaining a low profile, each taxpayer must find his happy medium between maximizing deductions and minimizing audit potential.

The tax laws have a lot of ambiguity and plenty of room for difference of opinion. Whenever your interpretation of the rules of the game favors your side, remember that the IRS will argue against you if you are audited. Compare the situation to that of buying a used car. The seller begins by asking a ridiculous price. If he knows you won't check under the hood, he will usually ask for more money than if he thinks you're a mechanic. Similarly, a taxpayer playing the audit lottery will start by asking for the most money by claiming everything he thinks he can get away with. If his return is questioned, he expects to end up with less money; but if it is not audited, he gets his inflated price for the car.

Want to play? It's simple. Give yourself the benefit of the doubt. As long as your interpretation of the law is based on some element of authoritative support, you have nothing to lose and everything to gain by playing the audit lottery.

Audit-Proofing Your Return

1. *Keep printed verification.* If you have tax information on a computer disk, get a printout. Make a photocopy of your return.
2. *Keep detailed records.* Note names, addresses, amount of payment, date, check number (or receipt for cash), purpose of payment, and photocopies of checks. *Save all checks.*
3. *Prove your income.* List number of shares or par value on investments, date acquired, cost or tax basis, dividends and interest received. Save all 1099 forms and W-2s.

    Record dividends or splits that affected the cost assigned to each share of stock. By allocating some of the original cost to each new share received in a dividend or split, you can minimize future taxes.

    Homeowners should keep records of original cost of property, improvements, balance of mortgages, total payments, real estate taxes, and interest. If you sold a previous home and invested the proceeds in your present home, be sure you save records on both the first and second homes.
4. *Keep records of all other deductions.* Save records of business-related expenses, pension or profit-sharing contributions, alimony or child support, and tax-shelter investments. It's better to have too many records than not enough in the case of an audit.

Auto Expense

If your car is economical to run and you do a lot of business driving, you are probably wise to claim the IRS mileage allowance of 22.5¢ per mile for the first 15,000 business miles and 11¢ per mile for additional mileage, plus parking and tolls. Otherwise, you have the choice of deducting actual operating costs rather than the standard mileage rate. Remember that any nonreimbursed auto expense is treated as a miscellaneous deduction and subject to a 2 percent floor.

If you own an automobile that is less than 4 years old, you will realize a larger savings by deducting actual costs plus depreciation. You must keep accurate records of gas, oil, parking fees, tolls, insurance premiums, and repairs.

Business vs. Hobby

If you have a part-time business (such as collecting and selling stamps or breeding cats), you are allowed to deduct the expenses of the activity as long as you show a profit. However, if you show a loss, the question will be raised as to whether the activity is a hobby or a genuine business.

Be prepared to prove that you operate in a businesslike manner; keep complete and accurate records. If you show a loss and are audited, be prepared to show (1) how much time and effort you have spent in the business; (2) that you expect your assets to appreciate in value; and (3) that you will make a profit in the near future. The IRS presumes that if you can show a profit for at least 3 out of 5 years, the activity is a business (as opposed to a hobby), and your losses are deductible.

You may prefer to wait until the fifth year to deal with the loss issue (in anticipation of realizing a profit for at least the 3 preceding years). You can file a special form with the IRS and waive the statute of limitations for the taxable years involved; if you race, breed, or show horses, the 5-year period becomes 7 years. This election to waive the statute of limitations may be made within 3 years of the date the return is due for the year in which you started the sideline business.

If you have not filed the election and your return is examined, you will have 60 days from the date you received the notice disallowing the loss to file the form.

Casualty Losses

In case of an audit, you must prove your casualty-loss deduction. Be prepared in case of a future casualty loss: take photographs of the interior and exterior of your home and save bills, receipts, and canceled checks. Put in your safe-deposit box those items plus appraisals of items for which you may not have receipts. Should you actually incur a casualty loss, save any repair bills. Because the loss is deductible in the year it occurred, regardless of when repairs are made, you will need written estimates to claim your loss if repairs are postponed.

Charitable Donations

If you know that your tax bracket will be lower next year and you need more deductions now, consider making donations during late December. Date your check or credit-card contribution before December 31 of the current tax year; that is the date that determines the year in which the contribution is deductible. If you are paying by other than check or credit card, get a receipt dated before December 31. If you are planning a donation of stock, begin early; it may take several weeks for the transfer to become effective.

A taxpayer giving property that has increased in value may deduct the fair market value, reduced by any amount that would be ordinary income (or short-term gain) if the property were sold for fair market value. In effect, this limits the deduction to the original cost of the property. A gift of securities to a college will result in a full deduction at fair market value, but the same gift made to a private foundation is limited to original cost.

More Deductible Contributions

• Civil Defense volunteers may claim deductions for unreimbursed travel and maintenance expenses.

• Scout leaders may deduct transportation and other nonreimbursed expenses, including materials purchased for the troop.

• Some charitable expenses are not deductible if they can be considered personal in nature. A Scout leader took his family on a one-week training seminar. Since the leader was not a delegate to the seminar, the IRS disallowed his expenses as being personal in nature. Unreimbursed travel expenses incurred by an Olympic skater's mother to help her daughter in competition were not deductible as contributions to the U.S. Olympic Committee, because the court felt that the personal motivation far exceeded any charitable motives. And the expenses of choir members' travel to and from the church for practice were held to be personal in nature and therefore not tax deductible.

• If you make a contribution that benefits you personally, it may be disallowed. A taxpayer made an unsolicited contribution to a church-affiliated school that his children attended. The school did not charge tuition but received funding from neighborhood churches and local residents. The courts ruled that the taxpayer's deduction was limited to the amount by which his contribution exceeded the presumed value of tuition. (If you want to support a church-affiliated school, make your contributions directly to the church. This should preserve your tax deduction.)

• The cost of unreimbursed meals, lodging, and commuting is deductible if you do volunteer charity work. Keep an accurate record of costs for gas, parking, and tolls. You may deduct 12¢ per mile or your actual expenses of driving for the charity, whichever is larger. You cannot deduct depreciation or repair and maintenance costs. Baby-sitting costs incurred while you are doing volunteer work are not deductible.

• The best way to make a charitable contribution is through your company. Donate some stock in a closely held corporation to charity and have it redeemed for cash. As long as there is no legal obligation for the charity to redeem the stock, you are allowed a deduction for the fair market value. (And it didn't cost you a penny!)

• You are entitled to a charitable deduction for up to $50 per month for the support of a full-time elementary or high school student living in your home who is not a relative or a dependent and who is staying with you by written agreement with a qualified charity. However, if the charity reimburses you for his or her expenses you will lose the deductions, so be sure that the charity gives any money directly to the student.

• You can get a charitable deduction for such out-of-pocket expenses as food and clothing if you provided temporary shelter for evacuees after a hurricane or flood. Save any correspondence with the agency that placed the person.

• You can give away your house to your church or alma mater, get a contribution deduction, and retain the right to live there until your death. The procedure is rather involved. Check with the church or school for the details.

• Beware of mail-order ministries. The Tax Court recently ruled that the Universal Life Church had no authority to allot tax exemptions. (Those who set up their own churches may not utilize them to save taxes.)

- If you want to leave a sum of money to charity without tying up your estate, name the charity as beneficiary on a life insurance policy that you place in an irrevocable trust. The life insurance premiums will be deductible on your tax return, and the charity will receive all proceeds from the policy upon your death.

Charitable Deductions for Future Payments

One taxpayer received an immediate deduction for cash to be paid in future years by writing an irrevocable letter of credit in favor of the charity. He was allowed to deduct the full value of the letter of credit on his return, even though the charity would collect installment payments in the future.

- *Valuing In-Kind Donations:* You can deduct the fair market *retail* value of property donations (valued at the price a *dealer* would get if he sold it to a customer instead of the lower price you would get if you sold directly to a dealer).

Unpaid public officials may deduct nonreimbursed job expenses. IRS considers the expenses deductible even though you don't intend to make a profit from your activity. Likewise, an unpaid officer of a charity can deduct out-of-pocket expenses as a charitable contribution.

- *Year-End Donations:* Only actual gifts are deductible; pledges and promissory notes are not deductible as donations until the payment is actually made. The cost of raffle tickets and games sponsored by charities is not deductible, and the cost of a ticket to a benefit is deductible only to the extent that the cost exceeds regular admission charge.

Gifts by check are considered deductible at time delivered or mailed, no matter when the check is cashed. Credit card donations are deductible on the date charged, regardless of when they're paid.

If you donate securities, a deductible contribution is considered made on the date the securities are mailed or delivered; however, if you deliver securities to a broker, the date of your contribution is the date the charity records receipt of the gift.

College Expenses

Considering the exorbitant costs of attending college, parents should be concerned with ways of getting any tax relief they can. If a parent (or grandparent) creates a custodial account for a child under age 14 and the child can be claimed as an exemption by the parents, the child's income will be taxed (to the child) at the parents' marginal tax rate. The exceptions are a $500 standard deduction to be used against unearned income with another $500 taxed at the child's tax rate. All income over $1,000 will be taxed at the parents' tax rate.

After age 14, the child's income will be taxable to the child, except for the $500 standard deduction to be offset against unearned income. Unearned income over $500 up to $17,850 will be taxed at 15 percent, with income over $17,850 taxed at the 28 percent bracket.

There is little incentive for a parent to transfer funds to a custodial account (for income-splitting purposes) with the small spread between the 15 percent rate and the 28 percent rate; however, if the parents are in the 33 percent marginal bracket (due to the phase-out of the 15 percent tax rate), the 18-point spread makes sense. If the spread between the brackets is even greater due to state and local taxes, there is even more of an incentive.

Playing With Children's Earnings

It may be best to look to the child's *earned* income to help plan for college expenses. The child can use the standard deduction ($2,540 in 1987 and $3,000 in 1988 for singles, adjusted for inflation after 1988).

Some infants are used for advertisements; others may earn big money as performers. One 9-year-old earned income for helping his parents keep up a trailer park. Many children's services are worthy of compensation—e.g., babysitting, mowing the lawn, washing the car, and the like.

If the child performs services for a family business, the amount may be deducted as ordinary and necessary business expense; however, if the family business is a corporation, there may be state work laws to be contended with.

Home Mortgage—College

If you have a considerable equity in a primary or second residence, consider mortgaging the home and using the proceeds for your child's college expenses. Home mortgage interest is deductible only up to the amount of the mortgage (not exceeding the original cost of the home plus improvements). However, there is an exception for qualified educational expenses paid within a reasonable time before (or after) the debt is incurred.

After a 5-year phase-in, no interest deduction will be allowed on a regular loan to cover college costs, since the loan itself will fall under the category of being a nondeductible consumer loan.

Gift Loan-Back

Assume a parent borrows $40,000 from a bank in late November. On December 31, he sets up an irrevocable trust with the child as beneficiary, and both parents transfer $20,000 to the trust. On January 15, another $20,000 is transferred to the trust. On January 20, the trust lends the parent $40,000 in return for an interest-bearing note with the parents' home as collateral. The parents pay off the bank with the $40,000, then begin paying interest on the note to the trust, and take a deduction for the interest. Assuming a 10 percent interest rate, $4,000 in interest will be payable as long as the principal remains $40,000; the resulting income tax would be $600 to a child in the 15 percent bracket. The remainder would be available for college costs.

Universal Life Insurance

Buying a single-premium universal life policy may be of benefit to a parent trying to put a child through college. Earnings on the investment portion of the policy will accumulate tax-free.

Deferred Annuities

Here's another good idea for saving toward college costs: Parent or grandparent buys a single-premium deferred annuity with payments geared toward when the child will enter college. The 10 percent withdrawal penalty will not apply in the case of distributions before age 59½ if the payments are spread out over the child's life expectancy.

Be careful in selecting an annuity. Take into account the period covered, the guaranteed yield, and the financial stability of the issuer.

College Zero Contract

Many colleges are offering contracts to pre-fund a child's future education. The amount initially paid on the contract will accumulate on a tax-deferred basis until the child graduates. Check with the schools of your choice to see if they have any programs in place.

Computers

Personal computers are treated specially under the tax law and fall under special requirements set up by the IRS. Use of a PC at home will be deductible only if it is (1) for the employer's convenience, (2) required as a condition of employment, and (3) necessary for the employee to perform properly the duties of his or her employment.

A statement by the employer that the use of the computer is a condition of employment is not enough to satisfy the IRS. You must also have clear and convincing evidence that your duties cannot be performed properly without the home computer. In one case, an engineer bought a PC for home use; he had a letter from his employer that he was required to buy the computer as a condition of employment. The IRS disallowed the deduction, since the engineer couldn't show that the PC was indispensable to his work, especially since he had access to a computer at his office.

However, if you have a sideline business that is run from a home office, you may be okay. Home offices are treated as your business premises, and a computer used there is assumed to be for business use. If you bought a computer in 1987, you can expense up to the first $10,000 (of cost) or claim depreciation using the new ACRS rules.

Conventions

As a general rule, a convention is considered a bona fide business meeting, but accurate and thorough records must be kept in order to prove that the convention trip was of a business nature. As a delegate to a convention, you must be able to prove that your attendance was in your own business interest—not that of the association—and that your attendance will benefit or advance your position. Fraternal organization conventions are not recognized as deductible meetings, but you may be able to deduct some of your expenses as a charitable contribution.

Convention costs include travel, food, tips, lodging, entertainment of business clients, display expenses, and other items essential to business dealings. Beginning in 1987 travel and other costs of attending a convention or seminar for investment purposes are no longer deductible. See page 130 for a full discussion.

Keep separate records for personal entertaining and sightseeing. If your spouse accompanies you, it is to your benefit to deduct the full amount it would have cost for you to attend alone, rather than divide total expenses in half. You may deduct the cost of your spouse's participation in entertaining business clients at the convention.

Divorce

Tax Reform has brought about changes that may fundamentally alter your tax and financial picture, and affect the manner in which divorces are settled. The high-income spouse paying alimony will be affected greatly by the lower rates. If he pays $20,000 annually (an after-tax cost of $10,000 in the 50 percent tax bracket) and is now in the 28 percent bracket, the net after-tax cost to him will be $14,400.

Taxpayers who have had long-term capital gains and find themselves in the 28 percent bracket will obviously be affected. Others will have increased taxes because of the passive-loss limitations, and loss of IRA deductions if they are covered by qualified company pension plans. Because of the substantial cost increases, some employers may decide to terminate their existing pension plan, and some taxpayers may find themselves out of pension plans completely.

Lower tax rates may provide more incentive for more housewives to enter the labor force, even though their earning capacity will be taken into account when alimony is awarded.

More emphasis will be placed on the use of property settlements and less placed on alimony as a tax-saving device. Because property settlements have been treated as tax-free transfers, the repeal of the capital gains deduction obviously affects tax planning. The Tax Reform Act makes bargaining more complicated because of the 40 percent increase on capital gains on sales of appreciated property.

Under the old law, it was common to place property in trust to provide child support; this won't work under Tax Reform. The income would become taxable to the trust at the parent's marginal rate, then would be taxable to the child without benefit of a personal exemption or standard deduction.

The $2,000 personal exemption may have some bearing on the decision of who will claim the children. However, child support will exceed the $2,000 allowance, and claiming exemptions will be more important.

The 6-year/$10,000 "front-loading" alimony rules have been drastically revised by a technical correction. If alimony paid in the first year exceeds the average payments in the second and third years by more than $15,000, the payor must include the excess in income in the third year. The recipient gets a deduction for that excess in computing adjusted gross income. To the extent that payments in the second year exceed the payments in the third year by more than $15,000, the same rule applies. The intent is to prevent spouses who divorce near year-end from making a deductible property settlement at the beginning of the following year. The new rule does not apply if (1) either party dies, or (2) the receiving spouse remarries by the end of the second calendar year after payments began. It also does not apply to temporary support or payments that are made for at least 3 years and are based on earnings of a business, property, or services.

Generally, this new law applies to divorce/support decrees executed after 1986, and to modifications of a prior agreement.

The Tax Reform Act eliminates the requirement that the divorce decree discontinue payments after the death of the receiving spouse. Under the old law, if the document failed to state this requirement specifically, the IRS took the position that none of the payments made during the payee's life would qualify. Payers of alimony can file a claim for refund for taxes paid as a result of loss of the deduction.

Educational Expenses

If you attend a college, university, or vocational school, take courses from a correspondence school, or have private tutoring, and the course maintains or improves your job skills (or was required by your employer), the educational costs (tuition, books, fees, transportation, and food and lodging if away from home) will be tax deductible.

If the school and your work location are in the same general area, you can deduct expenses for travel from work to school; if the school is farther away, the entire round-trip cost is deductible as a miscellaneous deduction and subject to the 2 percent floor.

Estate Planning

Three different federal taxes must be taken into account in estate planning: your present income tax situation, the estate tax, and the gift tax.

Estate Tax: Unified Credit

The estate tax is applied to property transferred to your heirs upon your death. Your executor may elect to have the estate tax based on the value of the property at the time of your death or 6 months later. The estate tax may include all taxable gifts made after 1976, plus certain property transferred within 3 years before the death (using fair market value as of the date of death). The estate tax also applies to property that was incompletely or improperly transferred before your death.

Although estate and gift tax rules have been liberalized, you still need proper estate tax planning. The estate tax exemption of $600,000 is fully phased in but may not be large enough to avoid estate taxes completely, due to inflation and increasing real estate values. The single unified credit for gift and estate tax exemptions will combine the two taxes into a single tax on transfers before and at death. The unified credit allots a tax exemption of $600,000 in 1987, allowing married couples to give away $1.2 million tax-free through their estates. The $100,000 estate tax exemption has been eliminated for participants in IRAs, Keoghs, and employee retirement plans.

Estate Tax: Marital Deduction

The gross value of an estate is reduced by the value of property passed to the surviving spouse. The surviving spouse may receive the property because of co-ownership, as insurance proceeds, as a gift or inheritance, under dower rights (a percentage of the property) created by state law, or as a survivor's interest in an annuity.

The marital deduction is not lost upon the occurrence of a certain and specific event (such as remarriage) or when property is to be transferred in accordance with the will or other instructions, or upon the death of the survivor. The deduction is unlimited; every married couple may avoid estate tax on the family fortune, regardless of the size of their estate, until the death of the surviving spouse. There is also no limit on gifts that can be made tax-free between spouses during their lifetimes. Although leaving all your property to a spouse will avoid immediate estate taxes, the decision could cause a heavy tax burden on the children upon the death of the second parent.

If you and your spouse are concerned that upon the surviving spouse's death the property will go to parties of the survivor's choice (which may not be the wish of the other spouse), consider writing a joint will. In a joint will, each spouse provides that his or her property (or a designated portion) will go to the surviving spouse and, upon the survivor's death, the property will be distributed as provided for in the joint will. Joint wills are not recommended, however, when the spouses' estates are large (and the method of asset disposition is complicated), since the life interest created by a joint will is subject to estate tax. Nonspousal bequests (to the extent of the unified credit—the excess going to the spouse) allow transfers to children and others, escaping estate tax.

Life Insurance

The amount of an estate includes life insurance proceeds if the benefits are payable to the executor (or estate) or if there are rights of ownership in the policy (i.e., to change the named beneficiary, to borrow against the policy, or to terminate the policy). Regardless of which spouse owns the insurance policy, proceeds will be received by the surviving spouse free of estate taxes. Although certain property (real estate, securities, business properties) requires specialized training to be handled by beneficiaries, life insurance is relatively simple. However, instead of lump-sum payments of life insurance proceeds, one could provide for payments over a period of years, earmark funds for college or mortgage payments, and provide some form of cash reserve for contingency use.

Trusts

If the value of property bequeathed to other than a spouse exceeds the unified credit deduction, it will be subject to estate tax and costs of probate. Also, the estate may quickly be dissipated due to the beneficiaries' inexperience, and it will be vulnerable to their creditors. In the final analysis, your estate will be subject to your beneficiaries' wishes upon your demise.

However, if you set up a trust while you are still living, you can transfer property that will not be part of your estate when you die. A qualified person or trust company will administer the trust for the benefit of your beneficiaries. Creditors will not be able to attach the principal, and, in addition, you can specify where the principal should be applied when the beneficiaries die. Benefits should be distributed annually; beneficiaries of an accumulation trust are taxed as though they received income during the tax year rather than the year in which they actually received the money.

Irrevocable Trusts

You may want to set up an irrevocable trust that will establish that your spouse will receive income for life and your children will receive the trust principal upon the death of your spouse. Your children will not be subject to estate tax. However, if the amount exceeds the annual exclusions of unified credit, they may have to pay gift tax.

Life Income Trust

You may prefer to establish a life income trust for your spouse (or another person), with the trust property to revert to a specific charity upon your beneficiaries' deaths. The amount of your estate will be credited with the value of the property on the date of your death less the calculated value of your beneficiaries' life interest (based on the value of the property when given).

Gift Tax: Annual Exclusion

The gift tax is applied to transfers made during your lifetime and valued on the date of the gift, less marital deductions and an annual gift-tax exclusion of $10,000 ($20,000 for marrieds filing jointly) for each recipient. The exclusion does not apply to gifts of a future interest—i.e., gifts which cannot be possessed (or enjoyed) by the donee until a given date in the future, except in the case of a minor who will not receive estate property until he or she comes of age (provided that the property is subject to the minor's disposition if the minor dies before age 21).

If you give a lifetime gift, income-producing assets and appreciated property can be transferred to family members in lower tax brackets, gifts can escape probate upon death (reducing commissions charged by the executor), and unified credit limitations can be avoided.

If you want to give property to family members but do not want to be left without income, you may want to consider an annuity in return for your gift. The annuity will not be taxed to your estate when you die if you establish a joint (or survivorship) annuity or have a minimum number of guaranteed payments (the actuarial value after your death will be taxed to your estate).

Estimated Tax (Form 1040-ES)

Estimated tax is basically the total of your estimated income tax, plus self-employment tax, less tax credits and an estimate of withholding tax. Every citizen of the United States or resident of the United States or its possessions must make a declaration of estimated tax if that tax is $500 or more and he or she: (1) can reasonably expect $500 income from sources where no withholding taxes were taken, and (2) can reasonably expect total income to exceed:

1. $20,000 for a single individual, head of household, widow or widower with surviving spouse privileges, or a married couple filing jointly where only one spouse has income
2. $10,000 for a married couple where both have income; or
3. $5,000 for a married person filing separately.

The estimated tax payments are due quarterly, on or before April 15, June 15, September 15, and January 15. The due date for declaration of those who will file estimated payments and payment in full for the preceding year is January 31.

Estimated tax payments are required only after you have received the income subject to the tax. If you do not receive income until April 15, you must make a payment by the due date for the period in which the income is received—i.e., by June 15. You have the option of either paying the tax in the remaining installments or paying it in full. In either case, make sure to pay enough tax during the year to avoid penalties. The period of estimated tax underpayment runs from the due date of the estimated tax installment to the date the election to apply the overpayment is made—usually the date of the filing of the return. The net effect: Filing extensions should be made as a result of careful calculations, not guessing.

Beginning this year, you must pay at least 90 percent of the current year's tax liability or 100 percent of last year's to avoid being penalized.

Every taxpayer who estimates that his tax will equal (or exceed) $500 for the year must pay in estimated tax. To begin with, estimate your taxable income for the year, then compute your tax. Add to that figure any taxes resulting from accumulated distributions or from use of the 5- or 10-year averaging for lump-sum distributions, and subtract any nonrefundable credits. Add to that amount alternative minimum tax, self-employment tax, tax from early withdrawal from an IRA, and tax from recapture of investment tax credit.

Even though you may have underpaid your estimated tax liability on a particular installment, you may escape any underpayment penalty under these conditions:

1. If the tax due after subtracting credits is less than $500
2. If you had no tax liability for the preceding year and were a citizen (or resident) of the United States for that period
3. If you use the annualized income installment alternative to calculate the amount of installment due.

File Form 2210 (Underpayment of Estimated Tax by Individuals) to compute any tax underpayment and to determine if a penalty is due or whether an exception may apply.

Executives—Financial Planning

It is important for executives to review all their compensation, benefits, estate planning, and investments, and in many cases make changes in accordance with Tax Reform. Employers will find that many of their executives need help in adjusting to the new tax laws and economic environment. Unfortunately, this employer-provided help will be fully taxable, since the value of financial and estate planning guidance offered by (or through) the employer must be listed as income. The cost will be fully deductible to the employer; however, lower tax rates will reduce the employer's after-tax cost of providing financial and estate planning advice.

Though investment advice is sought with a view to increasing income, the cost of the advice is no longer permitted as a deduction, which must be considered in evaluating employer-sponsored investment counseling. Employer-provided benefits—e.g., tax return preparation—create taxable income a possibly limited deduction.

Here are some of the tax changes that affect executives:

1. The basic 15 percent and 28 percent rates apply only after 1987.
2. Long-term capital gains are taxable at the same rate as ordinary income.
3. The married worker deduction is eliminated.
4. Extensive changes affect fringe benefits.
5. There are basically 5 tax rates for 1987, ranging from 11 percent to 38.5 percent; marrieds are taxed at 28 percent on $28,000 to $45,000 income, 35 percent over $45,000 up to $90,000, and 38.5 percent on taxable income over $90,000.
6. IRA contributions are nondeductible for taxpayers covered by qualified retirement plans and having $50,000 or more income on a joint return ($35,000 income if single).
7. There are extensive changes affecting retirement planning, including 401(k) plans.
8. The 15 percent rate, personal exemptions, and $25,000 rental real estate maximum for passive losses are phased out: 15 percent rate phase-out for marrieds filing jointly earning from $71,900 to $149,250; for head of household, $61,650 to $123,790; for singles, $25,950 to $113,300. Personal exemptions phase out starting where the 15 percent bracket phase-out ends by increasing tax by 5 percent; ranges vary with the number of exemptions. The $25,000 rental real estate maximum phase-out is from $100,000 to $150,000 adjusted gross income.

Although the 28 percent bracket sounds good for an executive who has been in (or near) the 50 percent bracket in the past, phase-outs as noted above can easily increase the 28 percent effective top rate to 33 percent or more after 1987. In 1987, when the dependency and 15 percent rate phase-outs don't apply, the top rate will be 38.5 percent except for capital gains (top rate of 28 percent). The loss on deductions due to changes effective January 1, 1987, may result in executives paying higher taxes than they would have under the 50 percent top rate. These higher rates may carry over to 1988 and beyond.

Even though Tax Reform increases personal exemptions and the standard deduction, the reduction in tax rates alone will not create lower taxes for the executive, because of fewer deductions and phase-outs. Here are some other changes that will increase taxes:

1. Loss of deduction for consumer interest (to be phased in over 5 years)
2. Loss of sales tax deduction
3. Repeal of income averaging
4. Phase-out of passive loss deductions in excess of passive income
5. Increase of the floor for medical expense deductions from 5 percent to 7.5 percent
6. New 2 percent floor on expenses connected with collection of income, management, or maintenance of property held for income, or preparation, collection, or refund of taxes, including tax preparation fees
7. Stiffer alternative minimum tax.

The treatment of capital gains as ordinary income and the denial of the passive-loss deductions, singly or in combination, will be a major concern to many high-income executives.

The 28 percent top rate is misleading if it fails to take into account marginal rates (the rate at which the top dollar of taxable income is taxed). High marginal rates one year and lower rates in another year, or vice versa, must be considered when determining acceleration or deferral of income or deductions for the executive. This makes tax planning even more important than it was before.

Compensation packages for executives need to be looked at closely. The use of phantom stock plans and stock appreciation rights should be reviewed. The effect will vary depending on the type of industry. Whereas ownership of stock in labor-intensive service businesses may be beneficial because of the 34 percent top corporate rate, investments in capital-intensive businesses may suffer.

Some deferred compensation plans may have been based on the assumption that at retirement the executive would be in a lower tax bracket; however, in light of the lower rates under reform, he may still be subject to the same tax rate at retirement as when the income was deferred.

An executive filing jointly will be taxed at the 28 percent rate on taxable income over $29,750 after 1987. Many executives who reach retirement will attain this maximum quickly due to pension benefits, Social Security, investment returns, and IRA benefits. Deferral compensation may retain some value for the executive, but not as much as previously, especially after the alternative minimum tax is taken into account.

The top rate of 28 percent on capital gains lessens the value of the capital gains aspect of many stock plans. The after-tax cost of financing stock purchases under company stock plans may be greater due to the tougher limitation deductions for investment interest.

There are some positive changes, however. There is no longer a need to hold stock acquired under incentive stock options in order to get long-term treatment because the gain on the sale will be taxed at the same rate after 1987. The only difference is that Tax Reform distinguishes between long-term gains for purposes other than tax on the gain realized on disposition. If the ISO stock is held for the required holding period, the gain should be treated as long-term gain, which could be offset by capital losses. Aside from this, Tax Reform gives added flexibility to the executive in disposing of his ISO stock.

He may also exercise the option and sell the stock acquired at the same time, which greatly eases the financing of the exercise. This could be done under the old law, but the new tax rates make it still better.

Tax Reform provides that ISOs do not have to be exercisable in the order granted. The employer is no longer restricted to $100,000 limit of ISOs it may grant to an employee per year. Tax Reform provides that the combined fair market value (determined at the time the option is granted) of the stock with respect to which the ISOs are exercisable for the first time under the plan is to be used.

Nonqualified stock options are devalued due to the higher tax rate on long-term gain along with the fact that Tax Reform will make the financing more costly (a deduction for interest paid may not be available under the investment interest deduction limitation). Also, some companies will be required to charge some value for nonqualified options against the company's earnings statement, so the companies may not want to use the options.

401(k) Plan

Under the old tax law, executives could put away up to $30,000 per year in 401(k) contributions to take advantage of tax deferral on the contributions *and* the income generated by them; but Tax Reform cuts this maximum to $7,000. Due to the limitations on IRA, if the employer does not have a 401(k) plan, the executive may want to try to get the employer to set up a salary-reduction-type 401(k) plan so he can make up for the loss of the IRA deduction.

Tax-free fringe benefits generally will have less after-tax value under the new law for individuals in lower tax brackets. Increasing the floor on medical expenses to 7.5 percent will make employer-provided tax-free medical benefits more attractive. Instead of relying on an itemized medical deduction, the executive might be better off under a salary-reduction arrangement.

Another worthwhile fringe benefit for the executive would be group-term life insurance.

Taxable fringe benefits increase in value to the extent that Tax Reform reduces the after-tax cost of the benefit. For example, if an executive is required to pay 28 percent of the cost of operating a company car for personal use and was formerly in the 50 percent bracket, he may actually benefit.

Employer-provided financial planning counseling will be available to the executive in the 28 percent bracket as long as it is reported as income, which is likely to be much less than if the executive sought counseling on an individual basis.

Due to the antidiscrimination rules, uncertainties, and complications built into the new tax law, many employers may eliminate some fringe benefits that are excludable from income. They can use the cash savings to provide taxable benefits to selected executives.

Split-Dollar Life Insurance

Tax Reform does not change the question of deductibility of interest by the employer in split-dollar assignment arrangements as distinguished from endorsement-type arrangements. Lower tax rates should create a lower after-tax cost to the executive in the early years of the arrangement, when he may be faced with some tax liability. It is apparent that life insurance will fare better than investments hard hit by the new law because to some extent the cash buildup in life insurance is tax-free. A universal life policy used in split-dollar arrangements will provide a greater buildup than whole life. Choose your policy carefully.

An Executive Checklist

To recapitulate, here are some important factors to consider in reviewing the executive's position and planning for the tax reform impact:

1. Elimination of income averaging.
2. Elimination of long-term capital gains deduction on the sale of capital assets. This change also affects stock redemptions, investments, and retirement plans.
3. Two basic rates, 15 percent and 28 percent, and the higher marginal rates caused by the phase-out of the 15 percent rate, personal exemptions, and the $25,000 real estate passive-loss exception.
4. Elimination of the married worker deduction.
5. Tougher alternative minimum tax.
6. Phase-out of long-term capital gains and 10-year averaging on lump-sum distributions from qualified plans; substitution of 5-year averaging.
7. Elimination of IRA deductions for high-income employees covered by pension plans.
8. Elimination of the $75,000 floor on retirement benefits and actuarial reduction of benefits for early retirement.

Financial planning for executives does not differ markedly from investors except in 2 areas: (1) The executive's investment portfolio may be heavily concentrated in employer stock and be in need of diversification; and (2) the executive probably knows more about his industry (and his company) than the average investor.

The executive faces the devaluation of employer stock holdings because of the less favorable tax treatment of appreciation under Tax Reform. Higher marginal rates may play a part in any decision the executive makes regarding sale of stock.

The devaluation of employer stock, plus the lower top rates, may create greater interest in cash compensation. This will place the executive in a better position to achieve diversification. Some employer-issuers of stock may be willing to buy it back from their executives, sometimes with excess cash that has become available to them due to the reduction of the top rate of corporate tax.

Retirement Planning

Tax Reform adversely affects executives with regard to retirement planning in ways that it does not affect rank-and-file employees:

1. Key employees generally cannot participate in a qualified cost-of-living arrangement.

2. The limit of compensation that can be taken into consideration under any retirement plan is $200,000.
3. There is a new 15 percent excise tax on annual benefit distributions in excess of $112,500 (indexed).
4. The $90,000 defined benefit limitation is phased in over the first 10 years of plan participation (not over the years of service with the employer).
5. When an employer determines an employee's maximum addition to a defined contribution plan (the lesser of $30,000 or 25 percent of compensation), all of the employee's contributions to the plan are taken into account (instead of the amount in excess of 6 percent of compensation).
6. The $75,000 floor on defined benefit plans for early retirees has been repealed. Actuarial reduction of benefits beginning before attaining Social Security retirement age is required.
7. Cost-of-living adjustments (COLA) to the $30,000 defined contribution dollar limit are suspended until that limit equals 25 percent of the defined benefit limit with a COLA adjustment ($120,000).

The $100,000 limit was previously applicable only to top-heavy plans and Self-Employed Plans (SEPs). It will increase as defined benefit limits increase. The purpose is to prevent contributions or benefits of middle- or low-income employees from being lowered by reductions in the maximum contributions or benefits. With the new Tax Reform's formula, the executive will not be able to contribute a maximum toward retirement out of proportion to the lower-paid employee.

It seems that this may result in nonqualified, unsecured excess benefits for executives earning more than $200,000 who are adversely affected; however, executives may prefer cash up front. Since such excess plans don't give the employer current deductions, some employers may seek to cut benefits and contributions for the middle- and low-income employees whenever possible.

Qualified cost-of-living arrangements incidental to defined benefit plans involve contributions by the employer and the employee. Provision must be made independently for cost-of-living protection through extra savings and excess benefit plans, due to the general exclusion of key employees from participation in these arrangements.

Pension planning generally is more difficult for employers due to additional coverage requirements, tighter antidiscrimination rules, and tougher integration rules. Many employers may consider terminating (or not starting) pension plans altogether.

The executive must consider whether he can depend on his employer to continue a qualified retirement plan.

IRAs

Although deductions for IRA contributions are disallowed over certain limits ($50,000 AGI for married filing jointly after phase-out starting at $40,000; and $35,000 AGI for singles with phase-out starting at $25,000), nondeductible contributions may still be made in the same amounts allowed under the old law. This will provide the benefit of tax deferral on the income generated by the IRA contributions. Executives may come out better under the new law, depending on the amount of IRA contributions made before withdrawal at age 59½ and considering the lower tax rate on payouts.

The use of rollover IRAs for lump-sum distributions from qualified plans to take advantage of the tax-deferred buildup and stretched-out distributions (made possible by annual recalculation of life expectancy and the use of younger individuals as beneficiaries) is more attractive under tax reform due to the lower rates.

The 10 percent excise tax for premature withdrawals has been retained by Tax Reform.

Family Members on the Payroll

If you are in a bona fide business, think about hiring your children for summer work. (A business is "an activity carried on for a livelihood or for profit." A profit motive must be evident, with regularity of activities as well as production of income.) As long as the compensation is reasonable, is based on actual services rendered, and is actually paid, it is deductible, even if the children use the money for part of their support. Of course, the value of meals and lodging furnished to a minor child by a parent is not deductible as wages or included in the child's income.

You cannot deduct money paid to your child for mowing the lawn or taking out the garbage, but you can deduct compensation to the child for actually helping you with your business.

If your child has a job that takes an hour a day during the summer and you pay him $15,000 to use for college expenses, this is definitely an unreasonable amount for the services performed. The IRS would not allow it.

For Social Security purposes, services performed by your child are not considered employment, which means that you need not take out taxes.

Filing Status Tax Tips

If you are divorced (or just thinking about it), you should be aware of subjects like filing status, tax consequences, legal fees paid in connection with the divorce, and claiming the children. If you are separated and have not obtained a decree of separate maintenance or a final decree of divorce, you are still considered married and would probably do best by filing jointly. If you received your final decree by December 31, you are considered single for the entire year; if you have children, you may be able to file as head of household.

Married couples living separately are permitted to file as single or unmarried heads of household, even though they may be married. Those in this special category are referred to as an abandoned spouse for the purposes of filing. You qualify if you file a separate return, if you paid more than half the cost of keeping up your home for the year, if your spouse did not live with you at any time during the year, and if you had a child or stepchild living with you for the entire taxable year.

In order to qualify for head-of-household tax rates, you must have been single as of the end of the year and you must have paid more than half the cost of maintaining a household that was the principal residence for your unmarried child, grandchild, adopted or foster child, stepchild (who need not have been your dependent), your parent (who must have been your dependent but need not have lived with you during the year), or any other relative who lived with you whom you can claim as a dependent.

If you were recently widowed, you may use joint return rates if you:

1. Maintained a home for the entire year for a child, adopted child, or stepchild, and are entitled to claim the child as a dependent
2. Furnished more than half the cost of maintaining the household
3. Could have filed a valid joint return with your spouse had he or she lived

4. Did not remarry before January 1 of this year.

Even if you cannot use joint return rates, you may qualify for head-of-household rates if:

1. You have not remarried by December 31
2. Your home was the residence of your child (or dependent relative) for the entire year
3. You provided more than half of the entire cost of your household
4. You have been a U.S. citizen or resident for the entire tax year.

In adding up household costs, remember to include rent, utilities, repairs, property taxes and insurance, mortgage interest, food, and the cost of domestic help. The costs of clothing, education, medical expenses, transportation, life insurance premiums, vacation expenses, and the value of your time working around the house do not count.

Fringe Benefits

It sometimes makes sense to look for a position with a company that offers fringe benefits as opposed to one that offers a higher salary. Fringe benefits are tax-free and may significantly increase after-tax take-home pay. Fringe benefits may include insurance (accident and health, group term life, and permanent life—if your employer pays most of the premium and is entitled to a portion of the proceeds upon your death), as well as stock options. If your employer offers a pension or profit-sharing plan, the funds contributed by you and your employer accumulate tax-free.

Other popular fringe benefits include: discounts on company products, low-cost meals in a company cafeteria; medical checkups paid for by the employer; legal services paid for by your employer; and use of company services at cost (e.g., company condo).

Gift Leasebacks

A gift leaseback is a way to have rents taxed at low rates by having rental property put in trust for low-income parents or children. The best type of property to use in a gift leaseback is fully depreciated property from which you have received all possible tax benefits. A typical gift leaseback works in this way: A taxpayer sets up a trust for his parents or children and gives the building to the trust. The taxpayer's company rents the building from the trust and deducts the rent as a business expense. The relatives in the low-income bracket receive the rent, and at the end of the trust period the taxpayer gets the building back. The Tax Court has made gift leasebacks legal only if the following requirements are met:

1. The taxpayer must have actually owned the property; the IRS may deny rent deductions where the donor was a partner or shareholder.
2. A gift leaseback may not use mortgaged property.
3. The taxpayer must not have control over the property. (Name a trustee and give him power to negotiate the lease and renewals. Don't name family members or employees as the trustee.)
4. The rent paid must be reasonable, and the lease must be in writing. (Compare average rentals in the area and settle on a reasonable figure.)
5. The leaseback must have a legitimate business purpose; i.e., the property must

actually be used in your business. A leaseback involving a personal auto is usually disallowed.
6. You may not keep the right to sell the property as long as the trust exists.

Trust income may not be used to escape support of your children. If the IRS judges that to be the case, you, not the beneficiaries, will be taxed on the trust income. In addition, there may be gift tax implications on property transferred to the trust.

Always seek professional advice if you are considering a gift leaseback.

Gifts of Appreciated Property

The Tax Reform Act still permits the deduction of appreciated property at fair market value without payment of capital gains tax that would have been paid if the property were sold. The donor will also avoid a higher capital gains tax: top rate 28 percent, as compared with 20 percent under the old law. And this 28 percent can go up to a marginal tax rate of 33 percent (or more) due to the phase-out of the 15 percent bracket. Gifts of appreciated property to charity are now a tax preference item under the revised alternative minimum tax.

The actual net price of a gift of appreciated property will be determined according to the following:

1. Taxable income of the donor over the income levels at which the marginal rate rises to 33 percent
2. Percent of appreciation in relation to the fair market value of the property
3. Combined federal, state, and local tax bracket of the donor; deductibility under state law; and tax treatment of the capital gains under state law.

The net after-tax cost of gifts of appreciated property is usually higher for those in lower tax brackets. The higher the combined federal, state, and local tax bracket of the donor, the lower the net after-tax cost of the contribution.

Net after-tax cost is determined by the difference between the amount that remains to the donor after making the gift compared to what would remain if the property were sold. If the sale would be in a later year, the savings would be less. If the sale of the property took place after the holder's death, there would be no tax saving on the appreciation up to the date of death, and the contribution of appreciated property would be identical to a gift of cash.

Some taxpayers who benefited from capital gains preference and tax shelters may be in higher brackets under the new tax law. As a result, the net after-tax cost of their charitable contributions may be less, unless they are affected by the new 21 percent alternative minimum tax.

Alternative Minimum Tax

Under Tax Reform, appreciation in charitable gifts is included in the base of AMT taxable income. This alternative minimum tax taxes more income and permits less in deductions. Although the rate is only 21 percent (as compared to the regular top rate of 28 percent), the resulting tax may be greater because the AMT permits a deduction for only the original cost of the property.

As a general rule, if you have no tax preferences (except gifts of appreciated property), you will be able to give appreciated property up to 25 percent of regular income without being subject to the alternative minimum tax.

Home Office

If you have a full-time job and operate a sideline business from your home, you may deduct home office expenses, provided your home is the principal place of business.

If you set aside one room of your house for exclusive use as a business office (furnishing it with a desk, filing cabinet, and so forth), you may deduct expenses applicable to the home office, but only if you use the room to meet patients, clients, or customers. If you can't set aside an entire room, perhaps you can separate the business area from the rest of the room. A physical partition, although not required, will make proving that a room in your home is used exclusively for business much easier.

Tax Reform has made home office deductions harder to come by than they have been in the past. There will be no more deductions when an employee leases a portion of his home to his employer for the premises to be used in performing services as an employee.

But what if the employee's spouse is the legal owner of the rental residence and is the sole person obligated to pay the mortgage and taxes? It would seem that if the spouse leases a portion of the home to the employer, it might qualify.

Allowable home office deductions are limited to the net income generated from the business. For example, if $7,000 of deductions are attributable to the business and $7,000 more pertain to depreciation, the direct expenses come off first, then the indirect expenses, but only up to the income. If the income was $10,000, the remaining $4,000 would be disallowed. However, this disallowed amount may be carried forward to a future year (again subject to the net income limitation).

An individual who owns 2 homes might consider this plan: If the principal residence (containing the home office) is heavily mortgaged, he might remortgage the secondary residence and reduce or pay off the mortgage on the primary residence. Then the interest deductions on the second home, which might have been disallowed under the new tax law, would be fully deductible.

Home Office "Focal Point" Test

The "focal point" of a home office is the place where goods or services are provided to customers or where income is produced, e.g., an owner-operator of a hot dog stand may not claim home office expenses for a home office to do bookkeeping for the business.

Benefiting from a Home Office

A business run out of your home can produce not only extra income but large tax benefits as well. To qualify for a home office deduction, you must set aside a room (or part of your home) exclusively for the primary place for your business. You may deduct part of your mortgage payment (or rent), taxes, repairs, utilities, depreciation, maintenance, and operating expenses—in proportion to the total size of your residence. Your home office writeoff, however, may not exceed your business's gross income.

Other legitimate business deductions include stationery, postage, magazines, legal expenses, salaries, and telephone charges as ordinary and necessary expenses.

All transportation expenses are deductible (e.g., trips to purchase supplies, attend a business lunch, meet a customer).

Equipment you purchase may qualify for a depreciation. Keep accurate, detailed records to show percentage of business use (a daily log is best).

Equipment you already own that is used in your business (e.g., car, furniture, etc.) may be depreciated, based on the lower of original cost or market value when placed in business use.

Deducting Start-Up Costs:

Money spent prior to going into business, (e.g., travel expenses to investigate the market or for financial or legal advice) may be written off over a period of 60 months, beginning with the month you started up the business—*if* the expenses are the type that would be deductible for an ongoing business.

Controlling Income and Expenses

By holding off year-end billings until January, you won't have to report the income until next year. On the other hand, you may purchase next year's supplies in December and claim the deduction this year.

Planning for Retirement

If you run an office out of your home, you're eligible to set up a Keogh retirement plan in addition to any retirement plan you have at your regular job or any IRAs you may own.

You may contribute up to 20 percent of your self-employment income (maximum of $30,000 per year).

Home Ownership

Your home may be the best tax shelter you have. Tax on the gain from the sale of a residence is deferred if the proceeds are reinvested in another residence within 2 years of the sale. If you are age 55 or older when you sell your house, you may have up to $125,000 of gain permanently excluded from tax. If you own the house when you die, the entire appreciation value escapes income tax (but may be subject to estate tax). Your beneficiaries inherit the property at fair market value on the date of your death and only the difference between that value and the selling price will be taxable.

Let your beneficiaries inherit the house. If an elderly person sells a house to a child for $1 to keep the property out of the estate, it is treated as a gift (rather than a sale), and the child assumes the tax basis that the parent has in the house. When the child sells, he must pay income tax on the full appreciation value. But if you let the child inherit the house, the appreciation is not taxed.

Another problem with the $1 sale is that if the child decides to rent the house back to the parents, the depreciation is based on the parents' tax basis in the house, not the property's current value.

Supporting Parents

If you are making payments toward your parents' support, here's a tax tip: Buy your parents' house from them, make monthly payments, and rent it back to them at a fair rental. Make the installment payments equal the rent plus the amount you had been giving them for support. The rent you receive is sheltered by depreciation, maintenance, and property taxes. If your adjusted gross income is less than $100,000 (and the writeoffs exceed the rent), you can deduct up to $25,000 of losses against taxable income. (If the AGI is between $100,000 and $150,000, you may deduct *some* of your losses.)

In addition, your parents' gain on the sale may be tax-free because of the $125,000 exclusion.

College Child

If you have a college-age child attending school in another city, buy a house (or apartment) and rent it back to your child (and possibly other students) at a fair rental. You get all the tax-shelter benefits of rental property and can write off up to $25,000 of losses if your AGI is under $100,000. In addition, your investment may appreciate while your child is attending school.

Sale under Age 55

If you are under age 55 and sell a house and do not intend to buy another, take back a note (or mortgage) and defer tax on a portion of your gain (the part that represents the money you did not receive immediately because you took back a mortgage). You pay tax on the gain only as you receive principal payments. (A 20-year mortgage would spread the tax on your gain over 20 years.) In addition, you collect interest on the full mortgage principal. Just be sure that a potential buyer is financially qualified.

Home Office

If you have a home office and claim depreciation on your home, when you sell your residence you may not defer the entire gain, since you claimed depreciation. Also, you may not claim the entire $125,000 exclusion. Only the personal use portion of the gain may be deferred (or excluded), not the business use portion. Claim depreciation for equipment and furniture used in the office but not for the home office itself. Under the new law, home office writeoffs are limited to income generated by the home office activity. Since the only writeoff likely to give you a loss is depreciation, why risk taking it when you may be better off tax-wise if you don't?

Vacation Property Traps

If you own vacation property that you rent out during the year, the Tax Reform Act has made deductions more difficult to come by. For instance:

1. A net loss on vacation property is no longer automatically deductible. If after taking taxes and casualty losses into account the rental property produces a profit, the interest expense generally will remain deductible. You can deduct a rental loss for the year (including interest) up to $25,000. If your adjusted gross income exceeds $100,000, your loss will be less; if your AGI is over $150,000, your loss is completely eliminated.
2. Transient rules apply if the average stay in your leased property is less than 30 days, in which case you can claim losses only if you actively manage it and provide substantial services.

You may want to avoid potential problems by considering your property as a second home (and not rental property) since there are lesser limits on interest, and taxes are personal in nature.

Home Rental

Consider renting your home in order to realize a greater profit on the sale; if you later sell the property at a loss, the loss will be deductible. If you rent a portion of your house and continue to live there, you may claim a loss on the sale of the rented portion only. But if you bought the property as an investment (with the intention of making a profit), your loss deduction will be allowed.

If you live in a house that was a gift or an inheritance, you can sell it at a loss, and the loss will be deductible; but you must offer it for sale or rent within a few weeks after inheritance. If you place an inherited residence up for sale only (no rental), you will be limited to a capital loss (up to $3,000 per year). But if you first try to rent but cannot and then sell, you will have an ordinary loss, which means that your entire loss will be deductible.

Income-Shifting

The Clifford Trust, which allowed a high-income taxpayer to shift income to a child or parent in a lower tax bracket, is gone under Tax Reform. The spousal remainder trust, which allowed the taxpayer to place income-producing property in a trust in order to keep gift taxes to a minimum, is also gone. Now unearned income of a child under the age of 14 over $1,000 annually will be taxed at the parents' rate.

Here are some pointers to consider with children under age 14:

1. Buy Series EE bonds and elect to defer tax on interest as it accrues.
2. Put a child to work in the family business to permit earned income to offset the standard deduction. Even a very young child can do some type of work.
3. If the child is the beneficiary of a trust, try to coordinate the trust income with other income earned outside the trust. Try to accumulate trust income up to $5,000 to take advantage of the 15 percent rate.
4. Invest in raw land with appreciation potential and low yield and keep it until the child reaches age 14.
5. Buy cash-surrender-value life insurance, which can accumulate income tax-free while permitting tax-free borrowing (e.g., single-premium, universal life, or whole life).
6. Place UGMA and UTMA funds in tax-exempt funds until the child reaches age 14. Check out zero-coupon tax-exempt bonds.
7. Consider gifts to a child under the annual $10,000 exclusion umbrella aside from any income-splitting considerations.
8. Buy annuities to provide income to the child at age 14, when the income will become taxable at the child's rate.
9. Invest in securities with strong appreciation potential and low yield, to be kept until the child becomes age 14.

Zero-Coupon Tax Exempts

Under the new law, tax-exempt zero-coupon bonds are very popular, since the other gifts to minors are no longer of benefit.

A principal advantage of the zero-coupon bonds is the low initial cost and the heavy discount from face value, which allows you to save a large initial outlay of funds. When the child goes to college, a $20,000 zero-coupon bond bought when the child was in preschool will pay for considerable tuition and room and board.

There is a new type of zero-coupon bond: a stripped municipal. These bonds try to offset some drawbacks of zero-coupon bonds. Large bond dealers have stripped interest payments from outstanding bonds. They are not callable and are backed by a pool of Treasury or federal agency securities to assure buyers that the bonds will not be called before the investor plans to receive the funds and that the money will be available at maturity.

The bond dealers strip a bond's semiannual interest coupons, each representing a fixed dollar amount payable at specified 6-month intervals. One stripped coupon bond develops into a whole series of zeros with staggered maturities at 6-month intervals.

The High/Low Spread

A senior family member can easily fall into a 33 percent marginal rate, although it appears on the surface that there is only a 13 percent difference between the 15 percent and 28 percent brackets. The 18 percent spread creates a much greater need for income splitting. For example, on a joint return filed after 1987 there is a 5 percent surtax on taxable income between $71,900 and $149,250 as the 15 percent rate is phased out.

A child may receive up to $500 in unearned income tax-free by using the standard deduction and another $500 taxable at the child's tax rate. If this under-age-14 child has $1,000 in unearned income and his parents are in the 28 percent bracket, the tax would be at 7.5 percent, creating a 20.5 percent spread instead of 13 percent.

If the child is 14 or older and has $1,500 in unearned income, the tax would be $150, or an average rate of 10 percent on the $1,500.

The Under-Age-14 Rules

Net unearned income means unearned income less $500 and the greater of (1) $500 standard deduction or $500 of itemized deductions and (2) the amount of allowable deductions directly connected with the production of income.

All net *unearned* income of a child under age 14 is taxed to the child at the top marginal rate of his parents.

Here are some examples:

1. The child has $480 of unearned income and no earned income; the standard deduction of $500 is applied to the child's unearned income, and he pays no tax.
2. The child has $950 unearned income and no earned income; a standard deduction of $500 is applied against the unearned income, so the net unearned income is $450. Because the net unearned income is less than $500, it is taxed at the child's rate.
3. The child has $1,300 unearned income and no earned income; a standard deduction of $500 is applied against the unearned income. Net unearned income is $750; the first $500 is taxed at the child's rate, and the other $250 is taxed at the parents' top tax rate.
4. The child has $300 of earned income and $1,200 of unearned income. Itemized deductions directly connected with the production of unearned income are

$400, and other deductions are $400. $500 is the maximum for deductions allowed against unearned income, so $500 of the $800 total deductions is allocated against the $1,200 unearned income. This leaves a net unearned income of $700, of which $500 is taxed at the child's rate, and $200 is taxed at the parents' rate.

5. The child has $700 earned income, $3,000 unearned income, and itemized deductions of $800 connected with production of unearned income, plus $200 other deductions. The entire $800 is applied against the unearned income, leaving a net unearned income of $2,200, of which $500 is taxed at the child's rate and $1,700 at the parents' top rate. The other $200 of deductions is allocated against his earned income, and the net earned income is taxed at the child's rate.

Incorporation

It may be advantageous for successful businessmen to incorporate, and even the smallest of corporations may benefit. Almost every self-employed person—plumber, artist, lawyer, writer—may be eligible to incorporate, save hard-earned dollars, and limit personal liability.

Among the many advantages of incorporation are:

1. *Medical reimbursement plans.* As a one-man or one-woman corporation, you can get tax-free medical benefits, with the corporation paying all the family medical and dental expenses.
2. *Tax-free dividends.* If a corporation invests in common stocks, 80 percent of all dividend income is tax-free.
3. *Group term life insurance.* The premiums for up to $50,000 in coverage are tax-free.
4. *Widow's/widower's award.* Up to $5,000 tax-free income goes to your spouse if you die.
5. *Disability insurance.* Premiums are tax-free.
6. *Limited liability.* Your corporation—not you personally—may be sued, and only to the extent of your investment in the business (except in the case of a professional corporation).

If you share your business profits and losses with someone else who works in the business (e.g., your spouse), it may be more desirable to file as a corporation than as a sole proprietorship. As a corporation, you will both be covered by Social Security. However, by operating as a sole proprietorship, you can reduce Social Security costs, since self-employment taxes are less than the FICA tax that must be paid by a corporation.

Operating a corporation can become expensive. There are franchise and legal fees, and the sheer volume of paperwork operating a corporation usually requires an accountant. Also, if you retain more than $250,000 in the corporation, you may be hit with an accumulated earnings penalty.

If you are incorporating an existing business, you must make certain changes in order to pass IRS scrutiny:

1. Your telephone listing and billing must be in the name of the corporation.
2. The corporate name must be added to all appropriate business signs and directories at your location.

3. All insurance policies must be revised to indicate the new corporate ownership.
4. Business cards must be printed with the name of the new corporation.
5. All stationery must reflect the new corporate name.
6. Suppliers must be notified of the name change.
7. All bank checking accounts must be altered to reflect the new corporate name.
8. Leases, if any, must be transferred to the corporation.
9. The board of directors must hold regular meetings on at least a quarterly basis.

Although professional one-man corporations offer considerable tax savings, the IRS will often dispute a professional's right to incorporate. In a recent case, a doctor incorporated his partnership and went through all the formalities (separate bank accounts, records, and minutes). Basically, he was performing the very same services for the corporation that he had for the partnership, with the exception that now he could build up a larger pension. According to the IRS, that purpose constituted tax avoidance—pure tax savings is not a sufficient reason to incorporate. The IRS capitalized on mistakes the doctor had made in incorporating his practice:

1. The taxpayer did not have a written partnership agreement acknowledging that the corporation was the new partner.
2. He failed to assign his interest in the partnership to the corporation.
3. There was neither an employment contract nor a covenant not to compete with the corporation.
4. He did not bother to endorse insurance policies to the corporation.
5. No new employees were added.
6. Although all the income of the corporation was not distributed to the doctor, the corporation made a sizable loan to him—probably the biggest mistake of all.

Individual Retirement Accounts

If you want to increase your retirement security, consider setting up an IRA to supplement Social Security and company pension plans. You may set aside and deduct a maximum of $2,000 per year plus an extra $250 for a nonworking spouse (or total earnings, if less than $2,000). No tax is paid on the income earned on the account until you withdraw the funds. You may not withdraw money from an IRA until you are 59½ years of age or become disabled, or you will be subject to a penalty tax. You must begin making withdrawals by age 70½; after that age contributions are not deductible.

Under the new law, if you are covered under a company plan, your IRA deduction may be limited. See page 132 for new limitations.

Interest Income

It is usually best to defer reporting bond interest if you think you may later be in a lower tax bracket. By deferring interest you also save the money you would have used to pay taxes now.

Interest credited to your savings and checking accounts generally has to be reported in the year of receipt; however, there are ways to defer interest to the next year. For example, if you buy a six-month certificate after June 30, you may be taxed on the interest when the certificate matures. If you buy Treasury bills, you will not be taxed until the year in which they mature.

The interest income on Series EE bonds is deferred until you cash the bond or until it matures, whichever comes first. Once you decide which way you will report the interest, you must continue reporting in that manner unless you get IRS permission to change. You can also defer income by swapping Series E for Series H bonds.

Intra-Family Loans

Under the old law, an older family member could lend a younger family member up to $10,000 interest-free, and the money could be used to buy a car, pay off a debt, or purchase other non-income-producing property.

Under the new tax law, intra-family loans are even more attractive. Because of the gradual repeal of the consumer interest deduction, the younger family member's after-tax cost of buying a big-ticket item will increase. An interest-free loan from the older family member may be used to offset the lost interest on an installment purchase.

An older family member in a lower (or zero) tax bracket may lend funds to a family member in a high bracket. The lending family member may incur less (or no) tax liability on the interest income received, and the borrower may be able to use the funds toward a great after-tax yield because of lower tax rates.

Investment Loss

Let us assume you hold some solid stocks bought at prices well above today's levels. Let us assume that you are in an income position in which it would be advantageous to take some of your paper losses for tax purposes. But like many of us, you are fairly confident that over the long term your stocks will eventually show a profit, and you do not want to get rid of these stocks at a loss. What can you do to get the benefit of the tax loss yet still keep the stock? There are a number of things that you may do, but you must take action before the end of the year.

What you may not do. You may not sell your stocks and buy back the identical securities within 30 days or less of the date of sale. This is referred to as a "wash sale," and the loss will be disallowed for tax purposes.

What you may do. You may buy back stocks in the same field, on the assumption that companies in equivalent positions in the same industry will move up or down with your stocks. You may also sell, wait the necessary 31 days, and repurchase the identical stock. You can only lose if your stock jumps in value during that period. You may also double up on your stocks for more than 30 days; after the waiting period, you can sell your original shares at a loss. You will not only avoid the "wash sale" rule; but, if your stock goes up in value during that time, you will have the benefit of both a tax loss and a paper profit.

Investments

Using IRAs to Save Taxes

Under the old tax law, there was no incentive to invest IRA funds in growth equities because the preferential treatment of capital gains would be lost (since IRA distributions would be taxed as ordinary income). Because of the repeal of the preferential capital gains treatment by Tax Reform, investing IRA funds in growth stocks is more attractive.

U.S. Government-Backed Securities

These are by far the safest investment vehicles available, and they are free of both state and local income taxes. Their yield varies with maturity.

Regardless of the maturity, the after-tax yield will increase due to the lower tax rates. If the yield on Treasuries is 6.95 percent before taxes, a taxpayer in the 28 percent bracket will receive an after-tax yield of 5 percent. Under the old law, a taxpayer in the 50 percent top tax bracket would receive a 3.475 percent yield.

Ginnie Maes

These mortgages are backed by the government and carry higher yields than Treasuries; however, Ginnie Maes are not exempt from state and local income taxes. If you assume a state income tax of 10 percent (net 7.2 percent after taxes at 28 percent), the net after-tax return is 6.156 percent.

The minimum investment in Ginnie Maes is $25,000, except for buying an interest in an older Ginnie Mae pool at a lower price (with the same yield) or buying into a mutual fund of Ginnie Maes. If interest rates decline, Ginnie Maes will appreciate (with some time lag due to risk that mortgagors will refinance if the interest reduction is large enough to warrant refinancing). If interest rates increase, the Ginnie Mae price will decline. Also, as the underlying mortgages are paid off, the investor receives a return of capital, depending on the turnover on the homes in the mortgage pool.

To protect yourself against the prepayment risk and/or a drop in yield of the Ginnie Maes, it may be wise to buy long-term zero-coupon Treasury bonds at the same time.

Series EE Bonds

Series EE bonds will continue to be popular due to the election provided to defer tax, but remember that the lower rates reduce the value of tax deferral. While Series EE bonds have a variable rate (geared to interest changes with a guaranteed floor) top yields must be held for a period of at least 5 years. Also, investments are limited to face amount of $30,000 (issue amount $15,000) per calendar year. Spouses could invest individually up to $30,000 each, or in co-ownership up to $60,000 in one year.

If you want to maximize safety, Treasuries and other government-backed securities may be the best bet.

Zero-Coupon Bonds

Zero-coupon bonds have been an effective way to lock in favorable interest rates for the term of the bond. Compare this with coupon bonds with which the investor could not be assured of investing the coupon proceeds at favorable rates. But, on the realistic side, who would want to lock in today's interest rates?

Interest income on zeroes is imputed to the owner annually, so an investor may incur tax liability without receiving any money. Under the old tax law, zero-coupon bonds were of prime use only when held by a tax-exempt entity (e.g., an IRA) or when the holder could use a personal exemption or zero bracket to shelter tax.

Under the new tax law, there is one major difference. When the holder is a minor (who may be claimed as a dependent on someone else's return), he does not get to use the personal exemption to shelter tax on unearned income. Instead, he or she can use

$500 of his or her standard deduction against unearned income. If the child is under 14 years of age, unearned income over $1,000 will be taxed at the parents' rate, and $500 will be taxable at the child's rate. Assuming a 15 percent tax rate for the child, there would be a tax of $75 on the imputed zero-bond income that is never seen.

A new kind of tax-exempt zero is being offered due to Tax Reform. The interest yield would normally be much lower than with a taxable zero. Buyers of taxable zeroes for minors before Tax Reform hoping to escape tax may now wish they had not acted so quickly.

Tax-Free Bonds

Tax Reform's lower rates also lower the value of the tax exemption provided by tax-free bonds. A tax-exempt yield of 7 percent is the same as a taxable yield of 14 percent to a taxpayer in the 50 percent bracket, but it is only the equivalent of a 9.72 percent after-tax yield to a taxpayer in the 28 percent bracket. If the investor is a resident of the state issuing the bonds, the 7 percent yield may be increased through exemption from state and local income taxes. You can no longer buy bonds below par and enjoy favorable capital gains treatment on the appreciation on bonds issued before July 18, 1984.

You could find yourself in a marginal rate of more than 50 percent if you fall into the 18 percent bracket, so you may be affected by 3 phase-outs: (1) the 15 percent rate, (2) personal exemptions, and (3) the $25,000 rental real estate exception from passive-loss restrictions. At the 50 percent bracket, a tax-exempt yield of 7 percent would be the equivalent of a 14 percent taxable yield.

Tax Reform has placed limitations on the ability of municipalities to issue private-purpose tax-exempt bonds. Reducing the supply of bonds could up the price and thus reduce the yield. Issuers may have to offer higher yields to induce investment because of lower tax rates reducing the value of tax exemption. The new top rates of 28 percent (or 33 percent) will not cover the costs of state taxes as much as the old 50 percent rate.

Most other tax shelters are severely restricted by Tax Reform, so this should increase investor demand for tax exempts, which may keep yields in check. Increased demand may increase the prospect of capital appreciation on bonds. With all the uncertainties, states and municipalities are waiting to see how reform affects the demand for their bonds.

Many states' income taxes are geared to federal law, in particular to adjusted gross income. Some admit that without a change in state law the state will enjoy a windfall, reducing pressures for issuing tax exempts to finance capital needs.

Many factors are involved in picking the type of tax exempts for investment: bills; short-term, intermediate, or long-term bonds; and the revenues pledged for payment. If an investor feels that interest rates and inflation will increase, he won't want to commit himself to long-term bonds because their value will decline if interest rates and inflation rise.

An investor must be concerned with the credit-worthiness of the bond insurer, so check out his credit rating. Also, take into consideration the prospect of future increases in the top federal tax rate. Although the value of the yield would increase, if higher tax rates are due to increased government deficits and inflation, any gain might be offset by other factors.

Minimum Tax and Tax Exempts

Under Tax Reform, the interest on private-purpose tax exempts is a preference item subject to the new 21 percent alternative minimum tax.

Short-Term Tax Exempts

Short-term investment in tax exempts may be appealing in light of two factors: (1) the uncertainty about Tax Reform, including whether federal and state top income tax rates will be adjusted soon; (2) the federal top tax rate for 1987 of 38.5 percent may make owning municipals a way to get high after-tax yields.

It's important to use a balanced approach to investments: Put some of your portfolio into equities, some in fixed debt, some in CDs and money-market funds, some into real estate, some into convertibles, some into government-backed securities, and some in life insurance and annuities. You may even want to invest in mutual funds or use put and call options. Since Tax Reform's results are still uncertain, this balanced approach is definitely best.

Job Hunting

You can deduct job-hunting expenses if you went job hunting in the same line of work, even if you did not get a new job; be sure to keep accurate records. Deductible costs include preparing, printing, and mailing résumés, travel expenses, and nonreimbursed fees paid to an employment agency. However, if you are looking for your first job, no expenses are deductible. Beginning in 1987, job-hunting expenses must exceed 2 percent of AGI to be deductible.

Loan Service Charges

Loan service charges (those charged by a bank or lender in the purchase of a principal residence—frequently called points) are deductible only if you receive the full amount of principal and pay the fee to the lender immediately. The loan fee is deductible as interest all in one year. If the loan fee is deducted from the loan itself, however, you must write off the fee over the life of the loan. You will get no immediate deduction.

If you are self-employed and have a loss in an unincorporated business or from a tax shelter, you may carry the excess loss back 3 years, then forward 15 years, until you have used it up completely. By carrying a loss back to the early year, you reduce your income for that year and are due a refund. Carrying a loss to a future year reduces income for that year. Determine whether it is to your advantage to carry a loss forward or back. If you are concerned that you might be audited for past years, you will want to carry the loss forward rather than first carrying it back. Once you decide which direction to go in, keep in mind that your decision is irrevocable.

If you want to carry back a loss, file Form 1045. This form is filed separately (it is not attached to your return) and must be filed not more than 12 months after the end of the tax year. The IRS will usually allow or reject your claim within 90 days of the filing.

Marriage vs. Living Together

As always, a two-earner couple living together without benefit of marriage will pay more taxes if they get married. In fact, under Tax Reform, it's worse: the $3,000 married worker deduction is gone. The two-bracket system (as opposed to the previous 11 brackets) should help some, but marrieds are severely hurt under Tax Reform. The bottom line: an increase of several thousand dollars in taxable income.

1. *Personal exemptions.* In 1988, personal exemptions will be $1,950, phased out for singles with an adjusted gross income above $89,560 and for marrieds above $149,250. (Two singles come out better than one couple by $29,870.)
2. *Standard deduction.* In 1988, the standard deduction will be $3,000 for singles and $5,000 for a married couple, a difference of $1,000.
3. *Passive losses.* There is a $25,000 maximum on losses from real estate activities in which there is active participation. The maximum in losses is the same for singles and marrieds, and it begins phasing out when income exceeds $100,000. Because the $25,000 maximum is the same for singles and marrieds, singles fare much better (by $25,000).
4. *IRAs.* If one spouse is an active participant in a qualified pension or profit-sharing plan, IRA contributions will be phased out for *both* spouses if AGI is over $40,000 and phased out entirely if income is over $50,000.

    For singles, the phase-out on IRA deductions begins at $25,000 and is completely phased out at $35,000. Singles living together would have a $50,000 to $70,000 IRA phase-out and come out better off tax-wise than marrieds.

Medical Expenses

In order to get a medical deduction, you must be able to identify the medical nature of a particular expense. For example, the cost of sending a physically handicapped person to a special school to improve his condition is deductible as a medical expense, but, in sending a problem child to a private school, you may deduct only the money charged specifically for psychological care. Ask the school to break down their charges to enable you to clearly identify which costs are of a medical nature.

Nurses' wages are deductible, including any payroll tax paid, but if the nurse also performed domestic duties, you are permitted to deduct only the portion of pay for medical services.

The cost of a nursing/convalescent home for a patient confined for a medical reason is deductible. The patient must have gone to the home on the advice of a doctor. In addition, the treatment must have a direct effect on the patient's condition, and the patient must be there for a specific ailment, not just generally poor health. If the patient is receiving general medical and nursing care (but not in connection with a specific ailment), have the home break down the charges so that you can claim everything as a medical expense with the exception of meals and lodging costs.

If you add special equipment or facilities to your home (due to a specific ailment), you may deduct the full cost of the special equipment only to the extent that it does not increase the value of your property. You must exceed 7.5 percent of AGI to deduct medical expenses.

Some Unusual Medical Tax Tips

- Telephone calls to your physician are tax deductible. A taxpayer had been under psychiatric care for 11 years and had sessions with her therapist via long-distance telephone calls. Since the calls were for the purpose of treating an illness, they were tax-deductible.

• Pay year-end medical expenses by credit card. The deduction is incurred when the charge is made.

• The cost of belonging to a computer data bank was deductible in a case where the bank was providing storage of personal medical information.

• A weight-loss program is deductible when prescribed by a doctor for a specific illness, such as obesity, emphysema, or hypertension, not just for losing weight.

• The added cost of salt-free products is deductible when such a diet is prescribed by a physician.

• Medical expenses incurred in a foreign country are deductible (as well as the costs of transportation if medical care was the reason for the trip).

• If a doctor recommends travel to a warm climate for an asthmatic, the cost may be deductible.

• All transportation expenses incurred by a kidney donor are tax deductible.

• A trip to Florida for a postoperative coronary patient is deductible.

• In a recent case, the courts permitted a tax deduction for the travel expenses of a wife who accompanied her husband on sales trips on his doctor's advice. The husband was a diabetic who had a heart condition, and the wife had been instructed on what to do in case of emergency. In another case, a mother was allowed to deduct travel expenses of accompanying her daughter to get medical care.

• Payments made to a baby-sitter to enable a woman to visit her sick husband in the hospital were not deductible.

• The cost of traveling to Alcoholics Anonymous meetings was deductible when attendance was prescribed by a doctor.

• A father was allowed to deduct the costs of driving his wheelchair-bound daughter to and from high school on a doctor's orders.

• School tuition may qualify as a medical expense. Parents paid for an extra program designed to help their children overcome their learning disabilities. Although the cost of the basic tuition was not deductible, the deduction for the extra program was permitted.

• The cost of prepaid lifetime care for the handicapped is tax deductible, even though the fee covers food and personal care.

• Legal fees necessary to authorize medical treatment for the mentally ill are deductible as medical expenses.

• An orthodontist suggested the clarinet as therapy for a child with a severe overbite; the cost of the instrument and the lessons were deductible.

• A dentist prescribed a device to add fluoride to home water; the cost of the unit was deductible.

• The cost of special filters to purify drinking water, ionizers to purify the air, and special air conditioning filters are tax deductible if prescribed by a doctor.

- The extra cost of a specially designed auto to accommodate wheelchairs, or one equipped with special hand controls, is deductible for the physically handicapped.

- The cost of a special reclining chair is deductible for a person suffering from a heart condition if it was prescribed by a doctor.

- The cost of a home elevator was deductible for a taxpayer who had a heart condition—but only to the extent that the cost did not increase the value of the property.

- The cost of special plumbing fixtures in a rented house is deductible for a handicapped person.

- A taxpayer, on the advice of his allergist, replaced the shingles on his house with wood to reduce contact with mold. The replacement was tax deductible—to the extent his cost exceeded the increase in the value to the home.

- The cost of new house siding for a taxpayer allergic to mold was deductible.

- The operating expenses of a home swimming pool, including repairs and chemicals, were tax deductible to a taxpayer with a pulmonary problem ordered by his physician to swim daily.

- The cost of a specially designed swimming pool as therapy for a polio patient was deductible.

- Swimming pool fees were deductible for an arthritic patient whose doctor prescribed swimming as therapy.

- The cost of a health spa installed in a home under doctor's orders was deductible for an arthritic.

- Health club fees, prescribed by a physician, qualify as a tax writeoff if related to a specific illness.

- Sorry, dancing lessons are not deductible. A taxpayer suffered from arthritis and nervous tension, and the doctor recommended dancing. Unfortunately, the IRS danced to a different drummer.

- Marital counseling fees, including sex clinics, are deductible. However, in a recent case, the couple was advised to stay at a nearby hotel to "work on their problems" because there was no room at the clinic. The expense of meals and lodging was not deductible, since the hotel was not engaged in providing medical care and their room was not specially furnished.

- Although the cost of psychiatric care is deductible, the cost of deprogramming a person by nonmedical personnel is not deductible.

- The costs of buying and training a dog for the hearing impaired were deductible. The dog was trained to listen to the phone ringing and to alert the taxpayer to any dangerous sounds. There was a similar case involving a cat.

- Special TV sets that print words on the screen (or adapters that do the same to existing sets) are deductible for the hard of hearing.

- A woman was afflicted with a disease which in a few years caused her to lose all her hair. The doctor decided that her mental health was at stake and prescribed a hairpiece. The cost of the wig was tax deductible. However, you may not deduct hairpieces purchased for cosmetic reasons only.

- The cost of a face-lift is deductible, even if a doctor does not suggest the surgery. The cost of all hair transplants and cosmetic surgery may therefore be deductible, but not the cost of removing facial hair. According to the IRS, a face-lift is an extensive operation requiring a surgeon; hair removal is performed in a hair-removal center by a technician with little or no training.

- *Special Schooling as a Medical Expense:* A taxpayer had two children who had language learning disabilities. He claimed a medical deduction for the extra cost of a language development program at a special school, even though it was not recommended by a doctor and there were no psychiatrists or psychologists on the staff.

The Tax Court ruled that the doctor's recommendation was not necessary to gain the deduction, since the learning disabilities were real, and the school's teachers had been trained to deal with the problems.

Medical Reimbursement Plan

If your adjusted gross income is high, you probably will not incur enough medical expenses to top 7.5 percent and will lose your writeoff; but if you have your own business, you can have family medical expenses paid directly by the company through a medical reimbursement plan. To qualify, a medical reimbursement plan must be in writing and nondiscriminatory to all employees.

A medical reimbursement plan may include tax-free payments for any permanent disfigurement or loss of a body part. Payments may be based on the type of injury or length of time out of work.

Miscellaneous Deductions

Miscellaneous deductions are allowed only to the extent that they exceed (in total) a floor of 2 percent of adjusted gross income. This includes professional and union dues, subscriptions to professional journals, employment agency fees, safe deposit rental, investment counsel fees, employment-related education, even the cost of tax preparation—all formerly claimed as miscellaneous deductions separately that must now total an amount that exceeds 2 percent of AGI. The only exceptions are (1) estate tax in case of income in respect of a decedent, (2) the deduction in which a taxpayer restores certain amounts held under a claim of right, and (3) gambling loss deductions (to the extent of winnings only).

Employee travel and transportation expenses and expenses of outside salespersons are allowed only as itemized deductions (and are included in the 2 percent floor).

These changes are supposed to save the taxpayer time, trouble, and the expense of keeping detailed records unless he or she thinks they will exceed the 2 percent floor, thus relieving the IRS of time-consuming audits. Although the changes were made in the name of simplicity, the bottom line is that the changes will increase tax collections by an estimated $23 billion through 1991.

If you are involved in the production (or collection) of income or the management of income-producing property, try to convert this income into a trade or business activity and report your income and expenses on Schedule C.

The IRS has defined a trade or business as an activity in which a profit motive is present and in which there is some economic activity—e.g., regular activities and transactions as well as production of income.

Converting other income to Schedule C would place the taxpayer in the position of having self-employment income, which permits a Keogh plan and some fringe benefits. However, on the negative side, you may be subject to self-employment tax.

Passive Income

Since Tax Reform limits the deduction of your losses from tax shelters, invest in activities that will produce passive income to offset those losses. Income and losses from all passive activities are combined.

If you have losses from previous tax shelter investments, new limited partnerships (which produce current income) may be a good idea to offset these losses. Consider investing in a general partnership of an S corporation that is currently showing a profit. You need not actively participate in order to claim passive income.

Passive Losses

When an individual actively participates in rental real estate, up to $25,000 of losses may be claimed against nonpassive income. However, this amount is phased out between $100,000 and $150,000 of adjusted gross income, without taking into account passive losses, taxable Social Security income, or IRA contributions. Thus it may be fairly easy to qualify under the active participation rules and get around the new passive-loss restrictions.

The $25,000 maximum loss is applied by first netting the income and loss from all rental real estate activities in which the taxpayer actively participates. If there is a net loss for the year, net passive income from other activities is then applied against it, determining the amount that will be eligible for the $25,000 allowance.

Record-Keeping

Keep bills that pertain to the production of income, such as commissions, rental for a safe deposit box, maintenance costs of property out of town, travel expenses to the property, and taxes and accounting fees. These are all deductible as investment expenses.

Be especially careful to keep full records for rental property: rents received, bills paid for utilities, repairs, taxes, salaries to janitors, legal fees for evictions, insurance premiums, and interest charges.

See page 127 for details of record keeping requirements for autos.

Here are some tips for keeping accurate, detailed records that will save you the most money at tax time.

1. Keep a daily diary for general items such as medical and charitable expenses and interest.
2. Keep separate special diaries for detailed expenses such as job-hunting or freelance business activities.
3. Keep expenses in separate envelopes or file folders. For infrequent expenses, a number 10 (business-size) envelope is usually enough for the entire year's receipts.

4. To document entertainment expenses, use a separate envelope for each occasion, putting the date and other information on the outside of the envelope.
5. Total each diary monthly, and you'll know where you stand as the year progresses. Keeping these running totals will also make it easier to fill out your return. Try to attach adding machine tapes to your diary whenever possible.

Refund Claims

File a refund claim for income taxes within 3 years from the time a return was filed or within 2 years from the time the tax was paid, whichever is later. (If you filed before April 15, that will be your filing date; if you filed for an extension, the actual date of filing is used.) If there are questionable items on your return, consider waiting until shortly before the statute of limitations is to expire to file your refund claim. This will limit any potential IRS assessment to the amount of your refund claim instead of your entire return. A separate claim for each year for which you are claiming a refund must be filed. Look over your return carefully; the IRS may choose to audit, and errors may end up costing you additional tax. Your maximum refund will be the amount of tax paid within the 3-year period (plus extensions) just before the refund claim or, if the claim is filed after the 3-year period, the amount of tax paid within the 2-year period just before filing the refund claim.

Form 1040X for individuals (Form 1120X for corporations) is the form used for filing refund claims. Be sure to adequately support your reasons for requesting the refund, including all the facts supporting the claim. If your claim for refund ever becomes a court case, only the grounds you have stated in filing the refund claim will be admitted as evidence; no others will be allowed.

Retirement Planning

Many taxpayers are concerned with the $200,000 compensation limit that now applies to all plans. Employers may choose to reduce benefit levels because benefits for highly paid employees will be reached with a lower percentage benefit for lower-paid workers. For example, an employee earning $200,000 may contribute only 3.5 percent of compensation to a salary reduction 401(k) plan before reaching the $7,000 maximum. For a higher-paid employee, the maximum plan contribution would require even a lower percentage of compensation. Since there will be no incentive for an employer to give the average worker a larger percentage retirement benefit than a highly paid executive, the lowered maximum benefit at the top will reduce the retirement benefits on the lower-paid workers.

Even though retirement plan contribution limits for elective deferrals under a 401(k) plan have been reduced from $30,000 to $7,000, this plan is still attractive. 401(k) contributions are excluded from current income and can be withdrawn in the event of hardship (before age 59½) without being subject to the 10 percent premature withdrawal penalty. In addition, making elective deferrals under cash and deferred plans does not prevent the use of nondeductible IRA contributions.

Tax on Distributions from Qualified Plans

The 10 percent premature withdrawal penalty for withdrawals prior to age 59½ (not due to death or disability or covered by an exception) now applies to distributions from qualified plans and covers distributions after 1986. One exception is the hardship withdrawal in a cash or deferred plan.

Other exceptions include (1) equal payments for life after separation from service, (2) early retirement at age 55, (3) distributions for medical expenses, (4) post-death distributions, and (5) certain employee stock ownership plan distributions.

Employees who frequently change jobs and cash in their pension benefits, agreeing to pay tax currently, may not take advantage of any of the exceptions.

Beginning January 1, 1989, all distributions from qualified plans must start no later than April 1 following the year in which the taxpayer becomes age 70½, regardless of when employment ceases. There is a new 50 percent penalty on the taxpayer required to take the distribution on the difference between amounts distributed and the amount *required* to be distributed, if greater. You can reduce distributions by using contingent beneficiaries and annually readjusting distributions based on life expectancy.

No More 10-Year Averaging

The 10-year averaging method has been replaced by 5-year averaging. Only one election to use 5-year averaging may be made with respect to a single lump-sum distribution after age 59½; however, if a taxpayer was age 50 on January 1, 1986, he or she may choose between 5-year or 10-year averaging.

Another change is the phase-out of capital gain treatment with respect to the pre-1974 portion of a lump-sum distribution; however, if the taxpayer was age 50 on January 1, 1986, he or she is exempt from this new provision. Others are bound by the phase-out of the capital gain treatment over a 6-year period beginning January 1, 1987.

Loans from Qualified Plans

The old tax law provided for borrowing the greater of $10,000 or 50 percent of accrued benefits in a qualified plan, not to exceed $50,000. Payback periods were limited to 5 years unless the loan was in connection with the purchase or improvement of a residence to be lived in by the participant or certain immediate family members.

Beginning December 31, 1986, the $50,000 loan ceiling is reduced by the participant's highest outstanding loan balance during the preceding loan period. The payback period over 5 years applies only to the purchase of a residence for the plan participant, not for home improvement loans for the taxpayer or for other family members.

Individual Retirement Accounts

There is still a tax deferral on IRA earnings, which offers an opportunity to build up retirement funds tax-free. The new tax law allows a $2,000 IRA deduction for taxpayers not covered by a qualified plan. For those who are covered by a qualified plan, the IRA deduction is phased out between $40,000 and $50,000 adjusted gross income on a joint return, and $25,000 to $35,000 for singles. Even if only one spouse is covered by a pension plan, the phase-out applies to both if the combined income exceeds $40,000.

The new 5-year averaging (and phase-out of preferential treatment for pre-1974 capital gains) makes IRA rollovers attractive to taxpayers who want to defer tax until the year after they become 70½ years of age—when distributions must begin.

Distributions from qualified pension or profit-sharing plans not covered by 5-year averaging (or the phase-out rule) will be taxed as ordinary income, and funds withdrawn from IRAs will be taxed as ordinary income. With a rollover, qualified plan distributions will continue to earn tax-deferred interest. Because of the 10 percent additional tax on early withdrawals, more of the distributions may be rolled over into IRAs to avoid the 10 percent penalty.

The owner of an IRA should not expect to be able to make tax-free withdrawals up to the amount of his nondeductible contributions. Withdrawals from an IRA will be taxable on a pro rata basis, taking into account the ratio of the nondeductible contributions to the entire amount in the IRA account.

Example

Nondeductible contributions over 6 years total $12,000, and earnings on the IRA equal $8,000, totaling $20,000 in the account. Withdraw $2,000, and $1,200 will be tax-free, with $800 taxable as ordinary income.

However, if the taxpayer also has $36,000 in a deductible IRA, for a total of $48,000 in both IRAs, and withdraws $1,000 from the nondeductible IRA, only one-fourth ($250) would be considered as coming from the nondeductible IRA; the balance of $750 would be presumed coming from the deductible IRA. $750 would be taxable as ordinary income, and only $250 would be considered tax-free. In the final analysis, the larger the deductible IRA is in relation to the nondeductible IRA, the greater the amount of withdrawal subject to tax.

If you continue thinking of your IRAs as a bank from which you can make constant withdrawals *at any time without penalty* after age 59½, you will be disappointed. If you have other funds to use, the nondeductible IRA contributions will come back tax-free. If you have a *deductible* IRA, be prepared to pay tax on withdrawals; but the *nondeductible* IRA as an additional source of tax-free income is still a viable savings plan.

Spousal IRAs

If you are not an active participant in a qualified plan (or if your joint income is less than $40,000) you can fund a spousal IRA of up to $250 for your nonworking spouse. The new tax law also permits your spouse to be treated as not having compensation, whereas the old law prevented the spousal IRA if the spouse had earned any compensation.

Company Retirement Plans

There are 2 basic methods of receiving benefits from your company's retirement plan:

1. Annuities—usually monthly payouts for the rest of your life
2. Lump sum—a lump-sum, one-time payout of all or part of your account balance.

Annuity payouts are fully taxed. Payments must start by April 1 of the year you reach age 70½, but not if you are still working and not if you own 5 percent or more of the firm. Beginning in 1989, however, age 70½ applies even if you are still employed.

Lump-sum payments may be rolled over to an IRA or other qualified plan in order to take advantage of tax deferral, or you may use 5-year averaging and get tax savings.

Rollovers. Partial payouts before age 59½ do not qualify if you stay on the job. At least one-half of your balance must be paid to you, and the part not rolled over is taxed as regular income. Rolling over the entire distribution may be done at any age.

Five-year averaging. This can be used for lump-sum distributions received within one year due to death, disability, leaving your job, or turning age 59½. Five-year averaging may not be elected unless you are age 59½ or were born prior to 1936. It can be done only once.

Limited capital gains. If you had coverage before 1974, this break is available. The top rate for payouts on contributions before 1974 is 28 percent. This is phased out, and none is allowed in 1991.

On withdrawals before age 59½, a penalty of 10 percent is added to the portion of the lump sum added to income. This applies only if you are on the job—not in cases of disability or death, or rollovers to IRAs, or if you are at least age 55 in the year you leave the job. Also, if the penalty is due to divorce or medical expenses, it does not apply.

On annual pension payouts of more than $150,000 or lump-sum payouts over $750,000, there is a 15 percent extra tax.

Taxpayers born prior to 1936 can use 10-year averaging at 1986 tax rates, but they cannot use 5-year averaging later. A 20 percent rate applies to capital gains.

Plan your pension and profit-sharing payouts; don't wait until the 60 days for making a rollover have started. If you revoke an IRA rollover and use 5-year averaging or capital gain instead, the lump sum is taxed as ordinary income.

IRA rollovers are flexible; you can put a lump sum from one employer's plan into an IRA, later move it to another plan if it accepts rollover funds. If it is later paid to you by lump sum, it qualifies as 5-year averaging.

Don't combine rollover IRAs with those funded by annual pay-ins, or you cannot later move the rolled-over portion to another plan.

Inherited IRAs

If the decedent had already started receiving payouts, the heirs cannot change unless to speed up schedule of payouts. If payouts had not started, widowed spouse can delay payouts until the decedent would have been age 70½.

If payouts begin within a year of the decedent's death, the payments may be spread over the life expectancy of the beneficiary. Otherwise, payments must be made in full within 5 years of death.

Salary Reduction Plans

If you are given the opportunity by your employer to participate in a 401(k) deferred-pay plan, you may benefit from substantial tax savings. To participate in the plan, you must agree to take a salary cut or forgo a raise, and an equal amount is placed in a trust account for your benefit. This amount is contributed by your employer; you don't have to report it on your taxes, and the income accumulates in the trust tax-free.

Sale of Residence

In order to defer tax on the sale of your home, you must keep accurate records of your costs. In addition to recording the original purchase price and costs paid at purchase time, be sure to list major improvements like room additions, central air conditioning, and landscaping. If you have sustained a casualty loss due to damage, deduct any loss in arriving at a tax basis. You need not increase your cost by any energy credits you may have claimed.

To properly report or defer your gain, you will need a sales contract showing sales price, statement of settlement costs at closing, amount of taxes and fire insurance, legal fees, broker's commission, a closing statement from the bank (showing all prorations and prepayment penalties), cost of improvements, and the charges for advertising your home for sale. In buying a replacement home, you will need the very same items; and if you have deferred the tax, you will need to reflect both the buying and selling costs on your return.

If you are over 55 and sell your home at a profit, it is not advisable to use up your one-time $125,000 exclusion; defer it for future use if there is the possibility you may sell this new home later and not replace it.

The $125,000 exclusion applies only once per couple, and each spouse does not have a separate exclusion. If you are single and about to marry someone who has already used the $125,000 exclusion, seriously consider selling before getting married. After marriage, you will be stopped from using your exclusion since your spouse has already done so; the IRS will look at your marital status as of the date of the sale.

Savings Bonds

Buy United States savings bonds for your child's future education, naming the child as the sole owner. File a tax return for the child each year and let the IRS know that the child is reporting the income. The child gets the savings bond earnings tax-free (only to the extent of his or her personal exemption) and can use the appreciated value to help pay for a future college education.

Single-Premium Life Insurance as a Tax Shelter

There are several advantages to owning single-premium life insurance; i.e., when you die, a tax-free death benefit is paid to your beneficiary. In fact, single-premium life insurance is one of the best tax-sheltered investments available.

If you need more life insurance and are considering an income-generating investment for retirement, consider buying single-premium life insurance for these reasons:

1. Your initial investment (single-premium payment) accumulates tax-free interest.
2. Since borrowing is not considered a taxable event, you can borrow against the policy for tax-free income.
3. When you die, your beneficiary receives life insurance proceeds as nontaxable income. You can set up the policy so that your spouse can continue to receive tax-free income over his or her lifetime.
4. Borrowed amounts are not included in calculations that tax up to half your Social Security benefits, as compared to earnings from tax-free municipal bonds.
5. The purchase of a single-premium policy and your borrowing are not reported to the IRS, and so there is no audit risk unless you *terminate* the policy.

Here's how it works: There's usually a minimum single-premium payment, say $10,000. Since there are no up-front fees, all your money starts earning tax-free interest immediately. Your life insurance coverage is a multiple of the policy's cash value and decreases as you get older; i.e.; if you are 40 years old, the coverage must be at least 600 percent of cash value; if you are 55, it must be at least 300 percent.

Borrowing from the Single-Premium Policy

If you invest a $10,000 initial payment earning 10 percent, you can borrow up to $1,000 a year and pay no tax on the proceeds. The interest charged is usually at the same rate as the interest earned, so you break even.

You must view the purchase of a single-premium life insurance policy as a lifetime investment to be passed on to your beneficiaries. If you terminate the policy, you will pay tax on the accumulated earnings at your highest rate. If you borrowed $1,000 a year for 20 years and terminated the policy, the IRS would tax you on $20,000 of previously untaxed earnings.

If you cash in your policy within 3 to 6 years of purchase, you will pay early-surrender penalties (usually 6 to 7 percent of interest earned).

If you borrow against the principal instead of the interest, you may not break even. You might be charged 7 percent on your loan but be paid only 4 percent on interest earned.

The issuing company of any single-premium policy should have a strong relationship with a major carrier and should be rated A+. The best policies are those in which future interest rates are geared to an outside index; e.g., 20-year T-bills, over which the insurance company has no control.

Tax Planning under Tax Reform

Tax Reform was supposed to be simple: eliminate deductions, reduce rates, tax more of our income, and tax it at lower rates. But it isn't simple at all.

In order to reach your financial goals, you have to increase your pretaxed income and reduce the taxes on that income.

Rates are lowered from 50 percent top rate in 1986 to 38.5 percent in 1987, dropping to 28 percent (or 33 percent) in 1988. Although we have among the lowest tax rates in the world, a number of experts feel that the best strategy is just to earn as much money as you can and pay the 28 percent tax.

Even with new restrictions under Tax Reform, real estate is considered by many to be a good investment. Although Tax Reform has increased the number of years over which you can depreciate real estate and has limited deductions to the amount for which you are at-risk (cash invested plus any debt for which you are personally liable), real estate generally continues to appreciate.

Rather than invest in a limited partnership, consider investing directly in real estate. Buy a house in a stable neighborhood and rent it out. Under the new law this is considered a passive activity. However, if your income is less than $100,000 and you actively participate in operating and managing rental real estate, you can deduct up to $25,000 of any net loss against your other income. To be actively participating, you must make management decisions, such as approving repairs and checking out prospective tenants. The $25,000 loss deduction is phased out between $100,000 and $150,000 AGI. If you owned the real estate prior to passage of the Tax Reform Act, you may deduct a decreasing share of any loss through 1990, no matter what your income bracket.

One of the best ways to end up with more money is to defer taxes. You can earn something on the money that IRS would have had and pay later with cheaper dollars. Since tax rates will drop in 1988, deferral makes even better sense in 1987.

The best choice may be a qualified retirement plan at work if it allows you to deduct the money you pay into it. Another good opportunity to defer taxes is to give money to a child under age 14. The first $500 of his or her unearned income is tax-free, and the next $500 is taxed at the child's rate.

Treasury bills, life insurance, U.S. Savings Bonds, and growth stocks offer a chance to defer income until the child reaches age 14 and pays income tax at his or her own rate.

Accelerating deductions produces the same effect as deferring income. Rates are dropping, and deductions are worth less when rates are low. If you are making an annual contribution to a charity for the next 5 years, think about making it all this year.

Although there's a 28 percent (or 33 percent) top rate for 1988, don't bet that these rates will hold up for the years after 1988. After the 1988 elections, Congress is going to be tempted to raise tax rates once again.

Life insurance is still a viable tax shelter. There is no tax on the investment buildup in the policy unless you cash it in during your lifetime; when your beneficiaries cash it in after your death, there will be no income tax to pay.

Consider purchasing a variable policy: You get a market rate of return, can borrow against the cash value tax-free, and the interest paid on the loan is partially offset by the interest earned on the policy.

The best idea may be the single-premium life insurance policy. You pay a single large sum (providing death protection and tax-deferred earnings immediately) instead of making periodic payments.

Don't buy single premium just as an investment, but only if you need the death protection. If you do buy insurance, plan to hold it for 5 years or more so you won't be charged for early policy surrender.

With the deduction for consumer interest (including policy loan interest) phasing out and with tax rates down, the cost of these policies is going up. Single-premium life also remains vulnerable to further tax change. Congress may even levy a tax on the investment buildup of all life insurance products.

Keep using your IRA to the maximum. Save as much as you can for retirement and forget taxes.

The maximum contribution for 401(k) plans has dropped from $30,000 to $7,000, but this is still a popular way to save for retirement. The $7,000 is tax deductible and tax-deferred. Middle-income taxpayers still like the 401(k) plans, and higher-paid executives and small-business owners are using nonqualified plans that defer part of their pay and often provide some form of life insurance.

The Tax Reform Act provides for a new 15 percent excise tax on large pension distributions (more than $150,000 a year or $750,000 lump sum). This new excise adds to income and estate taxes. This rule does not apply to money you had in your pension plan on August 1, 1986, or to any distributions you roll over into an IRA, or to any nondeductible contributions you make to your pension plan.

It's becoming a popular idea to use home mortgage loans to purchase items such as a car. Be careful how you do this. You may be paying interest long after the car is worn out, or you may even end up losing your home over a simple car loan.

Interest is deductible on investment debts only up to the amount of net investment income. The $10,000 allowance above net investment income that the old law provided will be phased out by 1990.

Consider borrowing against the margin account you have with your stockbroker, but be careful about spending the proceeds on consumer items. Many experts suggest using the cheapest source of credit you have at your disposal, especially if it is a deductible source. Your margin account charges may be 10 points less than your credit card.

Capital gains will be taxed as ordinary income after 1987, with a top rate of 33 percent. Consider taking long-term gains this year and postponing short-term gains until next year, but only if you do not expect a change in the market to offset this tax advantage.

Tax-Free Bonds

Yields on tax-exempt municipal bonds are expected to range between 85 percent and 100 percent of yields on long-term Treasury bonds. As these bonds become more popular, the price will go up and the return will go down.

If you plan to buy municipal bonds for a child, look at private-purpose municipals issued to finance multi-family housing and airports. These bonds currently yield about a point more than ordinary public-purpose municipals because interest on them is a preference item under the alternative minimum tax. If your child is not subject to the alternative minimum tax, these bonds are worth looking into.

Tax-Sheltered Investments

Tax shelters are not dead, but they have changed considerably. Lower tax rates will not eliminate the need for sheltering income. For example: under the old tax law, with a top tax rate of 50 percent, a tax-shelter writeoff of $1 costs the investor 50 cents after taxes. With a new maximum tax rate of 28 percent, the same investment will cost 72 cents net.

Consider profits. Assume a new top tax rate of 40 percent (including state and local taxes plus the effects of various phase-outs). With a 40 percent rate, $1 of income to the investor leaves 60 cents profit; if the $1 is tax-sheltered, the investor keeps the entire dollar. The extra 40 percent is still a strong enough incentive to seek out tax shelters. The degree of risk, personal needs, and other factors have to be taken into account. Individual investors will still need quality tax shelters. As a matter of fact, the number of closely held corporations seeking tax-sheltered investments may increase due to tax rate changes in combination with other tax-shelter provisions.

Some of the many changes in the new Tax Reform Act that were designed to kill tax shelters follow:

At-Risk Rules

The at-risk rules generally limit an investor's deductions (in an activity) to the amount the investor had at risk in the activity. Tax Reform now includes real estate investments in the at-risk rules.

Some nonrecourse financing still may qualify as at-risk, if the financing is by a person actively engaged in the business of lending who (1) is not the person from whom the taxpayer purchased the property, (2) is not related to the taxpayer, and (3) does not receive a fee with regard to the taxpayer's investment in the property. The lender *may* qualify even if related *if* the financing is commercially reasonable and on the same terms as loans involving unrelated persons.

Limitations on Passive Losses

New restrictions on the use of deductions and credits from passive activities are the most negative effect on tax shelters. Under the old law, tax shelters could be structured to provide deductions to offset income from other sources; however, deductions and credits from passive activities can only be used to offset income from passive activities. On the positive side, deductions and credits that are disallowed under the new rules may be carried over to apply against passive income in future years or taken when the tax shelter (which produces the losses) is finally disposed of.

Passive activities are not just traditional tax shelters but are defined as any trade or business in which the taxpayer does not materially participate as well as the rental of any tangible property.

These limitations are phased in for investments entered into before October 23, 1986. Losses and credits can still be claimed over several years: 65 percent for 1987; 40 percent for 1988; 20 percent for 1989; and 10 percent for 1990. Investments entered into after October 22, 1986, are faced with the new law immediately.

One way around the new law is to enter into various activities that will produce passive income as well as passive losses and use losses from one shelter against income from another.

Under the old law, an investor could benefit by investing in several shelters to obtain a higher success rate. Under Tax Reform, the idea of packaging different investments together to achieve better returns is a necessity. Deferral shelters will be packaged with investments generating taxable income.

This combination of offsetting income and losses is an opportunity for investors with "burned-out" existing tax shelters to realize tax deferral. Investors holding onto old tax shelters that have reached the crossover point may use newly generated passive losses to defer tax.

Oil and Gas

New tax law limitations don't apply to working interests in oil and gas wells, so investors in these ventures may continue offsetting salary and investment income with deductions —e.g., intangible drilling costs.

Closely Held Corporations

These corporations may use passive-activity losses and credits to offset income from business operations but not portfolio income. Under the old law, a closely held corporation was a tax shelter for its shareholders. Tax Reform reverses this setup, because the corporate tax rate will in many cases exceed the tax rates for individual shareholders.

Your Home as a Tax Shelter under Tax Reform

Here are some changes that affect home ownership in a *positive* way:

1. The 1986 Tax Reform Act limitations on the deductibility of home mortgage interest won't apply to mortgages obtained before August 17, 1986.
2. If a home loan is incurred for educational or medical purposes, interest on a loan (secured by a principal or second residence) in excess of the original purchase price of the home plus improvements will be deductible.
3. If a home loan is incurred for use in an unincorporated business, or if the proceeds of a home loan are used for investment purposes, the interest is deductible.
4. If loan proceeds are used for other purposes, the interest is deductible only on the portion that does not exceed the original purchase price of the residence plus cost of improvements.

5. Real estate taxes on homes are still tax deductible.
6. You can still sell your home and roll over the proceeds tax-free.
7. Taxpayers age 55 or over may still claim the exclusion on $125,000 of profit on the sale of a principal residence.
8. The stepped-up basis upon death of the homeowner is still in effect.

Homeowners should be familiar with what constitutes home improvements and keep detailed records on those improvements. This way they can maximize mortgage interest writeoffs. Some of the improvements that qualify are trees, shrubs, thermal windows, storm windows and doors, new insulation, and structural changes, as well as an asphalt driveway.

Be sure to keep detailed records to show how the mortgage loan proceeds were spent, whether for education, medical, business, or investment purposes.

Here are the changes that affect home ownership in a *negative* way.

1. The limitation of interest deductions applies to existing home equity loans, and deductions for the excess interest (over cost basis) will be phased out over 5 years; by 1991 there will be no deduction on the excess.
2. Long-term gains on the sale of a home will now be taxed as ordinary income.

Assume that a taxpayer bought a home for $180,000 several years ago, putting 25 percent down. Now the mortgage principal is down to $100,000. Assume that refinancing the property to fair market value will support a higher mortgage. Under the new tax law, the interest up to $180,000 (plus cost of improvements) would be fully deductible.

In calculating the alternative minimum tax under Tax Reform, the only interest deductible is the interest on the refinancing equal to the refinanced debt. So if you're thinking of refinancing, beware of this trap.

The proceeds from refinancing could be used for any purpose, including the purchase of a car or boat, and still be deductible when repaid. If the refinancing is connected with a home improvement, the cost of the home improvement will increase the interest deduction.

The educational exception may be very useful for taxpayers who want to finance college educations for their children; however, the IRS hasn't written new regulations yet.

Example

A taxpayer bought a new home 10 years ago for $210,000, subject to a $160,000 mortgage. The house has appreciated to a fair market value of $500,000. The taxpayer may refinance, get a new mortgage for $400,000, pay off the old mortgage (now down to $100,000), and have $300,000 left for personal expenses, including college funding. Expenses for education have to be incurred or paid within a reasonable time after incurring the refinancing. The same example could apply to medical expenses.

Reverse Annuity Mortgage

This arrangement is usually interest paid by elderly taxpayers who are not concerned with loss of an interest writeoff. The lender pays the elderly homeowner a monthly amount based on the equity in the home, and the loan is normally closed out when the owner dies or the property is sold.

An elderly taxpayer who has plenty of capital may wish to use a reverse annuity mortgage as a means of helping children by giving the annuity payments as gifts to them while reducing their estate at the same time.

Home Sales

If you sell a home and buy a more expensive one, there is no recognition of gain even though the value of your home has increased. The higher price of the new home determines your tax-deductible interest on the new mortgage.

Passive Losses

Passive losses on rental property can be used only to offset passive income. If an owner rents out a second home, the only tax benefit will be to the extent of $25,000 of losses through active participation in the management or maintenance of the property. Even this $25,000 maximum writeoff of losses is phased out for taxpayers with adjusted gross income over $100,000 and disappears completely for AGI over $150,000.

Active participation includes approving new tenants, deciding on rental terms, and approving capital expenditures or repairs. "A taxpayer who owns and rents out an apartment . . . that he uses as a part-time vacation home may be treated as actively participating even if he hires a rental agent."

Vacation Home

If you have limited personal use of your second home and have passive losses in excess of income from your second home (which you can use against salary and other nonpassive income), take note. If your second home is rented for 15 or more days during the taxable year and is used by you for personal purposes for more than 14 days (or more than 10 percent of the number of days during the year for which the home is rented, whichever is greater), your deductions are limited. They may not exceed the amount by which the rental exceeds the deductions for interest, taxes, and other expenses.

Any unused passive loss can be deducted when the property is sold. Any gain on the sale of the second residence will be taxed as ordinary income (at a top rate of 28 percent); however, because of the phase-outs of (1) the 15 percent rate above certain levels of income, (2) personal exemptions at still higher levels of income, and (3) the $25,000 rental real estate loss maximum starting at AGI of $100,000, the top marginal rate may be higher than 28 percent after 1987.

A Boat as a Second Home

According to the Internal Revenue Code, a dwelling unit includes a boat. In proposed Reg. 280A-1(d), one example of a boat as a home is one "suitable for overnight use." A boat with living accommodations should qualify as a second residence. Since large boat owners are usually fairly affluent (many have second land-based homes), it is not likely that they want to use their boats as a second residence.

However, the boat owner, like the owner of the vacation home, will feel this important difference. The depreciable life of a boat under the new tax law is 10 years, while the depreciable life of a second residence is 27.5 years. If the boat is rented and not used for personal use, the personal interest limitation would not apply; however, the passive-loss limitation would. This means that a loss disallowed in one year may be carried over to the next year.

Ten Tax Loopholes That Work

Even the courts admit that there's nothing wrong with trying to keep taxes as low as possible. Here are 10 tax loopholes that work:

1. *Hire the Best Tax Expert You Can Find.* Most professionals charge considerably less than they save you, so don't let the fee stop you.
2. *Buy a Vacation Home.* You can deduct mortgage interest and property taxes, and the appreciation in the property value is not taxed until you sell. You can rent out the place for up to 2 weeks each year without reporting the rent.
3. *Be Aggressive.* Take all the tax breaks to which you are entitled. Don't lose sleep over the possibility of being audited. Don't pre-audit yourself. Claim everything you can substantiate, no matter how large the deduction.
4. *Avoid Long-Term Deferred Compensation.* Tax rates will probably increase after 1988. If you defer income until 1989 (or later), you may be surprised when the time comes to report it.
5. *Buy Universal Life Insurance or Single-Premium Deferred Annuities.* Interest earned on these investments accumulates tax-free until you cash them in, and the interest rate often is over 10 percent. Single-premium insurance allows you a choice of a lump sum or payments over a few years. There may be a penalty for early withdrawal, and the fees and interest rates vary greatly, so shop around for the best deal.
6. *Create a Venture Partnership.* A limited partnership can be set up so that income and losses are allocated differently than the individual investor's actual capital contributions. Since the new business will need money up front (for deductible expenses), a greater share of losses can be allocated to the investor. If that person also has income from other passive investments, it can be sheltered by the partnership losses.
7. *Keep a Diary of All Tax-Deductible Expenses.* List unreimbursed business expenses and be sure to record details of travel and entertainment expenses at the time they are incurred. List gifts to charity, especially those you may overlook at tax time, e.g., volunteer expenses and donations of old clothing. Keep a list of unreimbursed medical expenses, including transportation costs.
8. *Let Family Members Inherit Appreciated Assets.* If you sell assets before your death, any increase in value will be taxable. However, if your beneficiaries inherit the property, the appreciation is not taxed until they sell. If you need cash now, consider borrowing against your property.
9. *Make the Maximum Contribution to Your Employer's 401(k) Plan.* The earnings are tax-deferred, and since you pay no tax on the deferred salary, you get the equivalent of a tax deduction for the contribution. You can put up to $7,000 into a 401(k) this year.
10. *Invest in Rental Real Estate.* Buy a home or small apartment building and actively manage it. If your AGI is under $100,000 and your writeoffs exceed the rent, you can deduct up to $25,000 of losses. For AGI between $100,000 and $150,000, some loss is allowed; over $150,000, there is no net rental loss.

Travel Deductions

Here's how to maximize your travel writeoffs under the new tax law.

Business Travel

If your trip is primarily for business, you may deduct the cost of getting to and from your destination, even if you take a side pleasure trip (or extend the trip for pleasure). During the business portion of your travel, you may deduct the cost of lodging, local transportation, and 80 percent of meals and entertainment that relate to business.

If your trip is made primarily for vacation (or pleasure), you may deduct some expenses if you conduct business while on the trip. For instance, while vacationing you take a customer out to lunch: 80 percent of the meal expense is deductible *if* business was discussed during the meal. Include tax, tips, and parking lot fees for the 80 percent deduction. Travel to the restaurant (e.g., by taxi) is 100 percent deductible.

Some circumstances may justify taking your spouse on a business trip and deducting his or her expenses. The IRS will not accept your taking a spouse along to answer the phone or type, but some of the acceptable circumstances are:

1. Your spouse is fluent in the language of the foreign country to which you are traveling, but you are not.
2. Your business is jointly owned by you and your spouse.

Education Travel

If you are in a trade (or business) and attend a related educational seminar, traveling costs to the seminar are deductible. You may not deduct the cost of attending a seminar to help you with your investments, but a stockbroker attending the same seminar might be able to deduct the travel as a business expense.

Teachers may no longer deduct costs of travel to a foreign country to improve teaching skills about that country.

Charitable Travel

If you serve as escort or chaperone for a charity, you may deduct the cost of traveling, but you must have a specific responsibility—e.g., helping the handicapped to get around or supervising a specific number of Scouts. While away from your tax home, all your lodging, meals, and other out-of-pocket expenses are deductible. You may not take deductions for expenses of accompanying family members.

Medical Travel

The cost of medical travel is tax deductible. If the person receiving medical treatment is too ill (or too young) to travel alone, expenses incurred for a traveling companion will be deductible.

Meals are not deductible for the companion, and lodging is allowed up to $50 per night *only* if it is absolutely necessary that the companion stay overnight.

Remember: Medical expense deductions are limited to the amount by which they exceed 7.5 percent of your adjusted gross income under Tax Reform.

Trusts

The purpose of trusts is to split income among various family members who may be in lower tax brackets. The net effect is to pay a lower combined tax.

An inter vivos trust is one created while you are still alive. A trust created upon your death is called a testamentary trust. In both cases, you transfer property to a trustee, who will manage the property for your beneficiaries.

An inter vivos trust may be either revocable or irrevocable. By conveying assets to a trust irrevocably, you no longer have to report the property income and are usually free from estate tax on the asset. Before you make an irrevocable trust, be sure that you will not need the funds in an emergency. A revocable trust, on the other hand, gives the right to revoke the trust but has no immediate income tax benefits; it does, however, minimize any delay in passing property to beneficiaries if you die while the trust is still in effect.

Almost any form of income-producing property may be transferred into a trust: savings accounts, dividend-producing stocks, even stock in a closely held corporation. The only type of property you would not want to transfer would be appreciated property that you may want to sell within 2 years. If the trust does sell appreciated property within 2 years of receipt, any gain will be taxed to the trust at your tax rates, undermining one of the primary reasons why you set up the trust in the first place.

If the taxpayer wants to split income with a minor child or someone to whom he does not wish to entrust property, he may convey the property in trust for the child, in effect splitting income between himself and the trust. A basic question is whether the taxpayer has transferred the income or the property or anything at all. The IRS has used 2 basic approaches in attempts to tax trust income back to the grantors. The first is a ruling that the funds do not exist for tax purposes; the second is an assignment of income back to the grantor.

Be careful when it comes to establishing family estate trusts. Since the IRS considers them illegal tax protests, they can lead to civil and possibly criminal penalties.

Union Membership

If you are a union member, you may find yourself making and receiving a variety of tax-related payments in connection with your union membership. A number of these payments are tax deductible and may have a significant effect on the size of your income tax refund. Remember, these deductions must be itemized and must exceed 2 percent of your adjusted gross income.

Initiation Fees and Dues

If you pay tuition fees and dues to acquire and maintain membership in a union, you are permitted a tax deduction, but only if you itemize.

Assessments for Sickness, Accident, and Death Benefits

Assessments to provide health, accident, and death benefits for union members are not deductible but are considered personal expenses. However, if you receive sickness and accident benefits, you may omit them from your income completely.

Unemployment Benefits

Assessments for out-of-work benefits payments to unemployed members are deductible to the extent that benefits are paid to unemployed union members who are physically capable of working. Conversely, voluntary payments into a separate fund for the purpose of paying unemployment benefits are not deductible. One hundred percent of unemployment compensation is taxable as income.

Pension Fund Payments

If you pay assessments to support a union's old-age pension fund, and if these payments are required as a condition of union membership, they are tax deductible. When you begin to collect retirement benefits from such a pension fund, they are taxable as ordinary income.

Tools, Work Clothes, and Work Shoes

If you are required to supply your own tools or to wear special work clothes and shoes, you are entitled to deduct not only their cost but also the cost of cleaning them. In a recent case, a painter who was required to wear white overalls was permitted a tax deduction.

Vacation Homes

You may deduct in full the interest on the mortgage and all property taxes on your second home, even under Tax Reform. (If you have more than 2 homes, you may take deductions on only 2 of them.) If you rent your vacation home, Tax Reform extends the depreciation life and limits your deductible losses. There are also limits on rental expenses, e.g., maintenance and utilities when you rent the home for part of the year and use it for personal purposes as well.

A vacation home is defined as a piece of property that is "a dwelling unit" with "basic living accommodations." This means that houses, condominiums, and even boats and house trailers may qualify under that broad definition.

If you use the home personally for the greater of (1) 14 days or (2) 10 percent of the total number of days your home is rented at fair rental value, you can claim a tax loss on part of the vacation home. In other words, you may always live in your second home up to 14 days each year; and, if it is rented at a fair value for, say, 180 days, you may spend 18 days in the house (10 percent of days rented).

If you exceed the 10 percent of the 14-day limit, the property will be considered a residence for the entire year, and your deductions will be limited to the rental income.

Using the home for personal purposes does not mean that you yourself have to occupy it. The property is used personally if occupied by (1) a person with an equity interest, (2) a person with whom you trade for another dwelling unit for a comparable period (e.g., time sharing), or (3) a spouse or blood relative, even if you charge a fair value rent. A person whom you do *not* charge a fair rental may occupy the home, but the personal purposes rule will apply; keep them in mind when counting the days of personal use.

Any day you spend in the unit for the principal purpose of repairing or maintaining the property will not count as a personal use day.

Under Tax Reform, your deduction for rental losses on your vacation home is limited, with the loss decreasing as your income increases over $100,000, based on the following:

1. If your AGI is under $100,000, you may deduct up to $25,000 in rental losses.

2. If your AGI is over $100,000, the maximum $25,000 writeoff is reduced by 50 percent of the amount your AGI is over $100,000.

For example, your AGI is $140,000. Subtract the $100,000 ceiling and have $40,000; take 50 percent of the $40,000 and get $20,000. Then subtract the $20,000 from the $25,000 limitation and have $5,000, your maximum writeoff.

In order to take up to $25,000 in vacation home losses, you must:

1. Be an active participant in rental operations.
2. Be involved in management decisions.
3. Have at least a 10 percent ownership stake in the property.

If you don't meet these requirements, you are subject to the passive loss rules.

Management decisions include your approving expenditures, establishing rental terms, and approving prospective tenants, even if you use a rental agent.

If you don't meet these requirements (and are then covered by the passive-loss rules), you may deduct your rental loss only against passive income.

For example, you live (and work) in one state but own and rent out a home in another and use that home part-time as a vacation home. Though you have an agent to collect rent and take care of maintenance, you personally approve leases and large expenditures. Therefore, you meet the active participation test.

Residential rental property depreciation has been increased from 19 years to 27½ years, using straight-line depreciation (no longer the accelerated method).

In addition, you must separate expenses for personal and rental purposes. Rental expenses must spell out: (1) taxes and interest, (2) operating expenses, and (3) depreciation. Deductible operating expenses include: insurance, advertising, repairs, maintenance, utilities, commissions, professional fees, and supplies.

Even if you use your vacation home *one day* out of the year, you must allocate expenses separately for personal and rental purposes. You have to allocate one day's worth of your vacation home's total expenses for the entire year to personal use.

Deduction for expenses (other than taxes and interest) is limited to the amount allocated to rental use; you get nothing for personal use.

Remember, if your adjusted gross income is over $100,000 and you want to carry forward unused rental losses, you must keep records of personal usage.

INDEX

Abandoned spouse, special rules, 56
Accelerated cost recovery system (ACRS), 88–89
Accident, see Casualty losses
Accountants, 128, 244
  choosing, 242–243
  conventions of, 89
Accounting methods, cash vs. accrual, 76
Accrual basis, as accounting method, 76
ACRS, see Accelerated cost recovery system
Actors and actresses, 73
Actual expense method, 77, 127
Adjusted gross income (AGI)
  and casualty losses, 175
  and employee business expenses, 184–188
  before IRA deduction, 27
Adjustments to income, 51, 122–148
  alimony, 122, 146–148
  business expenses, reimbursed, 51, 122, 123–132, 133
  IRA contributions, 22, 122, 132, 134–143, 144, 147
  Keogh retirement plan, 27, 122, 132, 144–145
  penalty on early withdrawal of savings, 122, 146
  self-employed health insurance deduction, 122, 143
  self-employed SEP deduction, 122, 144–145
  under Tax Reform Act, 27
  See also Form 2106; Form 8606
Adoption, and Tax Reform Act, 17
ADR, see Asset depreciation range
Advertising people, 32, 244–245
Age 55, see 55-or-older exclusion
Age 65 (or over), see Elderly
Agents, enrolled, 244
AGI, see Adjusted gross income
Airline pilots, 230
Alcoholics Anonymous, 276
Aliens, filing requirements for, 41, 54
Alimony, 122, 146–148
  back, 146
  vs. child support, 147
  deductible, 146
  and IRA, 132, 147
  and legal fees, 147
  and living together, 146
  periodic payments, 146
  and property settlements, 146
  recapture of, 148
  received, 69
  and Tax Reform Act, 148, 251–252
  and withholding exemptions, 147
Allergy, as medical expense, 32, 277

Alternative cost recovery system, 89
Alternative minimum tax (AMT), 32, 211–213
  and contributions, 212
  and depreciation, 211, 212
  and drilling costs, 212
  and gifts of appreciated property, 263
  and incentive stock option (ISO), 212, 213
  income for, 211–212
  and itemized deductions, 212
  and interest expense, 212
  and investment interest, 212
  and mortgage interest, 212
  and passive losses, 211
  and percentage depletion, 212
  research and experimentation for, 212
  and tax-free bonds, 212, 274, 287
  and tax-free municipal bonds, 287
  and Tax Reform Act, 12, 13, 17, 18, 263, 274
  and TMT, 212
  See also Form 6251
Alternative tax calculation, on new Schedule D, 97–98
Amended tax return, filing, 216, 231
  See also Form 1040X
Amortization, see Form 4562
AMT, see Alternative minimum tax
Anesthetists, 128
Annuities, 68, 195
  for children, 61, 267
  for company retirement plans, 382
  deferred, 16, 250, 291
  forms of, 9, 11
  in return for gifts, 254–255
  rollover to IRA, 142–143
  single-premium deferred, 291
  and Tax Reform Act, 9, 16, 23
  See also Pension plans; Reverse annuity mortgage
Apartment, fixing up, 115
Apartment buildings, 99
Appeals conference, 237
Appreciated assets, inherited by family members, 291
Appreciated property
  contributions with, 170
  gifts of, 263
Armed Forces, 181
  sale of home, deferring tax on, 100
Art, contributions of, 232
Assessments for sickness, accident, and death benefits, 293
Asset depreciation range (ADR), 88–89

Assets, and criminal tax cases, 38
   See also Appreciated assets; Business assets; Capital assets
Assets and investments checklist, 91
At-risk rules, 110
   and Tax Reform Act, 16, 26
   and tax shelters, 287
Attorneys, 128
   choosing, 244
   fees, 179, 186, 189
Audit, 223–235
   and accountants, 243
   after, 237
   asking for, 233
   avoiding, 233
   basic process, 227
   chances of, 230–231
   correspondence, 228
   dealing with, 233–234
   and deductions, 224–226, 230
   and expenses, documenting, 223
   field, 228
   how to handle, 233–234
   and income reporting, 223, 225–226
   lottery, 32, 245–246
   office, 228
   percentage by districts, 230
   postponing, 233
   random, 226, 227
   and red-flagging tax returns, 226–227
   settling dispute, 236–237
   and Tax Reform Act, 223, 226–227
   TCMP, 228
   tolerances, 231
   triggering, 228–231, 232–233
   types of, 228
   and unreported income notices, answering, 223–224
   See also Internal Revenue Service
Audit-proofing tax return, 246
Automobile expenses, 32, 127–128, 225, 246, 277
   See also Business auto; Car
Averaging, see Income averaging
Awards, 17, 19, 71

Baby-sitters, 32, 71, 202, 276
Back taxes, negotiating installment agreements, 219
Bad debts
   business, 95–96
   nonbusiness, 32, 36, 94–95
Bank deposits, 234
Bankruptcy, 165
Banks, and tax liens, 222
Benefits, see Fringe benefits; Social Security; Unemployment compensation benefits
Blind persons, 83–84
   exemptions for, 57
   and new standard deduction, 6–7, 57, 149, 192–193
   and Tax Reform Act, 6–7, 19, 25
Boat, as second home, 290
Bonds, 32, 97
   deep discount, 66
   discount, 66, 91
   and IRA, 135
   municipal tax-exempt, 189, 287
   Series EE, 61, 267, 272
   stripped municipal, 268
   taxable vs. tax-exempt, 240
   tax-exempt, 26, 37, 212, 240, 267, 273
   and Tax Reform Act, 26, 286–287
   zero-coupon tax-exempt, 267–268, 272–273
   See also Nonessential bonds; Savings bonds
Books, 171
Borrowing, from single-premium life insurance policy, 285
Buildings, see Apartment buildings; Historic structures
Burglary, see Theft
Business
   bad debt, 95–96
   car for, 232
   definition of, 278
   and family members, 32, 61, 85, 261, 267
   vs. hobby, 247
   home office, 264–265
   incorporation of, 35, 269–270
   property, loss of, 84–85
   purchases for, 86–87
   start-up costs, 84, 265
   travel for, 37, 77, 128, 129–132, 292
   See also Employee business expenses
Business assets, see Expensing business assets
Business auto, depreciation, 87–88
   See also Automobile expenses; Car
Business credits, 18
   general, 20, 208
Business expenses
   One-Minute Taxman, 75, 187
   reimbursed, 51, 122–132, 133
   See also employee business expenses
Business income or loss, reporting, 73–89
   accounting method, cash vs. accrual, 76
   actors and actresses, 73
   business expenses, 76
   cost of goods sold and/or operations, 86–87
   deductions reporting, 77–85, 224
   depreciation, 87–89
   income reporting, 76–77
   net operating losses, 73, 76
   See also Schedule C
Business travel, 37, 77, 87–88, 127–128, 130, 133, 292

Calendar year and Tax Reform Act, 10
Capital assets, 91, 94
Capital gains and losses, 90–105
   bonds, 91
   capital assets, 91, 94
   condemned property, avoiding gain on, 98
   dividend reinvestment plan stock, 96
   55-or-older exclusion, sale of home, 105
   homes, buying or selling, 102–103
   inherited property, sale of, 96
   inherited rental property, sale of, 96
   installment sales, 98–99, 110
   long-term, 6, 11, 94, 96, 195, 197, 199–200
   lump-sum distribution, company retirement plans, 282–283

nonbusiness bad debts, 94–95
nontaxable exchanges of property, 34, 99
options, 96
ownership, forms of, 90
patent, sale of, 36, 97, 114
phase-out of, 9, 281
recapture of tax benefits, 100, 148
rental property, conversion to, 104
residence, deferred gain on sale, 100, 104
securities, 91
short sales, 94–95
short-term, 6, 12, 94–95
stocks, 91
and Tax Reform Act, 6, 11, 12, 16, 17, 26, 197, 285, 286–287
where to report, 67
See also Form 2119; Losses; Schedule D

Car
business use of, 77, 232
for charitable work, 171
insurance on, 179
interest on loans, 169
mortgage loans for, 286
See also Automobile expenses; Business auto

Carry-backs
loss on, 274
of unused credits, 208

Carry-forwards, of unused credits, 208

Carry-overs
loss on, 274
and Tax Reform Act, 22

Cash basis, as accounting method, 76
Cash contributions, 169–170, 231
Cash-surrender-value life insurance, 267
Casualty losses, 33, 171, 175–180, 232–233
adjusted gross income, 175
and attorneys' fees, 179
and audit, 179, 246
computing, 175
insured, 175, 179
limitations on, 175
One-Minute Taxman, 128
proof for, 175
and psychological damage, 179–180
and record-keeping, 179
and Tax Reform Act, 15, 28
when deductible, 175
See also Form 4684; Theft

Certificates of deposit, 66
Certified historic structures, 17
Chairs (special), as medical expense, 277
Charitable contributions or deductions, *see* Contributions
Charitable travel, 292
and Tax Reform Act 15, 129
Child and dependent care credit, 202–203
computing, 202
employment-related expenses, 33, 202
limitation on, 202–203
See also Form 2441

Children, 33
annuities for, 61, 267
and casual labor, 115
college-age, 266
and college expenses, 249

earned income of, 7, 250
gifts to, 267
and inheritance of house, 265
securities for, 61, 267
for summer work, 261
tax-exempt municipal bonds for, 287
tax forms for, 42
and Tax Reform Act, 7, 15, 18
unearned income of, 7, 14, 18, 42, 61, 267–269, 272–273, 284–285, 287
See also Dependent children; Form 2441; Form 8615

Child support, 147, 252
Claiming everything, 240–241
Clifford Trusts, 18, 267
Closely held corporations, and Tax Reform Act, 288
Closing costs, 33
Clothes
old, 33, 171
work, 186
Coin collecting, 86
Collection information statement, 219
College-age children, 266
College expenses, 33, 249–251
College zero contract, 251
Commuting costs, 128–129
Companion, for medical travel, 292
Company retirement plans, 135, 282–283
annuities, 282–283
lump-sum distributions, 282–283
Compensation limit, for retirement plans, 280
See also Deferred compensation
Compliance failures, on tax returns, 235
Computer data bank, 276
Computers, 33, 251
Condemned property, avoiding gain on, 98
Condominiums, 155
Construction workers, 128
Consumer interest, 150, 164, 169
and Tax Reform Act, 28
Contingent interest, 163–164
Contractor, independent, 78
Contributions, 169–171
and AMT, 212
of art, 232
cash, 169–170, 225, 231
in-kind, 248
noncash, 170–171, 225
old clothes as, 33, 171
One-Minute Taxman, 174
out-of-pocket, 33, 169–170, 248
personal property as, 170–171, 231, 249
and private school, 33, 170, 248
and student support, 248
and Tax Reform Act, 11, 15, 18, 28
See also Form 8283; Gifts; Political contributions credit
Conventions, 33
accounting, 89
foreign travel expenses for, 83
and Tax Reform Act, 15, 251
Co-op, 166
Corporations, 77
See also Closely held corporations

Correspondence audits, 228
Cost depletion, 119
Cost of goods sold and/or operations, 77, 86–87
Credit card
    for contributions, 170, 249
    for medical expenses, 276
Credit rating, of bond insurer, 273
Credits, see Tax credits
Criminal tax cases, 238
Cruise costs, 129
Custodian accounts, 33
Custodial fees, 189
    for IRA, 35

Dancing lessons, 277
Dates, important to remember, 40
Death
    of dependent, 59
    and IRA, 134
    See also Form 1310
Debts
    business bad, 95–96
    nonbusiness bad, 32, 36, 94–95
Deductions
    for alimony, 122, 146–148
    and audit, 224–225, 231
    automobile, 32, 77, 87–89, 127–128, 169, 170, 179, 225, 232, 246, 286
    for baby-sitters, 32, 71, 202, 276
    for bad debts, 32, 36, 94–95
    for books, 170
    from business income or loss, 76–87, 224
    for business travel, 37, 77, 87–88, 128–129, 130, 133, 292
    claiming everything, 240–241
    for commuting costs, 128–129
    controlling, 265
    conventions, 15, 33, 83, 89, 251
    for cruise costs, 129
    for custodial fees, 189
    for drilling costs, 212
    for early withdrawal penalty, 16, 122, 142, 146, 280
    for educational travel, 11, 20, 34, 129, 183, 292
    for employing family members, 85
    for entertainment, 80–82, 122–123, 130–131, 132, 184–185, 225, 230, 233
    for foreign convention travel, 83
    for furniture, 100, 171
    for gambling winnings and losses, 34, 71, 279
    for health club fees, 277
    for health insurance, self-employed, 122, 143
    for hobby losses, 8, 15, 20, 86, 232
    for improvements, 80, 115, 162
    for IRA contributions, 22, 122, 132–143, 144, 187
    for IRA fees, 35, 189
    for Keogh retirement plan, 27, 122, 132, 144–145
    for lease costs, 181–183
    for legal fees, 36, 147, 186, 189, 276
    for loan service charges, 274
    for loss of business property, 84–85
    for margin account charges, 286
    marital, 253
    for marital counseling fees, 277
    married worker, 15, 22, 27
    for meals, 17, 71, 122–123, 130–132, 184–185, 186
    for mortgage interest, 11, 21, 78, 115, 156, 162–163, 164, 168, 212, 250, 266
    for professional dues, 186
    for professional expenses, 188
    for promotion, 225
    and recordkeeping, 247, 279–280
    for rental expenses, 117
    for rental property, 115, 117, 224
    for rent on business property, 78–80
    for repairs, 80, 115, 162–163
    return preparer fees, 24
    for safe, 189
    Section 179, 77
    for self-employed health insurance, 122, 143
    for self-employed SEP, 122, 144–145
    for start-up expenses, 84, 265
    for subscriptions, 189
    for supper money, 82
    and Tax Reform Act, 19, 129, 285–286
    for telephone calls, business-related, 186–188
    temporary away-from-home, 126–127
    for tools, 294
    trustees' fees, 189
    two-earner, 12
    and work clothes, 186, 294
    See also Depreciation; Home office; Itemized deductions; Miscellaneous deductions; Standard deduction
Deep discount bonds, 66
Deferred annuities, 16, 250
    single-premium, 291
Deferred compensation, long-term, 291
Deferred savings, see 401(k) plan
Defined benefit Keogh plan, 144–145
Defined contribution Keogh plan, 144–145
Dental expenses, 150–154
Dentists, 81, 276
Dependent child, widow(er) with, 56
Dependent children
    and earned income credit, 213
    filing returns for, 193
Dependents
    death of, 59
    defined, 58
    exemptions for, 34, 57, 58–59
    filing for, 58–59
    medical expenses of, 154
    See also Child and dependent care credit; Form 2120; Form 2441
Depletion, 118–119
    See also Percentage depletion
Depreciation, 34, 87–89, 116–118
    accelerated cost recovery system (ACRS), 88–89
    accelerated vs. straight-line, 212
    and accounting conventions, 89
    alternative cost recovery system (ACRS), 88–89
    and alternative minimum tax, 211–212
    and automobiles, 87–88, 127–129
    defined, 116
    and home office in residence, 266
    and improvements, 80
    lessee leasehold improvements, 89
    new rules, 88

and real estate, 116–119
and recapture of tax benefits, 100
and rental property, 104
and Section 179 deduction, 77
tables, 116, 118
and Tax Reform Act, 18, 116–118
vacation home, 295
See also Asset depreciation range; Form 4562
Diary, as tax record, 71, 279, 291
Disability
and child and dependent care credit, 202–203
exemptions for, 59
See also Permanently and totally disabled; Schedule R
Disability insurance, 269
Disaster loss, *see* Casualty loss
Discount, on mortgages, 163
Discount bonds, 91
deep, 66
Distributions
nontaxable, 67
from qualified plans, 280–281
See also Lump-sum distributions; Partial distribution; qualified total distribution
Dividends
exclusion, 16, 19
itemizing, 67
reinvestment plan stock, 96
tax-free, 269
and Tax Reform Act, 16, 18, 26
See also Schedule B
Divorce, 34, 54
and alimony, 146
and exemptions, 34, 59
and filing status, 261–262
and Tax Reform Act, 251–252
Dog for hearing impaired, as medical expense, 277
Donations, *see* Contributions
Drilling costs, and AMT, 212
Drugs, as medical expense, 154
Dues, *see* Initiation fees and dues

Early distribution tax, 200
Early withdrawal penalty
IRA, 134, 142
from qualified plans, 280–281
savings, 122, 145
and Tax Reform Act, 16
See also Hardship withdrawal
Earned income, of children, 7, 250
Earned income credit, 213–217
and Tax Reform Act, 18
Educational expenses, 188, 189, 252–253
One-Minute Taxman, 190
Educational travel, 34, 183–184, 292
and Tax Reform Act, 11, 19, 129
Elderly
exemptions for, 57
and 55-or-older exclusion, in sale of home, 105
and new standard deduction, 6–7, 57, 149, 192–193
and tax credit for, 204–207
and Tax Reform Act, 6–7, 19, 25
transportation barriers to, 83–84
See also Old age; Schedule R; Senior citizens

Elevator, as medical expense, 277
Employee awards, and Tax Reform Act, 15
Employee business expenses, 184–187
and adjusted gross income, 185–186
and audit, 225, 230–231
documentation for, 224–225
limitations on, 184–186
reimbursed, 51, 122–132
and Tax Reform Act, 19, 27, 28
See also Form 2106; Form 4852; Shareholder-employee loans
Employee business travel expenses, One-Minute Taxman, 133
Employer securities, net unrealized appreciation of distributed, 194–195
Employer stock, 259
Employment-related expenses, for child and dependent care credit, 202
See also Terminating employment
Energy tax credits, and Tax Reform Act, 19
Engineers, 28
Enrolled agents, 244
Entertainment expenses, 80–82, 122–123, 129–132, 184–186, 225, 230–231, 233
and audit, 80–81
home, 80–81
limitations on, 81
recordkeeping for, 80–81
and Tax Reform Act, 131–132
Envelopes, expenses in, 280
Equipment, 264–265
as medical expense, 275
Estate planning, 253–255
estate tax, 253
gift tax, 254–255
life insurance, 254
trusts, 254
See also Financial and estate planning
Estate tax, 253–254, 278
and marital deduction, 253–254
and Tax Reform Act, 21
unified credit, 253
Estimated tax, 255–256
declaration of, 255
filing dates for, 255
penalties for insufficient amounts, 34, 255–256
and Social Security, 70
and Tax Reform Act, 10, 15, 19
tolerance level for, 231
Excess distribution tax, 201
Exchanges, *see* Capital gains and losses
Excise tax, and Tax Reform Act, 286
Exclusion, 55-or-older, on sale of home, 105, 266, 284, 289–290
Executives
checklist, 259
compensation plans for, 257
and employer stock, 259–260
financial planning for, 256–261
401(k) plan for, 258
incentive stock options for, 258
and IRAs, 260–261
retirement planning for, 259–261
split-dollar life insurance, 259
stock plans for, 257–258

Executives (cont.)
   and Tax Reform Act, 256–261
Exemptions, 57–61
   for blind, 57
   for dependents, 57–59
   for disabled, 59
   and divorce, 34, 59
   for elderly, 57
   and multiple support agreements, 59
   and Tax Reform Act, 19, 51
   See also Personal exemptions
Expenses, documenting, and audits, 223
   See also Actual expense method; Deductions
Expensing business assets, and Tax Reform Act, 19
Experimentation and research, 212
Extensions, for filing, 34, 216
   See also Form 4868

Face-lifts, as medical expense, 278
Family
   bad debts, 95
   employing members of, 32, 61, 85, 261, 267
   and 55-or-older exclusion, in sale of home, 105
   gifts to members, 35, 104, 116, 254–255
   and inheritance of appreciated assets, 291
   See also Relatives
Family estate trusts, 34, 292–293
Farm financing and Tax Reform Act, 20
Fees
   custodial, 189
   health club, 277
   IRA, 35, 189
   legal, 35, 147, 187, 189, 276
   marital counseling, 277
   return/preparer, 24
   trustees', 189
   See also Initiation fees and clues
Fellowships and Tax Reform Act, 25
Field audits, 228
55-or-older exclusion, sale of home, 105, 266, 284, 289
Filing, 215–222
   amended return, 218
   and back taxes, 219, 222
   and dependent children, 193
   for dependents, 58–59
   and estimated tax dates, 255–256
   and IRS interest rates, 218
   last-minute tax forms, 215
   last-minute tips, 215
   late return, 216–218
   and money for taxes, 215
   penalty for not, 235
   and postage, 216
   and Problems Resolution Office, 218–219
   refund, checking on, 215
   special situations, 216–218
   status, 34, 54–56, 261–262
   See also Form 1040X; Form 4868; Income tax return
Filters, 276
Financial and estate planning, and Tax Reform Act, 14–15
Financial planning, for executives, 257–261
Financial publications, 189
Financing
   non-recourse, 287
   qualified nonrecourse, 110
Fire, damage from, 84
Firefighters, meals for, 186
Five-year averaging, 197, 199, 281
   company retirement plans, 282–283
   and Tax Reform Act, 196
   vs. ten-year averaging, 195, 196, 197, 199
Flight attendants, 230
Foreign convention travel, 83
Foreign country
   medical expenses in, 154, 276
   moving expenses to, 181
Foreign income, 72
   and Tax Reform Act, 8, 20
Foreign travel, 129–130, 131
Form W-2—Wage and Tax Statement, 44, 46, 47
Form W-4A—Employee's Withholding Allowance Certificate, 48
Form W-4EZ, 45–46
Form 1040—U.S. Individual Income Tax Return, 52–53
   adjustments to income, 51
   basic information, 51–61
   business expenses, reimbursed, 51
   changes in, 51–52
   exemptions, 51, 57–61
   filing status, 54–56
   income, 51
   income shifting, 61
   tax computation, 54
   See also Form 1310; Form 2120; Income tax return
Form 1040A ("short form"), 50
Form 1040X—Amended U.S. Individual Income Tax Return, 220–221
Form 1099-E, see Schedule D
Form 1310—Statement of Person Claiming Refund Due a Deceased Taxpayer, 59
Form 2106—Employee Business Expenses, 124–125
   changes on, 122–123
Form 2119—Sale or Exchange of Principal Residence, 101
Form 2120—Multiple Support Declaration, 59
Form 2441—Credit for Child and Dependent Care Expenses, 203
Form 3903—Moving Expenses, 182
Form 4562—Depreciation and Amortization, 120–121
Form 4684—Casualties and Thefts, 176–177
Form 4852—Employee's Substitute Wage and Tax Statement, 47
Form 4868—Application for Automatic Extension of Time to File U.S. Individual Income Tax Return, 217
Form 8283—Noncash Charitable Contributions, 172–173
Form 8582—Passive Activity Loss Limitations, 111–113
Form 8598—Computation of Deductible Home Mortgage Interest, 158–159

Form 8606—Nondeductible IRA Contributions, etc., 137
Form 8615—Computation of Tax for Children Under Age 14 Who Have Investment Income of More Than $1,000, 43
Forward averaging, 195, 196–198
401(k) plan, 258, 280, 283, 291
   and Tax Reform Act, 9, 24, 27, 286
   See also Salary reduction plans
403(b) annuities, and Tax Reform Act, 9
Fraud penalty, 235–236
Freelance income, 34
Fringe benefits, 34, 258, 262
Funding medium change, and tax-free rollovers, 141
Furniture, 100, 171

Gains, large, 232
   See also Capital gains and losses
Gambling winnings and losses, 34, 71, 278
Gas wells, 212, 288
   and Tax Reform Act, 10
General business credit, 208
   and Tax Reform Act, 20
Gifts
   of appreciated property, 35, 254, 263
   per business associate, 82
   to children, 267
   to college vs. private foundation, 248
   to family members, 34, 100, 116, 254
   leasebacks, 262–263
   loan-back, 250
   tax-free, from employer, 71
   and Tax Reform Act, 263
   at year-end, 249
   See also Contributions
Gift tax, 61, 254–255
Ginnie Maes, 272
Green card, and Tax Reform Act, 20
Gross income, determining, 64
   See also Adjusted gross income
Gross receipts, 76–77
Ground rent, 35, 164
Group term life insurance, 269
Growth stocks, 61
Guaranteed loans, 165

Hairpiece, as medical expense, 277
Hair removal, as medical expense, 278
Handicapped
   barriers to, 17, 83–84
   medical expenses for, 275, 276, 277, 278
   and Tax Reform Act, 17
   See also Physically handicapped
Hardship withdrawal, 281
   from salary reduction plan, 24
Head of household, 55–56
   requirements to qualify, 261–262
   and Tax Reform Act, 6–7, 12–13
   See also Schedule Z
Health club fees, 277
Health insurance
   self-employed deduction, 122, 148
   and Tax Reform Act, 20
Health spas as medical expense, 277

Hearing impaired persons, 277
High/low spread, in income-shifting, 268
Historic structures, certified
   rehabilitation of, 208–209
   and Tax Reform Act, 17
Hobby, 35
   vs. business, 247
   losses from, 8, 15, 20, 86, 232
   and Tax Reform Act, 8, 15, 20
Home
   buying or selling—One-Minute Taxman, 102–103
   converted to rental property, 104
   entertaining at, 81
   55-or-older exclusion, in sale of, 105, 266, 284, 289–290
   rental, 267
   security system, 189
   and Tax Reform Act, 288–289
   as tax shelter, 288–289
   See also Boat; Residence; Vacation home
Home improvements, 35, 162–163, 277, 288–289
   and mortgage interest, 162, 168
   for physically handicapped, 154
   vs. repairs, 162
Home mortgage, see Mortgages
Home office, 35, 36, 78–80, 224, 230
   benefits of, 264–265
   as business property, 104
   and commuting costs, 127–128
   and computers, 251
   for employees, 186
   and home ownership, 266
   for investor, 188–189
   and Tax Reform Act, 15, 20, 264
Home office "focal point" test, 264
Home ownership, 245, 265–267
   advantages of, 35, 265–266
   changing nondeductible interest to deductible, 266
   and children, inheritance of house, 265
   and college-age child, 266
   55-or-over exclusion on sale, 105, 266, 284, 289–290
   and home office, 266
   mortgage, then rent, 265–266
   and parents, supporting, 265–266
   and rental, 267
   and sale under age, 51, 266
Home sale, 290
   and 55-or-over exclusion, 35, 105
   at loss, 35, 105
Hospitalization insurance, 150
Housing, see Low-income housing credit
Housing co-op, 166
How to use Pay Less Tax Legally, 5–6

Improvements, vs. repairs, 80, 115, 162
Imputed interest, 67
Incentive stock option (ISO)
   and AMT, 212–213
   for executives, 257–258
   and Tax Reform Act, 258
Income, 51, 62–67
   adjusted gross, 27, 175, 185–186

Index

Income *(cont.)*
  alimony, 67
  for AMT, 211–213
  annuities, 68
  awards, 17, 19, 71
  controlling, 265
  deferred, 33
  and dependent children, 193
  from dividends, 67
  exclusions from, 71–72
  foreign, 8, 20, 72
  freelance, 34
  gambling winnings, 71
  gross, 64, 66
  interest, 26, 35, 66, 67, 270–271
  investment, 193
  nontaxable, 64
  ordinary, 195
  passive, 279
  pensions, 68
  portfolio, 107
  premiums, 71
  prizes, 19, 71
  proving, 245
  recordkeeping for, 279–280
  refunds of state and local income taxes, 67
  rental, 116, 265
  salaries, 66
  self-employment, 278
  Social Security benefits, 69–70
  taxable, 65
  tax-free, generating, 240
  and Tax Reform Act, 26–27
  tips, 66, 230
  trust, 267
  unemployment compensation benefits, 68
  unreported, answering notices, 223–224
  wages, 66
  See also Adjustments to income; Business income or loss; Earned income; Earned income credit; Form 4972; Schedule B; Supplemental income; Unearned income
Income averaging, 11, 15, 20
Income reporting, 76–77
  and audit, 223, 225
Income shifting, 37, 61, 267–269
  high/low spread, 268
  and Tax Reform Act, 21
  under-age-14 rules, 268–269
  zero-coupon tax-exempt bonds, 267–268
Income Tax
  computing, 30–31, 192, 194
  local, 67, 154–155
  questions on, 32–37
  state, 67, 154–155
Income tax return
  amended, 218
  audit-proofing, 246
  basic guidelines, 41–50
  children's income, 42–44
  children's tax forms, 43
  compliance failures, 235
  Form W-2, 43, 46
  Form W-4A, 48–49
  Form W-4EZ, 45–46, 50
  Form 1040A, 46, 50
  Form 1040EZ, 50
  and head of household, 6–7, 13, 55–56, 261–262
  late, 216
  preparation fee, 186
  red-flagging, 226–227
  "short forms," 50
  underwithholding, 45–46
  what you need to file, 42–43
  when to file, 45
  where to file and pay, 45
  whole dollars, 45
  who must file? 41–42
  See also Form 1040; Form 4852; Form 8615; Joint returns
Incorporation, of business, 35, 269–270
Incremental research tax credit, 18
Independent contractor, 78
Indexing, of exemptions and deductions, and Tax Reform Act, 21
Individual property, 90
Individual proprietor, *see* Schedule C
individual Retirement Account, *see* IRA
Industrial development bonds, 240
Information
  failure to file, 235
  and Tax Reform Act, 21
Inheritance, by family members of appreciated assets, 291
Inherited IRA, 134, 283
Inherited property, sale of, 96
Initial separate tax, 195
Initiation fees and dues, 293
In-kind contributions, 248
Installment agreements, on back taxes, 219–220
Installment sale, 98–99
  and passive loss rules, 111
Insurance
  on car, 179
  claims, 179
  disability, 269
  hospitalization, 150
  job, 188
  medical, 150, 154
  See also Health insurance; Life insurance
Insured casualty losses, 175, 179
Interest income, 35, 66–67, 270–271
  certificates of deposit, 66
  deep discount bonds, 66
  imputed, 67
  savings bonds, 66
  tax-exempt, 66
  and Tax Reform Act, 26
  Treasury bills and notes, 66
  See also Schedule B
Interest paid, 155–169
  and AMT, 212
  on car loans, 169
  changing nondeductible to deductible, 266
  computing, 166
  consumer, 28, 150, 164, 169
  contingent, 163–164
  on guaranteed loans, 165
  on housing co-op, 166
  investment, 15, 21–22, 26, 28, 166–167, 169, 212, 266, 286–287
  and IRA, 169

on life insurance, 15, 166
limitation on, 166
margin, 169
for mortgages, 11, 21, 28, 78, 114, 156–157, 162–163, 164, 168, 250, 266
in passive activity, 165
personal, 15, 165, 169
qualified residence, 156
and recordkeeping, 155–156
on SAM, 163–164
on student loans, 165–166
on tax deficiency, 166
and Tax Reform Act, 7, 11, 15, 16, 21, 26, 28, 29
timing, 155–156
Interest rates
IRS, 218
and Tax Reform Act, 21
Internal Revenue Service (IRS)
agents, 234–235
and appeals conference, 237
after audit, 237
and audit lottery, 245–246
audit staff, 223
and audit tolerances, 231
and audit types, 228
averages, 228–229
and basic audit process, 227
and compliance failures, 235
concentration of, 232–233
and criminal tax cases, 238
districts, 230
employee business expenses, 224–225
examination guidelines, 231
fallibility of, 235
and fraud penalty, 236
and income reporting, 225–226
and incorporation, 269–270
interest rates of, 218
and job titles, 230–231
and late returns, 216
paying off, 222
Problems Resolution Office, 218–219
and random auditing, 226
and red-flagging tax returns, 226–227
and refund claims, 280
and Tax Reform Act, 218
and unreported income notices, 223–224
See also Audit
Internal Revenue Service Center, where to file, 45
Inter vivos trust, 293
Intra-family loans, and Tax Reform Act, 271
Invention, see Patent
Inventories, 86–87
Investment club, 35, 189
Investment expenses, 188–189
One-Minute Taxman, 191
Investment income, and dependent children, 193
Investment interest, 165, 168, 169, 266
and AMT, 217
and Tax Reform Act, 16, 21–22, 26, 28, 266
Investment loss, 271
passive activity, 211
Investment property, and sales tax, 154–155
Investments, 271–274
Ginnie Maes, 272
Series EE bonds, 272

tax-free bonds, 273
and Tax Reform Act, 15–16
U.S. government-backed securities, 272
zero-coupon bonds, 272–273
See also Real estate; Tax shelters
Investments and assets checklist, 91
Investment seminars, and Tax Reform Act, 22
Investment tax credit, 209
IRA (Individual Retirement Account), 132–145, 144–145, 281–282, 286
and alimony, 171, 132, 147
borrowing for, 134, 169
contributions, 22, 132–142, 144, 147
deductible vs. nondeductible, 281–282
early withdrawals, 142
excess contributions, 141
and executives, 260–261
fees with, 35, 188–189
inherited, 134, 283
married couples vs. living together singles, 275
penalty, 141, 142–143
rollover, 141–143, 198–199, 260, 282, 283–284
self-directed, 134
spousal, 142, 282
and Tax Reform Act, 8–9, 11, 22, 27, 135–142, 270, 272
where to invest funds, 141
See also Form 8606
Irrevocable trusts, 254, 293
IRS Service Centers, 235
See also Internal Revenue Service
IRS Tele-Tax service, 219
ISO, see Incentive stock option
Itemized deductions, 149–191
and AMT, 212
casualty and theft, 15, 28, 33, 84–85, 171, 175–180, 232–233, 247
changes in, 150
for charitable travel, 292
contributions, 11, 14, 15, 18, 28, 33, 169–171, 174, 172–173, 212, 225, 231, 232, 248–249
dental expenses, 150–154
medical expenses, 8, 11, 15, 22–23, 28, 36, 150–154, 275–278
for medical travel, 292
miscellaneous, 8, 11, 15, 23, 28, 184–191, 224, 278–279
moving expenses, 15, 23, 27, 28, 36, 150, 180–184
vs. new standard deduction, 149, 192–193
taxes, 154–155
and Tax Reform Act, 14, 23, 28
See also Form 3903; Form 4684; Form 8283; Interest paid; Schedule A
Items no longer included, in Tax Reform Act, 7

Job, temporary vs. indefinite, 126–127
Job hunting, 35, 188, 274
Job insurance, 35, 188
Jobs credit, 18
targeted, 25
Job skills, 36, 188
Joint returns
and divorce, 146–147
filing status, 261–262
for married couples, 24, 116

Joint returns *(cont.)*
   and Tax Reform Act, 6–7, 24
Joint tenancy, 90

Keogh retirement plan, 122, 144–145
   date for contribution, 132–134
   defined benefit, 144–145
   defined contribution, 144–145
   and Tax Reform Act, 27

Labor, casual, 115
Land, 116, 267
Late payment charges, 163
Late return, filing, 281
Lawyers, *see* Attorneys
Learning disabilities, 278
Leasebacks, gift, 262–263
Lease costs, 181–183
Leasing, of home office, 20
Legal fees, 36, 186, 189, 276
   and alimony, 147
Lessee leasehold improvements, 89
Liability, *see* Limited liability; Tax liability
Life income trust, 254
Life insurance, 249, 254
   cash-surrender-value, 267
   group term, 269
   interest on installment payments, 15, 165–166
   loans, 165–166
   single-premium, 284–285, 286
   split-dollar, 259
   and Tax Reform Act, 15, 286
   universal, 250, 291
   variable, 286
Limited liability, 269
Limited partnerships, 230
Living together singles, vs. married couples, 274–275
Loan-back gift, 250
Loans
   bad debts, 32, 36, 94–95
   guaranteed, 165
   interest on car, 169
   interest on student, 165
   intra-family, 271
   life insurance, 165
   mortgage for car, 286
   from parents, 67
   from qualified plans, 281
   shareholder-employee, 232
Loan service charges, 274
Local income taxes, 155
   refunds of, 67
Local sales tax and Tax Reform Act, 14, 28
Local taxes and Tax Reform Act, 12
Lodging, excluded from income, 71–72
Long-term capital gains, 94–95, 97
   for lump-sum distributions, 194–195, 197–198, 199–201
   and Tax Reform Act, 6, 11
Long-term capital losses, 97
Long-term deferred compensation, 291
Loopholes, *see* Tax loopholes
Losses
   business property, 84–85

   on carry-backs, 274
   on carry-overs, 274
   casualty and theft, 15, 33, 84, 171, 175–180, 232–233, 247
   gambling, 34, 71, 278
   hobby, 8, 15, 20, 86, 232
   home sale at, 35, 104
   investment, 211–212, 271–272
   large, 232
   long-term, 6, 11, 94, 97, 195, 197–198, 199
   net operating, 76
   passive, 9–10, 16, 106–107, 110–114, 167, 211, 275, 279, 288, 290
   rental, 26–27
   residence, sale of, 104
   short-term capital, 94–95
   vacation home, 294–295
   See also Business income or loss; Capital gains and losses
Lottery, audit, 32, 245–246
Lottery winnings, 71
Low-income housing credit, 209
   and Tax Reform Act, 16, 22, 27
Lump-sum distributions, 36, 195–201
   and company retirement plans, 282–283
   5-year averaging, 195, 196–197, 199, 200, 281, 282–283
   forward averaging, 195–197
   long-term capital gain for, 194–195, 197, 199–200
   one-time election, 200
   and ordinary income, 195
   and participation in other plans, 200
   reporting, 105
   and rollovers, tax-free, 141–142, 198–199
   special tax treatment for, 199–201
   and Tax Reform Act, 22
   ten-year averaging, 195, 196–197, 199, 200, 281
   and terminating employment, 200
Luxury cars, 89
Luxury-water transportation, and Tax Reform Act, 129

Mail-order ministries, 248
Margin account charges, and Tax Reform Act, 286
Margin interest, 169
Marital counseling fees, 277
Marital deduction, and estate tax, 253
Marital status, for filing, 261–262
Married couples
   and 55-or-older exclusion, in sale of home, 105
   filing requirements for, 41
   filing separately, 6–7, 55, 193
   and installment sale, 99
   joint returns, 6–7, 24, 116
   living apart, 116
   living together singles, 274–275
   moving expenses for, 183
   and Tax Reform Act, 13, 274–275
   See also Schedule Y
Married worker deduction, and Tax Reform Act, 15, 22, 27
   See also Two-earner deduction
Maximum tax liability, and general business credit, 208

Meals, 122–123, 130–132, 184–185
  excluded from income, 71–72
  for firefighters, 186
  and Tax Reform Act, 17
Medical expenses, 150–154, 275–278
  auto, 276
  chairs, special, 277
  dog for hearing impaired, 277
  drugs, 150
  elevator, 277
  equipment, 275
  face-lift, 278
  in foreign country, 154, 276
  for handicapped, 275, 276, 277, 278
  health club fees, 277
  legal fees as, 276
  marital counseling fees, 277
  nursing care, 275
  nursing/convalescent home, 275
  One-Minute Taxman, 152–153
  prepaid, 276
  psychiatric care, 277
  salt-free products, 276
  schools, special, 36, 276, 278
  swimming pool, 277
  and Tax Reform Act, 1, 11, 15, 23, 28, 150
  telephone calls, 275
  therapy, 276
  transportation, 154, 276
  TV set (special), 277
  for water, 276
  weight-loss program, 276
  wig, 277
Medical insurance, 150, 154
Medical reimbursement plan, 269, 278
Medical travel, 276, 292
Medicare, 150
Minimum tax, see Alternative minimum tax
Ministries, mail-order, 248
Miscellaneous deductions, 150, 184–191, 278–279
  educational expenses, 188, 190, 252–253
  employee business expenses, 19, 28, 51, 122–133
  investment expenses, 188–189, 191
  job hunting, 35, 188, 274
  One-Minute Taxman, 187, 190
  and Tax Reform Act, 1, 11, 15, 23, 28
Money, for taxes, 215
Mortgage interest, 156–161, 162–164, 250
  and AMT, 212
  and financial institution, 78, 114
  and home improvements, 162–163, 168–169
  and Tax Reform Act, 11, 21, 28, 162, 266
Mortgages
  discount on, 163
  late payment charges, 163
  limitations of, 21
  loan for car, 286
  points, 163–164, 168
  prepayment of, 162
  refinancing, 165
  and rental, 265–266
  reverse annuity, 289–290
  and Tax Reform Act, 21, 286
  wraparound, 98–99
  zero-rate, 163
  See also Form 8598; Shared appreciation mortgage
Moving expenses, 36, 150, 180–184
  to foreign country, 181
  limitations on, 183–184
  and married couples, 183–184
  and self-employed persons, 180, 183
  and Tax Reform Act, 15, 23, 27, 28
  and unemployed persons, 183
  See also Form 3903
Multiple support agreements, 59, 61
Municipal bonds
  stripped, 268
  tax-exempt, 189, 287
  and Tax Reform Act, 287
Musicians, 80, 127–128

Natural gas, and percentage depletion, 119
Negligence penalty, 235
Net lease provisions, 22
Net operating losses, 73, 76
New standard deduction, vs. itemized deductions, 149–150, 192–193
90-day letter, 237
Nonbusiness bad debts, 94–95
Noncash contributions, 170–171, 226
Nonessential bonds, 212
Nonrecourse financing, 287
  qualified, 110
Nonrefundable credits, 201
Nonrental activities, and passive loss rules, 110
Nonresidents, filing requirements for, 41–42, 54
Nontaxable distributions, 67
Nontaxable exchanges of property, 35, 99
Nontaxable income, One-Minute Taxman, 64
Nurse, 188, 276
Nursing/convalescent home, 276

Occupations, and audits, 230–231
Office, see Home office
Office audits, 228
Office expenses, see Home office
Oil investments
  and cost depletion, 119
  and Tax Reform Act, 10
Oil royalties, see Windfall profits tax credits
Oil wells, 212, 288
Old age, see Elderly; Senior citizens
Old clothes, as contribution, 171
Operating losses, see Net operating losses
Optional expense method, 77, 127–128
Options, 96
  See also Incentive stock option
Ordinary income, and lump-sum distribution, 195
Out-of-pocket contributions, 33, 169–170, 248
Outside salespersons, 126, 184
Overpayment of tax, computed, 192
Ownership, forms of, 90

Painters, 294
Parents, 116
  and 55-or-older exclusion, in sale of home, 105
  loans from, 67
  single, 37, 54

Parents *(cont.)*
  supporting, 56, 202–203
Partial distribution, 198–199
  and tax-free rollovers, 141–142
  and Tax Reform Act, 142–143
Partner, retiring, 114
Partnership, 36
  limited, 230
  venture, 291
Passive activity, interest in, 165
Passive income, and Tax Reform Act, 279
Passive losses
  and active participation, 106–107, 110–111, 279, 290
  and AMT, 211–212
  and investment interest, 167
  limitations on, 287–288
  married couples vs. living together singles, 274–275
  and Tax Reform Act, 9–10, 16, 107, 287–288
  and vacation home, 290
Passive tax credits, 106–107, 110–111
Patent, sale of, 36, 97, 114
PC, *see* Personal computer
Penalties
  avoiding, 235–236, 242
  for early withdrawal from qualified plans, 280–281
  for early withdrawal of savings, 122, 146
  for estimated tax, insufficient amounts, 34, 255–256
  for compliance failures, 235
  fraud, 235–236
  IRA, 141, 142–143
  on mortgages, 163
  prepayment, 36, 163
  and recordkeeping, 126
  and Tax Reform Act, 23
Pension plans
  benefits, 12
  distributions—premature, 23, 68
  and excise tax, 286
  payments, 294
  Simplified Employee Pension (SEP) plan, 122, 145
  and Tax Reform Act, 9, 12, 23
  termination of, 252, 260
  See also IRA; Keogh retirement plan
Percentage depletion, 119
  and AMT, 212
Permanently and totally disabled, tax credit for, 204–205
  See also Schedule R
Personal computer (PC), 251
Personal exemptions
  additional, for blind persons and old age, 57
  married couples vs. living together singles, 274–275
  for spouse, 56–57
  vs. standard deduction, 193
  and Tax Reform Act, 7, 12, 15, 19, 29
Personal interest, 164, 169
  and Tax Reform Act, 15
Personal property, as contribution, 170–171
Personal property tax, 155

Phase-in and investment interest, 22
Phase-out of capital gains and losses, 281
  and Tax Reform Act, 9
Physically handicapped, 277
  home improvements for, 154
Planning, *see* Estate planning; Retirement planning; Tax planning
Points, 36, 163, 164, 167–168
Policeman, 128–129
Policies, *see* Insurance
Political contributions credit, and Tax Reform Act, 24
Portfolio income, 107
Postage, 216
Premiums, 71
Prepayment penalties, 36, 163
Private-purpose municipals, 287
Private school, and contributions, 33, 171, 248
Prizes, 71
  and Tax Reform Act, 19
Problems Resolution Office (IRS), 218–219
Professional, incorporation by, 269–270
  See also Business income or loss; Schedule C
Professional adviser, 188
Professional dues, 186
Professional expenses, and One-Minute Taxman, 187
Professors, 28
Profits, *see* Capital gains and losses
Promotion, 225
Property
  appreciated, 169–170, 263
  business, loss of, 84–85
  condemned, 98
  as gift, 248
  individual, 90
  inherited, 96
  investment, 154–155
  nontaxable exchanges, 34, 99
  personal, as contributions, 170–171, 231, 248
  renting, 267
  sale of, by realtors, 100
  vacation, 266
  See also Rental property
Property settlements, 252
  and alimony, 146–147
Psychiatric care, 277
Publications, financial, 189
Public-purpose municipals, 287
Purchases, for business, 86–87

Qualified plans
  distributions from, 280–281
  loans from, 281
Qualified residence interest, 161
Qualified total distribution, 198–199

Railroad retirement benefits, 70
Random audits, 226, 227
Real estate
  and depreciation, 116–118
  large gains or losses from, 232
  nontaxable exchanges, 99
  rental, 291
  taxes, 154–155

and Tax Reform Act, 9, 110, 285
  See also Apartment buildings; Historic structures; Property
Realtors, and sale of property, 100
Recapture of tax benefits
  alimony, 148
  depreciation, 99–100
Recordkeeping
  and audit, 234, 246
  for automobile expenses, 128
  and casualty or theft losses, 179
  for deductions, 246, 279
  diary for, 279
  for income, 279
  and interest paid, 160–161
  and IRS, 226
  and penalties, 126
  and travel expenses, 82–83
  and vacation home, 295
Recovery period, 26
Recreational vehicle, 36
Red-flagging tax returns, 226–227
Reform, *see* Tax Reform Act
Refund
  checking on, 216, 218
  claims, 280
  delayed, 33, 218
  and IRAs, 134
  of state and local income taxes, 67
  See also Form 1310
Refundable credits, 201
Rehabilitation of historic structures, and Tax Reform Act, 208–209
Rehabilitation tax credit, 208–209
  and Tax Reform Act, 16, 24, 26
Reimbursed business expenses, 51, 122–132
  automobile deductions, 127–128
  commuting costs, 128–129
  entertainment, 130–132
  meals, 130–132
  travel, 129–130, 131–132
Relatives
  employment of, 202
  as exemption, 55–56
  renting to, 36, 116
  See also Family
Rent
  on business property, 78–79
  ground, 35, 164
Rental, home, 267
Rental expenses, and One-Minute Taxman, 117
Rental housing (Low-income) tax credit, 209
Rental income, 266
  One-Minute Taxman, 117
Rental losses, and Tax Reform Act, 27
Rental property
  conversion to, 104
  deductions for, 115, 117, 224–225
  income or loss, 114
  and mortgage interest, 114
  passive losses and credits, 106–107, 110–111
  and relatives, 36, 116
  repairs vs. improvements, 115–116
  sale of inherited, 96
  vacation home as, 294–295

Rental real estate, 291
Repairs
  vs. home improvements, 162
  vs. improvements, 80, 115
Research, 212
Research and development, and Tax Reform Act, 24
Residence
  deferring tax on sale of, 100, 284
  55-or-over exclusion, on sale of, 104–105, 266, 284, 289–290
  loss on sale of, 104
  primary vs. secondary, 264
  qualified interest, 161
  sale of, 100, 104–105, 266, 283–284, 290
  second, 266
  See also Form 2119; Home
Retirement
  and home office business, 265
  payout options, 23, 68
  and Tax Reform Act, 23
Retirement planning, 280–283
  company retirement plans, 282–283
  compensation limit, 280
  distributions from qualified plans, 280–281
  for executives, 259–260
  401(k) plan, 280
  inherited IRAs, 283
  IRAs, 281–282, 283
  loans from qualified plans, 281
  10-year averaging vs. 5-year averaging, 281
  See also Annuities; Keogh retirement plan; Pension plans; Simplified Employee Pension (SEP) plan
Return/preparer fees, and Tax Reform Act, 24
Returns, *see* Income tax return
Reverse annuity mortgage, 289–290
Revocable trust, 293
Rollovers
  IRA, 141–143, 198–199, 260–261, 281–283
  lump-sum distributions, company retirement plans, 282–283
Royalties, from patent or invention, 114
Royalties, oil, *see* Windfall profits tax credits

Safe, cost of, 189
Salaries, 66
Salary reduction plans, 36, 283
  and hardship withdrawal, 24
  and Tax Reform Act, 24
  See also 401(k) plan
Sale
  of home, 55-or-older exclusion, 105, 266, 283–284, 290
  of inherited property, 96
  of inherited rental property, 96
  installment, 98–99, 110
  of residence, 100, 102–103, 104–105, 266, 283–284, 290
  under age, 51, 266
  wash, 271
Sales and exchanges, *see* Capital gains and losses
Salespersons, 126–129
  and entertainment expenses, 230–231
  and traveling expenses, 128–129, 230

Salespersons (cont.)
　See also Outside salespersons
Sales tax, 36, 150
　and investment property, 155
　state and local, 14, 28
　and Tax Reform Act, 14, 25, 28
Salt-free products, as medical expense, 276
SAM, see Shared appreciation mortgage
Savings
　deferred, 11
　early withdrawal penalty on, 122, 146
　and Tax Reform Act, 11
Savings bonds, 284
　interest, 66
Schedule A—Itemized Deductions, 151
Schedule B—Interest and Dividend Income, 62, 63
Schedule C—Profit (or Loss) From Business or Profession, 73, 74–75
　See also Business income or loss
Schedule D—Capital Gains and Losses and Reconciliation of Forms 1099-E, 92–93
　alternative tax calculation on new, 97–98
Schedule E—Supplemental Income Schedule, 108–109
Schedule R—Credit for the Elderly or for the Permanently and Totally Disabled, 206–207
Schedule SE—Computation of Social Security Self-Employment Tax, 210
Schedule X—Single Taxpayers, 321
Schedule Y—Married Taxpayers and Qualifying Widows and Widowers, 321
Schedule Z—Heads of Household, 321
Scholarships, and Tax Reform Act, 8, 25
Schools
　church-affiliated, 248
　private, 33, 171, 248
　special, 36, 275, 278
　tuition, 276
　See also Educational expenses
Scouts, 248
Section 179 deduction, 77–78
Securities
　for children, 61, 268
　gift of, 248
　tax-exempt, 61, 267–268
　tax planning for, 91
　U.S. government-backed, 272
　at year-end, 36, 248
　See also Capital gains and losses; Employer securities
Security deposits
　as lease cost, 181–182
　separate bank account for, 114
Security system, home, 189
Self-employed health insurance deduction, 122, 143
Self-employed persons
　filing requirements for, 41
　and moving expenses, 180–181, 183
　See also Schedule SE
Self-employed retirement plans, see Keogh retirement plan; Simplified Employee Pension (SEP) plan
Self-employment income, 278
Self-employment tax, 36, 209–210

Seminars, 233
　educational, 292
　investment, 189
Senior citizens, Social Security benefits for, 70
　See also Elderly; Old age
Separate returns, for married persons, 6–7, 55, 192–193
Separate tax, initial, 195
SEP plan, see Simplified Employee Pension (SEP) plan
Series EE bonds, 61, 267–268, 272
Settling dispute, with IRS, 236–237
Sex clinics, 277
Shared appreciation mortgage (SAM), interest on, 163–164
Shareholder-employee loans, 232
Shareholders, 189
Shelters, see Tax shelters
Shoes, see Work shoes
"Short forms," 50
Short sales, 94–95
Short-term capital gains and losses, 94–95
　and Tax Reform Act, 6, 7, 12
Short-term tax-exempt bonds, 274
Simplified Employee Pension (SEP) plan, self-employed, 122, 144, 145
Single parents, 37, 54
Single persons
　filing requirements for, 41–42
　living-together, 274–275
　tax planning for, 37, 54
　tax rates for, 6–7, 24
　and Tax Reform Act, 6–7, 12–13, 24
　See also Schedule X
Single-premium deferred annuities, 291
Single-premium life insurance, 286
　and tax shelter, 284–285
Social Security
　benefits, 27, 37, 62, 69–70, 145
　as partially taxable, 37, 62, 69–70, 145
　self-employment tax, 73
　and Tax Reform Act, 27
　See also Schedule SE
Sole proprietorship, see Schedule C
Split-dollar life insurance, 259
Spouse
　abandoned, special rules, 56
　and business travel, 133, 292
　and 55-or-over exclusion, on sale of residence, 284
　hiring, 85
　and IRA, 142, 282
　personal exemptions for, 57
　and remainder trust, 267
　surviving, 6–7, 56, 253
　travel expenses of, 133, 292
Standard deduction
　married couples vs. living together singles, 274–275
　vs. personal exemptions, 192–193
　and Tax Reform Act, 6–7, 12, 14, 25, 28
　See also New standard deduction
Start-up expenses, for business, 84, 265
State income tax, 154–155
　refunds of, 67

State sales tax, and Tax Reform Act, 14, 28
State taxes, and Tax Reform Act, 12
Status, filing, 34, 54–57, 261–262
Stock, 91
   company plans, 257–258
   as contribution, 248
   cost of shares, 246
   dividend reinvestment plan, 96
   employer, 259
   for executives, 257–258
   growth, 61
   holding period for, 37, 96
   and Tax Reform Act, 258, 260
   See also Capital gains and losses; Securities
Stockbroker, 292
Straddles, and Tax Reform Act, 25
Stripped municipal bond, 268
Student
   and child and dependent care credit, 202–203
   full-time, 248
   part-time work for, 126, 127
   support for, 248
Student loans, interest on, 165–166
Subscriptions, 189
Supper money, 82
Supplemental income, 106–119
   depletion, 118–119
   depreciation, 116–118
   passive losses and credits, 106–107, 110–111
   rental property, 111–114
   royalties, 111
   See also Form 4562; Form 8582; Schedule E
Support, 37
Surviving spouse, 56, 253
   and Tax Reform Act, 6–7
Swimming pool, as medical expense, 277

Targeted jobs credit, 83–84
   and Tax Reform Act, 25
Taxable income, and One-Minute Taxman, 65
Tax benefits, see Recapture of tax benefits
Tax brackets, 14
   lowering, 24
   and tax-exempt bonds, 37, 240
Tax computation, 54, 192
Tax credits, 201–209
   carry-backs and carry-forwards of unused, 208
   child and dependent care, 33, 34, 202–203
   earned income, 18, 213–214
   for elderly, 204–205
   energy, 19
   general business, 20, 208
   incremental research, 18
   investment, 209
   low-income housing, 16, 22, 26, 209
   nonrefundable, 201
   passive, 106–107, 110–114
   for permanently and totally disabled, 204–205
   political contributions, 24
   refundable, 201
   rehabilitation, 24, 26, 208
   targeted jobs, 183–84
   and Tax Reform Act, 18
   windfall profits, 209
Tax dates, important to remember, 40

Tax deferral, 241
   and Tax Reform Act, 285–286
Tax deficiency, 166
Taxes, 154–155
   local, 12
   local income, 67, 154
   local sales, 14
   money for, 215
   personal property, 155
   real estate, 155
   sales, and investment property, 155
   state income, 67, 154–155
   See also Back taxes
Tax-exempt bonds, 272–274
   and AMT, 212, 273
   municipal, 189, 287
   short-term, 274
   and tax bracket, 37, 240
   and Tax Reform Act, 26, 287
   zero-coupon, 267–268, 272–273
Tax-exempt interest income, 66
Tax expert, 291
Tax forms, last-minute, 215
Tax-free dividends, 269
Tax-free income, generating, 240
Tax home, locating, 133
Tax liability
   maximum, 208
   understating, 235
Tax lien, 222
Tax loopholes, 291
   diary of tax-deductible expenses, 291
   family members inheritance of appreciated assets, 291
   401(k) plan, 291
   long-term deferred compensation, 291
   rental real estate, 291
   single-premium deferred annuities, 291
   tax expert, 291
   universal life insurance, 291
   vacation home, 291
   venture partnership, 291
   See also Tax shelters
Taxpayer compliance, 227
Taxpayer Compliance Measurement Program (TCMP), 226, 227, 228
Tax planning, 240–242
   claiming everything, 240–241
   combining, 241–242
   tax bracket, lowering, 241
   tax deferral, 241
   tax-free income, generating, 240
   and Tax Reform Act, 285–287
   year-end, 37, 249
   See also Planning; Year-end tax planning
Tax preparers, 244
Tax rates, and Tax Reform Act, 6–7, 12–13, 14–15, 24, 285–286
Tax rate schedules, 194, 315–20
   Schedule X—Single Taxpayers, 321
   Schedule Y—married Taxpayers and Qualified Widows and Widowers, 321
   Schedule Z—Heads of Household, 321
Tax rate tables, 31
Tax reform, 11–12, 37

Tax Reform Act, 6–31
   and adjustments to income, 28
   and adoptions, 17
   and alimony, 146–147, 251–252
   and AMT, 14, 17, 263, 273
   and annuities, 9, 16, 23
   and at-risk rules, 16, 26
   and audits, 223, 226–227
   and awards, 17, 19
   and blind persons, 6–7, 19, 25
   and bonds, 26, 287
   and calendar year, 10
   and capital gains and losses, 6–7, 9, 11, 12, 16, 17, 26, 197, 281, 285, 286–287
   and carry-overs, 22
   and casualty losses, nonbusiness, 15, 28
   and charitable travel, 15, 129
   and children's earnings, 7
   and children's unearned income, 15, 18
   and closely held corporations, 288
   and compliance failures, 235
   and consumer interest, 28
   and contributions, 11, 15, 18, 28
   and conventions, 15, 251
   and deductions, 19, 129, 286
   and depreciation, 18, 116
   and dividends, 15, 18, 26
   and divorce, 251–252
   and early withdrawal penalty, 16
   and earned income credit, 18
   and educational travel, 11, 19, 129
   and elderly, 6–7, 19, 25
   and employee awards, 15
   and employee business expenses, 19, 27, 28
   and energy tax credits, 19
   and entertainment expenses, 131–132
   and estate tax, 21
   and estimated tax, 10, 15, 19
   and excise tax, 286
   and executives, 256–260
   and exemptions, 20, 51
   and expensing business assets, 19
   and farm financing, 20
   and fellowships, 25
   and financial and estate planning, 14–15
   and 5-year averaging, 196–197
   and foreign income, 8, 20
   and 401(k) plan, 9, 24, 27, 286
   and 403(b) plan, 9
   and general business credit, 20
   and gifts, 263
   and green card, 20
   and handicapped, barriers to, 17
   and head of household, 6–7, 13
   and health insurance, 20
   and historic structures, certified, 17
   and hobby, 8, 15, 20
   and home, 288–289
   and home office, 15, 20, 264
   and income, 26–27
   and income averaging, 11, 15, 20
   and income shifting, 21
   and indexing, 21
   and information, 21
   and interest expenses, 8, 11, 15, 17, 21, 26, 28, 286
   and interest income, 26, 35, 66–67, 270–271
   and interest rates, 21
   and intra-family loans, 271
   and investment interest, 15, 22, 27, 28, 266, 285
   and investments, 15–16
   and investment seminars, 22
   and IRA, 9, 11, 22, 27–28, 135–142, 270, 271
   and IRS, 218
   and ISO, 257–258
   and items no longer included, 7
   and joint returns, 6, 24
   and Keogh retirement plan, 27
   and life insurance, 15, 286
   and local sales tax, 14, 28
   and local taxes, 12
   and long-term capital gains, 6, 11
   and low-income housing credit, 16, 22, 26, 27
   and lump-sum distributions, 22
   and margin account charges, 286
   and married couples, 13, 274–275
   and married worker deduction, 15, 22, 27
   and meals, 17
   and medical expenses, 8, 11, 15, 22–23, 28, 150
   and miscellaneous deductions, 8, 11, 15, 23, 28
   and mortgage interest, 11, 21, 28, 162, 266
   and mortgages, 21, 286
   and moving expenses, 15, 23, 27, 28
   and municipal bonds, 287
   overview, 13–14
   oil investments, 10
   and partial rollovers (IRA), 143
   and passive income, 279
   and passive losses, 9–10, 16, 107, 287–288
   and penalties, 23
   and pension plans, 9, 12, 23
   and personal exemptions, 7, 12, 14, 19, 31
   and personal interest, 15
   and political contributions credit, 23
   and prizes, 19
   and real estate, 10, 110, 285–286
   and rehabilitation of historic structures, 208–209
   and rehabilitation tax credit, 16, 24, 26
   and rental losses, 27
   and research and development, 24
   and retirement, 23
   and return-preparer fees, 24
   and salary reduction plans, 24
   and sales tax, 14, 25, 28
   and savings, 11
   and scholarships, 8, 25
   and SEP, 145
   and single persons, 6–7, 12–13, 24
   and Social Security, 27
   and standard deduction, 6–7, 12, 14, 25, 28
   and state sales tax, 12, 28
   and state taxes, 12
   and stock, 358, 359
   and straddles, 25
   summary of, 11–13
   and targeted jobs credit, 25
   and tax credits, 18
   and tax deferral, 285
   and tax-exempt bonds, 26, 287
   and tax-free bonds, 272–273
   tax planning under, 285–287

Index

and tax rates, 6–7, 12–13, 14–15, 24, 285–286
and tax shelters, 12, 25–26, 287–290
and travel expenses, 15, 26, 129–132
and unemployment compensation benefits, 15, 26, 27
and vacation home, 294–295
and vacation property, 266
and widows, 26
worksheet calculations under, 26–31
and zero-coupon tax-exempt bonds, 267–268, 272–273
Tax return, see Income tax return
Tax savings, 242
  with IRAs, 134
Tax shelters, 230, 287–290
  annuity as rollover to IRA, 142
  and at-risk rules, 287
  boat as second home, 290
  closely held corporations, 288
  failure to register, 235
  gas wells, 288
  home as, 288–290
  home sales, 290
  and IRS, 238
  oil wells, 288
  and passive losses, 211–212, 287–288, 290
  reverse annuity mortgage, 289–290
  single-premium life insurance as, 284–285
  and Tax Reform Act, 12, 25–26, 287–290
  vacation home, 290
  See also Tax loopholes
Tax tables, 193–194, 315–21
TCMP, see Taxpayer Compliance Measurement Program
TCMP audits, 228
Teachers, 126, 188, 292
Telephone calls
  business-related, 186
  as medical expense, 275–276
Tele-Tax service (IRS), 219
Temporary away-from-home deductions, 126–127
Tenancy-in-common, 90
Tentative disallowance, 167
Tentative minimum tax (TMT), 212
Ten-year averaging, 281
  vs. 5-year averaging, 195, 196–197, 199
  See also Form 4972
Terminating employment, and lump-sum distributions, 200
Testamentary trust, 293
Theft, losses from, 84–85, 171, 179–180
  and Tax Reform Act, 28
  See also Form 4684
Therapy, as medical expense, 276
30-day letter, 237
Tips, 66, 230
TMT, see Tentative minimum tax
Tools, deduction for, 294
Total distribution, qualified, 198
Trade, defined, 278
Tradesman carrying bulky tools, 128
Transportation
  as medical expense, 154, 276
  and new business location, 82–83
Travel expenses, 291–292
  away from home, 82–83
  for business, 37, 77, 82–83, 128–130, 133, 292
  charitable, 15, 129, 292
  and conventions, foreign, 83
  educational, 11, 19, 34, 129, 183, 292
  as employee, 82–83, 129–130, 132, 184–185
  foreign, 133
  medical, 276, 292
  to new job location, 82–83
  and recordkeeping, 82
  and salespersons, 128–129, 230–231
  and seminars, 233
  of spouse, 133, 292
  and Tax Reform Act, 15, 26, 129, 131–132
Treasury bills, 66
Treasury notes, 66
Trustees' fees, 189
Trust income, 267
Trusts, 37, 254
  Clifford, 267
  family estate, 34, 293
  inter vivos, 293
  irrevocable, 254, 293
  life income, 254
  purpose of, 292
  revocable, 293
  spousal remainder, 267
  testamentary, 293
Tuition, school, 276
TV set, as medical expense, 277
Two-earner deduction, and Tax Reform Act, 12
  See also Married worker deduction

UGMA funds, 267
Under-age-14 rules, 268–269
Underwithholding, 45–46
Unearned income, of children, 7, 15, 18, 44, 61, 267–269, 272–273, 285, 287
Unemployed persons, and moving expenses, 183–184
Unemployment compensation benefits
  taxable as income, 37, 68, 293
  and Tax Reform Act, 15, 26, 27
Union membership, 293–294
  assessments for sickness, accident, and death benefits, 294
  dues, 186, 293
  initiation fees, 293
  pension fund payments, 294
  unemployment benefits, 293
  tools, 294
  work clothes, 294
  work shoes, 294
Universal life insurance, 250, 291
Unreported income, answering notices, 223–224
U.S. government-backed securities, 262
UTMA funds, 267

Vacation, 37
Vacation home, 37, 161, 291, 294–295
  defined, 294
  management decisions, 295
  and passive losses, 290
  personal purposes rule on, 294

Vacation home *(cont.)*
   and recordkeeping, 295
   renting, 294–295
   and Tax Reform Act, 294–295
Vacation property, and Tax Reform Act, 266
Vandalism, 171, 175
Variable life insurance, 286
Venture partnership, 291

Wagering, *see* Gambling winnings and losses
Wages, 66
   See also Form W-2
Waiters, 66
Waitresses, 66
Wash sale, 271
Water, as medical expense, 276
Weight-loss program, as medical expense, 276
Wells, *see* Gas wells; Oil wells
What you need in order to file, 44–45
When to file, 45
Where to file and pay, 45
Whole dollars, reporting, 45
Who must file?, 41–42
Widowers
   award, 269
   with dependent child, 56
   See also Schedule Y
Widows
   award, 269
   with dependent child, 56
   exclusion, 26
   and Tax Reform Act, 26
   See also Schedule Y
Wife, *see* Spouse
Wig, as medical expense, 277
Windfall profits tax credits, 209
Winnings, gambling, 34, 70, 278
Withdrawal, *see* Early withdrawal penalty; Hardship withdrawal
Withhholding on wages
   and alimony, 146–147
   exemptions from, 146–147
   See also Form W-4A; Form W-4EZ; Underwithholding
Work clothes, 186, 294
Working couples, married worker's deduction, and Tax Reform Act, 12, 15, 22, 27–28
Worksheet calculations, and Tax Reform Act, 26–29
Work shoes, 294
Wraparound mortgage, 98–99
Writing off property, *see* Depreciation

Yacht, 104
Year-end tax planning, 37, 249

Zero contract, college, 251
Zero-coupon tax-exempt bonds, 267, 272–273
   and Tax Reform Act, 267–268, 272–273
Zero-rate mortgages, 163

1987 Tax Table

Based on Taxable Income

For persons with taxable incomes of less than $50,000.

Example: Mr. and Mrs. Brown are filing a joint return. Their taxable income on line 36 of Form 1040 is $25,325. First, they find the $25,300-$25,350 income line. Next, they find the column for married filing jointly and read down the column. The amount shown where the income line and filing status column meet is $3,679. This is the tax amount they must write on line 37 of their return.

At least	But less than	Single	Married filing jointly*	Married filing separately	Head of a household
			Your tax is—		
25,200	25,250	4,807	3,664	5,374	3,973
25,250	25,300	4,821	3,671	5,391	3,987
25,300	25,350	4,835	(3,679)	5,409	4,001
25,350	25,400	4,849	3,686	5,426	4,015

If line 36 (taxable income) is—		And you are—				If line 36 (taxable income) is—		And you are—				If line 36 (taxable income) is—		And you are—			
At least	But less than	Single	Married filing jointly*	Married filing separately	Head of a household	At least	But less than	Single	Married filing jointly*	Married filing separately	Head of a household	At least	But less than	Single	Married filing jointly*	Married filing separately	Head of a household
			Your tax is—						Your tax is—						Your tax is—		
0	5	0	0	0	0	1,400	1,425	155	155	155	155	2,700	2,725	335	298	347	307
5	15	1	1	1	1	1,425	1,450	158	158	158	158	2,725	2,750	339	301	351	311
15	25	2	2	2	2	1,450	1,475	161	161	161	161	2,750	2,775	342	304	354	314
25	50	4	4	4	4	1,475	1,500	164	164	164	164	2,775	2,800	346	307	358	318
50	75	7	7	7	7	1,500	1,525	166	166	167	166	2,800	2,825	350	309	362	322
75	100	10	10	10	10	1,525	1,550	169	169	171	169	2,825	2,850	354	312	366	326
100	125	12	12	12	12	1,550	1,575	172	172	174	172	2,850	2,875	357	315	369	329
125	150	15	15	15	15	1,575	1,600	175	175	178	175	2,875	2,900	361	318	373	333
150	175	18	18	18	18	1,600	1,625	177	177	182	177	2,900	2,925	365	320	377	337
175	200	21	21	21	21	1,625	1,650	180	180	186	180	2,925	2,950	369	323	381	341
200	225	23	23	23	23	1,650	1,675	183	183	189	183	2,950	2,975	372	326	384	344
225	250	26	26	26	26	1,675	1,700	186	186	193	186	2,975	3,000	376	329	388	348
250	275	29	29	29	29	1,700	1,725	188	188	197	188	**3,000**					
275	300	32	32	32	32	1,725	1,750	191	191	201	191	3,000	3,050	382	334	394	354
300	325	34	34	34	34	1,750	1,775	194	194	204	194	3,050	3,100	389	341	401	361
325	350	37	37	37	37	1,775	1,800	197	197	208	197	3,100	3,150	397	349	409	369
350	375	40	40	40	40	1,800	1,825	200	199	212	199	3,150	3,200	404	356	416	376
375	400	43	43	43	43	1,825	1,850	204	202	216	202	3,200	3,250	412	364	424	384
400	425	45	45	45	45	1,850	1,875	207	205	219	205	3,250	3,300	419	371	431	391
425	450	48	48	48	48	1,875	1,900	211	208	223	208	3,300	3,350	427	379	439	399
450	475	51	51	51	51	1,900	1,925	215	210	227	210	3,350	3,400	434	386	446	406
475	500	54	54	54	54	1,925	1,950	219	213	231	213	3,400	3,450	442	394	454	414
500	525	56	56	56	56	1,950	1,975	222	216	234	216	3,450	3,500	449	401	461	421
525	550	59	59	59	59	1,975	2,000	226	219	238	219	3,500	3,550	457	409	469	429
550	575	62	62	62	62	**2,000**						3,550	3,600	464	416	476	436
575	600	65	65	65	65	2,000	2,025	230	221	242	221	3,600	3,650	472	424	484	444
600	625	67	67	67	67	2,025	2,050	234	224	246	224	3,650	3,700	479	431	491	451
625	650	70	70	70	70	2,050	2,075	237	227	249	227	3,700	3,750	487	439	499	459
650	675	73	73	73	73	2,075	2,100	241	230	253	230	3,750	3,800	494	446	506	466
675	700	76	76	76	76	2,100	2,125	245	232	257	232	3,800	3,850	502	454	514	474
700	725	78	78	78	78	2,125	2,150	249	235	261	235	3,850	3,900	509	461	521	481
725	750	81	81	81	81	2,150	2,175	252	238	264	238	3,900	3,950	517	469	529	489
750	775	84	84	84	84	2,175	2,200	256	241	268	241	3,950	4,000	524	476	536	496
775	800	87	87	87	87	2,200	2,225	260	243	272	243	**4,000**					
800	825	89	89	89	89	2,225	2,250	264	246	276	246	4,000	4,050	532	484	544	504
825	850	92	92	92	92	2,250	2,275	267	249	279	249	4,050	4,100	539	491	551	511
850	875	95	95	95	95	2,275	2,300	271	252	283	252	4,100	4,150	547	499	559	519
875	900	98	98	98	98	2,300	2,325	275	254	287	254	4,150	4,200	554	506	566	526
900	925	100	100	100	100	2,325	2,350	279	257	291	257	4,200	4,250	562	514	574	534
925	950	103	103	103	103	2,350	2,375	282	260	294	260	4,250	4,300	569	521	581	541
950	975	106	106	106	106	2,375	2,400	286	263	298	263	4,300	4,350	577	529	589	549
975	1,000	109	109	109	109	2,400	2,425	290	265	302	265	4,350	4,400	584	536	596	556
1,000						2,425	2,450	294	268	306	268	4,400	4,450	592	544	604	564
1,000	1,025	111	111	111	111	2,450	2,475	297	271	309	271	4,450	4,500	599	551	611	571
1,025	1,050	114	114	114	114	2,475	2,500	301	274	313	274	4,500	4,550	607	559	619	579
1,050	1,075	117	117	117	117	2,500	2,525	305	276	317	277	4,550	4,600	614	566	626	586
1,075	1,100	120	120	120	120	2,525	2,550	309	279	321	281	4,600	4,650	622	574	634	594
1,100	1,125	122	122	122	122	2,550	2,575	312	282	324	284	4,650	4,700	629	581	641	601
1,125	1,150	125	125	125	125	2,575	2,600	316	285	328	288	4,700	4,750	637	589	649	609
1,150	1,175	128	128	128	128	2,600	2,625	320	287	332	292	4,750	4,800	644	596	656	616
1,175	1,200	131	131	131	131	2,625	2,650	324	290	336	296	4,800	4,850	652	604	664	624
1,200	1,225	133	133	133	133	2,650	2,675	327	293	339	299	4,850	4,900	659	611	671	631
1,225	1,250	136	136	136	136	2,675	2,700	331	296	343	303	4,900	4,950	667	619	679	639
1,250	1,275	139	139	139	139							4,950	5,000	674	626	686	646
1,275	1,300	142	142	142	142												
1,300	1,325	144	144	144	144												
1,325	1,350	147	147	147	147												
1,350	1,375	150	150	150	150												
1,375	1,400	153	153	153	153												

* This column must also be used by a qualifying widow(er).

Continued on next page

1987 Tax Table—Continued

If line 36 (taxable income) is—		And you are—				If line 36 (taxable income) is—		And you are—				If line 36 (taxable income) is—		And you are—			
At least	But less than	Single	Married filing jointly *	Married filing separately	Head of a household	At least	But less than	Single	Married filing jointly *	Married filing separately	Head of a household	At least	But less than	Single	Married filing jointly *	Married filing separately	Head of a household
			Your tax is—					Your tax is—					Your tax is—		
5,000						**8,000**						**11,000**					
5,000	5,050	682	634	694	654	8,000	8,050	1,132	1,084	1,144	1,104	11,000	11,050	1,582	1,534	1,594	1,554
5,050	5,100	689	641	701	661	8,050	8,100	1,139	1,091	1,151	1,111	11,050	11,100	1,589	1,541	1,601	1,561
5,100	5,150	697	649	709	669	8,100	8,150	1,147	1,099	1,159	1,119	11,100	11,150	1,597	1,549	1,609	1,569
5,150	5,200	704	656	716	676	8,150	8,200	1,154	1,106	1,166	1,126	11,150	11,200	1,604	1,556	1,616	1,576
5,200	5,250	712	664	724	684	8,200	8,250	1,162	1,114	1,174	1,134	11,200	11,250	1,612	1,564	1,624	1,584
5,250	5,300	719	671	731	691	8,250	8,300	1,169	1,121	1,181	1,141	11,250	11,300	1,619	1,571	1,631	1,591
5,300	5,350	727	679	739	699	8,300	8,350	1,177	1,129	1,189	1,149	11,300	11,350	1,627	1,579	1,639	1,599
5,350	5,400	734	686	746	706	8,350	8,400	1,184	1,136	1,196	1,156	11,350	11,400	1,634	1,586	1,646	1,606
5,400	5,450	742	694	754	714	8,400	8,450	1,192	1,144	1,204	1,164	11,400	11,450	1,642	1,594	1,654	1,614
5,450	5,500	749	701	761	721	8,450	8,500	1,199	1,151	1,211	1,171	11,450	11,500	1,649	1,601	1,661	1,621
5,500	5,550	757	709	769	729	8,500	8,550	1,207	1,159	1,219	1,179	11,500	11,550	1,657	1,609	1,669	1,629
5,550	5,600	764	716	776	736	8,550	8,600	1,214	1,166	1,226	1,186	11,550	11,600	1,664	1,616	1,676	1,636
5,600	5,650	772	724	784	744	8,600	8,650	1,222	1,174	1,234	1,194	11,600	11,650	1,672	1,624	1,684	1,644
5,650	5,700	779	731	791	751	8,650	8,700	1,229	1,181	1,241	1,201	11,650	11,700	1,679	1,631	1,691	1,651
5,700	5,750	787	739	799	759	8,700	8,750	1,237	1,189	1,249	1,209	11,700	11,750	1,687	1,639	1,699	1,659
5,750	5,800	794	746	806	766	8,750	8,800	1,244	1,196	1,256	1,216	11,750	11,800	1,694	1,646	1,706	1,666
5,800	5,850	802	754	814	774	8,800	8,850	1,252	1,204	1,264	1,224	11,800	11,850	1,702	1,654	1,714	1,674
5,850	5,900	809	761	821	781	8,850	8,900	1,259	1,211	1,271	1,231	11,850	11,900	1,709	1,661	1,721	1,681
5,900	5,950	817	769	829	789	8,900	8,950	1,267	1,219	1,279	1,239	11,900	11,950	1,717	1,669	1,729	1,689
5,950	6,000	824	776	836	796	8,950	9,000	1,274	1,226	1,286	1,246	11,950	12,000	1,724	1,676	1,736	1,696
6,000						**9,000**						**12,000**					
6,000	6,050	832	784	844	804	9,000	9,050	1,282	1,234	1,294	1,254	12,000	12,050	1,732	1,684	1,744	1,704
6,050	6,100	839	791	851	811	9,050	9,100	1,289	1,241	1,301	1,261	12,050	12,100	1,739	1,691	1,751	1,711
6,100	6,150	847	799	859	819	9,100	9,150	1,297	1,249	1,309	1,269	12,100	12,150	1,747	1,699	1,759	1,719
6,150	6,200	854	806	866	826	9,150	9,200	1,304	1,256	1,316	1,276	12,150	12,200	1,754	1,706	1,766	1,726
6,200	6,250	862	814	874	834	9,200	9,250	1,312	1,264	1,324	1,284	12,200	12,250	1,762	1,714	1,774	1,734
6,250	6,300	869	821	881	841	9,250	9,300	1,319	1,271	1,331	1,291	12,250	12,300	1,769	1,721	1,781	1,741
6,300	6,350	877	829	889	849	9,300	9,350	1,327	1,279	1,339	1,299	12,300	12,350	1,777	1,729	1,789	1,749
6,350	6,400	884	836	896	856	9,350	9,400	1,334	1,286	1,346	1,306	12,350	12,400	1,784	1,736	1,796	1,756
6,400	6,450	892	844	904	864	9,400	9,450	1,342	1,294	1,354	1,314	12,400	12,450	1,792	1,744	1,804	1,764
6,450	6,500	899	851	911	871	9,450	9,500	1,349	1,301	1,361	1,321	12,450	12,500	1,799	1,751	1,811	1,771
6,500	6,550	907	859	919	879	9,500	9,550	1,357	1,309	1,369	1,329	12,500	12,550	1,807	1,759	1,819	1,779
6,550	6,600	914	866	926	886	9,550	9,600	1,364	1,316	1,376	1,336	12,550	12,600	1,814	1,766	1,826	1,786
6,600	6,650	922	874	934	894	9,600	9,650	1,372	1,324	1,384	1,344	12,600	12,650	1,822	1,774	1,834	1,794
6,650	6,700	929	881	941	901	9,650	9,700	1,379	1,331	1,391	1,351	12,650	12,700	1,829	1,781	1,841	1,801
6,700	6,750	937	889	949	909	9,700	9,750	1,387	1,339	1,399	1,359	12,700	12,750	1,837	1,789	1,849	1,809
6,750	6,800	944	896	956	916	9,750	9,800	1,394	1,346	1,406	1,366	12,750	12,800	1,844	1,796	1,856	1,816
6,800	6,850	952	904	964	924	9,800	9,850	1,402	1,354	1,414	1,374	12,800	12,850	1,852	1,804	1,864	1,824
6,850	6,900	959	911	971	931	9,850	9,900	1,409	1,361	1,421	1,381	12,850	12,900	1,859	1,811	1,871	1,831
6,900	6,950	967	919	979	939	9,900	9,950	1,417	1,369	1,429	1,389	12,900	12,950	1,867	1,819	1,879	1,839
6,950	7,000	974	926	986	946	9,950	10,000	1,424	1,376	1,436	1,396	12,950	13,000	1,874	1,826	1,886	1,846
7,000						**10,000**						**13,000**					
7,000	7,050	982	934	994	954	10,000	10,050	1,432	1,384	1,444	1,404	13,000	13,050	1,882	1,834	1,894	1,854
7,050	7,100	989	941	1,001	961	10,050	10,100	1,439	1,391	1,451	1,411	13,050	13,100	1,889	1,841	1,901	1,861
7,100	7,150	997	949	1,009	969	10,100	10,150	1,447	1,399	1,459	1,419	13,100	13,150	1,897	1,849	1,909	1,869
7,150	7,200	1,004	956	1,016	976	10,150	10,200	1,454	1,406	1,466	1,426	13,150	13,200	1,904	1,856	1,916	1,876
7,200	7,250	1,012	964	1,024	984	10,200	10,250	1,462	1,414	1,474	1,434	13,200	13,250	1,912	1,864	1,924	1,884
7,250	7,300	1,019	971	1,031	991	10,250	10,300	1,469	1,421	1,481	1,441	13,250	13,300	1,919	1,871	1,931	1,891
7,300	7,350	1,027	979	1,039	999	10,300	10,350	1,477	1,429	1,489	1,449	13,300	13,350	1,927	1,879	1,939	1,899
7,350	7,400	1,034	986	1,046	1,006	10,350	10,400	1,484	1,436	1,496	1,456	13,350	13,400	1,934	1,886	1,946	1,906
7,400	7,450	1,042	994	1,054	1,014	10,400	10,450	1,492	1,444	1,504	1,464	13,400	13,450	1,942	1,894	1,954	1,914
7,450	7,500	1,049	1,001	1,061	1,021	10,450	10,500	1,499	1,451	1,511	1,471	13,450	13,500	1,949	1,901	1,961	1,921
7,500	7,550	1,057	1,009	1,069	1,029	10,500	10,550	1,507	1,459	1,519	1,479	13,500	13,550	1,957	1,909	1,969	1,929
7,550	7,600	1,064	1,016	1,076	1,036	10,550	10,600	1,514	1,466	1,526	1,486	13,550	13,600	1,964	1,916	1,976	1,936
7,600	7,650	1,072	1,024	1,084	1,044	10,600	10,650	1,522	1,474	1,534	1,494	13,600	13,650	1,972	1,924	1,984	1,944
7,650	7,700	1,079	1,031	1,091	1,051	10,650	10,700	1,529	1,481	1,541	1,501	13,650	13,700	1,979	1,931	1,991	1,951
7,700	7,750	1,087	1,039	1,099	1,059	10,700	10,750	1,537	1,489	1,549	1,509	13,700	13,750	1,987	1,939	1,999	1,959
7,750	7,800	1,094	1,046	1,106	1,066	10,750	10,800	1,544	1,496	1,556	1,516	13,750	13,800	1,994	1,946	2,006	1,966
7,800	7,850	1,102	1,054	1,114	1,074	10,800	10,850	1,552	1,504	1,564	1,524	13,800	13,850	2,002	1,954	2,014	1,974
7,850	7,900	1,109	1,061	1,121	1,081	10,850	10,900	1,559	1,511	1,571	1,531	13,850	13,900	2,009	1,961	2,021	1,981
7,900	7,950	1,117	1,069	1,129	1,089	10,900	10,950	1,567	1,519	1,579	1,539	13,900	13,950	2,017	1,969	2,029	1,989
7,950	8,000	1,124	1,076	1,136	1,096	10,950	11,000	1,574	1,526	1,586	1,546	13,950	14,000	2,024	1,976	2,036	1,996

* This column must also be used by a qualifying widow(er).

Continued on next page

1987 Tax Table—Continued

If line 36 (taxable income) is—		And you are—				If line 36 (taxable income) is—		And you are—				If line 36 (taxable income) is—		And you are—			
At least	But less than	Single	Married filing jointly *	Married filing separately	Head of a household	At least	But less than	Single	Married filing jointly *	Married filing separately	Head of a household	At least	But less than	Single	Married filing jointly *	Married filing separately	Head of a household
		Your tax is—						Your tax is—						Your tax is—			
14,000						**17,000**						**20,000**					
14,000	14,050	2,032	1,984	2,047	2,004	17,000	17,050	2,511	2,434	2,887	2,454	20,000	20,050	3,351	2,884	3,727	2,904
14,050	14,100	2,039	1,991	2,061	2,011	17,050	17,100	2,525	2,441	2,901	2,461	20,050	20,100	3,365	2,891	3,741	2,911
14,100	14,150	2,047	1,999	2,075	2,019	17,100	17,150	2,539	2,449	2,915	2,469	20,100	20,150	3,379	2,899	3,755	2,919
14,150	14,200	2,054	2,006	2,089	2,026	17,150	17,200	2,553	2,456	2,929	2,476	20,150	20,200	3,393	2,906	3,769	2,926
14,200	14,250	2,062	2,014	2,103	2,034	17,200	17,250	2,567	2,464	2,943	2,484	20,200	20,250	3,407	2,914	3,783	2,934
14,250	14,300	2,069	2,021	2,117	2,041	17,250	17,300	2,581	2,471	2,957	2,491	20,250	20,300	3,421	2,921	3,797	2,941
14,300	14,350	2,077	2,029	2,131	2,049	17,300	17,350	2,595	2,479	2,971	2,499	20,300	20,350	3,435	2,929	3,811	2,949
14,350	14,400	2,084	2,036	2,145	2,056	17,350	17,400	2,609	2,486	2,985	2,506	20,350	20,400	3,449	2,936	3,825	2,956
14,400	14,450	2,092	2,044	2,159	2,064	17,400	17,450	2,623	2,494	2,999	2,514	20,400	20,450	3,463	2,944	3,839	2,964
14,450	14,500	2,099	2,051	2,173	2,071	17,450	17,500	2,637	2,501	3,013	2,521	20,450	20,500	3,477	2,951	3,853	2,971
14,500	14,550	2,107	2,059	2,187	2,079	17,500	17,550	2,651	2,509	3,027	2,529	20,500	20,550	3,491	2,959	3,867	2,979
14,550	14,600	2,114	2,066	2,201	2,086	17,550	17,600	2,665	2,516	3,041	2,536	20,550	20,600	3,505	2,966	3,881	2,986
14,600	14,650	2,122	2,074	2,215	2,094	17,600	17,650	2,679	2,524	3,055	2,544	20,600	20,650	3,519	2,974	3,895	2,994
14,650	14,700	2,129	2,081	2,229	2,101	17,650	17,700	2,693	2,531	3,069	2,551	20,650	20,700	3,533	2,981	3,909	3,001
14,700	14,750	2,137	2,089	2,243	2,109	17,700	17,750	2,707	2,539	3,083	2,559	20,700	20,750	3,547	2,989	3,923	3,009
14,750	14,800	2,144	2,096	2,257	2,116	17,750	17,800	2,721	2,546	3,097	2,566	20,750	20,800	3,561	2,996	3,937	3,016
14,800	14,850	2,152	2,104	2,271	2,124	17,800	17,850	2,735	2,554	3,111	2,574	20,800	20,850	3,575	3,004	3,951	3,024
14,850	14,900	2,159	2,111	2,285	2,131	17,850	17,900	2,749	2,561	3,125	2,581	20,850	20,900	3,589	3,011	3,965	3,031
14,900	14,950	2,167	2,119	2,299	2,139	17,900	17,950	2,763	2,569	3,139	2,589	20,900	20,950	3,603	3,019	3,979	3,039
14,950	15,000	2,174	2,126	2,313	2,146	17,950	18,000	2,777	2,576	3,153	2,596	20,950	21,000	3,617	3,026	3,993	3,046
15,000						**18,000**						**21,000**					
15,000	15,050	2,182	2,134	2,327	2,154	18,000	18,050	2,791	2,584	3,167	2,604	21,000	21,050	3,631	3,034	4,007	3,054
15,050	15,100	2,189	2,141	2,341	2,161	18,050	18,100	2,805	2,591	3,181	2,611	21,050	21,100	3,645	3,041	4,021	3,061
15,100	15,150	2,197	2,149	2,355	2,169	18,100	18,150	2,819	2,599	3,195	2,619	21,100	21,150	3,659	3,049	4,035	3,069
15,150	15,200	2,204	2,156	2,369	2,176	18,150	18,200	2,833	2,606	3,209	2,626	21,150	21,200	3,673	3,056	4,049	3,076
15,200	15,250	2,212	2,164	2,383	2,184	18,200	18,250	2,847	2,614	3,223	2,634	21,200	21,250	3,687	3,064	4,063	3,084
15,250	15,300	2,219	2,171	2,397	2,191	18,250	18,300	2,861	2,621	3,237	2,641	21,250	21,300	3,701	3,071	4,077	3,091
15,300	15,350	2,227	2,179	2,411	2,199	18,300	18,350	2,875	2,629	3,251	2,649	21,300	21,350	3,715	3,079	4,091	3,099
15,350	15,400	2,234	2,186	2,425	2,206	18,350	18,400	2,889	2,636	3,265	2,656	21,350	21,400	3,729	3,086	4,105	3,106
15,400	15,450	2,242	2,194	2,439	2,214	18,400	18,450	2,903	2,644	3,279	2,664	21,400	21,450	3,743	3,094	4,119	3,114
15,450	15,500	2,249	2,201	2,453	2,221	18,450	18,500	2,917	2,651	3,293	2,671	21,450	21,500	3,757	3,101	4,133	3,121
15,500	15,550	2,257	2,209	2,467	2,229	18,500	18,550	2,931	2,659	3,307	2,679	21,500	21,550	3,771	3,109	4,147	3,129
15,550	15,600	2,264	2,216	2,481	2,236	18,550	18,600	2,945	2,666	3,321	2,686	21,550	21,600	3,785	3,116	4,161	3,136
15,600	15,650	2,272	2,224	2,495	2,244	18,600	18,650	2,959	2,674	3,335	2,694	21,600	21,650	3,799	3,124	4,175	3,144
15,650	15,700	2,279	2,231	2,509	2,251	18,650	18,700	2,973	2,681	3,349	2,701	21,650	21,700	3,813	3,131	4,189	3,151
15,700	15,750	2,287	2,239	2,523	2,259	18,700	18,750	2,987	2,689	3,363	2,709	21,700	21,750	3,827	3,139	4,203	3,159
15,750	15,800	2,294	2,246	2,537	2,266	18,750	18,800	3,001	2,696	3,377	2,716	21,750	21,800	3,841	3,146	4,217	3,166
15,800	15,850	2,302	2,254	2,551	2,274	18,800	18,850	3,015	2,704	3,391	2,724	21,800	21,850	3,855	3,154	4,231	3,174
15,850	15,900	2,309	2,261	2,565	2,281	18,850	18,900	3,029	2,711	3,405	2,731	21,850	21,900	3,869	3,161	4,245	3,181
15,900	15,950	2,317	2,269	2,579	2,289	18,900	18,950	3,043	2,719	3,419	2,739	21,900	21,950	3,883	3,169	4,259	3,189
15,950	16,000	2,324	2,276	2,593	2,296	18,950	19,000	3,057	2,726	3,433	2,746	21,950	22,000	3,897	3,176	4,273	3,196
16,000						**19,000**						**22,000**					
16,000	16,050	2,332	2,284	2,607	2,304	19,000	19,050	3,071	2,734	3,447	2,754	22,000	22,050	3,911	3,184	4,287	3,204
16,050	16,100	2,339	2,291	2,621	2,311	19,050	19,100	3,085	2,741	3,461	2,761	22,050	22,100	3,925	3,191	4,301	3,211
16,100	16,150	2,347	2,299	2,635	2,319	19,100	19,150	3,099	2,749	3,475	2,769	22,100	22,150	3,939	3,199	4,315	3,219
16,150	16,200	2,354	2,306	2,649	2,326	19,150	19,200	3,113	2,756	3,489	2,776	22,150	22,200	3,953	3,206	4,329	3,226
16,200	16,250	2,362	2,314	2,663	2,334	19,200	19,250	3,127	2,764	3,503	2,784	22,200	22,250	3,967	3,214	4,343	3,234
16,250	16,300	2,369	2,321	2,677	2,341	19,250	19,300	3,141	2,771	3,517	2,791	22,250	22,300	3,981	3,221	4,357	3,241
16,300	16,350	2,377	2,329	2,691	2,349	19,300	19,350	3,155	2,779	3,531	2,799	22,300	22,350	3,995	3,229	4,371	3,249
16,350	16,400	2,384	2,336	2,705	2,356	19,350	19,400	3,169	2,786	3,545	2,806	22,350	22,400	4,009	3,236	4,385	3,256
16,400	16,450	2,392	2,344	2,719	2,364	19,400	19,450	3,183	2,794	3,559	2,814	22,400	22,450	4,023	3,244	4,399	3,264
16,450	16,500	2,399	2,351	2,733	2,371	19,450	19,500	3,197	2,801	3,573	2,821	22,450	22,500	4,037	3,251	4,413	3,271
16,500	16,550	2,407	2,359	2,747	2,379	19,500	19,550	3,211	2,809	3,587	2,829	22,500	22,550	4,051	3,259	4,429	3,279
16,550	16,600	2,414	2,366	2,761	2,386	19,550	19,600	3,225	2,816	3,601	2,836	22,550	22,600	4,065	3,266	4,446	3,286
16,600	16,650	2,422	2,374	2,775	2,394	19,600	19,650	3,239	2,824	3,615	2,844	22,600	22,650	4,079	3,274	4,464	3,294
16,650	16,700	2,429	2,381	2,789	2,401	19,650	19,700	3,253	2,831	3,629	2,851	22,650	22,700	4,093	3,281	4,481	3,301
16,700	16,750	2,437	2,389	2,803	2,409	19,700	19,750	3,267	2,839	3,643	2,859	22,700	22,750	4,107	3,289	4,499	3,309
16,750	16,800	2,444	2,396	2,817	2,416	19,750	19,800	3,281	2,846	3,657	2,866	22,750	22,800	4,121	3,296	4,516	3,316
16,800	16,850	2,455	2,404	2,831	2,424	19,800	19,850	3,295	2,854	3,671	2,874	22,800	22,850	4,135	3,304	4,534	3,324
16,850	16,900	2,469	2,411	2,845	2,431	19,850	19,900	3,309	2,861	3,685	2,881	22,850	22,900	4,149	3,311	4,551	3,331
16,900	16,950	2,483	2,419	2,859	2,439	19,900	19,950	3,323	2,869	3,699	2,889	22,900	22,950	4,163	3,319	4,569	3,339
16,950	17,000	2,497	2,426	2,873	2,446	19,950	20,000	3,337	2,876	3,713	2,896	22,950	23,000	4,177	3,326	4,586	3,346

* This column must also be used by a qualifying widow(er).

Continued on next page

1987 Tax Table—Continued

If line 36 (taxable income) is—		And you are—				If line 36 (taxable income) is—		And you are—				If line 36 (taxable income) is—		And you are—			
At least	But less than	Single	Married filing jointly *	Married filing separately	Head of a household	At least	But less than	Single	Married filing jointly *	Married filing separately	Head of a household	At least	But less than	Single	Married filing jointly *	Married filing separately	Head of a household
		Your tax is—						Your tax is—						Your tax is—			
23,000						**26,000**						**29,000**					
23,000	23,050	4,191	3,334	4,604	3,357	26,000	26,050	5,031	3,784	5,654	4,197	29,000	29,050	6,013	4,367	6,704	5,037
23,050	23,100	4,205	3,341	4,621	3,371	26,050	26,100	5,045	3,791	5,671	4,211	29,050	29,100	6,030	4,381	6,721	5,051
23,100	23,150	4,219	3,349	4,639	3,385	26,100	26,150	5,059	3,799	5,689	4,225	29,100	29,150	6,048	4,395	6,739	5,065
23,150	23,200	4,233	3,356	4,656	3,399	26,150	26,200	5,073	3,806	5,706	4,239	29,150	29,200	6,065	4,409	6,756	5,079
23,200	23,250	4,247	3,364	4,674	3,413	26,200	26,250	5,087	3,814	5,724	4,253	29,200	29,250	6,083	4,423	6,774	5,093
23,250	23,300	4,261	3,371	4,691	3,427	26,250	26,300	5,101	3,821	5,741	4,267	29,250	29,300	6,100	4,437	6,791	5,107
23,300	23,350	4,275	3,379	4,709	3,441	26,300	26,350	5,115	3,829	5,759	4,281	29,300	29,350	6,118	4,451	6,809	5,121
23,350	23,400	4,289	3,386	4,726	3,455	26,350	26,400	5,129	3,836	5,776	4,295	29,350	29,400	6,135	4,465	6,826	5,135
23,400	23,450	4,303	3,394	4,744	3,469	26,400	26,450	5,143	3,844	5,794	4,309	29,400	29,450	6,153	4,479	6,844	5,149
23,450	23,500	4,317	3,401	4,761	3,483	26,450	26,500	5,157	3,851	5,811	4,323	29,450	29,500	6,170	4,493	6,861	5,163
23,500	23,550	4,331	3,409	4,779	3,497	26,500	26,550	5,171	3,859	5,829	4,337	29,500	29,550	6,188	4,507	6,879	5,177
23,550	23,600	4,345	3,416	4,796	3,511	26,550	26,600	5,185	3,866	5,846	4,351	29,550	29,600	6,205	4,521	6,896	5,191
23,600	23,650	4,359	3,424	4,814	3,525	26,600	26,650	5,199	3,874	5,864	4,365	29,600	29,650	6,223	4,535	6,914	5,205
23,650	23,700	4,373	3,431	4,831	3,539	26,650	26,700	5,213	3,881	5,881	4,379	29,650	29,700	6,240	4,549	6,931	5,219
23,700	23,750	4,387	3,439	4,849	3,553	26,700	26,750	5,227	3,889	5,899	4,393	29,700	29,750	6,258	4,563	6,949	5,233
23,750	23,800	4,401	3,446	4,866	3,567	26,750	26,800	5,241	3,896	5,916	4,407	29,750	29,800	6,275	4,577	6,966	5,247
23,800	23,850	4,415	3,454	4,884	3,581	26,800	26,850	5,255	3,904	5,934	4,421	29,800	29,850	6,293	4,591	6,984	5,261
23,850	23,900	4,429	3,461	4,901	3,595	26,850	26,900	5,269	3,911	5,951	4,435	29,850	29,900	6,310	4,605	7,001	5,275
23,900	23,950	4,443	3,469	4,919	3,609	26,900	26,950	5,283	3,919	5,969	4,449	29,900	29,950	6,328	4,619	7,019	5,289
23,950	24,000	4,457	3,476	4,936	3,623	26,950	27,000	5,297	3,926	5,986	4,463	29,950	30,000	6,345	4,633	7,036	5,303
24,000						**27,000**						**30,000**					
24,000	24,050	4,471	3,484	4,954	3,637	27,000	27,050	5,318	3,934	6,004	4,477	30,000	30,050	6,363	4,647	7,054	5,317
24,050	24,100	4,485	3,491	4,971	3,651	27,050	27,100	5,330	3,941	6,021	4,491	30,050	30,100	6,380	4,661	7,071	5,331
24,100	24,150	4,499	3,499	4,989	3,665	27,100	27,150	5,348	3,949	6,039	4,505	30,100	30,150	6,398	4,675	7,089	5,345
24,150	24,200	4,513	3,506	5,006	3,679	27,150	27,200	5,365	3,956	6,056	4,519	30,150	30,200	6,415	4,689	7,106	5,359
24,200	24,250	4,527	3,514	5,024	3,693	27,200	27,250	5,383	3,964	6,074	4,533	30,200	30,250	6,433	4,703	7,124	5,373
24,250	24,300	4,541	3,521	5,041	3,707	27,250	27,300	5,400	3,971	6,091	4,547	30,250	30,300	6,450	4,717	7,141	5,387
24,300	24,350	4,555	3,529	5,059	3,721	27,300	27,350	5,418	3,979	6,109	4,561	30,300	30,350	6,468	4,731	7,159	5,401
24,350	24,400	4,569	3,536	5,076	3,735	27,350	27,400	5,435	3,986	6,126	4,575	30,350	30,400	6,485	4,745	7,176	5,415
24,400	24,450	4,583	3,544	5,094	3,749	27,400	27,450	5,453	3,994	6,144	4,589	30,400	30,450	6,503	4,759	7,194	5,429
24,450	24,500	4,597	3,551	5,111	3,763	27,450	27,500	5,470	4,001	6,161	4,603	30,450	30,500	6,520	4,773	7,211	5,443
24,500	24,550	4,611	3,559	5,129	3,777	27,500	27,550	5,488	4,009	6,179	4,617	30,500	30,550	6,538	4,787	7,229	5,457
24,550	24,600	4,625	3,566	5,146	3,791	27,550	27,600	5,505	4,016	6,196	4,631	30,550	30,600	6,555	4,801	7,246	5,471
24,600	24,650	4,639	3,574	5,164	3,805	27,600	27,650	5,523	4,024	6,214	4,645	30,600	30,650	6,573	4,815	7,264	5,485
24,650	24,700	4,653	3,581	5,181	3,819	27,650	27,700	5,540	4,031	6,231	4,659	30,650	30,700	6,590	4,829	7,281	5,499
24,700	24,750	4,667	3,589	5,199	3,833	27,700	27,750	5,558	4,039	6,249	4,673	30,700	30,750	6,608	4,843	7,299	5,513
24,750	24,800	4,681	3,596	5,216	3,847	27,750	27,800	5,575	4,046	6,266	4,687	30,750	30,800	6,625	4,857	7,316	5,527
24,800	24,850	4,695	3,604	5,234	3,861	27,800	27,850	5,593	4,054	6,284	4,701	30,800	30,850	6,643	4,871	7,334	5,541
24,850	24,900	4,709	3,611	5,251	3,875	27,850	27,900	5,610	4,061	6,301	4,715	30,850	30,900	6,660	4,885	7,351	5,555
24,900	24,950	4,723	3,619	5,269	3,889	27,900	27,950	5,628	4,069	6,319	4,729	30,900	30,950	6,678	4,899	7,369	5,569
24,950	25,000	4,737	3,626	5,286	3,903	27,950	28,000	5,645	4,076	6,336	4,743	30,950	31,000	6,695	4,913	7,386	5,583
25,000						**28,000**						**31,000**					
25,000	25,050	4,751	3,634	5,304	3,917	28,000	28,050	5,663	4,087	6,354	4,757	31,000	31,050	6,713	4,927	7,404	5,597
25,050	25,100	4,765	3,641	5,321	3,931	28,050	28,100	5,680	4,101	6,371	4,771	31,050	31,100	6,730	4,941	7,421	5,611
25,100	25,150	4,779	3,649	5,339	3,945	28,100	28,150	5,698	4,115	6,389	4,785	31,100	31,150	6,748	4,955	7,439	5,625
25,150	25,200	4,793	3,656	5,356	3,959	28,150	28,200	5,715	4,129	6,406	4,799	31,150	31,200	6,765	4,969	7,456	5,639
25,200	25,250	4,807	3,664	5,374	3,973	28,200	28,250	5,733	4,143	6,424	4,813	31,200	31,250	6,783	4,983	7,474	5,653
25,250	25,300	4,821	3,671	5,391	3,987	28,250	28,300	5,750	4,157	6,441	4,827	31,250	31,300	6,800	4,997	7,491	5,667
25,300	25,350	4,835	3,679	5,409	4,001	28,300	28,350	5,768	4,171	6,459	4,841	31,300	31,350	6,818	5,011	7,509	5,681
25,350	25,400	4,849	3,686	5,426	4,015	28,350	28,400	5,785	4,185	6,476	4,855	31,350	31,400	6,835	5,025	7,526	5,695
25,400	25,450	4,863	3,694	5,444	4,029	28,400	28,450	5,803	4,199	6,494	4,869	31,400	31,450	6,853	5,039	7,544	5,709
25,450	25,500	4,877	3,701	5,461	4,043	28,450	28,500	5,820	4,213	6,511	4,883	31,450	31,500	6,870	5,053	7,561	5,723
25,500	25,550	4,891	3,709	5,479	4,057	28,500	28,550	5,838	4,227	6,529	4,897	31,500	31,550	6,888	5,067	7,579	5,737
25,550	25,600	4,905	3,716	5,496	4,071	28,550	28,600	5,855	4,241	6,546	4,911	31,550	31,600	6,905	5,081	7,596	5,751
25,600	25,650	4,919	3,724	5,514	4,085	28,600	28,650	5,873	4,255	6,564	4,925	31,600	31,650	6,923	5,095	7,614	5,765
25,650	25,700	4,933	3,731	5,531	4,099	28,650	28,700	5,890	4,269	6,581	4,939	31,650	31,700	6,940	5,109	7,631	5,779
25,700	25,750	4,947	3,739	5,549	4,113	28,700	28,750	5,908	4,283	6,599	4,953	31,700	31,750	6,958	5,123	7,649	5,793
25,750	25,800	4,961	3,746	5,566	4,127	28,750	28,800	5,925	4,297	6,616	4,967	31,750	31,800	6,975	5,137	7,666	5,807
25,800	25,850	4,975	3,754	5,584	4,141	28,800	28,850	5,943	4,311	6,634	4,981	31,800	31,850	6,993	5,151	7,684	5,821
25,850	25,900	4,989	3,761	5,601	4,155	28,850	28,900	5,960	4,325	6,651	4,995	31,850	31,900	7,010	5,165	7,701	5,835
25,900	25,950	5,003	3,769	5,619	4,169	28,900	28,950	5,978	4,339	6,669	5,009	31,900	31,950	7,028	5,179	7,719	5,849
25,950	26,000	5,017	3,776	5,636	4,183	28,950	29,000	5,995	4,353	6,686	5,023	31,950	32,000	7,045	5,193	7,736	5,863

* This column must also be used by a qualifying widow(er).

Continued on next page

1987 Tax Table—Continued

If line 36 (taxable income) is—		And you are—				If line 36 (taxable income) is—		And you are—				If line 36 (taxable income) is—		And you are—			
At least	But less than	Single	Married filing jointly *	Married filing separately	Head of a household	At least	But less than	Single	Married filing jointly *	Married filing separately	Head of a household	At least	But less than	Single	Married filing jointly *	Married filing separately	Head of a household
		Your tax is—						Your tax is—						Your tax is—			
32,000						**35,000**						**38,000**					
32,000	32,050	7,063	5,207	7,754	5,877	35,000	35,050	8,113	6,047	8,804	6,717	38,000	38,050	9,163	6,887	9,854	7,559
32,050	32,100	7,080	5,221	7,771	5,891	35,050	35,100	8,130	6,061	8,821	6,731	38,050	38,100	9,180	6,901	9,871	7,576
32,100	32,150	7,098	5,235	7,789	5,905	35,100	35,150	8,148	6,075	8,839	6,745	38,100	38,150	9,198	6,915	9,889	7,594
32,150	32,200	7,115	5,249	7,806	5,919	35,150	35,200	8,165	6,089	8,856	6,759	38,150	38,200	9,215	6,929	9,906	7,611
32,200	32,250	7,133	5,263	7,824	5,933	35,200	35,250	8,183	6,103	8,874	6,773	38,200	38,250	9,233	6,943	9,924	7,629
32,250	32,300	7,150	5,277	7,841	5,947	35,250	35,300	8,200	6,117	8,891	6,787	38,250	38,300	9,250	6,957	9,941	7,646
32,300	32,350	7,168	5,291	7,859	5,961	35,300	35,350	8,218	6,131	8,909	6,801	38,300	38,350	9,268	6,971	9,959	7,664
32,350	32,400	7,185	5,305	7,876	5,975	35,350	35,400	8,235	6,145	8,926	6,815	38,350	38,400	9,285	6,985	9,976	7,681
32,400	32,450	7,203	5,319	7,894	5,989	35,400	35,450	8,253	6,159	8,944	6,829	38,400	38,450	9,303	6,999	9,994	7,699
32,450	32,500	7,220	5,333	7,911	6,003	35,450	35,500	8,270	6,173	8,961	6,843	38,450	38,500	9,320	7,013	10,011	7,716
32,500	32,550	7,238	5,347	7,929	6,017	35,500	35,550	8,288	6,187	8,979	6,857	38,500	38,550	9,338	7,027	10,029	7,734
32,550	32,600	7,255	5,361	7,946	6,031	35,550	35,600	8,305	6,201	8,996	6,871	38,550	38,600	9,355	7,041	10,046	7,751
32,600	32,650	7,273	5,375	7,964	6,045	35,600	35,650	8,323	6,215	9,014	6,885	38,600	38,650	9,373	7,055	10,064	7,769
32,650	32,700	7,290	5,389	7,981	6,059	35,650	35,700	8,340	6,229	9,031	6,899	38,650	38,700	9,390	7,069	10,081	7,786
32,700	32,750	7,308	5,403	7,999	6,073	35,700	35,750	8,358	6,243	9,049	6,913	38,700	38,750	9,408	7,083	10,099	7,804
32,750	32,800	7,325	5,417	8,016	6,087	35,750	35,800	8,375	6,257	9,066	6,927	38,750	38,800	9,425	7,097	10,116	7,821
32,800	32,850	7,343	5,431	8,034	6,101	35,800	35,850	8,393	6,271	9,084	6,941	38,800	38,850	9,443	7,111	10,134	7,839
32,850	32,900	7,360	5,445	8,051	6,115	35,850	35,900	8,410	6,285	9,101	6,955	38,850	38,900	9,460	7,125	10,151	7,856
32,900	32,950	7,378	5,459	8,069	6,129	35,900	35,950	8,428	6,299	9,119	6,969	38,900	38,950	9,478	7,139	10,169	7,874
32,950	33,000	7,395	5,473	8,086	6,143	35,950	36,000	8,445	6,313	9,136	6,983	38,950	39,000	9,495	7,153	10,186	7,891
33,000						**36,000**						**39,000**					
33,000	33,050	7,413	5,487	8,104	6,157	36,000	36,050	8,463	6,327	9,154	6,997	39,000	39,050	9,513	7,167	10,204	7,909
33,050	33,100	7,430	5,501	8,121	6,171	36,050	36,100	8,480	6,341	9,171	7,011	39,050	39,100	9,530	7,181	10,221	7,926
33,100	33,150	7,448	5,515	8,139	6,185	36,100	36,150	8,498	6,355	9,189	7,025	39,100	39,150	9,548	7,195	10,239	7,944
33,150	33,200	7,465	5,529	8,156	6,199	36,150	36,200	8,515	6,369	9,206	7,039	39,150	39,200	9,565	7,209	10,256	7,961
33,200	33,250	7,483	5,543	8,174	6,213	36,200	36,250	8,533	6,383	9,224	7,053	39,200	39,250	9,583	7,223	10,274	7,979
33,250	33,300	7,500	5,557	8,191	6,227	36,250	36,300	8,550	6,397	9,241	7,067	39,250	39,300	9,600	7,237	10,291	7,996
33,300	33,350	7,518	5,571	8,209	6,241	36,300	36,350	8,568	6,411	9,259	7,081	39,300	39,350	9,618	7,251	10,309	8,014
33,350	33,400	7,535	5,585	8,226	6,255	36,350	36,400	8,585	6,425	9,276	7,095	39,350	39,400	9,635	7,265	10,326	8,031
33,400	33,450	7,553	5,599	8,244	6,269	36,400	36,450	8,603	6,439	9,294	7,109	39,400	39,450	9,653	7,279	10,344	8,049
33,450	33,500	7,570	5,613	8,261	6,283	36,450	36,500	8,620	6,453	9,311	7,123	39,450	39,500	9,670	7,293	10,361	8,066
33,500	33,550	7,588	5,627	8,279	6,297	36,500	36,550	8,638	6,467	9,329	7,137	39,500	39,550	9,688	7,307	10,379	8,084
33,550	33,600	7,605	5,641	8,296	6,311	36,550	36,600	8,655	6,481	9,346	7,151	39,550	39,600	9,705	7,321	10,396	8,101
33,600	33,650	7,623	5,655	8,314	6,325	36,600	36,650	8,673	6,495	9,364	7,165	39,600	39,650	9,723	7,335	10,414	8,119
33,650	33,700	7,640	5,669	8,331	6,339	36,650	36,700	8,690	6,509	9,381	7,179	39,650	39,700	9,740	7,349	10,431	8,136
33,700	33,750	7,658	5,683	8,349	6,353	36,700	36,750	8,708	6,523	9,399	7,193	39,700	39,750	9,758	7,363	10,449	8,154
33,750	33,800	7,675	5,697	8,366	6,367	36,750	36,800	8,725	6,537	9,416	7,207	39,750	39,800	9,775	7,377	10,466	8,171
33,800	33,850	7,693	5,711	8,384	6,381	36,800	36,850	8,743	6,551	9,434	7,221	39,800	39,850	9,793	7,391	10,484	8,189
33,850	33,900	7,710	5,725	8,401	6,395	36,850	36,900	8,760	6,565	9,451	7,235	39,850	39,900	9,810	7,405	10,501	8,206
33,900	33,950	7,728	5,739	8,419	6,409	36,900	36,950	8,778	6,579	9,469	7,249	39,900	39,950	9,828	7,419	10,519	8,224
33,950	34,000	7,745	5,753	8,436	6,423	36,950	37,000	8,795	6,593	9,486	7,263	39,950	40,000	9,845	7,433	10,536	8,241
34,000						**37,000**						**40,000**					
34,000	34,050	7,763	5,767	8,454	6,437	37,000	37,050	8,813	6,607	9,504	7,277	40,000	40,050	9,863	7,447	10,554	8,259
34,050	34,100	7,780	5,781	8,471	6,451	37,050	37,100	8,830	6,621	9,521	7,291	40,050	40,100	9,880	7,461	10,571	8,276
34,100	34,150	7,798	5,795	8,489	6,465	37,100	37,150	8,848	6,635	9,539	7,305	40,100	40,150	9,898	7,475	10,589	8,294
34,150	34,200	7,815	5,809	8,506	6,479	37,150	37,200	8,865	6,649	9,556	7,319	40,150	40,200	9,915	7,489	10,606	8,311
34,200	34,250	7,833	5,823	8,524	6,493	37,200	37,250	8,883	6,663	9,574	7,333	40,200	40,250	9,933	7,503	10,624	8,329
34,250	34,300	7,850	5,837	8,541	6,507	37,250	37,300	8,900	6,677	9,591	7,347	40,250	40,300	9,950	7,517	10,641	8,346
34,300	34,350	7,868	5,851	8,559	6,521	37,300	37,350	8,918	6,691	9,609	7,361	40,300	40,350	9,968	7,531	10,659	8,364
34,350	34,400	7,885	5,865	8,576	6,535	37,350	37,400	8,935	6,705	9,626	7,375	40,350	40,400	9,985	7,545	10,676	8,381
34,400	34,450	7,903	5,879	8,594	6,549	37,400	37,450	8,953	6,719	9,644	7,389	40,400	40,450	10,003	7,559	10,694	8,399
34,450	34,500	7,920	5,893	8,611	6,563	37,450	37,500	8,970	6,733	9,661	7,403	40,450	40,500	10,020	7,573	10,711	8,416
34,500	34,550	7,938	5,907	8,629	6,577	37,500	37,550	8,988	6,747	9,679	7,417	40,500	40,550	10,038	7,587	10,729	8,434
34,550	34,600	7,955	5,921	8,646	6,591	37,550	37,600	9,005	6,761	9,696	7,431	40,550	40,600	10,055	7,601	10,746	8,451
34,600	34,650	7,973	5,935	8,664	6,605	37,600	37,650	9,023	6,775	9,714	7,445	40,600	40,650	10,073	7,615	10,764	8,469
34,650	34,700	7,990	5,949	8,681	6,619	37,650	37,700	9,040	6,789	9,731	7,459	40,650	40,700	10,090	7,629	10,781	8,486
34,700	34,750	8,008	5,963	8,699	6,633	37,700	37,750	9,058	6,803	9,749	7,473	40,700	40,750	10,108	7,643	10,799	8,504
34,750	34,800	8,025	5,977	8,716	6,647	37,750	37,800	9,075	6,817	9,766	7,487	40,750	40,800	10,125	7,657	10,816	8,521
34,800	34,850	8,043	5,991	8,734	6,661	37,800	37,850	9,093	6,831	9,784	7,501	40,800	40,850	10,143	7,671	10,834	8,539
34,850	34,900	8,060	6,005	8,751	6,675	37,850	37,900	9,110	6,845	9,801	7,515	40,850	40,900	10,160	7,685	10,851	8,556
34,900	34,950	8,078	6,019	8,769	6,689	37,900	37,950	9,128	6,859	9,819	7,529	40,900	40,950	10,178	7,699	10,869	8,574
34,950	35,000	8,095	6,033	8,786	6,703	37,950	38,000	9,145	6,873	9,836	7,543	40,950	41,000	10,195	7,713	10,886	8,591

* This column must also be used by a qualifying widow(er).

Continued on next page

1987 Tax Table—Continued

If line 36 (taxable income) is—		And you are—				If line 36 (taxable income) is—		And you are—				If line 36 (taxable income) is—		And you are—			
At least	But less than	Single	Married filing jointly *	Married filing separately	Head of a house-hold	At least	But less than	Single	Married filing jointly *	Married filing separately	Head of a house-hold	At least	But less than	Single	Married filing jointly *	Married filing separately	Head of a house-hold
		Your tax is—						Your tax is—						Your tax is—			
41,000						**44,000**						**47,000**					
41,000	41,050	10,213	7,727	10,904	8,609	44,000	44,050	11,263	8,567	11,954	9,659	47,000	47,050	12,313	9,549	13,075	10,709
41,050	41,100	10,230	7,741	10,921	8,626	44,050	44,100	11,280	8,581	11,971	9,676	47,050	47,100	12,330	9,566	13,094	10,726
41,100	41,150	10,248	7,755	10,939	8,644	44,100	44,150	11,298	8,595	11,989	9,694	47,100	47,150	12,348	9,584	13,113	10,744
41,150	41,200	10,265	7,769	10,956	8,661	44,150	44,200	11,315	8,609	12,006	9,711	47,150	47,200	12,365	9,601	13,132	10,761
41,200	41,250	10,283	7,783	10,974	8,679	44,200	44,250	11,333	8,623	12,024	9,729	47,200	47,250	12,383	9,619	13,152	10,779
41,250	41,300	10,300	7,797	10,991	8,696	44,250	44,300	11,350	8,637	12,041	9,746	47,250	47,300	12,400	9,636	13,171	10,796
41,300	41,350	10,318	7,811	11,009	8,714	44,300	44,350	11,368	8,651	12,059	9,764	47,300	47,350	12,418	9,654	13,190	10,814
41,350	41,400	10,335	7,825	11,026	8,731	44,350	44,400	11,385	8,665	12,076	9,781	47,350	47,400	12,435	9,671	13,209	10,831
41,400	41,450	10,353	7,839	11,044	8,749	44,400	44,450	11,403	8,679	12,094	9,799	47,400	47,450	12,453	9,689	13,229	10,849
41,450	41,500	10,370	7,853	11,061	8,766	44,450	44,500	11,420	8,693	12,111	9,816	47,450	47,500	12,470	9,706	13,248	10,866
41,500	41,550	10,388	7,867	11,079	8,784	44,500	44,550	11,438	8,707	12,129	9,834	47,500	47,550	12,488	9,724	13,267	10,884
41,550	41,600	10,405	7,881	11,096	8,801	44,550	44,600	11,455	8,721	12,146	9,851	47,550	47,600	12,505	9,741	13,286	10,901
41,600	41,650	10,423	7,895	11,114	8,819	44,600	44,650	11,473	8,735	12,164	9,869	47,600	47,650	12,523	9,759	13,306	10,919
41,650	41,700	10,440	7,909	11,131	8,836	44,650	44,700	11,490	8,749	12,181	9,886	47,650	47,700	12,540	9,776	13,325	10,936
41,700	41,750	10,458	7,923	11,149	8,854	44,700	44,750	11,508	8,763	12,199	9,904	47,700	47,750	12,558	9,794	13,344	10,954
41,750	41,800	10,475	7,937	11,166	8,871	44,750	44,800	11,525	8,777	12,216	9,921	47,750	47,800	12,575	9,811	13,363	10,971
41,800	41,850	10,493	7,951	11,184	8,889	44,800	44,850	11,543	8,791	12,234	9,939	47,800	47,850	12,593	9,829	13,383	10,989
41,850	41,900	10,510	7,965	11,201	8,906	44,850	44,900	11,560	8,805	12,251	9,956	47,850	47,900	12,610	9,846	13,402	11,006
41,900	41,950	10,528	7,979	11,219	8,924	44,900	44,950	11,578	8,819	12,269	9,974	47,900	47,950	12,628	9,864	13,421	11,024
41,950	42,000	10,545	7,993	11,236	8,941	44,950	45,000	11,595	8,833	12,286	9,991	47,950	48,000	12,645	9,881	13,440	11,041
42,000						**45,000**						**48,000**					
42,000	42,050	10,563	8,007	11,254	8,959	45,000	45,050	11,613	8,849	12,305	10,009	48,000	48,050	12,663	9,899	13,460	11,059
42,050	42,100	10,580	8,021	11,271	8,976	45,050	45,100	11,630	8,866	12,324	10,026	48,050	48,100	12,680	9,916	13,479	11,076
42,100	42,150	10,598	8,035	11,289	8,994	45,100	45,150	11,648	8,884	12,343	10,044	48,100	48,150	12,698	9,934	13,498	11,094
42,150	42,200	10,615	8,049	11,306	9,011	45,150	45,200	11,665	8,901	12,362	10,061	48,150	48,200	12,715	9,951	13,517	11,111
42,200	42,250	10,633	8,063	11,324	9,029	45,200	45,250	11,683	8,919	12,382	10,079	48,200	48,250	12,733	9,969	13,537	11,129
42,250	42,300	10,650	8,077	11,341	9,046	45,250	45,300	11,700	8,936	12,401	10,096	48,250	48,300	12,750	9,986	13,556	11,146
42,300	42,350	10,668	8,091	11,359	9,064	45,300	45,350	11,718	8,954	12,420	10,114	48,300	48,350	12,768	10,004	13,575	11,164
42,350	42,400	10,685	8,105	11,376	9,081	45,350	45,400	11,735	8,971	12,439	10,131	48,350	48,400	12,785	10,021	13,594	11,181
42,400	42,450	10,703	8,119	11,394	9,099	45,400	45,450	11,753	8,989	12,459	10,149	48,400	48,450	12,803	10,039	13,614	11,199
42,450	42,500	10,720	8,133	11,411	9,116	45,450	45,500	11,770	9,006	12,478	10,166	48,450	48,500	12,820	10,056	13,633	11,216
42,500	42,550	10,738	8,147	11,429	9,134	45,500	45,550	11,788	9,024	12,497	10,184	48,500	48,550	12,838	10,074	13,652	11,234
42,550	42,600	10,755	8,161	11,446	9,151	45,550	45,600	11,805	9,041	12,516	10,201	48,550	48,600	12,855	10,091	13,671	11,251
42,600	42,650	10,773	8,175	11,464	9,169	45,600	45,650	11,823	9,059	12,536	10,219	48,600	48,650	12,873	10,109	13,691	11,269
42,650	42,700	10,790	8,189	11,481	9,186	45,650	45,700	11,840	9,076	12,555	10,236	48,650	48,700	12,890	10,126	13,710	11,286
42,700	42,750	10,808	8,203	11,499	9,204	45,700	45,750	11,858	9,094	12,574	10,254	48,700	48,750	12,908	10,144	13,729	11,304
42,750	42,800	10,825	8,217	11,516	9,221	45,750	45,800	11,875	9,111	12,593	10,271	48,750	48,800	12,925	10,161	13,748	11,321
42,800	42,850	10,843	8,231	11,534	9,239	45,800	45,850	11,893	9,129	12,613	10,289	48,800	48,850	12,943	10,179	13,768	11,339
42,850	42,900	10,860	8,245	11,551	9,256	45,850	45,900	11,910	9,146	12,632	10,306	48,850	48,900	12,960	10,196	13,787	11,356
42,900	42,950	10,878	8,259	11,569	9,274	45,900	45,950	11,928	9,164	12,651	10,324	48,900	48,950	12,978	10,214	13,806	11,374
42,950	43,000	10,895	8,273	11,586	9,291	45,950	46,000	11,945	9,181	12,670	10,341	48,950	49,000	12,995	10,231	13,825	11,391
43,000						**46,000**						**49,000**					
43,000	43,050	10,913	8,287	11,604	9,309	46,000	46,050	11,963	9,199	12,690	10,359	49,000	49,050	13,013	10,249	13,845	11,409
43,050	43,100	10,930	8,301	11,621	9,326	46,050	46,100	11,980	9,216	12,709	10,376	49,050	49,100	13,030	10,266	13,864	11,426
43,100	43,150	10,948	8,315	11,639	9,344	46,100	46,150	11,998	9,234	12,728	10,394	49,100	49,150	13,048	10,284	13,883	11,444
43,150	43,200	10,965	8,329	11,656	9,361	46,150	46,200	12,015	9,251	12,747	10,411	49,150	49,200	13,065	10,301	13,902	11,461
43,200	43,250	10,983	8,343	11,674	9,379	46,200	46,250	12,033	9,269	12,767	10,429	49,200	49,250	13,083	10,319	13,922	11,479
43,250	43,300	11,000	8,357	11,691	9,396	46,250	46,300	12,050	9,286	12,786	10,446	49,250	49,300	13,100	10,336	13,941	11,496
43,300	43,350	11,018	8,371	11,709	9,414	46,300	46,350	12,068	9,304	12,805	10,464	49,300	49,350	13,118	10,354	13,960	11,514
43,350	43,400	11,035	8,385	11,726	9,431	46,350	46,400	12,085	9,321	12,824	10,481	49,350	49,400	13,135	10,371	13,979	11,531
43,400	43,450	11,053	8,399	11,744	9,449	46,400	46,450	12,103	9,339	12,844	10,499	49,400	49,450	13,153	10,389	13,999	11,549
43,450	43,500	11,070	8,413	11,761	9,466	46,450	46,500	12,120	9,356	12,863	10,516	49,450	49,500	13,170	10,406	14,018	11,566
43,500	43,550	11,088	8,427	11,779	9,484	46,500	46,550	12,138	9,374	12,882	10,534	49,500	49,550	13,188	10,424	14,037	11,584
43,550	43,600	11,105	8,441	11,796	9,501	46,550	46,600	12,155	9,391	12,901	10,551	49,550	49,600	13,205	10,441	14,056	11,601
43,600	43,650	11,123	8,455	11,814	9,519	46,600	46,650	12,173	9,409	12,921	10,569	49,600	49,650	13,223	10,459	14,076	11,619
43,650	43,700	11,140	8,469	11,831	9,536	46,650	46,700	12,190	9,426	12,940	10,586	49,650	49,700	13,240	10,476	14,095	11,636
43,700	43,750	11,158	8,483	11,849	9,554	46,700	46,750	12,208	9,444	12,959	10,604	49,700	49,750	13,258	10,494	14,114	11,654
43,750	43,800	11,175	8,497	11,866	9,571	46,750	46,800	12,225	9,461	12,978	10,621	49,750	49,800	13,275	10,511	14,133	11,671
43,800	43,850	11,193	8,511	11,884	9,589	46,800	46,850	12,243	9,479	12,998	10,639	49,800	49,850	13,293	10,529	14,153	11,689
43,850	43,900	11,210	8,525	11,901	9,606	46,850	46,900	12,260	9,496	13,017	10,656	49,850	49,900	13,310	10,546	14,172	11,706
43,900	43,950	11,228	8,539	11,919	9,624	46,900	46,950	12,278	9,514	13,036	10,674	49,900	49,950	13,328	10,564	14,191	11,724
43,950	44,000	11,245	8,553	11,936	9,641	46,950	47,000	12,295	9,531	13,055	10,691	49,950	50,000	13,345	10,581	14,210	11,741

* This column must also be used by a qualifying widow(er).

50,000 or over—use tax rate schedules

1987 Tax Rate Schedules

Caution: You may use these schedules **ONLY** if your taxable income (Form 1040, line 36) is $50,000 or more.

Example: Mr. Jones is single. His taxable income on Form 1040, line 36, is $53,525. First, he finds the schedule (Schedule X) for single taxpayers. Next, he finds the $27,000–54,000 income line. Then, he subtracts $27,000 from $53,525 and multiplies the result ($26,525) by 35%. He then adds $9,283.75 ($26,525 × .35) to $5,304 and enters the result ($14,587.75) on Form 1040, line 37.

Schedule X—Single Taxpayers

Use this schedule if you checked **Filing Status Box 1** on Form 1040—

If the amount on Form 1040, line 36 is: Over—	But not over—	Enter on Form 1040, line 37	of the amount over—
$0	$1,800	........11%	$0
1,800	16,800	$198 + 15%	1,800
16,800	27,000	2,448 + 28%	16,800
27,000	54,000	5,304 + 35%	27,000
54,000	-------	14,754 + 38.5%	54,000

Schedule Z—Heads of Household

(including certain married persons who live apart—see page 5 of the Instructions)

Use this schedule if you checked **Filing Status Box 4** on Form 1040—

If the amount on Form 1040, line 36 is: Over—	But not over—	Enter on Form 1040, line 37	of the amount over—
$0	$2,500	........11%	$0
2,500	23,000	$275 + 15%	2,500
23,000	38,000	3,350 + 28%	23,000
38,000	80,000	7,550 + 35%	38,000
80,000	-------	22,250 + 38.5%	80,000

Schedule Y—Married Taxpayers and Qualifying Widows and Widowers

Married Filing Joint Returns and Qualifying Widows and Widowers

Use this schedule if you checked **Filing Status Box 2 or 5** on Form 1040—

If the amount on Form 1040, line 36 is: Over—	But not over—	Enter on Form 1040, line 37	of the amount over—
$0	$3,000	........11%	$0
3,000	28,000	$330 + 15%	3,000
28,000	45,000	4,080 + 28%	28,000
45,000	90,000	8,840 + 35%	45,000
90,000	-------	24,590 + 38.5%	90,000

Married Filing Separate Returns

Use this schedule if you checked **Filing Status Box 3** on Form 1040—

If the amount on Form 1040, line 36 is: Over—	But not over—	Enter on Form 1040, line 37	of the amount over—
$0	$1,500	........11%	$0
1,500	14,000	$165 + 15%	1,500
14,000	22,500	2,040 + 28%	14,000
22,500	45,000	4,420 + 35%	22,500
45,000	-------	12,295 + 38.5%	45,000